MAN AND MEANING

MAN AND MEANING

A SUCCESSOR TO MAN AND HIS NATURE

James E. Royce, S.J.
Seattle University

McGraw-Hill Book Company
New York   St. Louis   San Francisco   Toronto   London   Sydney

*Library of Congress Catalog
Card Number* 68–31664

ISBN 07-054167-1

890 KPKP 7987

Acknowledgments

The following publishers deserve thanks
for kind permission to quote from
copyrighted material: Appleton-Century-
Crofts, Inc., Barnes & Noble, Inc.,
Harcourt, Brace & Company, Harper &
Brothers, Henry Holt-Dryden Press,
Alfred A. Knopf, Inc., McGraw-Hill Book
Company, and World Book Company.

PREFACE

For, since the one who writes recognizes,
by the very fact that he takes the trouble to write,
the freedom of his readers, and since the one who reads,
by the mere fact of his opening the book,
recognizes the freedom of the writer, the work of art,
from whichever side you approach it,
is an act of confidence in the freedom of man. Sartre

 One's philosophy must be his own, freely chosen. Teacher and textbook can only be signposts pointing directions, not police directing traffic. By the same right, this book is my philosophy, freely chosen. Indebted greatly to previous and contemporary thinkers, it rests on no authority either past or present. In the final event, it must stand or fall on its own merits, on whether it squares with the student's own experience and with the facts as he knows them. Such a philosophy begins not with definitions or syllogisms but inductively, exploring the world of human experience. Is man "noble in reason," as Hamlet says, or the only irrational animal, or both? The student must decide for himself.

This book is immersed in the second half of the twentieth century. It does not demand any prerequisite science, but students come to philosophy today with greater scientific sophistication and with problems which did not confront Plato or Aquinas or Kant or Hegel. Hence the need for philosophy which goes beyond all of these. If the philosopher talks about man and his behavior without some awareness of what modern biology and psychology are saying, he is open to exactly the charge he resents most—that of working in a vacuum. We cannot afford to prepare students for life in a hypothetical English-speaking thirteenth century.

Different students have different needs, and one advantage of a textbook is that it releases the instructor for discussion and individual attention. The problem at the undergraduate level is what to discuss, since no one course can cover everything. There is something here to challenge the superior student or elicit comment from the teacher, while providing the average student with some orderly notion of man —rather than leaving him bewildered by a smörgasbord of unrelated tidbits, perhaps chronologically arranged but not organized and made relevant to his contemporary world.

The new chapters "The Mystery of Man" and "Man as Person" and new material on the contributions of "ordinary-language" analysis, existentialism, phenomenology, and other current trends, plus a rewriting of the entire book in the light of these themes, called for a new title to this book, which was formerly *Man and His Nature*. Elimination of much outmoded scholasticism has resulted in retaining approximately the same size. The original plan for the revision was to eliminate the word "soul" entirely. But since the word is going to be in common speech for a long time, it was thought more helpful to the student to make it intelligible instead, partly by rejecting the Cartesian pseudo-Thomism of many scholastic manuals of the past few centuries.

The book is primarily a text for the philosophy-of-man course, now sometimes called philosophical anthropology, but it should also be of interest to the general reader who has some knowledge of the biosocial sciences. The superiority of intellect, freedom of choice, and the ultimate nature of the human person are deemed the three pivotal problems for the undergraduate, and space is allotted accordingly. Philosophical orientation is given for the study of topics important to modern social science, such as emotion, motivation, habit, evolution, cultural diversity, subjective factors in perception, and communication.

This orientation is especially relevant because in symposia, presidential addresses, and other official activities, the members of the American Psychological Association disagree more and more with the narrow empiricism of early twentieth-century psychology; they frankly recognize that scientific psychology is "replete with metaphysical commitments" (Berenda, 1957, p. 726).[1] Philosophy cannot solve the problems of science as science, but it can make the scientist's task easier. Because philosophy is not enmeshed in the intricacies of scientific hypothesis and verification, it can help by eliminating blind alleys, clarifying the subject matter of experiment, and giving meaning to the finished product. The psychologist will find in this book no dualism, no "little man in the head" who chooses or guides, no straw man of psychoanalysis pictured as mere pansexualism, no need to abandon any established fact about human physiology or psychology.

My thanks are due to John Boler of the University of Washington, F. Torrens Hecht of Loyola in Chicago, and the many others whose stimulating and helpful criticisms have contributed so much to this new effort.

James E. Royce, S.J.

---

[1] For easy reading, only the briefest identification of sources is given in the text of this book. Full identification of each reference will be found in the General Bibliography at the end of the book. There the above citation, for example, will be seen to refer to page 726 of an article by Carlton W. Berenda, "Is Clinical Psychology a Science?" in *American Psychologist* for 1957, volume 12, pages 725–729. If there is more than one book or article by the same author published during the same year, they are listed as 1957a, 1957b, etc.

CONTENTS

MAN IN THE WORLD

I

1 THE MYSTERY OF MAN

Confrontation with man's being can cause dizziness,
but philosophy is not a hospital.   Merleau-Ponty

 "The world is a mess, man is a mess—what does it all mean?" is likely to be the typical attitude of the thinking young person of today. Not really a cynic or a pessimist, he or she is inclined to view the contemporary situation with a reaction reminiscent of *The King and I*: "It's a puzzlement!" He is not sure, and he sometimes doubts that anyone is very sure, as to what life really means and where it is all going. He tends to be disillusioned about Christianity, communism, democracy, science, philosophy, war, the Boy Scouts, his parents, and himself. He is fairly confident that he won't make quite as much of a mess of things as did the older generation, but he is rather vague as to the grounds for that confidence.

Very acute is the personal question, "What am I?" It is clear I had nothing to do with getting here. But here I am, and the only certain thing about my future is that eventually it will involve death. Psychologists talk about an identity crisis, and even though I may have some idea of who I am, this does not tell me much about *what* I am, or why. To say that I am a human being brings

3

little comfort. Jean-Paul Sartre says, "There is no such thing as human nature," and there are days when we wish there weren't. Human beings can be such weak, confused, inconsistent antiquated contraptions that you wonder if they can ever cope with the complexities of the world that surrounds them, even the modern world their own technology has created.

Even more disturbing is the question, "Why should they?" One wonders what pragmatic value all this has anyway, whether life is worth the effort. Why not go the easy route and escape to a more comfortable world accessible by the simple expedient of drugs or daydreaming? In asking why I exist, I am asking in what man's ultimate happiness really consists. Life can be boring at best, and completely puzzling if you question it hard enough. Albert Camus concludes that suicide is the only logical attitude in an absurd world.

Even those who are not inclined to go quite that far find it hard to discover satisfactory solutions to their basic questions. Those whose religious faith provides some answers want to have the intellectual satisfaction of understanding these things better. They want more than mere theory or sentimentalism. Late adolescence usually brings some questioning of faith, for the simple reason that the intelligent man needs to feel that his faith is reasonable, compatible with the facts and an intelligent interpretation of those facts which will stand up under questioning by those who will not accept faith or divine revelation as a source of knowledge. Quoting texts from the Bible is of little use for one who does not accept the Bible.

Philosophy and being

If we turn to philosophy, we find a bewildering disharmony of voices. Logical positivism, pragmatism, linguistic analysis, existentialism, and phenomenology have discredited both the naïve realism and the airy idealism of older philosophies, but are not at all agreed on what to put in their place. Both science and scholastic metaphysics are looked upon by some as mere sets of constructs. There is not even a category which can be called existentialism, for example: J. P. Sartre and Albert Camus are atheists, Karl Jaspers is neutral but open to religion, Gabriel Marcel is a Catholic, Martin Buber a Jew, and the originator, Søren Kierkegaard, a Lutheran.

Besides, today's inquirer is not interested in talking about philosophy and philosophers; he would agree wholeheartedly with Kierkegaard: "First live, then philosophize." He wants to talk about living, about himself and the world he must live in, about the meaning of it all for him. More important, he does not want a ready-made answer handed him by any philosopher. He wants to discover what he can for himself.

The above-mentioned welter of philosophical opinions makes him skeptical whether even the whole body of philosophers collectively can possess the truth. He would echo the statement of Maurice Merleau-Ponty, "Knowledge is never finished." He sees philosophy as a striving, an approximation, a lifetime task of groping constantly toward a better and better grasp of things we will never understand fully.

The reason for this is that he senses naturally what Marcel refers to as the Mystery of Being. Reality is indeed mysterious, full of paradoxes that do not fit into the neat boxes of Aristotle's categories which he may have learned in logic. He values logic, of course, as a necessary and useful tool in both science and philosophy, and resents being called illogical. But he feels, and rightly, that philosophy in its more profound moments goes beyond (not contrary to) logic and comes to grips with Being in a more intuitive manner. Though both he and his professors might have misgivings about the word "intuition," he understands without realizing it what the phenomenologists are talking about when they insist that knowledge is an immediate presence, a union that denies separation of knower (subject) and known (object). In contrast to the outmoded introspection of earlier experimental psychology, he sees that his most elementary experience contains implicitly within it the basic mystery of being: the awareness of self and other as existing, in an intimate relation in which self is known only in the contrast to other, and the other is known only as it reveals itself to the knower.

The important fact here is that one knows this somehow in the most elementary act of awareness, without ever formulating the word "existence" or dreaming of philosophy as such. Yet this is what philosophy is: wonder that anything *is*, that there is anything to know and that we can know anything about it. We may later ask why it is, *why* things exist rather than not exist. But the basic philosophic wonder is *that* they exist. What do we mean when we say something *is*? The scientists may wonder about something specific, but not about the wonder of being itself.

The phenomenologist Martin Heidegger uses this example to answer those who might feel that "being" is an empty word. Just substitute "tree"; is it empty? To avoid a supposed emptiness, we turn to specific trees, and to individual trees of those species. But if the word "tree" is really empty, why don't we turn to specific or individual rabbits, or motor cars? Only because the word tree does tell us something. Similarly, we can distinguish being from nonbeing. Even to deny something is to assert a difference between existence and nonexistence.

The way we use words in everyday conversation suggests a connection between phenomenology and another important approach in modern philosophy: linguistic analysis, especially in the hands of the "ordinary-language" philosophers. Just as the phenomenologist tries to dig meaning out of his immediate experience, so the analyst tries to get at the meaning of words by observing how we use them, and to disentangle the mysteries of philosophy by exposing the traps we fall into by our unwary use of words. We must discover the ways in which man deceives himself when he tires to grapple with reality through language. At one point, Ludwig J. Wittgenstein, one of the most influential analytic philosophers, suggests that we use language as we play a game.

Perhaps the biggest trap man falls into is what the mathematician-philosopher Alfred North Whitehead has called "the fallacy of misplaced concreteness," or tending to mistake abstractions for things. Although useful, concepts cause untold confusion in both philosophy and science when people forget that constructs are only abstractions, convenient ways of expressing some facet of reality, a handy way to summarize something inferred from the data. They are not things. Thus mind, matter, atomic power, race, conditioning, drive, mass, IQ do not exist as such. What exist are things and people. There is no behavior "out there" but only a behaving organism. There is no gravity as such, but only bodies which act in certain describable ways.

PERSONS

Once the beginning philosopher is alerted to the games people play with the language of both science and philosophy, he seeks a more personal encounter. Not constructs but people are important. He agrees with Sartre that there is no such "thing" as an abstract human nature, some Platonic Idea or Aristotelian essence of man, some universal stereotype with uniform laws of behavior he can codify on a computer. He resents being treated as impersonally as an IBM punch card. He is conscious of his rights as a free man, his responsibility as a person. But he is not very clear as to the source of this personality. Whence the much-heralded dignity of man?

The old definition of man as a rational animal leaves him unimpressed, for the simple reason that he sees so many of his fellowmen who act in downright irrational ways, and discovers much of the irrational even in himself. A person can be emotional, capricious, sometimes in error, lovable, stupid, artistic—none of which strikes him as particularly rational. Animal, yes; but he is quite sure there is more to a person than just being an animal. People are important in a way that other animals are not. But what precisely gives personal value? Not just what they have done, for we love our little son as a person, and would not dream of drowning him as we might drown an extra kitten merely because he has not achieved much as yet. We demand human rights for people regardless of race or color or talent, simply because they are human beings. But we stumble when asked what makes a human being human, and why this fact guarantees him certain inalienable rights. We are not sure what it means to be a human being. Yet it seems to mean a great deal to us, and to trigger huge involvements, from the local urban scene to international conflicts.

Change

One of the most disturbing aspects of the situation is that we are in a world of change. Thanks to men such as Charles Darwin, Henri Bergson, and Teilhard de Chardin, we are conscious as never before of the evolving nature of man and his world. Add the seemingly fantastic facts of space exploration, the instant communication and rapid travel which make a sinister incident in any remote corner of the world a personal threat to us, ecumenism, the ever-present threat of annihilation through atomic fission, the population explosion, and the even more dramatic knowledge explosion in which we have doubled the world's knowledge in the last twenty years and may double it again in the next ten. The result is exciting but almost terrifying. Things are changing so fast we despair of keeping up. Yet we are part of things. Our knowledge, if it be knowledge at all, is not of some separate world mirrored in static concepts, but of this very world as it evolves.

If things are changing, it behooves our knowledge to change right along with them. But if we are changing too, our inquiry into the meaning of man begins to feel like walking on the well-greased surface of one of those amusement park "rides" which consists of a spinning platform and no handholds. Biological evolution, developmental and "depth" psychology, cultural anthropology, and our own contacts with people tell us that human nature is not a stable entity but changing, evolving, dynamic, varied. We use expressions like, "He is not himself today," and, "I'm not like I used to be," and, "That is normal for that culture." Sociology tells of the differences between urban and rural people, various socioeconomic levels, cultural shifts, and different civilizations. It seems as if our quest for man's nature is doomed to failure for lack of a real target.

Meaning and experience

Perhaps the most honest place to begin is with our own experience; or, as we have seen above, with an analysis of our attempts to communicate these experiences through language. The first approach may throw some light on my own nature, and the latter may give some clue as to whether at least some features of it are shared by others in my language community.

We know man chiefly by examining man. Now there is no more immediate specimen of man around than myself. If I doubt the honesty of the report, I can only blame my own lack of authenticity. True, I am capable of self-deception, but that is where analysis of communication can be a check, along with scientific studies of others' behavior and the knowledge of unconscious motivation given us by Freud and others. We understand self by knowing others, and understand others largely in the light of our own experiences. I see that a rock is a thing because my body is a thing; indeed, as we will see, I am "a body that knows." I can guess something of what a rat might feel because I feel. And I know what you mean when you say, "I have a toothache," largely in terms of the fact that I have had a toothache, a difference we shall have to explore later. We may not understand ourselves fully, but what understanding we have must begin with what is immediately present in our own awareness of things as they reveal themselves to us.

Nor is there any danger of this approach ending in solipsism (from two Latin words meaning "one's self alone"), the doctrine that I alone am reality and everything else exists just in my mind. For any careful analysis of human knowing reveals right in the experience itself an intimate relation or presence of knower and known, a union so intimate that it defies analysis and yet is immediately evident to everyone in the very fact of experiencing at all. In this way contemporary philosophers avoid the impossible task of getting out of the mind once you start inside it. Reality cannot be attained by deduction from what goes on in the mind. Nor is truth some Platonic world of Ideas which we can grasp by sheer intellect. On the other hand consciousness is not a thing, an object to be analyzed or the premise of a syllogism. Neither thought (rationalism) nor experience (empiricism) is an absolute. Whatever meaning they yield is given by our existence, our living in a world in which we can interact with our environment, where everything lends itself to a dialogue with man: a sunset, a rose, a dog or cat, another person.

WHAT IS MAN?

This encounter with our surroundings initiates a dialogue which soon leads us into fascinating questions. It starts with a distinction between my body-as-knower and other things, which eventually leads into questions about what is meant when we say that I *have a* body rather than *am* a body, why we talk about *my body* instead of just about *me.* Biology and psychology as well as modern philosophy rightly abhor any dualism, any making of man into two things instead of a unified whole. Yet there is obvious diversity and complexity in man's makeup. Precisely what does it mean to be a part of a whole? Is a part a thing? Or is only the whole a thing, with parts having no existence other than the existence of the whole? When you pinch my arm or step on my toe we say that you pinched or stepped on *me.* Yet I am not just an arm or a toe. How does the child differentiate between me and not-me?

Analysis of our everyday expressions reveals a profound difference in the way we refer to things and persons. We do not apologize to the door when we bump it, not reprimand the typewriter when it misspells a word, nor refer to a man as "it" or to a thing as "you." In fact, the use of "he" and "you" suggests that your presence or absence makes a real difference, whereas I speak of "it" whether it is present or absent. Even if we do not speak, your presence is a very real factor in my behavior; I am terribly conscious of someone staring at me, even though he be a perfect stranger whom I could rightly ignore. Two persons in love can be quite content at times in each other's presence merely knowing that the other is there, without a word or other exchange.

This mutuality between persons suggests a social dimension to man. It is not merely that he is gregarious as other animals are: he craves communication to the point that he feels sometimes he just has to tell somebody about something, even a total stranger. He needs love, recognition, a sharing not only of goods but of feelings, thoughts, ambitions. He cares about others, and this care goes deeper than the results of societal conditioning or his choice to form a group. Without accepting any such notion as a group mind, he feels obligated by a treaty made before he was born or by a ruler he never voted for. The American Indian has claims against all of us (which our government is still paying) for the events of over a century ago. That these are not mere legal fictions is evidenced by the fact that we feel ashamed of what our parent or brother does, even though we know the act was done without our knowledge or at least without our personal culpability. Society is thus a whole which is more than the sum of its parts, and independent of their number or simultaneity in time.

We speak of time, yet cannot define it satisfactorily even to ourselves. We speak of man having a history and a destiny; we do not speak of either of these concepts with regard to other animals. Time is intimately tied up with our sense of identity, of who we are as well as what we are. Some dimension of man seems to transcend time, though we are immersed in it. The past is no longer existent, yet we cannot escape the historical context in which we live our lives, or deny its real presence. Any commitment has a time implication, even though we do not know the future or what it will bring. Time is for us not merely the measurable factor it is for the physicist, but the setting for our personal involvement with the world.

All this is very mysterious, even though it is a part of our ordinary daily experience and in that sense quite obvious. This dual fact of mystery and immediacy indicates both the task ahead of us and the principal method we shall use. To try to unravel these complexities and unveil these mysteries we cannot call upon arguments from authority, be it of the greatest philosophers or even (if we are philosophers and not theologians) of God. We must begin with that complex, mysterious being we see in the mirror and observe communicating through language with his fellow beings. We can discover nothing which is not at least implicitly contained in our own experience: the past and future are known only in the present, the most distant star or most abstruse theory is known by me only as somehow contained in being as it exists for me.

A final mystery we must mention before we embark upon this challenging task is the question of freedom. Materialistic philosophers and behavioristic psychologists talk much of determinism, while other philosophers speak constantly of freedom and the existentialists even complain about being "condemned to freedom." Our whole legal system assumes responsibility for normal acts, while some psychoanalysts tell us that our sense of responsibility only betrays ignorance as to the real unconscious determiners of our behavior. It is clear that I am not responsible for my acts if they are totally the product of heredity and environment. Yet our convictions about democracy, law, crime, rights, human dignity, liberty, and the authenticity of our own actions are based on the assumption that man is free, within limits, to determine his own choices. Human personality seems inextricably bound up with the question of freedom.

Meaningful questions

These are questions fundamental to that democratic way of life which we like to think is the core of Western civilization, but we do not find universal agreement on how they can be answered. At first glance, it would appear that the brute animals are more competent than men in almost every area. We use bloodhounds instead of deputy sheriffs because dogs can smell and discriminate between odors better than man. Eagles can see farther, deer can run faster, elephants are more powerful physically, bats have their own built-in radar, cats can solve puzzle boxes, rats can learn to run a maze perfectly, and chimpanzees seem to solve problems in mechanical engineering. And now we have computing machines which calculate more reliably than brains and faster than scores of statisticians working frantically. Where do these facts leave man?

These questions must be answered if our ideals are to have any meaning. With all due respect to the engineers, if our civilization breaks down it will not be because our bridges collapse, but because we have not formulated an adequate and satisfactory theory of man. It is hard to be reassuring if you are not sure. We must know that we are different from the brute animals if we are to have adequate reason for not acting like them. What man *should* do must be correlative to what man *is*.

REVIEW QUESTIONS

A summary of each chapter might tempt the student not to think through the material for himself. On the other hand, the following questions should help him to get the most from his reading.

1. Have you ever wondered about who you are? about what you are?
2. Can you remember when you first discovered that you were different from other things? that things are different from people?
3. One of the great thinkers of this century has said, "The real issue in both world wars was the nature of man." Why is the philosophy of man the basis for political science and ethics? What are the political consequences of denying the special nature of man?
4. What similarity or connection do you see between analysis of ordinary language and analysis of our immediate experience?
5. What important dimension does the fact of language add?
6. If man is constantly evolving, does this mean we can know nothing about him for certain?

FOR FURTHER READING

For full identification of sources mentioned here or in the text, consult the General Bibliography at the end of the book. These suggestions for each chapter do not pretend to be exhaustive but merely list some possibilities for further information or alternative views. Inclusion of a book here obviously does not mean full agreement; as a philosopher the student must decide for himself on the basis of evidence and reasoning.

Readings in the Philosophy of Man, edited by **Wm. L. Kelly** and **Andrew Tallon** (McGraw-Hill, 1967, paper), is a handy source of supplementary readings and will be referred to henceforth as **Kelly & Tallon.** Suggested here are the chapters from **Kierkegaard, Marcel,** and **Schutz.**

E. Cassirer, *An Essay on Man,* especially pp. 15–41: a neo-Kantian philosopher surveys various approaches to man.

The Murder of the Missing Link (also under title *You Shall Know Them*), by **Vercors** (pseudonym for **J. Bruller**), is an interesting short bit of science fiction about the discovery of a whole tribe of "missing links," which has as its central problem the question of how we know whether a being is human or not.

B. F. Skinner, in *Walden Two,* stirred up a controversy with his utopian society run wholly by conditioning. **John Dewey** raises some problems in *Human Nature and Conduct.*

W. Barrett, in *Irrational Man,* points up the mystery of man as a setting for existentialism. Some suggestions for a start in primary existentialist sources are **Søren Kierkegaard,** *The Sickness unto Death;* **Jean-Paul Sartre,** *Nausea;* **Albert Camus,** *The Myth of Sisyphus;* **Gabriel Marcel,** *Homo Viator* and *Man against Mass Society;* **Karl Jaspers,** *Man in the Modern Age,* and a popular presentation of his views, *Way to Wisdom.*

Many of the readings listed at the end of Chapter 13 are pertinent for this and the following chapter. A useful bibliographical source is **Mortimer J. Adler** (Ed.), *The Great Ideas: A Syntopicon of the Great Books of the Western World* (Chicago: Encyclopaedia Britannica, Inc., 1952), vol. II, chap. 51.

2 VIEWING MAN WHOLE

*How to give birth to those vital and procreative ideas which
multiply into a thousand forms and diffuse themselves
everywhere, advancing civilization and making the dignity of
man, is an art not yet reduced to rules, but the secret
of which the history of science affords some hints.*   Peirce

Whether from science or philosophy, the picture of man
portrayed in books too often strikes the college student as
having scant resemblance to the people in the world
around him. He wants a philosophy of man that fits in
with his own experience, not some abstract or universal
formula. The American pragmatists such as James,
Dewey, and Peirce reacted against the otherworldliness
of the early American puritanical ethic by a philosophy
practical with the values of this world. The existentialists
in their concern with the individual person, the concrete
human situation, have reacted strongly against the ex-
cessively elaborate systematizing of older philosophies,
especially that of Hegel.

A similar reaction is generated by the sciences of man.
These have tended to use rigorously formal techniques
to investigate rather unimportant problems. The feeling
of the Freshman in his introductory psychology class is re-

flected in the farewell editorial of a distinguished psychologist (Smith, 1961, p. 462): "It seems, having reviewed some 2,825 manuscripts, that a remarkably high proportion of the research reported is clean, stringently conceived and effectively executed, reflective of rigorous and painstaking thought and experimentation—and remarkably trivial!" If one asks the wrong question or a trivial one, getting an answer even at the .001 level of statistical accuracy is not enough.

Throughout this book we shall try to wonder about the meaning of man by starting always with our own experience, with the data which seem relevant. This will not be so easy as it sounds, as evidenced by the history of philosophy. Like love, having an open mind is one of the easiest things to talk about and the hardest to achieve; paradoxically, in both cases what should be the most spontaneous actually demands the most hard work.

Analytic philosophers, phenomenologists, and a host of others all agree in their own varying ways on this. Our approach to reality must be a "disciplined naïveté"—the open-eyed wonder of a child combined with the utmost cunning we can cull from the accumulated philosophical experience of all that has gone before. We must analyze our use of ordinary language for clues as to what we really mean, and constantly check our observations against those from the sciences of man.

This openness is all the less easy because any observation begins with some previous assumption or knowledge, some scheme into which we perhaps unconsciously fit the present fact. Moreover, some systematization, some attempt to order the bewildering panorama of facts about man into some kind of coherent structure, seems necessary if our study is to make any sense and be more than a mere hodgepodge of unrelated facts. But we must try not to let system dictate observation, never prostitute data to preconceived theory. In the first instance and in the last analysis we come down to the basic question: "Does this square with my experience?" Relevance to the actual world in which I live is a pragmatic criterion to be constantly applied.

Knower and known

One matter which bothers most philosophers now is the fragmentation of both man and the universe into bits and parts. Even the distinction between man and the universe seems slightly artificial, since man is part of the universe. There is no knowledge apart from the knower, and equally no knowledge apart from something to be known. Subject (knower) and object (known) form a continuum rather than a dichotomy.

It is precisely because I am a part of the world that I can know it.

As experiencing subject, I am not something apart, a disembodied knower. It is precisely through my body that I know, and we do not know fully just when and how the infant first gets clear the distinction between his own body and the rest of physical reality. Moreover, we know with our whole body, not just our sense organs. We turn toward a sound, we strain and squint, we hold ourselves breathless to listen, our heart speeds up with the rhythm of an exciting dance or piece of ballet music. A blind man picks up cues which tell him not only where he is but even the attitude of the person addressing him. The hostess walks into a room after an unpleasant incident and senses the tension or embarrassment among her guests. She cannot explain to her husband how she knows. That "the air is blue" is obviously not to be taken literally, and may have escaped him entirely; but she is right about the fact.

These facts illustrate not only the totality of the knower but also the total nature of the object. In perception, "The whole is more than the sum of the parts." The net total impression is more than you would get from adding up the elements. Familiar optical illusions have their basis in this fact, as we shall see when discussing perception later. Experimental psychologists have to rig a most artificial laboratory situation to try to isolate a "pure sensation" as opposed to the total perception as we normally experience it.

This totality principle has been carried over into larger areas: that of personality, where it is seen that the total person is more than what you might expect from merely adding his components; and that of society, where the group will do what you could never predict from a knowledge of the individuals taken singly. In every instance the object known is a complex totality with multiple relations to the rest of reality, and to which the knower brings much of himself. So the artist "lives" his work, identifying with nature as he absorbs it, yet projecting much of his own ideas and ideals into nature as he molds it creatively. So we have expressions about how much of himself the artist put into his work, and likewise how much of his boyhood milieu has gone into the artist.

Whole versus parts

Throughout all this we have stressed wholeness: whole body, whole knower, whole object, whole universe, whole knower-object situation. Yet are we to make no distinctions? Does close interrelationship mean identity? Historically, we can discover that excessive separation of knower and known has given rise to idealism and positivism, exaggerated realism and skepticism. These we are happy to avoid. Similarly, undue emphasis on the distinction between sense knowledge and intellectual understanding has given rise in past centuries to the same errors.

Others argue that to talk simply of "man in the world," without any distinctions, can result in our making man nothing more than a blob of mush in a sea of pea soup. My stomach is not my imagination, no matter how true it is that certain images cause me to vomit. Intellection is not hearing; otherwise I would understand Chinese. I am not my father, no matter how much I psychologically identify with him. Cabbages are not kings, and ships and shoes are not sealing wax, even for Alice in Wonderland.

Ironically, one must use concepts even to reject concepts. Mental constructs of some kind are essential for any kind of thinking, including both scientific and philosophical, for the simple reason that no finite mind can grasp all of the intelligible universe in one intuitive vision. Man must break up reality into smaller units that he can manipulate in a meaningful way. Since we cannot know everything at once by one comprehensive act of understanding, human knowledge always comes piecemeal; this is the old problem that medieval philosophers tried to solve by means of universal concepts, and the same difficulty at which Camus and other existentialists have more recently chafed. Reality may be whole, but we know it by parts.

Every poet, philosopher, and psychologist—Plato, St. Paul, Shakespeare, Freud, Sartre—has described in his own terms the warring factions within man. If man had only one kind of operation, it would be clear that he is one being. But in view of the complexity of human operation, the unity of man's nature presents a real problem. Man is too varied in activity to be studied all at once, so it seems logical to take him part by part. This method, through the measurement of particular responses, has contributed much to our knowledge of human activity.

But how can we understand the parts except in view of the whole? A partial view could give us a false knowledge, which is worse than no knowledge at all. Moreover, there are many facts about man's operations which are total, i.e., of their very nature they involve the whole man and we see them incorrectly when we try to take them apart. This has been the argument of the personalistic, holistic, and Gestalt psychologists, who insist that the whole is more than the sum of the parts. Their experiments on perception and theories of personality are quite at variance with the part by part approach. Even the operationalists, who want to define the "intervening variables" between stimulus and response purely in terms of the operations by which we try to study them, soon find that this approach involves a leap in the dark from observed data to concepts intelligible only in the light of the total personality or total organism. The same heat which melts the butter hardens the egg: response is rarely explainable by stimulus alone.

Which side shall we take in this perennial debate? We shall try to maintain balance by looking at the facts on both sides. We shall study man as a whole composed of many parts and try to look at the parts without losing sight of the whole. Here is a man who trembles with anger at the thought of some outrageous injustice. His trembling, his anger, his thoughts about injustice are all different, yet all are the acts of the same one man. To isolate them from one another or from the man is to make them not only meaningless but nonexistent. They can exist only in the man who is angry. There is a totality here which is undeniable, yet thinking about injustice is not the same as trembling.

METHOD OR METHODS?

Perhaps now the pertinence of the quotation from C. S. Peirce at the head of this chapter begins to become apparent. In view of the diversity of method and approach among philosophers, we might take a hint from the history of science. In spite of constant use of the term "the scientific method," we soon learn that there is no one procedure which merits that epithet. Einstein suggests that if we ignore what scientists *say* they do, and pay attention to what they actually do, we will find them using many different methods and not following the procedures outlined so neatly in the textbooks on the logic of science. Taking an operational definition of science as what scientists do, we see that scientific discovery includes all the idiosyncrasies of the individual scientists as they struggle by every possible means to wrest from nature her secrets.

Similarly, instead of trying to use just one philosophical method, it may be wise to avail ourselves of all possible avenues in our quest for man. The picture seen above of man as part of the universe, evolving with it and interacting with it as he comes to know it, enmeshed in a complex totality in which he is both observer and observed, suggests that there is no one magic key to this puzzle. There is no one avenue to truth as something "out there" when we are included in both the means and the goal. Yet we cannot start wholly within ourselves, since we know ourselves only in contrast to other things and persons in the total universe of which both they and we are a part. It is a little like trying to put ourselves under a microscope and then look at ourselves with our own eyes. Moreover, we must use the very operations we are studying in order to study them. We must also use the behavior of others, and their experiences as reported in human language, as a sort of mirror in which we can see and interpret our observations of ourself.

Challenging? Yes. Impossible? Some philosophers have said so. At least it seems man can never know himself perfectly. Not only is our knowledge always to some extent inadequate, but man's potentialities may be unlimited so that we can never know to what heights he might evolve and hence can never encompass him fully. Nevertheless we know something of what he can do, which will tell us at least that much about the kind of being he is. We never know a nature as such; we know individual beings behaving in certain ways, communicating in a given language community, achieving certain pragmatic results— all of this meaningful to us in terms of our own experience. The task of the philosopher is to analyze what is implicit in all these sources of information, in whatever facts shed light on what man is. The facts are there; what is implicit in them is that man could not do these things if he did not have the ability to do them, if he were not that kind of being.

We know a being from its properties and performance. If it quacks, waddles, has down feathers, and all the other characteristics of a duck, we do not say that it is a cabbage. Similarly, from the fact that man lives, we say he is an organism in some basic sense of the term; since this organism is observed to feel, see, hear, etc., we call him an animal; if it is observed to reason and make responsible choices, we call him a person. (This merely illustrates the general trend of our procedure; we do not pretend to have settled anything at this point.) If we wish to investigate the question of whether man is one being or several, we must investigate whether he functions as one or not. If we inquire as to whether man has some value or destiny beyond that of other organisms, we must analyze what is implied by his behavior, language, and experience.

The nature of this analysis, as well as the data from which it proceeds, may take many forms. In general, it involves making explicit what is implicit in the rudimentary facts themselves. For instance, our awareness of ourselves as particular thinking subjects is implicit in any act of knowing that is not wholly irrational. But to make this awareness an explicit part of the general knowledge about the nature of the thinker requires a diligent and subtle investigation.

Reason or insight?

The precise nature of the inference involved in this investigation is now being reexamined (Lonergan, 1956; Maurer, 1958). Although it

may be hard work, it seems to be less a matter of rationalistic deduction than older textbooks of scholastic philosophy might suggest. The
student must realize that a syllogistic "proof" is not a description of
how a conclusion was arrived at, but the subsequent formulation of
an insight at first grasped inductively and intuitively. As will appear
later when we reject the "ghost in the machine" notion of soul, there
is nothing in man which is not implicitly apprehended in some way in
any full, direct experience. Man is not so much an object beyond our
total human experience as rather a subject contained within it. Experience is not to be transcended but rather explicated, opened up,
dis-closed. This is not deduction so much as a sort of experiential induction—a fuller realization of facts we already knew, implicitly and
confusedly, about man from observing his actions and our own experiences.

This is done by a series of analyses of various activities which are
mutually complementary and corrective. As Heidegger says, "Precisely because man is man, man's essence is always to some extent
unconcealed from man himself." I am immediately present to myself.
The word "unconcealed" here could be translated unveiled, unhidden,
uncovered. What he is saying is that any experience that something *is*
contains implicitly a host of relations about man, knowledge, and
being. But man is a being, and knowledge is a special kind of being.
The task is to make these relations explicit, and to analyze what is
involved in the terms of the relations, i.e., what justifies our talking
this way at all. Likewise, the fact that man has certain abilities is
unintelligible apart from some awareness of the person or subject
operating on the one hand, and of the operation on the other. But what
is explicitly observed is the operation, and the implied ability is not
a thing separate from the person who operates.

A start

We begin, then, with the most elementary fact of human experience:
"Here I am!" Not "I am here," for this would immediately involve us
in questions of where: New York or Chicago, and about this there
could be error and delusion. But here I am, whatever and whoever I
may be. The expression exhibits the basic facts of experience: I exist,
I am not-other, I am located somehow in space, I expect you to understand my exclamation.

This is not the "Cogito, ergo sum" of Descartes. There is no question
of *proving* that I exist, or that you exist. That is impossible, for there
is no prior premise, no more fundamental notion, to use as a starting
point. Even to raise the question implies the answer. Not only could

you never ask the question if you did not exist, but your very asking implies that you already understand the difference between being and nonbeing. If we say nobody can explain it to anyone, this is not due to a lack of ability but due to the fact that there is nothing more simple in terms of which it can be explained, nothing more immediate to which it can be reduced. Demand for a step-by-step proof only leads to an infinite process. Eventually you have to get down to something so directly and immediately known that it needs no proof. Yet somehow each budding philosopher seems to have to go through the agonizing process of wrestling with this problem. This is philosophy, which takes nothing for granted and must examine what other types of knowledge may leave implicit (unexamined). This start is not a naïve realism or blind assumption, precisely because it is examined.

But we are interested in man, not being in general. What can we know about man from this fact? A great deal. "Here I am!" immediately implies not only that you and I exist, and that you and I know being, but that you and I can communicate: we can somehow share these experiences by means of a set of symbols called language. This implies both a commonality of experiences and something common in our makeup. We could not share experiences if we did not have basically the same equipment for having them. Neither could we have an I-thou relationship. When a man "communicates" with a computer and it "talks back" to him, it is clear that he is doing something *to* it, not sharing an experience *with* it. Even when man "communicates" with a dolphin, it is different from a man-to-man communication. The relationship lacks the mutuality or reciprocity of personal interchange. And in those areas of prelinguistic or nonlinguistic experience which language analysis cannot handle, man often is able through some art form or empathy to share with his fellowman. An elderly couple can communicate and share understandings without a word spoken.

From facts such as these we can gain many insights into human nature. The modern approaches indicated here seem to lack the precision and order of some of the older systematic philosophies, but they have definite advantages. Man is both unique and complex. If we reduce him to a common nature, we miss his uniqueness as a person. If we separate him into various parts, we miss the dynamic complexity of his total unified being. The Gestalt psychologists made some excellent studies of the total nature of sense perception, but they did not carry the holistic approach far enough into the realm of the total person and indeed the whole universe of which the person is just a part. Modern philosophers have tried to explicate man's experience without fragmenting it. As we destroy a living thing when we dissect it, so we lose something of human experience when we divide it into neat categories. Definitions are useful and even necessary for certain phases of human investigation, but no definition can convey the beauty of a rose or the distinctiveness of a human personality. A detailed description of a man raising his arm at such an angle with so many dynes of force and so on would perhaps never convey to me what he is doing; but if you tell me that he is laying bricks I understand at once. Human actions have a depth value which requires a third-dimension picture, an insight into feelings and goals. Ten pages of behavioral analysis may never tell me *why* she slammed the door, just as a photograph might tell me what Van Gogh saw but never convey how Van Gogh *felt* about it.

The effort to capture the simultaneous personal intersubjectivity, the spontaneous, the fluid unity and dynamic intentionality of human action is what characterizes much of modern philosophy—and what would have dismayed the overly systematic philosopher of other centuries. Take the phenomenon of loneliness. What a wealth of implications are there: man's social nature, his desire to communicate, his capacity for feeling, his hunger for fulfillment, his precarious sense of self-identity, his passionate need for meaning in his life. Yet to put all this in words and to analyze it at the time seems vapid in comparison with just being there, visiting a lonely person and being able to understand. How can we examine without destroying? Can we not simply behold or regard with sufficient insight to wrest the meaning from the fact or situation? Sometimes it seems we thus understand better, that something is lost by analysis.

POINTS OF VIEW

Perhaps the biggest problem here is the matter of perspective, the point from which we view man. In the microuniverse of subatomic particles, the organized bundle of molecules we know as man is a giant. In the macrouniverse of galaxies beyond our Milky Way, man is tinier than an amoeba in our solar system. The history of both science and philosophy is replete with examples of lack of perspective, one restricted viewpoint cutting even intelligent men off from large and important areas of knowledge. To the early Christians "the whole world" meant the Mediterranean Basin. For some philosophers the world was made up of only one element: water, for instance (Thales). For others, the entire universe was only a projection of their own mind. Similarly in science, where Jenner's notion of vaccination was ridiculed, and where a committee appointed by the French academy, with Lavoisier as a member, reported that meteorites did not exist, with the result that many museums in Western Europe threw away their meteorite collections. As we shall see in discussing sensory perception, we can fail to see what is unpleasant or unacceptable to the group (Asch), or "see" what we expect to see even though it is not happening (e.g., the rotating trapezoid of Ames).

This is important because man, who lives in a world of meaning and is always seeking meaning, still is terribly limited by his viewpoint as to what meaning he will derive. Reading the pointer on a galvanometer means nothing to a person ignorant of what it is or how it works; to a scientist it might mean the answer to a year's research. So true is this that Einstein and Eddington insist that no scientist really proceeds on "hard facts" because observation without theory is meaningless. The latter goes so far as to say that the hard-headed experimentalist is more swayed by his theories than anyone else because he is less accustomed to scrutinizing them. "Experimentation is generally the last step in the acquisition of knowledge rather than the first. Much theorizing and naturalistic observing has to be done before worthwhile experiments are possible. The experimenter is the last member of a relay team." (Maslow, 1955, p. 2)

Theoretical constructs seem to play a similar role in both philosophy and science: they are useful, but limiting because they are never expressive of the whole of reality. No collection of experts will add up to a wise man. Removal of limits will allow other aspects for added perspective, but only the removal of all limits will allow all other aspects. This is what philosophy should be, but individual philosophers can only approach this unlimited perspective. At least we can be on our guard lest our pet constructs lead to exclusiveness or reductionism, by which man becomes nothing but mind, or nothing but matter, or nothing but any one particular aspect emphasized in this or that philosophy. Otherwise we will end up like the reductionist who says that Beethoven's symphonies are nothing but sound waves, a Rembrandt masterpiece is nothing but oil paint—and man becomes nothing but atomic particles. A widely accepted reductionist philosophy, which has also had great impact on psychology, is positivism.

Positivism is a theory of knowledge proposed by Comte, following Locke and Hume, which holds that we can know only the facts of immediate sense perception, only externally observable physical realities: we can know nothing of ultimate causes or natures or essences, only empirical phenomena (appearances). Positivism generally rejected metaphysics; Ernst Mach rejected all theory, even in science. "Logical positivism," as found in Bertrand Russell and the Vienna circle, marks the apex of antimetaphysical thought: we know neither substance nor process worth talking about. The philosophy of science for these men is concerned only with the logic of procedure and the rules of discourse: the formal structure of logical relations, not their referents (the realities to which they refer).

Operationism is an outgrowth of positivism which teaches that the only way we can define anything is to describe the operations by which we measure it: thus, we define horsepower or ergs or dynes in terms of the operations involved in arriving at these measures. Operationism was a healthy influence in science, especially psychology, because it forced people to be precise and eliminated a lot of vague theorizing. In this sense it was largely a modern form of Ockham's razor (or Lloyd Morgan's canon, or the law of parsimony) which states: don't postulate more hypothetical entities than the data call for. For example, the behaviorists used operationism against Freudian psychoanalysis with some effect, by forcing them to reduce constructs like the Oedipus complex to observable data.

Contemporary scientific view

But Einstein himself was only the first of an impressive list of outstanding physical scientists who came to see that such reductionism can go too far, that even physical science goes well beyond the confines laid down for it by positivism. Newton's laws seemed so logical, so palpable, that Kant and lesser thinkers for several centuries tended to assume that physical laws constitute an absolute description of reality instead of a convenient abstraction, as the subsequent work of Heisenberg, Planck, and Einstein was to show. We have already mentioned Whitehead's scolding about the fallacy of misplaced concreteness; he includes the positivists, who forgot that many of their own constructs were not empirical.

Percy Bridgman, the physicist whose 1927 essay had launched both physicists and psychologists on a cult of operationism,[1] had occasion decades later to regret this fact openly (1954, 1959). He and other eminent physicists have reprimanded the psychologists for patterning their science on classic Newtonian physics when the physicists themselves have long since abandoned it. Bridgman, Rudolf Carnap, Herbert Feigl, and other logical positivists have abandoned at least the extreme of that position and have recognized that science is much more than the description of the concretely observable, mere correlations of physical data. Science is to a great extent a matter of theoretical constructs, often highly abstract and speculative.

---

[1] Though grounded in scientific caution, operationism approached the absurd point where "Aptitude is how one performs on this test," or "Love is two people kissing," or "I'm hungry" is the same as "I eat a lot."

Some of the reasons for this shift have been the following. Relativity, indeterminancy, subjectivism (even in physics), molar or quantum theories, and similar developments have exploded the old view of science as a mechanical model of reality. Analogy is playing an increased role in science, and to think in analogy requires the ability to abstract the similarity between two sets of relations (somewhat, but not exactly, like a mathematical proportion as an equality between two ratios). Most important, theory has had fertility beyond expectation: it has led to results not dreamed of by the original theorizer, and not contained in his data. Conversely, it has enabled us to predict new kinds of events before they were observed. Prediction is a great hallmark of science, but statements about future events are not verifiable according to strict positivism. Lastly, there is the convergence of theories developed by Russian and American scientists working on opposite sides of the iron curtain and from different data. All this shows most strikingly that science itself is a way of conceptualizing reality, not merely correlating data.

One result of this is that scientists are beginning to reexamine their own assumptions. In so doing they are becoming philosophically much more sophisticated than ever before. For it is the philosopher who takes nothing for granted, who must cut down to the very bedrock on which all knowledge has its footings. It is precisely because the scientist in his theory or model goes beyond data that he can never be sure of *exact* correspondence of his theory with reality, even though the theory provides more than the mere correlations to which the positivist limited him. Hence the value of a sound philosophy. While not productive of scientific theory as such, it can aid the scientist in formulating theory and protect him from the sterility which comes from a faulty perspective in the search for both data and interpretation.

Paradoxically, science is more dialectical than is philosophy: the more specialized a scientific investigation becomes, the more it involves theory and deduction. The scientist invents intriguing hypotheses and laboriously tries to substantiate them by experiment and analogy with ingenious models. The danger, of course, is of "not being able to see the forest for the trees," of getting lost in a realm of minute details or theoretical constructs.

CONSCIOUSNESS

The point at which positivism has had its greatest impact on the study of man is a controversy in which both philosophers and psychologists have been aligned on both sides. We use it to conclude this chapter because it illustrates a problem in both subject matter and method.

So far we have been using words such as consciousness and experience without any analysis of their precise meaning, relying on the commonsense understanding of these terms to carry the discussion. Actually, the analysis of human experience has a long and controversial history, and is still a matter of considerable dispute.

Consciousness has many different meanings. First, it may mean any activity whose nature connotes awareness. Thus I am focally conscious of this page in front of me. I am aware to a lesser extent of things in marginal or liminal consciousness, as the fact that there is light in the room or traffic outside (which may shift from the margin to the focus of consciousness if the light goes off or if the traffic noise suddenly stops). It may refer to states of diminished or dissociated consciousness, as during a dream when I am "aware" that a dinosaur is chasing me. It may refer not only to knowledge activities, as in the above examples, but also to affective or feeling activities: "I felt like hitting that boor," and to conative or volitional activities: "I wanted to choose the best." All this is usually subsumed under the general term experience.

But *consciousness* has a second and special meaning. For the older philosophers it meant an *explicit* reflection on our subjective states. Our awareness is now focused on the experience itself, rather than on the page or the dinosaur or the boor. I am aware that I am aware. I examine my conscious act itself: the perception, the dream, the feeling, the wish. In modern times this process has been called introspection (to look within), but as we shall see this term took on a further specialized meaning in the hands of certain psychologists.

The student should note that introspection is not psychoanalysis, i.e., it is not an attempt to understand or delve into the why and wherefore of our experiences, but simply a description of the experience itself. Again, we must not confuse consciousness, which is the simple fact of awareness, with conscience, which is one very small and restricted part of consciousness, viz., awareness of moral right and wrong. And introspection tells us nothing of brain activity, since we are aware of what is going on in the brain only from a study of physiology, not from our own consciousness.

Lastly, it must be noted that midway between the above first two senses, *consciousness* may mean the *implicit* awareness of myself as the subject in any and every experience. While I may not advert to it, I am at least dimly aware of myself, as other than that of which I am conscious. It is I who see, I who think, I who feel and digest and move. We have already noted this implicit consciousness of self as subject in every act of knowing. Try to describe a morning's activities purely in terms of "sciousness"—i.e., as purely objective without the "con" (with) of the agent who knows ("scious"). In other words, consciousness means that I am *with* the object. But we do not always explicitly advert to this being-with.

This "I" as conscious agent is often called "ego" in psychology, but this term causes trouble because of a tendency to think of it as some hypothetical construct or separate entity within man instead of simply as the total person who experiences. I am quite sure that I am real, not a mental construct. Similarly, the word "self" has taken on special connotations of a value to be enhanced or defended, a self-concept, instead of the meaning we have here of my total being—as when we identify that "it was not he but myself who did it."[2]

Difficulties regarding the reliability of consciousness in the first sense of the word come under that part of philosophy which is called "epistemology," which studies whether man can really know. Although it is assumed in all scientific endeavor that he can, we shall have to examine the problem briefly at the end of Chapter 6. Certainly things are not always quite what they seem. Appearances are deceiving; error, illusion, delusion, hallucination, and uncertainty are facts. I cannot always trust my consciousness of things.

Objectivism

But the real controversy today centers around the second meaning of consciousness; i.e., the degree to which my analysis or reflection on my own experiences is to be trusted—in other words, whether examining consciousness can furnish valid factual data. The present attitude of modern psychology toward the experience of knowing can only be understood in the light of its history. As we shall see later, Descartes (died 1650) split man into two beings, a mind and a body. Mind became a substance, and ideas were associated by some sort of mental chemistry. Consciousness, instead of being an operation of the whole man, became some mysterious "mind stuff." Thus the philosophical stage was badly set before modern psychology made its entrance. The early experimental psychologists at the end of the nineteenth century began to study this "mind" experimentally in their laboratories, by the process of introspection.

But this introspection differs from the "disciplined naïveté" of current phenomenology, which wishes to investigate experience free of all implicit and explicit assumptions. Instead of starting with a complete openness, the introspectionist psychologists approached the phenomena of consciousness with some preconceived ideas as to the structure of the human mind—hence they were called structuralists.

[2] See James E. Royce, S.J., *Personality and Mental Health,* rev. ed. (Milwaukee: Bruce, 1964), pp. 94–96, on different meanings of self.

They proceeded to impose their theoretical structure categories on the data, instead of simply observing what they found in their acts of awareness. Thus some tried to reduce all conscious experience to three elements: sensation, image, and feeling. Other psychologists said that analysis of the content of consciousness revealed thinking as a component not reducible to the above three elements.

On top of this quibbling about consciousness, Freud's followers were offering conjectures about unconscious motivation which raised doubt whether consciousness was very significant after all. Finally Watson, quite understandably disgusted with the abuses and theorizing, decided to throw out introspection entirely and make psychology merely a study of external behavior. During the 1920s it was fashionable to think of psychology as scientific only if it dealt exclusively with externally observable behavior and ignored consciousness entirely (behaviorism).

Although classic Watsonian behaviorism in its extreme view was abandoned within two decades,[3] the behavioristic approach is still vigorously upheld by many positivistic and analytic philosophers as well as by a large number of psychologists following B. F. Skinner, and continues to flavor strongly the terminology of American psychology (behaviorism was not widely accepted in Europe). It maintains that the purely objective and quantitative method is the only scientific one. Skinner argues forcibly not only from the unreliability of introspection and the contradictory evidence it can produce, but even more from the fact that his objective science of behavior works. He prefers to stay with this pragmatic criterion and avoid the philosophical implications of an "-ism" by speaking simply of a science of behavior rather than of behaviorism. This objective approach avoids all the epistemological difficulties of the introspectionist psychology. Not only does it work, but its results can be replicated anywhere and the facts observed by all, whereas nobody else can observe my thoughts or feelings. Hence the data of consciousness are both superfluous and unverifiable.

Subjective data

Other psychologists and philosophers disagree, while not rejecting objective behavior as data. Although they are unfair in painting

---

[3] S. Koch gives the history graphically in the first chapter of *Behaviorism and Phenomenology*, the Rice symposium edited by T. W. Wann (Chicago: The University of Chicago Press, 1964), which also contains a chapter by B. F. Skinner. Cf. W. Harrell & J. R. Harrison, "The Rise and Fall of Behaviorism," *J. gen. Psychol.*, 1938, 18:401–402; Marvin M. Black, *The Pendulum Swings Back* (London: Cokesbury Press, 1937).

Skinner's *Walden Two* as the proposal of a monstrous Frankenstein, they present many arguments for a phenomenological and humanistic approach which would include also the data of consciousness as primary raw material in the study of man. Wittgenstein later at Cambridge, in his *Philosophical Investigations* (1953), uses linguistic analysis in a vein which is a far cry from the positivistic tone of his earlier Vienna *Tractatus* (1921).

Man has many activities, and they are of many different kinds. It would be begging the question at this point to determine which are specifically human and which are not. At least it is obvious that man's operations include some which are distinctly physical, for his body obeys the laws of gravity and motion, and some which are distinctively psychological, for man has conscious experiences of various kinds. If it is a fact that he has conscious experiences, it would be most unscientific to ignore them. Consequently this side argues that both the philosopher and the scientist must take into account both man's external behavior and his inner experience.

Language communicates personal experiences, implies that we know reality and can share our knowledge of it with others in a meaningful way—that there is meaning to be communicated. That human communication is successful at all is evidence that man can report his subjective experiences. He may not ordinarily reflect on them, unless he is in a philosophic mood. But he does make observations which he can make intelligible to others, which would be impossible if one were incapable of reliably reporting the data of consciousness. This is constantly reflected in our ordinary speech: "I have a toothache," has real meaning for you, even though it reports my purely subjective state. You know that it is I, not you, who has it, yet you know quite well what it is that I am experiencing. After all, a language that is totally private would not be a language; communication necessarily implies some commonality of what is expressed, or the communication could never occur. Similarly, it has been often noted that we cannot even make the distinction between public and private experience unless we all understand what private experience is; in which case it has something public about it. Conversely, every public experience is in a true sense private, or it would not be an experience.

Although an animal, man has many experiences which he does not share with other animals: the fact that he cares and is very much bothered by the "care-less" man means that he is committed to his fellow beings in a special relationship. He has emotions which are closely connected with his role as artist, as poet, as hero; yet neither artistry nor heroism is experienced as the result of mere emotion. Whatever we may know about animals by conjecture and analogy, only man has a sense of history: he is aware of the heritage of the past, and he knows that his own acts transcend the present and leave some footprints on the sands of time. He is conscious of his own mortality, yet because of his awareness of it he reaches out for relationships beyond himself: he wants to be remembered, to have relations with others that surpass his own contingent existence.

These facts of human experience are studied by modern existentialist and phenomenological philosophers, as well as by pragmatists such as James and Dewey, to throw light on the meaning of man. They are the common and repeatable observations of all men. Moreover, we can constantly check our experience against observable behavior. Since the report of subjective experiences is always liable to error, it must be used with care and constantly supplemented with other knowledge. To verify our own experiences, we must search outside ourselves and appeal to evidence in the external world, as apprehended by the senses. We examine the experiences of others during various periods of life from infancy to old age, in different races and different levels of civilization, in both normal and abnormal conditions, and in the light of the functioning of the brain, the nervous system, and the other physiological organs that mediate these processes. These findings may be supplemented by observations of animals other than man, but the data thus obtained are not in our direct experience and can give us information about human activities only by analogy. Experience remains our primary source of knowledge. Even the "tough-minded" experimentalist finds himself interpreting his data with reference to his own experience: operational definitions are really aimed at what is measured, though seemingly aimed at how we measure it.

This side argues further that the subjective are not the only data liable to error. Every scientist must trust his ability to report on his own conscious impressions. Even when he reads his thermometers and dials or looks into his microscope, what he records is really the result of his knowing process. If it is argued that he can always check his observations against those of others, the answer is obvious: since he knows the reports of others only through his conscious experience of hearing or reading them, he is again assuming the trustworthiness of his own experience as well as that of others. As mentioned earlier, no fact is entirely public because it always depends on a human report, and no fact is entirely private if it can be intelligibly reported to another.

Many facts cannot be known directly except by our own experience: e.g., the fact that two railroad tracks seem to converge in the distance, or the feeling of sadness. To convince yourself of this, try to imagine how you would explain what it means to have an idea or emotion to a being which never had one. Yet these experiences are commonly accepted and shared; we may disagree as to why the railroad tracks seem to converge, but we all admit they do seem to.

Such philosophers argue that just because the study of subjective processes is difficult is no reason to ignore them if they are facts. Arsenic is dangerous to work with, and a chemist would gladly prefer not to have to; the resulting chemistry without arsenic compounds would be easier, but hardly true. The mere fact that the subjective method is difficult does not justify abandoning it. Watching a white rat may be almost as easy as watching a ball roll down an inclined plane; but psychology is not physics, however much the early psychologists wished to pattern their science after physics. "Objective" must not be made synonymous with "true," for this implies that subjective experiences are not also facts.

Objective and subjective combined?

And so the argument goes. One professor does a classroom demonstration in which students "observe" varying and even contradictory details of the same incident which all have just witnessed. He concludes that consciousness is unreliable and we had better stick to observing objective behavior. His colleague in the next classroom takes the same facts and concludes that since we cannot trust even our observation of objective data, we must study phenomenology all the more intensely to make *any* reported data reliable. Some argue that neither method is sufficient by itself and that one must be checked against the other. Since consciousness is the only direct avenue to certain facts, it must be used in as sophisticated a manner as possible. Although by no means unanimous, many of those currently writing psychology seem to favor this middle course.

> *[Modern psychology has outgrown] the widespread feeling in some quarters that the admission of human feelings, attitudes, and perceptions as behavioral data flirts with the mystical and runs the risk of being "unscientific." No real science, however, can afford to ignore data relevant to its purposes simply because they are difficult to measure or do not lend themselves to treatment by orthodox means. If behavior is a function of perception, then a science of human relationships must concern itself with the meaning of events for the behaver as well as for the observer. Human feelings, attitudes, fears, hopes, wants, likes and aversions cannot be set aside while we deal with objective events. The subjective aspects of human experience cannot be suspended from operation.*

Perceptions are the very fabric of which human relationships are made (Combs & Snygg, 1959, p. 308).

J. P. Guilford (1950, p. 445) exemplifies this trend away from the extreme behavioristic position: "What I am saying is that the quest for easily objectifiable testing and scoring has directed us away from the attempt to measure some of the most precious qualities of individuals and hence to ignore those qualities." E. G. Boring (1951, pp. 360–363) in a review of Gibson's book on perception, which he considers very valuable and scholarly although it is not quantitative, remarks that many facts of experience are undeniable and as such should be the property of some science. He asks the question, "What science takes account of these facts if psychology does not?" He says that Gibson, to suit the behavioristic operationists, should have removed all doubt about his position by describing the operations by which it is verified of chimpanzees. But "How can we be sure that *Zeitgeist* is set eventually to make behavioristics the indisputable scientific truth? All in all the reviewer finds this book a remarkably keen, clear and wise description of just how it is that people see things. The chimpanzee phenomenology of vision, moreover, may need to wait until we have trained a chimpanzee to write it."

Many psychologists are unwilling to use words like consciousness, mind, mental, and introspection, which lost scientific respectability during the era of behaviorism. However they still wish to recognize that these psychological facts must be included in any description of human activity, so they now use such expressions as experience, covert behavior, or inner behavior. For many, the important thing is that both sets of data must be taken into account.

REVIEW QUESTIONS

1. Is the problem of the unity of man a question of (*a*) whether he has only one operation or one kind of operation, or (*b*) whether he operates as one being or many? Why?
2. Can you prove your own existence? Do you doubt it? Is it a blind assumption?
3. Why is a systematic approach to philosophy of man misleading? Has it any advantages?
4. Why do we begin the study of man with distinctively human experience instead of something simpler and more basic like biological functioning or animal behavior?

5. How are the dangers of pure phenomenology and introspectionism encountered in your answer to question 4 eliminated?
6. What is logical positivism? Is logical positivism a scientific or a philosophical position?
7. Why was operationism a healthy influence in psychology?
8. Why do you think psychology would lag behind physics by clinging to positivistic operationism and a Newtonian model of physics?
9. What is introspection? How does it differ from psychoanalysis? from philosophical analysis? from physiology? from phenomenology?
10. Could an observation of objective behavior be false? Could an observation of subjective experience be true? What do you conclude from this as to whether objective and true are synonymous?
11. List all the reasons you can why the philosophy of human nature should include man's organic functioning.

FOR FURTHER READING

Kelly & Tallon: the selection from **Heidegger** on pp. 164–173, and the chapters from **Jaspers** and **Newman.**

Two very handy sources of readings for this chapter, and for the entire book, are paperback collections. One edited by **Frank T. Severin,** *Humanistic Viewpoints in Psychology* (McGraw-Hill, 1965), includes selections from **D. O. Hebb, Percy Bridgman, Robert Oppenheimer, Werner Heisenberg, Henry Margenau,** and other scientists who point out the error of reducing philosophy to physical science. The other, *Challenges of Humanistic Psychology,* edited by **J. F. T. Bugental** (McGraw-Hill, 1967), answers the question of positivistic behaviorism, "What other kinds of knowledge are there?" Especially useful are the chapters by Bugental himself, **Hadley Cantril, Charlotte Buhler, Hubert Bonner,** and particularly that by **Willis Harman. Bonner's** own book *On Being Mindful of Man* amplifies his plea here for a more personalistic view.

Alfred North Whitehead in *Science and the Modern World,* **Werner Heisenberg** in *Physics and Philosophy,* and **Ernan McMullin** (in all of his writings listed in the General Bibliography) are examples of physicists who recognize that science deals at least as much with mental constructs as it does with physical data, to which latter the philosopher might actually be closer. **Michael Polanyi** is another physicist-turned-philosopher who, in *Personal Knowledge* and *The Study of*

Man, stresses the subjective factors in even physical science. **E. F. Caldin,** in *The Power and Limits of Science,* presents a balanced view of where excessive scientism had led.

Joseph R. Royce in *The Encapsulated Man* makes an eloquent plea for breaking out of the limited viewpoints within which man has entrenched himself.

Paul Ricoeur is a leading French phenomenologist who analyzes human finitude in *Fallible Man.* **Edmund Husserl,** the father of modern phenomenology, is very difficult to read. Perhaps a good place to start is *Phenomenology and the Crisis of Philosophy.* Nor is *Insight* by **Bernard Lonergan** easy reading, though it is rewarding. Some useful items on the phenomenological approach are the following:

> de Finance, Joseph, S.J. "Being and Subjectivity," *Cross Currents,* 1956, 6:163–178.
>
> Johann, Robert O., S.J. "Subjectivity," *Rev. Metaphysics,* 1958, 12:200–234.
>
> Kuenzli, Alfred E. (Ed.) *The Phenomenological Problem,* especially the chapters by **Carl Rogers, Robert MacLeod,** and **Combs & Snygg.**
>
> Kwant, Remy C. *The Phenomenological Philosophy of Merleau-Ponty.*
>
> Lauer, J. Quentin. *Phenomenology: Its Genesis and Prospect;* also published as *The Triumph of Subjectivity.*
>
> Luijpen, Wm. A. *Existential Phenomenology,* and *Phenomenology and Humanism.*
>
> Wann, T. W. (Ed.) *Behaviorism and Phenomenology.* The chapters by **Rogers** and **MacLeod.**

B. F. Skinner, besides his chapter in *Behaviorism and Phenomenology,* states his case well in *Science and Human Behavior* and in *Cumulative Record.* The student should evaluate whether **Joseph W. Krutch's** *The Measure of Man* is too narrow and opinionated an attack on Skinner. **Arthur Pap,** in his *An Introduction to the Philosophy of Science* (1963), has some interesting sections: "Theoretical Constructs and the Limitations of Operationism," pp. 39–57; "Behaviorism and the Postulate of Public Verifiability," pp. 67–74; "Mind and Behaviorism," pp. 374–409. **H. H. Price** of Oxford gives "**Some Objections to Behaviorism,**" in the symposium edited by **Sidney Hook** on *Dimensions of Mind.* A symposium expressing many points of view is that edited by **Herbert Feigl,** "**The Foundations of Science and the Concepts of Psychology and Psychoanalysis,**" in *Minnesota Studies in the Philosophy of Science,* vol. I. Note **Carnap's** shift away from logical positivism, pp. 38–76. Other discussions of the positivist-behaviorist approach are these:

Bakan, David. *The Duality of Human Experience* and his *On Method.*

Chein, Isidor. *The Image of Man,* final chapter.

Copleston, Frederick. *Contemporary Philosophy: Studies of Logical Positivism and Existentialism.*

Joad, C. E. M. *A Critique of Logical Positivism.*

MacPartland, John. *The March toward Matter.*

Martin, Oliver. "An Examination of Contemporary Naturalism and Materialism," in John Wild (Ed.) *The Return to Reason.*

Stotland, Ezra. "Mentalism Revisited," *J. gen. Psychol.,* 1966, 75:229–241.

Walker, Leslie J., S.J. *Theories of Knowledge.*

Wellmuth, John J. *The Nature and Origins of Scientism.*

Wild, John. *Introduction to Realistic Philosophy.*

3 PHILOSOPHY, SCIENCE, AND MAN

Those who ignore history are doomed to repeat it.   Santayana

Each student must start from scratch in the sense that a true philosopher does not accept anything just on someone's say-so. He must work out his own philosophy if it is to have real meaning for him. But although personal conviction can not be communicated, information can. Man has been described as an animal incapable of learning from his own history, and in the matter of world wars there seems to be all too much truth in that. But there is nothing wrong in taking advantage of what has gone before, or at least considering it as part of the data.

The history of philosophy is sometimes to the philosopher what the experimental laboratory is to the scientist. When the scientist wishes to know what would happen if two chemicals are mixed, he takes a beaker and mixes them. When the philosopher wishes to know what will happen when this theory is proposed or that line of reasoning pursued, he does not have to speculate. He can delve into the history of philosophy and find recorded there the accumulated experiences of the human mind in dealing with these problems over the centuries.

The student does not want to be told answers, but at least he can be helped to avoid asking the wrong questions, or asking them in a way that leads down blind alleys. The history of the philosophy of man especially has all too often been a matter of, "Ask a foolish question and you get a foolish answer." The eventual outcome of an initial position or faulty question is rarely foreseen by its originator, nor can the originator control the trend of a thought developed over several generations. Given the fact that philosophers, too, are human beings with emotions, fears, ambitions, and resentments, it is not surprising that many developments in the history of ideas are really historical accidents rather than the result of orderly planning. Not only are there lessons for all of us in this; there may be a thread of unity in philosophical experience, a least common denominator that has filtered out, of which we can take advantage in building our own views.

Indifference of the scientist toward the history of ideas is in striking contrast to his attitude toward the history of his own science. He does not simply lead the beginning psychology student into a well-equipped laboratory and tell him, "Now go ahead and discover the laws of learning," or perception, as the case may be, any more than the chemistry professor would turn his neophyte chemists loose in a laboratory full of reagents and have them "discover" oxygen, blissfully ignorant of the fact that Lavoisier and Cavendish ever lived. If, in the sciences, we give the beginning student the benefit of the accumulated experiences and achievements of the past, why should we naïvely hope to start from scratch in philosophy and ignore what has gone before?

Thus, the psychologist's disdain for philosophy has often robbed him of the fruits of over 2,300 years of human experience with the very problems to which his science almost always leads. The result is sometimes almost amusing. One quite competent American psychologist, in discussing the monism-dualism problem which occurs perennially, tried to show his awareness of history by stating that the problem was not a new one, for its history "goes as far back as Spinoza." What he seemed to be unaware of is that the problem was raised by the ancient Greeks and thoroughly discussed in the Middle Ages. To go back only as far as Spinoza (A.D. 1677) fails to take advantage of historical perspective and over 2,000 years of earlier philosophy. "We are dwarfs, but standing on the shoulders of giants" is the attitude we prefer to assume. The giants of the past give us a vision superior to the limited perspective we would have, were we unwilling to profit from previous experimenting.

Spearman spends much of his two-volume *Psychology down the Ages* showing how often the psychologists of a later generation brought in the back door under a new name what had previously been thrown out the front door. The facts remain; rejection of a name usually means correcting a faulty conception with which the facts have become entangled. Spearman shows how "faculty" is thrown out and *ability* brought in a decade later; "instinct" goes out and *drives* comes in; "intellect" falls into disrepute and fifty years later we see a great revival of interest in *thinking;* "free will" was rejected as unscientific nonsense and now psychologists talk of *selective inhibition, client responsibility, self-determination,* and *choice-behavior.* And J. McV. Hunt, after surveying the past history and present status of psychology, concluded his presidential address to the American Psychological Association (1952) with a prediction that psychology would rediscover the soul.

In addition to this value of the history of philosophy as a laboratory for testing the perennial worth of ideas and validity of questions, history can also give us broad balance in the face of philosophical conflict. Great tolerance for the divergent opinions found among even good minds flows from an awareness of "how they got that way."

Knowledge of history will thus help us over one of philosophy's biggest hurdles: "How can I be right and very intelligent men be wrong?" Sentimentally distorted ideas of democracy can lead one to avoid facing the fact that contradictory opinions cannot both be right. It is necessary to distinguish between a person's right to an opinion and the opinion itself. The stand that "everything is just a matter of opinion" is itself merely an opinion, and it opens up the possibility that the opposite is true. If one tries to settle his bank balance on the basis of an opinion that two plus two equals five, he will find the teller tolerant of him as a person, but the truth quite intolerant—as history bears witness.

PHILOSOPHY AND SCIENCE

There have been many ways of seeking the answer to man's meaning. Many sciences study man: psychology, anthropology, sociology, biochemistry. Can they give us the answers we seek? No, our questions do not fall within the scope of the sciences as such. Are we, then, to jump to the supernatural? Not if we are to stay in philosophy. Occupying the middle ground between science and theology, philosophy has not always been fully appreciated. During the last several centuries, first theological controversies and then the progress of science have held a dominant position in our culture. Philosophy, meanwhile, has been belittled as mere empty speculation from a prescientific era. (Philosophy may be called a science in an older sense of the term, but as with the word psychology, we prefer to conform with current usage and equate the term science with the positive or natural sciences, physical and behavioral.)

How then does philosophy differ from science, and specifically, how does the philosophy of man differ from modern scientific psychology? To begin with, it should be noted that the word "psychology" had for many centuries been used to designate that part of philosophy which deals with man and his ultimate nature. The Greek word "psyche" usually meant soul, and it was used because those philosophers found the ultimate characteristic of man to be that he was a be-souled organism. (Aristotle's *De Anima* is really $\pi\epsilon\rho\grave{\iota}\ \Psi\nu\chi\hat{\eta}s$.) Ironically enough, the Greek symbol for the psyche (Ψ) is still used by the American Psychological Association on all its publications, although they contain no discussion of the soul. The reason is that after the modern biosocial science which we now know as psychology was born, about 1879, it took over this word for itself. The philosopher, who might have argued his right to the word on the grounds of "who was there first," has had to search out a new term for that part of philosophy now called philosophy of man, philosophy of human nature, or philosophical anthropology.[1]

Briefly, philosophy differs from science in three ways: the kind of facts used, the method of procedure, and the type of knowledge obtained. We are here speaking of philosophy in general as opposed to science; we have seen in the previous chapters that there are many different philosophical approaches.

Kind of facts used

First, let us be clear that both the philosopher and the scientist start with facts. Philosophy which is not grounded on facts is not worth considering. It must also be broad enough to be compatible with all the facts. At this point it may be asked how any of the earlier philosophies about man could be valid today, since they were unaware of the many facts which have been uncovered by the modern techniques of biology and experimental psychology. The answer is that the philosopher and the scientist work from different kinds of facts.

The *scientist* uses complex experimental facts whose discovery may involve highly elaborate technological equipment, experimental labora-

[1] The term "rational psychology" seems an inappropriate title for the philosophy of man. It has two unfortunate implications. It implies that scientific psychology does not study man's rational operations; yet thinking and choice-behavior are unavoidable psychological facts, as we have seen. And it implies that philosophy studies *only* the rational operations; yet the sensory and organic aspect must be included or a false picture of man will result.

tories, or refined statistical procedures. He usually makes exact measurements and presents his data quantitatively. For instance, the scientist may want to measure precisely the relation between the intensity of a stimulus and the intensity of a resulting sensation, or how a certain manner of learning affects the quantity of the result. He must control variable conditions and take many readings.

The *philosopher* begins with simple, primary facts which are commonly observable and which require no technology to discover. Of these he can be absolutely certain, and he need not worry about the precision of his measurements. He bases his conclusions on general facts which are directly observable in the common experience and behavior of all mankind: the facts that people live and die, think, feel, digest their dinners, see and hear. When discussing the important problem of the unity of man, we come back time and time again to two easily observable facts: this man understands, this man dies. The fact that people know or that people die need not be learned in a laboratory or through elaborate statistical investigation. There is nothing closer to us than the experience of knowing, and we are all quite certain that man is the sort of being that dies.

These general facts, so readily observable, are quite different from so-called "commonsense" notions which are often mere folklore. Most psychology books begin with a list of such common impressions, which they rightly show to be unwarranted: purported differences between men and women, misconceptions about the influence of heredity, and the like. These are not observed facts, but theories illogically inferred from haphazard observation. They demand critical, scientific investigation. We are talking about facts so directly observable that they are not a matter of inference—facts that are admittedly broad and general, leaving details to the scientist—but that are so incontestably evident that they need no further verification and are universally admitted. For example, it is unscientific to say that people with red hair get more angry than others, but it is a commonly admitted fact that people do get angry. This is the type of general fact which the philosopher uses.

These facts are the common property of philosopher and scientist alike. The experimental psychologist carries such certitude with him when he enters his laboratory. He could not even begin to set up an experiment on hearing or vision if he did not first know the difference between seeing and hearing, or that there are such processes. This is why we are not called upon to revise our philosophical conclusions every time a new article refuting the claims of a previous article is published in one of the scientific journals. Facts of the type that the philosopher uses simply do not change, although the causes underlying them may be understood more and more clearly.

Method of procedure

Besides this difference in kind of facts used, philosophy and science differ in method. The scientist uses his elaborate techniques of observation and his laboratory instruments to gather a very wide and valid sampling of detailed facts. He is concerned about the adequacy of his coverage of cases, and from them he develops an explanatory hypothesis, which he then proceeds to verify through experiments. The philosopher does not proceed in this way, but his method must be, if possible, even more certain. Beginning with commonly observable facts about man's behavior and experience, he proceeds upon an investigation such as we have indicated in the two previous chapters. Note that the philosopher is not opposed to scientific methodology. He favors it, and opposes only the unscientific assumption that the scientific method is the only road to knowledge, or that it is always the best.

The philosopher cannot afford to have his conclusions couched in approximations such as those with which the scientist emerges from his laboratory. We may take an example from geometry to illustrate the difference (while noting that mathematics is not philosophy). A boy trained exclusively in the methods of the physical sciences would try to "prove" theorems by laying out lines and triangles carefully on gold foil, measuring them with a micrometer caliper for uniform thickness, weighing them on a delicate scale, or measuring them many times with precise instruments. At best he would emerge with the conclusion that angle A equalled angle B $\pm$ 0.0018°, or that the sum of the squares of the sides of a right triangle equalled the square of the hypotenuse plus or minus some respectable margin of error. In contrast, by some orderly reasoning about the congruence of triangles, we can conclude that these angles or squares are equal exactly and certainly, with no "plus or minus."

The average college student thinks of philosophy as some very abstruse, mysterious, and difficult study which is far beyond his powers. Actually it is much simpler and much easier than the physical sciences. The basic conclusions of this course can be reached much more easily than the molecular structure of a polymer or DNA, though they are not always agreed upon for a variety of reasons, often historical.

Contrary to the false impression some have of philosophic procedure, we cannot begin with the essence or nature of man any more than does the scientist. Likewise, we do not deduce the existence of anything from its definition. Rather we begin with the facts of man's behavior and experience and see where these facts lead as a necessary ultimate explanation. In doing so we shall often avail ourselves of data discovered in experimental science in so far as they clarify, confirm, and enrich common experience. For example, Gestalt psychology and Ames's illusion experiments enlarge our knowledge of the subjective factors in perception. It may be that on some points the refined details of science may give us factual basis for modifying minor philosophical conclusions, but they cannot alter the general lines of our argument. This is because the commonly observable facts of which we spoke above are prior to both science and philosophy.

It should be noted that the philosophy of man is not just "applied metaphysics," i.e., the philosopher does not take some preconceived philosophical principles and from them deduce conclusions about the nature of man. Rather, he begins with the facts and from them discovers what kind of being man is. Neither can the philosopher begin with blind assumptions; however, here he may legitimately accept as true some things which have been established elsewhere, e.g., in logic, just as the professor of biochemistry may assume the facts of general chemistry and anatomy.

When we say that the philosopher proceeds from the facts of what man does to an understanding of what man is, this does not imply that he attempts to decide whether a given trait or need is "natural" in a sense of being inherited or acquired. This is a problem for the scientific psychologist. The philosopher is content with the fact that man exhibits the trait, that he is clearly capable of this activity, whether because he is born with the capability or is the kind of being which can learn or acquire it. Much controversy among psychologists is thus irrelevant to the philosopher if he properly understands the limits of his investigation. This will be clear from the discussion in the next section of this chapter, on the nature of philosophical knowledge.

Thus the method of the philosopher is simpler than the hypothetical-deductive-verification method which the scientist must use. Is there, then, no verification for the philosopher's conclusions? Besides the tests of consistency with the rest of his philosophy and pragmatic relation to the experienced world of facts, there is the further test of time. This is the importance of the history of philosophy.

Type of knowledge sought

Philosophy differs from science also in the type of conclusion to be sought. The subject matter may be the same; for instance, man. The difference is in the aspect under which man is studied. Thus sociology deals with man under the group aspect, biochemistry deals with him from the viewpoint of chemistry, the psychologist is interested in the laws of human behavior and experience. These sciences consider man socially, chemically, and psychologically. In contrast to these limited aspects, the philosopher takes an unlimited view. The former give expert knowledge, but he seeks wisdom. He wishes to understand the very being of man *as man*. Concerned with meaning rather than data, he wishes to achieve at least a limited understanding of man's being, of what man *is*.

But how much can the philosopher know? Here opinions range from the one extreme of logical positivism, which would give us mere behavioral correlations, mere descriptions of the laws of man's operations, all the way to the naïve essentialism of some Aristotelians, who would imply that the philosopher can know the essences of many things. We must not be deluded into the optimism of this latter position by the shift away from extreme positivism noted at the end of the previous chapter. We never know any essence completely, not even that of man.

If philosophy here is easier than science, it is perhaps because it has a broader target. The philosopher, because he relies more on common facts, can move more easily within the existential order. But his conclusions are also going to be more general than those of the scientist, even if more certain. He must humbly go about the sublime task of investigating man's fundamental nature, his essential properties. What he seeks is understanding in terms of basic principles: a viewpoint from which he can see all the facts in a balanced and meaningful relationship. By way of analogy, we could say that a microscope is useful, but the bacteriologist cannot use it to tell whether his child has a smile or frown for daddy; he can see meaning in the arrangement of face muscles only by getting away from individual cells and looking at the pattern as a whole. Again, a mosaic has meaning never revealed by examination only of the individual stones that make it up.

Similarly, the philosopher in using only the most common and accessible facts misses much of the richness of detail uncovered by science. He must be content to paint with broad strokes a picture substantially correct in its bold outline, which can then be filled in by the scientist's researches. His picture will not be exhaustive, nor does he naïvely expect an exact replica of man's nature; but it will be existential in the best sense of that word, for he moves directly from his experience of what man actually does to what man is.[2] His picture

[2] The Judaeo-Christian conception is much more existential than Aristotle's, for its thought is more concerned with the existing individual than with abstract essences. (This does not mean that religious belief is invoked as philosophical proof: we simply call attention to the admitted fact that different traditions may suggest different avenues for philosophical investigation.)

will not be stagnant, for he will be constantly at work to make it a more and more nearly perfect represention of reality; yet it will have a certain stability, for it is based on facts which cannot change.

SPECIAL RELATION OF PSYCHOLOGY TO PHILOSOPHY

The peculiar nature of the subject matter of psychology, viz., man, seems to place it in a very special relation to philosophy, even though now it is a distinct science. This seems to be true not only of psychology as applied (clinical), but even as a pure or theoretical science. The existence of this special relation is evidenced by (1) the nature of psychology and (2) the writings of psychologists.

1. One fact peculiar to psychology is that the scientist is his own data: his nature is too close to the facts concerning his study to escape notice. Whereas the chemist can be proficient in his subject matter without elaborating a cosmology, the same does not seem to be true of the psychologist and a philosophy of man. The chemist can study structures and valences without asking why they should be that way, what is their purpose or goal. But goals and purposes are so much a part of every man's experience that the psychologist is led inevitably to philosophical considerations (pp. 28–31 above). Moreover, the concepts used in the empirical approach (the terms of the induction) usually have meaning only within a philosophical structure.

Because of the complexity of man, you can hardly control all the variables, or know when you have an adequate induction, unless you have as a guide a basic understanding of the nature of man. Again, philosophical presuppositions determine our choice of the phenomena to be studied. The queer mixture of facts about man, viz., his mental or conscious experience and his observable organic behavior, lead at least to suspicions that his nature must be complex even though we avoid any dualism.

2. This special relationship is confirmed by the history and present status of scientific psychology, as seen in statements by the psychologists themselves.

J. L. McCary in *Psychology of Personality: Six Modern Approaches* (1956, pp. xiii–xiv) points out how modern psychology, which has never been able to stomach Cartesian dualism, has had to wrestle constantly with the apparent dichotomy between organic and mental, a split which is only now disappearing in favor in integration. These problems are inescapably philosophical. Likewise, the fact that man has some control and direction of his drives or responses to stimuli suggests that other laws of nature must apply to his behavior than those which control the activity of beings which do not have this inner regulation.

Cole concludes his rather lengthy book *Human Behavior: Psychology as a Bio-social Science* (1953, p. 822, italics his), with a summary restatement of Erich Fromm's position as follows: "There is an *essential Homo sapiens*. The essence is discoverable. . . . In a sense this is a kind of neo-Thomism, a new-Aristotelian affirmation of an essential nature of man, an affirmation of the worthwhileness of the quest for a kind of absolute psychology, a super-cultural understanding on whose groundwork we could draw up a new *rights of man* that would form the charter for right living. . . ."

This type of statement would not be found in a science textbook written before the middle of this century, but there is a growing awareness among psychologists of the need for philosophy. American psychologists are coming more and more to recognize explicitly the relation of their science to philosophy and the distinctly philosophical nature of some of the problems which have plagued them in the construction of their theories.

Most significant of this is the fact that since 1963 the American Psychological Association has had a very active Division (24) on Philosophical Psychology, involving a broad spectrum of members from the other divisions.

As a matter of fact, psychologists rarely succeed in avoiding at least an implicit reliance on philosophy, in spite of professing to stay in the realm of pure science. "Every psychology of personality is also a philosophy of the person," says Gordon Allport (1961). Reviewing the results of a symposium of outstanding psychologists attempting to work "Toward a Unified Theory of Human Behavior," Cartwright (1957, p. 122) observes:

> It should come as no surprise, then, to find the same ancient problems causing trouble. They were rarely taken on deliberately; they just had a way of slipping into the conference room. The mind-body problem was there in all of its manifestations, for the conference was trying to arrange a compatible marriage between soma and psyche. Teleology reared its ugly head, and much time was consumed worrying about the propriety of using the word "goal" in polite scientific society. Reductionism insisted on being heard, but there never was agreement on what was to be reduced to what. For a time it did appear, though, that psychology might be dispensed with as long as biology and sociology were kept. And meaning persisted in sneaking in. . . . And yet a gnawing uneasiness remained to the end. Do these concepts provide mere analogies? Has a unity of science been achieved? Is the result really a monism, or a socio-psychophysical parallelism? What is actually accomplished by noting that cells and societies both have boundaries and steady states? What is the proper role of analogy in science?

These are all philosophical questions, whose answers deserve a philosophical competence few psychologists even strive to attain. Psychologists often forget that the denial of metaphysics is itself a metaphysical position, and materialism is every bit as much a philosophy as is an attitude that goes beyond matter. Now that psychology has dropped the adolescent defensiveness which characterized its earlier struggle to emancipate itself from philosophy, it is time to acknowledge its awareness of interdisciplinary relations. Boring editorialized in *Contemporary Psychology* (1958, 3:362), ". . . the psychologists resist the humanizing deviations that would bring their science over toward scholarship and wisdom and understanding, resist them sometimes because they are dedicated to a narrow empiricism."

Although it would be quite legitimate simply to ignore philosophy, most psychologists of the first half of the twentieth century were not entirely nonphilosophical. Rather, in their desire to *avoid* philosophy, they failed to take it seriously enough to achieve the competence necessary to develop any explicit philosophy, and simply indulged in some implicit and often lamentable philosophizing of their own.

The various behavioristic schools of psychology in the first half of this century were inclined to imply that we can know nothing but external behavior, or nothing but operations. Now the denial of other kinds of knowledge is an epistemology, a philosophical position rather than a scientific one. Again, some tended to imply that man and indeed all reality is composed of nothing but matter. But any assertion or denial of the ultimate principles of all being is a metaphysics. Hence the reductionist "nothing-but" positions of these schools of psychology were really philosophical. Moreover, they were assumptions that were not based on data. Materialism is not a conclusion from a laboratory experiment, but a metaphysics. There is always danger that the prestige merited in one field will be thought a proof of competence in all: neither the Pope nor a Beethoven is an authority on baseball, nor is the scientist *as scientist* an expert on philosophy.

The present endeavor differs at least in being frankly philosophical instead of surreptitiously so. Even were this study of little aid to the scientific psychologist, it has in itself the value of all philosophy: pursuit of that simpler truth which is wisdom.

REVIEW QUESTIONS

1. Why is the history of philosophy like a laboratory?
2. If philosophy is based on facts, how could earlier philosophies of man be valid since the facts of modern biology and psychology were unknown then?
3. What events in the history of the last 400 years would explain why many scientists are unwilling to look toward the Middle Ages as sources of valid knowledge?
4. How does philosophy differ from theology?
5. Are philosophy and psychology distinct? Have they always been kept separate?
6. Does modern psychology *as a science* take a position with regard to the existence of the soul?
7. Can we establish the nature of man from a definition?
8. Does the philosopher argue that *because* man has a soul as a principle of unity, therefore man is one being? Why? Show the connection between the question and your answer to question 7.
9. Would it be correct to say that philosophy studies man's soul, whereas science studies his body?

FOR FURTHER READING

Kelly & Tallon: the selection from **Heidegger** on pp. 159–164.

In addition to **C. Spearman's** *Psychology Down the Ages,* mentioned in this chapter, a fascinating book on the history of philosophy as the laboratory of thought is **E. Gilson's** *The Unity of Philosophical Experience,* wherein he concludes in Part IV that "metaphysics always buries its undertakers." **Ray Hyman,** in *The Nature of Psychological In-*

quiry, and **T. S. Kuhn,** in tracing *The Structure of Scientific Revolutions,* show how intimately the history of science is bound up with the philosophies and personalities of the times. **B. Wolman** and **E. Nagel,** in *Scientific Psychology,* quote the great psychologist **E. C. Tolman** as saying that "all human knowledge, including my theory, results from and is limited by behavioral needs." Two more books illustrating the human side of the history of science are **Karl Popper's** *Conjectures and Refutations: The Growth of Scientific Knowledge* and **A. H. Maslow's** *The Psychology of Science: A Reconnaissance.*

Mary Hesse discusses *Models and Analogies in Science,* and **Errol Harris** talks about *The Foundation of Metaphysics in Science.* The following shed further light on the relations between philosophy and science:

> Friedrich, L. W., S.J. (Ed.) *The Nature of Physical Knowledge.*
> Koren, Henry J. *Research in Philosophy.*
> Lee, Otis. *Existence and Inquiry.* Pp. 307–309 contain a clear statement on the difference between philosophy and science.
> McCall, Raymond J. *Preface to Scientific Psychology.* A good explanation of the nature of scientific psychology.
> Martin, Oliver. *The Order and Integration of Knowledge.* Chap. 9.

Michael Scriven, *Primary Philosophy,* and **E. H. Madden,** *Philosophical Problems in Psychology,* explore various aspects of the relation between philosophy and psychology from the viewpoint of analytic philosophy. Other views on this point are:

> Feigl, Herbert. "Philosophical Embarrassments of Psychology" (invited address to the 1958 convention of the American Psychological Association), *Am. Psychologist,* 1959, 14:115–128.
> Gustafson, Donald F. (Ed.) *Essays in Philosophical Psychology.*
> Mercier, J. *The Origins of Contemporary Psychology.*
> Misiak, Henryk. *The Philosophical Roots of Scientific Psychology.*
> Müller-Freienfels, Richard. *The Evolution of Modern Psychology.*
> Murphy, Gardner. *An Historical Introduction to Modern Psychology.*

See also the presidential addresses of **J. McV. Hunt, O. H. Mowrer, Fred McKinney, J. P. Guilford, K. S. Lashley,** and **J. E. Royce,** listed in the General Bibliography.

II
MAN THE KNOWER

4   ORIGINS OF KNOWLEDGE

. . . the things which exist around us, which we touch, see, hear and taste, are regarded as interrogations for which an answer must be sought. . . .   Dewey

A fundamental fact about man is his ability to know, to be aware of things, of himself, and even of his own awareness. We could not even begin to discuss the whole question of knowledge if we were not already aware by direct experience of what it means to know. All science presumes this ability, for science is simply one kind of knowledge. We may only infer that other animals know; but in the case of man the fact that he knows is clear, however we may explain it or whether we are able to explain it at all.

But whereas the scientist may concentrate on the objects he knows, the philosopher must penetrate into this mysterious realm of knowing itself and try to understand what the process involves. The marvel of radar is nothing without the power of sight we take for granted as we examine the screen or read about the usefulness of this discovery. We shall begin by examining the facts concerning human knowledge, leaving to Chapter 8 the philosophical explanation of its nature. In the investigation of the knowing processes themselves we shall rely largely on data known by common or general observation, and supplement them with the findings of experimental psychology when useful.

KNOWERS VERSUS NONKNOWERS

To begin with, knowing differs from nonknowing qualitatively, not merely in degree. As John Dewey says, "No inanimate thing reacts to things *as* problematic. Its behavior to other things is capable of description in terms of what is determinately there. Under given conditions, it just reacts or does not react" (1929, p. 345). If we analyze even the activity of plants or the physiological level of operation which men and other animals share with the vegetable kingdom, we see that the quantity of the response is the important factor. There is always a direct relation or correspondence between the quantity of stimulus and the quantity of the response. There may be qualities which distinguish these reactions from those of nonliving things, but measurement is always possible. But in psychological activity it is the *quality* of the response that is most important. There need not be any correspondence between the quantity of the stimulus and the quantity of the response; e.g., a dog may react in the same way whether he sees his master 100 yards away or 10 feet away.

The amoeba can learn by experience that it can entrap living prey by putting out its pseudopod in a circular way instead of directly, whereas the fly-catcher plant never achieves this qualitative modification of response.

The fly-catcher plant *Dionaea muscipula* (Venus's-flytrap) has leaves which curl up at a slight touch and thus trap insects, but there is no more evidence for its being aware than there is for the morning glory or the heliotrope being aware of the sun; these reactions are in the category of vegetative tropisms. The mere fact of response is not evidence of consciousness. "How does the fly-catcher plant know that the fly is there?" can be answered by asking, "How does the rat trap know that the rat is there?"

The difference in quality between a knowing and a nonknowing being may be clear enough in theory, but we do not pretend that it is always easy to apply the theory in all instances. The details of the application are the work of the scientists. Our present knowledge does not enable us to tell for sure whether certain organisms are vegetative or animal. The student must decide whether this proves that there is no difference between a vegetable and an animal. There might never be agreement on the precise point at which green shades into blue on the spectrum, yet no one would argue that therefore green is blue. The essential difference between plant and higher forms of life is not the possession of a nervous system or locomotion, nor is it a matter of photosynthesis, chlorophyll, or the direction of carbon dioxide interchange. Nor is it simply a matter of irritability or adaptive response. The difference lies in the possession of that unique and qualitative experience we call consciousness, awareness, or knowing. Either a being has at least the elemental sense of touch or taste, or it does not. We have no right to assert the existence of such abilities when there is no evidence of their operation.

SENSATION

It is now time to begin a detailed exploration of our knowing experience. "Here I am" implies first of all an existing presence, a presence somwhere in the world of physical space. Though I may not know where the "here" is, it is quite clear that this elementary awareness contains some relation to reality other than myself, whatever that reality may consist of. If I start to explore that reality, it is obvious that I must have some ability to be in contact with it. The word "contact" literally means touch, which suggests that touch is a very fundamental avenue of approach. The infant explores his own body by feeling it long before he looks in a mirror, and lower animals which lack most or all of the other kinds of sensation at least seem to have touch receptors. We use expressions like "get the feel of it" when examining a new golf club or even trying out a new car.

Is touching the only way I can know? Appropriate as this question might be for a worm, it is quite apparent that man has other kinds of awareness. The blind man who recovers his sight by a surgical operation may tell us that at first he seems to experience things touching his eyes when he sees. But his subsequent accounts as well as our normal visual sensations indicate that this was due to a lifetime depending on touch as a primary source of information. Both he and ourselves find little difficulty in recognizing that seeing is a different kind of sensation than touching. When something does actually touch our eye it is clearly a different matter from when we see it.

Here we have grounds for our first distinction among kinds of knowing. Up to now we have been impressed by the totality and complexity of the knowing process, and that something is lost by dissection. Without losing sight of this totality, we may briefly examine the various kinds of sensation. The inquiry can be brief because the philosopher may leave detailed investigation to the experimental psychologists. The philosopher is interested in the nature of sensation and its relation to the rest of knowledge, and what its analysis can tell us about man. All human knowledge seems to begin in some way from the senses, which suggests that man's body is a primary avenue of information. For this reason the sensist and positivist philosophers are preoccupied with sensory data. But the precise number of senses and their mode of operation is of more scientific than philosophical interest. The old popular tendency to restrict the number to five, and group under the general name of touch all the others besides sight, hearing, taste, and smell, is unfortunate and is due to a misreading of Aristotle. Philosophically, it makes no difference whether man has five or five hundred senses.

The word sensation here connotes not what is meant by calling a Hollywood movie "sensational" but only the simple awareness resulting from the stimulation of a receptor organ. It practically never occurs in isolation, as noted before, but as part of a total perceptual process. Details of its connection with specific end organs are again left to the scientist, but in general our experience tells us that we somehow see with our eyes, hear with our ears, and so forth.

Proper object

Even when we are uncertain as to the precise bodily organ, we can distinguish sensations from one another by the distinct quality of the experience. The color-blind physicist may describe red in terms of wavelengths, but he cannot have the unique sensory experience of this particular sensible quality. Try to explain to a man born blind the difference between red and green. He may understand intellectually, but this does not have the quality of the sensory awareness itself. Our attempt convinces us that a color such as red or green or blue is not warm or cold, soft or hard, sweet or sour or stinky, except by association. Some things are known only by one precise knowing ability. A flower may look as though it will smell sweet, but only by my nose can I really tell (as a novice hiker will discover when he whiffs the pretty "skunk cabbage"). We may refer to this fact by saying that color is the *proper object* of vision, odor the proper object of our sense of smell, and so forth. It is that which is directly and uniquely attained by that activity and no other. In the case of the senses it is some sensible quality of the object, sometimes referred to simply as a proper sensible.

Other meanings of "object"

We say "properly" and "uniquely" because some sensible qualities can be known through the operation of two or more senses. For instance, I may know the round shape of an object by looking at it, by pressing it against my skin, or by running my finger around its edges. Thus shape is not proper to any one sense, but *common* to sight, touch, and kinesthesis (sense of motion). Similarly with the movement of an object, or its distance from the viewer, and many other common sensible qualities. Again, if I strike the eyeball I may see a flash of light, but one would hardly argue that this is a proper function of the organ of seeing. Some qualities proper to one mode of knowing are only incidental to another.

Further linguistic analysis reveals that there are still other different meanings of the word "object." Object in general means that with which any operation deals or with which an operation is concerned. Note that in this context the word object does *not* mean end or purpose, as it does in the expression, "What was his object in going downtown?" Rather, it simply refers to that toward which the activity is essentially ordered. Thus the object of knowledge is that which is known, the object of desire is that which is desired.

Formal object is the precise aspect under which the object is attained. Thus we saw in Chapter 3 that man is known under the different aspects of biochemistry, anthropology, philosophy of man, and so forth. It is clear then that the same thing may have many different formal objects, i.e., it can be attained or operated upon in many different ways or under different aspects. Thus the material food on my plate may be considered under the formality of color, desirability, or calorie content, depending on whether I am discussing visual perception, appetite, or nutrition.

Formal object may be proper, common, or even incidental as we discovered above in analyzing sensations. In this sense "object" is not a *thing*, but only data for further knowing.

Activities classified by their proper objects

Man's abilities and activities are sometimes said to be *specified* (classified, recognized, identified as to species) by their proper objects. This simply means that how many different *kinds* of operation we have depends on how many different proper formal objects we can discern. We may see trees, houses, cars; but this does not give three powers of sight, since all these are seen by the same kind of operation (seeing) and under the same formal aspect or quality, color. But color and odor, even in the same thing, are not attainable in the same way: smelling is a different kind of operation from vision. It has a different proper object.

THE SPECIAL SENSES IN DETAIL

We usually designate by the term *special sense* the ability we have to experience a proper quality resulting from present stimulation of a sense organ. There are many different classifications of the special senses. The one given below is fairly common and representative of our present knowledge. Since this matter is not the subject of any great philosophical controversy, it seems suitable to our brief exploration.

Distance senses
  Visual
  Auditory
Chemical senses
  Taste
  Smell
Somesthetic (body) senses
  Cutaneous (skin)
    Pressure or touch
    Warmth
    Cold
    Pain
  Kinesthetic (active movement)
  Vestibular (body motion and position)
  Organic

VISION The most well-known of our special senses is probably vision. Its proper object is color, which the psychologists usually divide into chromatic (the colors of the spectrum) and achromatic (the black-gray-white tones). Although, according to the physicist, black is the absence of wavelength, the psychologists recognize a certain sensation designated as black. The specific receptor or end organ for vision is the rods and cones which form the endings of the optic nerve in the retina at the back of the eyeball. The organ also includes the optic nerve itself and the occipital areas of the cerebral cortex which form the visual center in the brain. Note that many extended things are not visible at all, including light itself under certain conditions. The object, then, is color, which is light as reflected or refracted by a surface, rather than light itself.

HEARING The object of hearing is either tone or noise, the difference being largely a matter of the regularity of vibration in the air waves. The specific receptor is the organ of Corti in the inner ear, where the endings of the auditory nerve are arranged along the inner windings of a small bony structure called the cochlea, because it is shaped something like a snail shell. The marvel of hearing is perhaps less appreciated than that of seeing; actually, the ear is capable of extremely fine discriminations of pitch, intensity, and timbre or quality, and in some ways surpasses the eye.

TASTE Gustatory sensations have as their object the flavors usually designated under the categories of sweet, salt, sour, and bitter. The taste receptors are found on the taste buds, chiefly on the edges and around the surface of the tongue.

SMELL The proper object of olfactory sensations is odor. Attempts to standardize the terminology and classify odors have so far been only moderately successful. The receptor is the olfactory nerve endings high in the nose which are directly connected to the olfactory bulbs of the brain, lying just below the frontal lobes. Although smell has less importance in the life of man than in that of the lower animals, it does play a very important part in warning us of dangers and helping to identify objects. A great deal of what is mistakenly thought to be taste is actually a matter of odor. The common evidence for this is the lack of taste when one holds one's nose.

CUTANEOUS The skin senses generally inform us of objects having the qualities of warmth, cold, smoothness, hardness, and others which may affect us by exerting pressure on the skin. This pressure may even become painful. It is a matter of indifference whether pain be considered a special category of sensation or a quality of all sensations, since it seems that any of them can become painful if the stimulus is too intense. The receptors for the skin senses have been very carefully studied. Different types of nerve endings in the skin have been identified anatomically, and some success has been achieved in relating them to different sensory qualities. But the results of these investigations are by no means certain and adequate. Seldom have scientists worked so assiduously at a problem with so little success. Recent experiments have indicated that sensations of both pressure and temperature are the result not so much of the contact itself but rather of a change in contact. Thus pressure and temperature become relative to the previous stimulus rather than absolute, as far as sensation is concerned.

KINESTHESIS The word "kinesthesis," from the Greek words meaning feeling and motion, refers to the active movement of the parts of our body. The receptors are nerve endings in the muscles, tendons, and joints, which report the movement. The importance of this sense quality is readily seen when we consider the conditions in which it is absent: when our foot has gone to sleep, or when some disease makes us unable to feel the position and movement of our limbs, we find such movements as walking very difficult, even though the motor nerves are intact.

VESTIBULAR The sense of equilibrium has to do with body position in relation to gravity and passive motion of the body as a whole. It is concerned with starting or stopping movements, balance, position, and turning. The receptors are the semicircular canals and the vestibules of the inner ear. Although anatomically very closely related to the auditory nerves, these organs are not a part of hearing. They consist of bony cavities which contain liquids and otoliths, tiny particles of calcium. The equilibratory nerves end in tiny hair cells on the inner surface of the cavities and pick up stimulations from these liquids and particles.

ORGANIC Lastly, there are sensations of ache, pressure, nausea, thirst, and so forth, which seem to arise from within the body. These sensations are called intraorganic or visceral or interoceptive. Their origin and function is rather obscure in some details as yet.

Some of these bodily senses might be reducible to others; for instance pressure might include the kinesthetic and some aspects of the organic. Other divisions, such as exteroceptive, proprioceptive, and interoceptive have been suggested, but these divisions categorize the senses by material rather than by formal object. At least it is obvious that there are several clearly distinct sensible qualities.

Not all animals have all the special senses, but the somesthetic senses seem to be basic, as all animals seem to have at least some elementary awareness of touch or pressure. Smell is also quite fundamental. Animals higher on the evolutionary scale, those vertebrates with well-developed nervous systems (dogs, cats, apes, etc.), appear to have the same number of special senses as man.

Spatial relations

Those sensible qualities such as time, motion, and tridimensional space which are the common and incidental objects of sense arouse some interesting problems. Apparent movement (which is called the *Phi phenomenon*) must be distinguished from real motion. Awareness of time involves many subtle physiological factors: fatigue, amount and variation of intervening stimulation, hunger, fullness of the bladder, and many others. Depth is a function of both binocular retinal disparity and more subtle perceptual cues. Ingenious experimentation has been done with binaural cues for perceiving the location and motion of sound, with sounds from the right being funneled to the left ear and vice versa (Young's pseudophone) or transmitted electrically to separate earphones on the opposite sides from the pickup.[1] Again, psychologists have worn glasses with prisms which rectified from its normal inverted position the physical image projected on the retina of the eye.[2]

The upshot of these and hundreds of other experiments has been essentially the confirmation of the traditional position. Sensation is not a purely mechanical or neurophysiological process, nor are these "judgments" of distance, etc., a matter of intellectual deduction from sensory cues. Rather, a middle course seems indicated which places these operations definitely in the realm of animal knowledge, between the rational and the purely physiological. Likewise, the basic powers are inborn, but learning plays a large part in the development of their use. It is not purely a matter of inborn responses nor entirely a matter of learning.

Trends in the study of the senses

A shift has taken place in the manner in which the special senses are being approached by experimental psychology. Once its main preoccupation, they were neglected later when the emphasis turned to more dynamic processes. Since World War II there has been renewed interest, but from a different viewpoint.

Their connection with adjustment and learning is emphasized more, and there is added interest in the subjective and emotional factors which modify our perceptions. Second, although the physics and physiology of sensation are inseparable from the total process, there is increased emphasis on the distinctly psychological or conscious aspects of the process in the new approach. Third, psychologists now seem to be more aware of the dynamic and self-actualizing nature of the sense power. Sensation is looked upon less as a purely mechanical or passive impression. This of course accords with the conception of earlier philosophers, who realized that the cognitive power is not purely mechanical, but the ability to react vitally and consciously to a stimulus.

[1] P. T. Young, "Auditory Localization with Acoustical Transposition of the Ears," *J. exp. Psychol.*, 1928, 11:399–429.
[2] G. M. Stratton, "Vision without Inversion of the Retinal Image," *Psychol. Rev.*, 1897, 4:341–360; 463–481.

Fourth, where the earlier psychologists, in their anxiety to ape pure classical physics, concentrated exclusively on efficient causality and ignored final cause or purpose, the recent approach to the special senses has been quite teleological. Hilgard stresses the adaptive or purposeful approach, mentioning four functions of the senses: information, protection, orientation, and appreciation. He also notes that the knowledge of the workings of the special senses has been utilized by both the military and industrial psychologists to make working conditions more efficient and safe.

Lastly, the senses have recently been approached from the viewpoint of the whole, rather than from the aspect of the part. Even though the older psychologists tried to distinguish psychology from physiology on the basis of their concern with wholes and not with parts, they seemed to contradict this distinction by trying to explain sensation in terms of units of the nervous system, making conditioned reflexes the building blocks or atoms of psychology. It is now recognized that this molecular view is inadequate. The current molar view considers sensation psychologically, as a total response even though concerned with a specific receptor, whereas metabolism may take place in the entire body but is still physiological.

STIMULUS DEPRIVATION OR SENSORY ISOLATION Experiments in which persons are isolated as far as technically possible from all sensory stimuli of any kind in a dark, soundproof room demonstrate strikingly how important to man is some sense contact with his environment. Although well paid, these subjects rarely persevere for long, and report not mere loneliness but hallucinations and gross disorientation. Later we shall mention how cultural deprivation can have crippling effects on the development of intellect.

Summary of sensation

From the data in this chapter we can distinguish three aspects of the process of sensation: physical, physiological, and psychological.

1. The *physical* phase consists of the object with its material qualities of size, shape, color, odor, temperature, and the manner in which the quality is put into contract with the sense organ, usually through some medium such as light waves or sound waves. This aspect is the proper domain of the physicist, with his investigation of wavelengths and other physical properties. Note that in sensation the object is present and actually stimulating the sense organ here and now.

2. The *physiological* stage includes the activity of the receptor organ, the sensory nerves, and usually certain areas of the cerebral cortex or gray matter of the brain. The word organ means instrument, and many facts illustrate that the physiological processes themselves are not the sensation, but only the instruments of the sense power. The sensory organs may be physiologically active, yet consciousness may not result. This will be seen more clearly in the next chapter.

3. The *psychological* stage is that of actual awareness, when the sense vitally reacts to the stimulation and issues in knowledge or awareness. This will be discussed more fully in Chapter 8, on the nature of knowledge.

These three phases may be summarized by saying that in sensation an object by physically activating a sense organ impresses a sense power, which reacts with awareness of sensible qualities.

The sensory experience (3) will usually have attributes which correspond to the attributes of the physical stimulus: quality, intensity, and duration.

OPERATIVE POWERS OR ABILITIES

It has become apparent that the same person has many abilities and many operations. That he has many operations is obvious. That these flow from different abilities is clear from the fact that they are different *kinds* of operations: we do not see by means of our power of hearing, nor think by means of our ability to digest. Therefore man must have abilities such as those of seeing, digestion, imagination, understanding. The fact that man acts in certain ways implies that he has the ability to do so. Ability is not a thing, but simply refers to the fact that man "can do" a given activity or operation, whether he is actually doing it at the moment or not. But it is *man* who performs the operation, not some mythical entity. The power is not *that which* acts, but that *by which* man acts. When we say "the intellect knows" this is a loose expression for "man knows by means of his intellect."

Now it would seem quite obvious that the power by which I digest is not the same as that by which I imagine. But unfortunately, this simple notion became badly distorted in the eighteenth century by the introduction of the word "faculty" to designate these various abilities, with the implication that faculties were separate little things or substances within man. Thus we have the caricature of the will as a little man inside us pulling levers, the intellect as a little man inside us who thinks or guides. Gall and Spurzheim further confused the concept in the nineteenth century by associating faculties with brain areas in the pseudoscience of phrenology. Personality diagnosis was a matter of feeling the head for bumps which purportedly contained knowledge, will, etc. Faculty psychology became even worse. Certain of the faculty psychologists began enumerating long lists and quibbling about the exact number, distinguishing a faculty for making friends, a faculty for altruistic behavior, a faculty for making successful business deals, and whatever.

Modern psychologists quite rightly rejected this preposterous conception, pointing out that it was impossible to discover any such entities within man. Unfortunately, they confused the concept of "faculty" with the commonsense notion of ability which we have described above and to which they would all consent. For this reason it seems better to avoid the term "faculty" and use current expressions such as "operative power" or "ability" (Spearman, Thurstone) or "potentialities of man" (G. Murphy).

We shall return to a more philosophical analysis of this concept in Chapter 12, where we shall see that abilities are permanent properties, as opposed to contingent operations which can begin and cease. Abilities have not been offered as an explanation of behavior or to cover up our scientific ignorance. To say that a cat sees because he has the power of sight is no explanation; rather, we know he has the power of sight because he sees. The philosopher sees the obvious implication; the scientists makes the detailed investigation.

Distinct but not separate We must discern the difference between being distinct and being separate. It is important to understand that although we recognize the operations, the abilities, and the man as distinct, we insist that they are not separate. It is true that separation is often one sign of distinction; and thus the fact that the man can cease thinking, i.e., that man and his thought can be separated, is clear proof that they are distinct. But even if two things are never separated (and we see this to be true of the man and his abilities) they may still be distinct. Distinct means not identical: that one is not the other. Two things may be distinct even though they are inseparable. Thus the man is not his thinking or his digestion, even if these operations were never separated from the man. An understanding of this difference between distinct and separate will prevent the student from becoming a victim of the fallacy that because two things are inseparable they are therefore identical; for instance, because certain mental operations cannot exist without an organ, we need not necessarily conclude that they *are* the organ.

One being, many activities The distinction between man and his activities is also obvious in man's own experience, for his thoughts and actions come and go, yet he is conscious of being the same self who has the various thoughts and actions. At this point we do not presume anything about the nature of this self except that it must be subsistent, since activities cannot exist independently of the one acting. As we shall see, this distinction makes it possible to understand the unity of man as a being in spite of the multiplicity of his operations. But it should be clear that this is no naïve wall-and-paint theory of substance and accident, as will be seen from Chapter 12, which may be taken up at this time if desired. Confining ourselves here to a phenomenological and operational approach, we shall return to the nature of the self in Part IV of this book.

REVIEW QUESTIONS

1. Why do we prefer the term "special senses" to "external senses?"
2. Does the designation of three phases imply that sensation is three activities?

3. If I strike the closed eyelid, I may see a flash of light. Does this response fulfill the definition of sensation?
4. Philosophically, does it make any difference whether there are five senses or fifty?
5. Would you guess that a dog has the same special senses as yourself? Does a fish? Does a worm?
6. When we see, do we see images on the retina, or sensations, or visible objects? How does the experiment of wearing prisms which rectify the normally inverted images verify your answer?
7. If rationality is what is distinctive of man, why do we begin with sensation?
8. What is the difference between proper and common object? Give your own examples.
9. Is odor a common, proper, or incidental object of hearing?
10. How do we know how many different abilities man has?

FOR FURTHER READING

Kelly & Tallon: the chapter from **Berkeley,** and the selection from **Merleau-Ponty** on pp. 219–228.

The philosophical implications of this chapter are developed in Chapter 6. What goes beyond common observation here is more a matter of physiology and experimental psychology. Of special note is *The Senses Considered as Perceptual Systems,* a later work of **James J. Gibson,** author of the classic *The Perception of the Visual World.* We add a few items:

Adrian, Edgar D. *The Physical Background of Perception.*

Aristotle. *On the Soul.* Book II, chap. 5, to Book III, chap. 2.

Boring, E. G. *Sensation and Perception in the History of Experimental Psychology.*

Buddenbrock, Wolfgang von. *The Senses.*

Geldard, F. A. *The Human Senses.*

Graham, C. H. *Vision and Visual Perception.*

Ledvina, J. P. *Philosophy and Psychology of Sensation.*

Meissner, W. W., S.J. "Neurological Aspects of the Sense Powers of Man," *The Thomist,* 1963, 26:35–66.

Moore, Thomas Verner, *Cognitive Psychology.* Pp. 93–130, 209–271.

Simon, Yves, & Peghaire, Julien. "The Philosophical Study of Sensation," *The Modern Schoolman,* 1945, 23:111–119.

5 SENSORY KNOWING

*Perception is an achievement. . . . All
verbs of perceiving, as used in reference to acts
of perception, are achievement words.* Ryle

 We must constantly remind ourselves that these processes, which must be spread over several chapters for the purpose of study, do not take place in isolation. Except in highly artificial laboratory situations created by the experimental psychologist, or in certain brain-injury or other abnormal states, one never has just sensation alone, but always the total perceptual experience involving the activity of several knowing powers acting all at once. Thus I know red (sensation), apple (perception), and existing (intellection) all in the same instant.

Perception

Our sensory experience is not limited to awareness of colors, sounds, odors, and other qualities. Daydreaming, remembering, and the perception of a round, red, sweet, smooth apple are obviously more than a simple sensation. It is a basic fact of human behavior that we react not to a single stimulus but to patterns of stimuli. Our perception of the world as composed of objects (tree) rather than of mere sensory qualities (green, large) demands further investigation.

How then do sensation and perception differ? Both are sensory, animal types of knowledge. Both are psychological experiences, not merely physiological. Both are concerned with a present object. They differ in the same way that seeing the parts of the jigsaw puzzle differs from awareness of the whole picture they make up, or in the way that seeing daubs of paint on canvas differs from awareness of the scene they portray. Note that there is no question here of intellectual awareness of the nature or essence of the object, but merely of a total awareness of the material object in a sensory way, as opposed to the individual sensible quality known in simple sensation.

In modern times Gestalt psychology has most extensively experimented on perception. Beginning with the fact that we perceive not isolated notes but the pattern which makes a melody, not isolated bits of color but the pattern which makes a picture or a sunset, not individual still pictures but apparent movement in the moving pictures, these psychologists went on to investigate in great detail how the pattern of stimuli gives a total impression which is more than the sum of the parts. The parts may even be entirely replaced and the total impression still remain, as when a tune played in another key is recognizable as the same melody, even though not a single note would be the same.

The Gestaltists themselves assert and many experiments make it clear that these total impressions are not the result of intellectual deduction from data given by the special senses: the process of forming the impressions is a sensory one. It is not a question of knowing the *nature* of the object, but rather of organizing simple sensations into perceptual wholes.

Both to explore the problem of whether even sense knowledge involves more than sensation, and to enrich our appreciation of the subjective factors in perception, it may be useful to review briefly some facts from experimental psychology which illustrate how perception molds, elaborates, and even distorts the data of the special senses.

AMBIGUITY Ambiguous figures are those which give exactly the same stimulus to the special senses and yet can be perceived as two entirely different objects. Jastrow's rabbit-duck figure (Figure 1) is a common example. Whether we see it as a rabbit facing one direction or a duck facing the other cannot be due to the special sense of vision; it must be due to internal factors. Often the ambiguity flows from a reversal of figure and ground: the same stimulus is seen as the main figure at one time and as background at another.

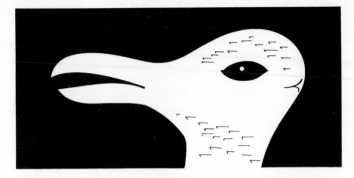

Figure 1   Jastrow's Rabbit-Duck

CONTRAST   If a piece of gray paper is cut in half and one half is pasted on a large sheet of black paper, the other on a large sheet of white paper, it will be seen that the same gray no longer produces an equal shade in our total impression. By contrast, the gray on the white will seem darker, that on the black will seem whiter. Yet the one gray is hardly giving off a different physical stimulus. This is called simultaneous contrast; the same can be observed in successive contrast where the same pickle, for instance, tastes more sour after eating candy than it would otherwise.

ILLUSION   We are all familiar with the optical illusions which make straight lines seem crooked and equal lines seem unequal, and so forth. Whereas in the case of ambiguity the same stimulus could give rise to two percepts, each equally true, in an illusion we get a false impression because of the distortion of the sense data. Here again the addition of other lines or background does not change the physical or physiological nature of the original stimulus and its impression on the special senses; the distortion must come from further psychological processes.

Illusion is distinguished from hallucination in that the former has a real object which is distorted, whereas hallucination mistakes an image for reality when there is no object present at all. Thus if I see a man as larger than an elephant because of distorted perspective, this is an illusion; if I see pink elephants on the ceiling where there is nothing, that is an hallucination. Both these processes are sensory and thus are distinguished from delusion, which is an erroneous intellectual conviction; for instance, delusions of persecution or delusions of grandeur. Phi phenomenon or the perception of apparent movement in a series of still pictures, such as in the movies or on an electric display sign, is an example of normal illusion.

SECONDARY PERCEPTUAL CUES   Color-blind people distinguish colors only by the texture or grain of the various shades of gray which they see; this fact was utilized in World War II when color-blind men were employed to read aerial photographs to distinguish a brown plowed field from a green pasture or stand of grain. The Ames experiments in perception[1] are based largely on the importance of secondary cues and background. Relative posi-

[1] See A. Ames, Jr., "Visual Perception and the Rotating Trapezoidal Window," *Psychol. Monogr.*, 1951, 65, No. 7 (Whole No. 324), and many current psychology texts.

tion is a cue to size, but we can be fooled, as in those experiments where the distorted trapezoidal room gives a false perspective or where cards actually all of the same size are arranged so as to suggest relative difference of position, making some seem larger. Stage scenery does not represent objects, but gives us perceptual cues from which we construct the impression of objects. Three-dimensional movies and stereoscopic pictures involve the utilization of secondary perceptual cues of depth.

CONSTANCY   An object tends to give a fairly consistent perceptual impression in spite of very divergent stimulations: for instance, the image striking the retina from a man close up is immense in comparison with the image on the retina from a man three blocks away, yet the former is not seen as a giant and the latter as a midget (size constancy). A red rose or a piece of white paper will actually give off highly different physical stimulations in bright sunshine and at dusk, yet we see them as having about the same color under either condition (color constancy). Likewise, a ring is seen as round even when the image striking the eye from an angle is really elliptical (shape constancy).

SELECTIVITY   We tend to see what we want to see, rather than all that is there. Witnesses to an auto accident usually give highly different versions, depending on their personal interest in the plaintiff or defendant.

SET   We tend to see what we expect to see. Experiments in which a black six-of-hearts or a red ten-of-spades is shown betray that we often report not what is actually there but what we assume or expect to see.

MOTIVATION   Lastly, experiments have shown that our needs and the value we set on things can influence greatly how we perceive objects. Poor children who are asked to estimate the size of a dime according to carefully controlled measures were found to make it much larger than rich children did in the same experiment. Adult subjects in another experiment were shown vague pictures on a screen which they interpreted as food twice as often when hungry as when they had just finished a meal, and estimated the size of hamburgers shown on the screen to be 50 to 75 percent larger when they had not eaten recently.

A central sense?

This rather lengthy excursion into the vagaries of perception seems to indicate that even sensory knowledge is not a simple matter of sensation as examined in the previous chapter. Other experiences further complicate the picture.

We can distinguish between the proper objects of the various special senses: between color and sound, for instance. How? This distinction cannot be made by means of either the special sense of sight or that of hearing, since we saw that neither is a channel for the proper object of the other. Since as a matter of fact we do know the difference, our ability to do so must depend on something other than either of these special senses—and obviously not on some other special sense which again would be restricted to its own proper sensible quality.

Also, we are able to combine the sensations of various special senses, as when we put together the impressions of red, smooth, firm, savory, and round to get the percept of apple. This is not a function of vision, for through it we can know nothing of firmness or taste. Again, can we combine odor and color by means of the sense of touch? Each sense is restricted, yet to combine these qualities requires the ability to know all of them. Otherwise we would only know a number of unrelated qualities of color, sound, and taste. (We speak here of combining the qualities of only one thing; association of one thing with another is a function of imagination.) Phi phenomenon or apparent movement is possible using two different special senses: e.g., a bell seen in one position and heard in another seems to have moved. This ability to combine sensations is clear in the case of man, and seems to be readily inferred from the actions of the higher animals, as when you whistle at a dog and he turns his head to look in the direction of the sound. It would seem that neither vision nor hearing alone could account for this, but only some central sense.

For some the most impressive evidence in this direction is the fact that we can be aware that we are sensing. Now sight is not visible; only color or colored objects can be seen. The object of a special sense is some material quality, not sensation itself. Yet I am aware that I am seeing. This again suggests some central knowing power which is not restricted like the special senses, but can embrace all sensations.

Be that as it may, *consciousness* could be called in a very special way the function of this central sense, for by it we know concretely that we are actually awake and sensing. Being sensory, this power is organic and its organ is probably located in the brain; a knockout blow produces a mild temporary concussion which interferes with the organ of the central sense. Sleep, on the other hand, is not the cessation of all conscious functioning but is a state of partial consciousness in which chiefly the imagination is at work and the central sense is not.

All this evidence has led some philosophers to conclude that implied in these operations is an ability called the *central sense,* or synthetic or unifying sense. It has sometimes been called the common sense, from its Latin name, but this is very misleading in English: we do not refer to good judgment, which is implied by the English term "common sense." Synthetic suggests its combining power, but not its function as a discriminator between sensations, or its basic function of general consciousness.

In light of the above evidence, *central* sense might be defined as the power by which we apprehend, distinguish, and combine sensations into total sensory awareness of a present object. By "present object," we mean one that is actually stimulating the sense organs here and now.

According to this view perception is a function of the central sense plus one or more of the special senses and usually also shows influence of the imagination and the other internal senses. In practice it is impossible to know how much intellectual influence might also be there, but at least the term always refers to our total impression of a *sensed* object.

IMAGINATION

So far we have been speaking only of perception, which occurs only in the presence of an object actually stimulating a receptor. But we can also "know" objects in their absence by forming an image of them. (If I close my eyes and imagine this table, it is physically present but perceptually absent.) This image might be simply a re-production of some previous sensory experience, as in the case of the imagined table. More importantly, I can combine previous perceptions or parts of them into new images, as when I imagine a flying cow. Thus imagination is thought of by many philosophers as the avenue to the fantastic, the illusory, and the absurd. So it is, but as we shall see, the influence of imagination on sensation may actually result in a more accurate perception than otherwise. And certainly it would be a dull world without the poetry, humor, and creativity which come through imagination.

Because imagination makes us independent of present sensory stimu-lation and allows us to soar beyond reality, it is a great tool of the intellect and is usually found well developed in poets, scientists, in-ventors, and other creative thinkers. But imagination can also con-tribute to illusion, neurosis, and overemotionalism, and is a partial explanation for much of the purported success of fortune-telling, telepathy, and similar phenomena.

Images may be evoked by physiological causes, by motivational urges, or by associations which vary from the apparently random to those which are directly the result of choice. Fantasy or daydreams as well as dreams during sleep will often reflect our wishes and fears; hence the distinction between the manifest and the latent con-tent of dreams. But there is no proof that all dreams are symbolic, much less that all dream symbols are sexual or that the symbolism all follows one pattern. One of the interests of psychologists is to study the various ways and laws by which images may be associated.

It is to be noted that the imagination can reproduce not only visual perceptions, as is suggested by the word image, but any previous sensory experience. Hence we have not only visual images, but also auditory, olfactory, gustatory, kinesthetic, tactual, etc. Individuals vary greatly in their power of auditory imagination, for instance; some can hear a whole symphony orchestra in their imagination, while others find it difficult to imagine the simplest tune.

Some philosophers distinguish between reproductive imagination and creative imagination, depending on whether it merely evokes a previous experience or combines several elements, as in the case of the flying cow. Others call the former a function of memory. In any case they do not seem to be distinct powers but just different activities of my ability to reproduce the absent. Thus when a person says he "has no imagination" he does not really mean that he lacks this power entirely, but rather that his imagination has a low degree of creativity.

MEMORY

When reproducing certain previous perceptual experiences, there is sometimes more than the fact that they are imagined, i.e., not present. I recognize them as part of my past experience. If some one is describing a certain city, he may enable me to build up a rather good picture in my imagination; then suddenly it dawns on me, "I was there." It is no longer a mere picture, it is identified precisely as part of my past. We say, "I remember that." The image now has a personal relation to me, and I may recall the sequence of events in which it was located.

Both imagination and memory reproduce past sensory impressions, and their functions are so similar and interwoven that many philosophers do not consider them as distinct powers; others think them to be distinct because of their difference in respect to the formal aspect of pastness, i.e., the actual identification and recognition of this experience in relation to me. Usually the word "memory" refers to not only this activity but also to imagination. Memory may also mean the retention of ideas, and this is simply another function of the intellect.

The organic nature of sensory memory is clear from the manner in which it represents objects clothed with material qualities, and also from the relationships between memory function and brain injury.[2] Since both imagination and memory store impressions by way of habit, their functions also pertain to the discussion in the latter half of Chapter 12 on habit and learning.

INSTINCTIVE AWARENESS

The word "instinct" unfortunately has been associated with certain theories of the past two centuries in which behavior was ascribed to hypothetical entities such as "instinct of mother love," or a "food-

[2] Wilder Penfield, "The Permanent Record of the Stream of Consciousness," *Proc. 14th Int. Congr. Psychol.*, Montreal, 1954. Although questionable in some of his philosophical implications, this and more recent accounts bring out the organic yet psychological nature of memory. See Halstead & Rucker (1968).

gathering instinct." To appeal to such an entity as an explanation of behavior, as when people say, "This happened by instinct," is of course meaningless. For this reason we prefer not to use this noun.

But there is clear evidence that there are certain activities, especially in insects and lower animals but also to some extent in higher vertebrates and even in man, which seem to merit the adjective "instinctive" because of characteristics now well established by experimentation. Animals raised in complete isolation from all others will, at maturity, display distinctive patterns of behavior in mating, nest building, and other activities, which are peculiar to their own species and which could not possibly have been learned by imitation or trial and error. Although the word "instinct" was rejected in the first half of the twentieth century because it had been used to cloak our ignorance of just how animals function, recently the term has come into use again (Hilgard, Munn, Morgan) but in a more cautious and scientific way. We prefer the adjective "instinctive" to designate the behavior, without implying that instinct is a substance. This behavior is unlearned, impulsive, useful, complex, and modifiable by conditioning although basic to a given species.

Because instinctive tendencies are modifiable by learning and circumstances, it is absurd to look for examples of purely instinctive behavior at least among higher vertebrates, including man. But there must be something there to modify. Instincts cannot be classified and enumerated as if they were things, but we do have tendencies to act in accordance with our recognition of the usefulness or harmfulness of certain objects, without intellectual understanding or previous experience. The classic examples are the instinctive activities of ants, bees, and other insects.

These activities cannot be explained merely as a reaction to pleasant or unpleasant sensation caused by the object, since the animal often continues activity even though unpleasant. Again, this activity can hardly be a mere chain of reflexes,[3] since it is not mechanical but clearly psychological in origin. There is much evidence of at least sensory cognition, awareness of *what* is to be done, if not *why*. The activity is not automatic and stereotyped like reflex, but highly modifiable, irregular, and impulsive.

Ingenious experiments have shown that animals respond to certain internal stimuli such as changes in their blood chemistry with the gradual lengthening of the days in spring. But rather than being an explanation, these facts need to be explained. Why does the bird

---

[3] Karl S. Lashley shows the inadequacy of the reflex theory in "Experimental Analysis of Instinctive Behavior," *Psychol. Rev.*, 1938, 45:453.

fly north rather than south when the days grow longer? Such responses are beyond any reflexes known to physiology. Some are so impressed by the nonmechanical nature of these responses that they go to the opposite extreme and ascribe to the brute animal possession of intelligence in the strict sense. This question is treated in the Appendix.

What excites this drive activity? If it is neither merely reflex nor truly intellectual, the explanation must be at the sensory level. But the special senses cannot account for it, for "what to do with it" is not their proper object. The evidence points to the existence of a power which is different from all of these, whose proper object is the usefulness (or harm) of a perceived object. This is only one factor in a complex process, but seems necessary to account for the unlearned, cognitive aspects. In animals below man this power has been called by some the *estimative* power, and defined as the power by which an animal recognizes, prior to learning and without understanding, suitable behavior regarding a sensed object. It is the cognitive element of what may be called instinctive behavior, which also involves physiological, appetitive, and motor factors. "Suitable" in this definition does not imply moral rightness, but merely what is to be done: by this power the animal knows whether to eat, build a nest out of, run from, or mate with the object it perceives.

In man?

The above description of instinctive behavior emphasized that it is never found in a pure form even in the higher vertebrates with their great capacity for learning, much less in man. In man there is the further complication of the so-called higher thought processes, so that it becomes even more difficult to determine whether there is an instinctive component in human behavior. But the work of Freud and others has uncovered much evidence that man is impelled to some extent by drives which are animal, unlearned, instinctive at least in part. True, Watson and the behaviorists proved that much of what was thought to be inborn was actually acquired by learning or conditioning, but they kept the term "drive." The Freudian contribution has not been wholly invalid, in spite of linguistic difficulties with the terms "instinct." (E. C. Wilm, in *Theories of Instinct*, shows how many meanings there are to the term.) In addition to the evidence from psychoanalysis we can observe times when human beings seem to be acting in purely instinctive, animal fashion: the newborn baby, the grossly deranged who lashes out with little or no evidence of either reason or learning, the degenerated senile who reverts to infantile activity. And much human thinking exhibits a very earthy, animal-like awareness of concrete exigencies.

For these reasons the medieval philosophers (who of course did not know Freud but had some of these insights from the ascetical writers) postulated something in man analogous to the estimative power in other animals. It was called by other names such as the *cogitative power,* the discursive power, the comparative sense, or even particular reason. Some of these names were coined by the Arabian commentators on Aristotle; their development of the notion of this sense power in man greatly influenced Aquinas. These names are used to emphasize that in man this sense power works very intimately with the intellect and to that extent differs from that of other animals. They considered its function a sort of concrete reasoning. (Similarly, the word reminiscence was sometimes used to refer to the activity of memory when under the guidance and direction of intellection.)

INTERNAL SENSE

The evidence accumulated in this chapter seems to imply that man has sensory abilities beyond those of simple sensation. The special senses appear to be the first avenues of stimulation of the organism by its environment, but we have seen here many types of awareness which do not fall under the formal aspect of their proper objects. Perceptual synthesis, combining and distinguishing sensations as well as reflex consciousness of sensation itself, imagination, memory, and what some have called "concrete reasoning" all seem to be functions of a more general sensory ability. *Internal sense* is the name used in this connection by many philosophers, to contrast with the special senses.

What is distinctive about the special senses is that each has its own receptor organ and has as its proper object some particular material quality. Perception and imagination deal not with single qualities but with total objects. Sensation is always a matter of present stimulation, whereas in imagination and memory I can be aware of objects even in their absence. The special senses were called the external senses by the medieval philosophers, but because many of the sensations arise within the body itself, the name was unfortunate. Kinesthetic, vestibular, and organic sensations all arise from within the body. Hence the modern term "special" seems more precise than the older term "external."

An internal sense might be defined as the ability to know concrete objects in a material way, from sensible qualities experienced through the special senses. It is called internal not because of having no organ on the surface of the body, for as we saw that is true of certain special senses. A special sense puts us in contact directly with its object, in contrast to internal sense which receives data through the special senses. Because these data are present in the special senses and therefore internally present to the knower, they are internal data for further elaboration. The organ is probably those large areas of the brain called the association areas of the cerebral cortex. We say "in a material way" because the object is always known in and with its sensible qualities, whether absent or present, real or imaginary. It is never abstract or universal, always concrete and particular.

Distinct? The medieval philosophers disputed as to whether there were four distinct internal senses corresponding to the four types of activity we have examined in this chapter. We know in general we have the ability if we experience the activities, but whether it is one or multiple need not detain us. Aquinas and many of his followers feel that these activities have sufficiently different proper objects to make them distinct. Suarez and others disagree. We leave it an open question.

In any case the operations are so closely interwoven among themselves, with sensation, and with intellection in the case of man, that pragmatically it makes no difference. It is unfortunate that we must examine them separately for purposes of study, but we cannot say all at once what in fact is happening all at once.

Although we have good evidence for all four types of activity in the higher vertebrates, we do not say that all animals have this complete panoply of sensory operations: one could hardly assert much evidence for imagination in an oyster. Man's sensory activities show much greater scope and flexibility because of their close cooperation with intellect, but this does not change the essentially animal or sensory nature of the operations themselves. Through them even man's most abstract thinking is kept in a concrete time-space relation with physical reality.

REVIEW QUESTIONS

1. List all the ways in which the internal senses differ from the special senses.
2. List all the ways in which they are similar.
3. Does the stress on subjective distortions of perception militate against the idea that man can know reality?
4. Are these distortions due only to the activity of the central sense? If not, what other factors are involved?
5. If other factors are involved, what characteristic of perception indicates that they be discussed there?

6. When one has "a song on the brain" what power is operating? Is this experience sensory, even though we cannot visualize it?
7. How does imagination differ from central sense?
8. Why would there be a tendency for intelligence to correspond with degree of imagination?
9. How does memory differ from imagination? Give examples.
10. Is an animal born with knowledge or only with the power of knowing?
11. Some call the action of the estimative power a sense judgment. Does this mean that the animal understands? Is judgment here a univocal or analogous term?

FOR FURTHER READING

Kelly & Tallon: the selections from **Augustine** starting on p. 26, and from **Luijpen** on pp. 273–281.

Maurice Merleau-Ponty has two books pertinent here: *Phenomenology of Perception,* and *The Structure of Behavior.* Erwin Straus, *Phenomenological Psychology,* and Silvan Tomkins, *Affect, Imagery, Consciousness,* are two examples of applying the contents of this chapter to personality study. **Harold Rugg** in describing *Imagination* uses a multidiscipline approach.

Irving Block's article in *Phronesis,* 1964, 9:58–63, argues that it is in **Aristotle's** later small works rather than in his *On the Soul* that we find his mature statement on the internal senses. A critical study of the Aristotelian tradition is made by **John Gasson,** S.J., and **Magda Arnold** in "The Internal Senses—Functions or Powers?" *The Thomist,* 1963, 26:1–34. **Mark Gaffney's** *Psychology of the Interior Senses* is semipopular, often anecdotal.

The literature on perception is vast. We list some significant works:

Ames, A., Jr. "Reconsideration of the Origin and Nature of Perception," in S. Ratner (Ed.) *Vision and Action.* Pp. 251–274.

Bier, W. C., S.J. (Ed.) *Perception in Present-day Psychology: A Symposium* (Fordham University). Good presentation of current experimental research in Europe and America. Includes discussions of implications for epistemology and for clinical, experimental, and social psychology.

Combs, Arthur W., & Snygg, Donald. *Individual Behavior: A Perceptual Approach to Behavior.* (Rev. ed.)

Forgus, Ronald H. *Perception: The Basic Process in Cognitive Development.* An excellent survey, reflecting the work of R. MacLeod, J. J. Gibson, and D. Hebb.

Gibson, J. J. *The Perception of the Visual World.*

Ittleson, W. H., & Cantril, H. *Perception: A Transactional Approach.*

Moore, Thomas Verner. "A Scholastic Theory of Perception," *The New Scholasticism,* 1933, 7:222–238.

Gestalt psychology

Angyal, Anders. *Foundations for a Science of Personality.*

Brunswik, Egon. *The Concept and Framework of Psychology.*

Hamlyn, D. W. *The Psychology of Perception: A Philosophical Examination of Gestalt Theory and Derivative Theories of Perception.*

Helson, H. (Ed.) *Theoretical Foundations of Psychology.*

Herr, Vincent., S.J. "Gestalt Psychology: Empirical or Rational?" in Anton C. Pegis (Ed.) *Essays in Modern Scholasticism.*

Katz, David. *Gestalt Psychology.* This authoritative presentation shows that Köhler did not claim that animal Gestalten were intellectual processes.

Lastly, some items on the problem of instinctive behavior in human beings:

Allers, Rudolf. "The Vis Cogitativa and Evaluation," *The New Scholasticism,* 1941, 15:195–221. Also pertinent is his article, "The Intellectual Cognition of Particulars," *The Thomist,* 1941, 3:95–163.

Bernard, L. L. *Instinct: A Study in Social Psychology.* Good presentation of the behavioristic viewpoint opposing instinct, though it is given some restricted place. Unfortunately uses uniformity of action pattern as the criterion of instinctive behavior, which of course cannot apply to human beings because of social and learning factors.

Cattell, Raymond B. "The Discovery of Ergic Structures in Man in Terms of Common Attitudes," *J. abnorm. soc. Psychol.,* 1950, 45:598–618.

Fletcher, Ronald. *Instinct in Man: In the Light of Recent Work in Comparative Psychology.* Good criticism of behavioristic position.

Flynn, Thomas V., O.P. "The Cogitative Power," *The Thomist,* 1953, 16: 542–563.

Klubertanz, George P., S.J. *The Discursive Power.*

Moore, Thomas Verner. *The Driving Forces of Human Nature and Their Adjustment.* Pp. 231–242.

Peghaire, Julien. "A Forgotten Sense, the Cogitative, According to St. Thomas Aquinas," *The Modern Schoolman,* 1943, 20:123–140, 210–229.

Wilm, E. C. *Theories of Instinct.*

For additional data on the activity of the estimative power in animals, see the further readings listed in the Appendix.

6 HUMAN KNOWLEDGE

Without hypotheses there can be no useful observation.   Darwin

We must now complete our account of human knowing by exploring those activities referred to as thinking or understanding, or cognitive in the fullest sense. We say, "I hear you, but I don't understand." This suggests that there is more to knowing than the sensory experience.

INTELLECTUAL ACTIVITIES

Idea or concept   Many philosophers are impressed by the evidence that our understanding has different characteristics from those we discovered in sense knowledge. The sensory is always concrete and never abstract, particular rather than universal, and always limited. It is clothed with sensible qualities (such as green, square, moving, large), rather than devoid of them. Even when not so located actually, as in the daydream or the image of the flying cow, the object is always known as able to be located in space, subject to time, physically extended, and in some way quantitatively measurable. In contrast, philosophers contend that understanding can be universal, independent of time or location, unlimited in representative capacity—in short, immaterial (which here means "nonphysical," not "irrelevant").

Mostly, they stress the lack of sensible, i.e., material or physical, qualities in the intellectual experience. They argue that any percept or image of a horse must picture it as brown or white or black, large or small, moving or still, racehorse or workhorse; but the concept or idea of horse, my understanding of what a horse is, applies equally well to all horses regardless of color or position or even kind. And when their opponents, the sensists, postulate some neutral-gray image which would stand for all horses, they reply that my understanding of "what a horse is" does not involve gray, nor would this image apply equally well to gray and brown horses, as does the concept. Aside from the fact that my concept of a horse does not involve neutral gray, the theory of sensism seems to break down completely if we push the generalization a step further. We understand clearly what a mammal is, yet we have no vague image which would apply equally well to elephant, cow, rabbit, and mouse. No sense experience can, yet the concept does.

Idea is the broad term for this elemental act of understanding. It is often called concept when it represents the objects of a general category. It is some awareness of *what* a thing is. It is usually so imperfect and incomplete that we hesitate to say that the idea is awareness of essence, or nature. For this reason the medieval philosophers called the object of an idea by the deliberately vague term "whatness" (Latin *quid,* hence the barbarism "quiddity").

We have been using the term *intellect* simply to refer to the fact that man has the ability to have these and other understanding-type experiences, much as we used the term sense to refer to his sensory abilities. Since it is man who knows, we do not attribute these activities to any separate entity called intellect, but use it as a sort of shorthand term for the fact that man can do them. Many philosophers deny that we can, and we shall devote the next chapter to this controversy. First we must complete our survey of knowing activities.

Judgment In real life the concept never happens in isolation but as an intimate part of a much more elaborate process, or complex of activities. This is true not only because it is not separated from bodily contact with the environment, but also because intellection itself is much more varied than the investigation has yielded so far.

In logic we analyze the reasoning process into elements for the purpose of checking on its correctness. The terms of a proposition express the concepts which make up the judgment. The form of a proposition is somewhat artificial, and we must not think of the concepts joined in the judgment as isolated acts or elements glued together by some sort of mental chemistry.

Reasoning   Similarly, the reduction of a line of reasoning to syllogistic form to study its logical correctness must not be mistaken for a psychological description of how we think. In practice we may skip many of the steps, as in hunches or intuitions. Or we may wander, with or without guiding principle, through many unnecessary steps.

Insight   The discrepancy between logic and our actual intellectual processes is bothersome only if we assume that our thinking is always formal reasoning. Maritain, Chevalier, Bergson, and others are probably right in stressing the intuitive aspects of intellection, which Aquinas neglected in his emphasis on reasoning. According to Kapp (1942), Aristotle on this point was closer to Plato, who insisted on the superiority of νοῦς (*intellectus*, understanding) over διανοία (*ratio*, reasoning).

This emphasis on the rational aspects of human intellection in Aquinas is counterbalanced by many trends in contemporary philosophy. We mentioned several of these trends in Chapter 2 when we talked about method in philosophy itself and the growing philosophical sophistication about what is really involved in scientific discovery, and will see them in Chapter 7 when we talk about recent studies in the development of language and thought.

Aristotle's world has been described as a block universe, a neat system of essences which fall into distinct and immutable categories. Aquinas tended to think that the whatness or quiddity which the intellect abstracts from sensible things is a Platonic form, or Idea, somehow embedded in and extractable from matter; he was saved from this view only by Aristotle's more empirical emphasis. All this is hardly typical of how ideas are actually formed.

The child's first conscious contact with the world yields him a variety of initial impressions which he must gradually conceptualize. The process literally takes a lifetime, and is never finished. "There is no meaning that is pregiven in fully finished form in man's interiority" (Kwant, 1965).

We distinguish between meaning and referent. Referent is simply what the word refers to, and indicates the subject of a sentence; meaning or significance is more, and is usually a predicate. Thus the predicates "George Washington" and "first president of the United States" have the same referent, but different meanings. The nominal or referent use of a word by the child may indicate no more than that he knows it is there, exists, is a being. It is like seeing a man on a distant hill: at first all you know is that there is an object, a physical being of some kind, then you see it moving and decide it is not a tree, it comes closer and you see it is a man rather than a woman, and finally you may identify it as farmer Jones.

The name he learns for it is so bound up with the first, concrete, existential awareness of an object that the child thinks the name is part of the referent at first, and separates them in thought only later. Thus a child may call all men "Daddy" until he learns to sort them out. This is the beginning of descriptive (and hence classificatory) thought which develops gradually with speech. He is beginning to get predicates, meaning instead of mere referents. But any nominal or referent use presumes some experiential, concrete awareness at least of the being of the thing, grasped in the sensory-intellective initial act of knowledge. Ordinary language expresses this referent use first. Development of more precise predicates goes beyond the mere pointing function of words, perhaps into what Lonergan calls explanatory rather than mere descriptive definitions.

Concept formation is not always a simple matter of abstracting a common element out of repeated experiences. The whatness is grasped somewhat intuitively by the intellect in the initial perceptual experience of the object, in a complex and confused way which is only gradually made more explicit. Any intelligible form that is there is so immersed in matter that it can be known only through its properties, not in any direct intellectual grasp of the whole essence in its pure intelligibility. We can define a construct like triangle, but it may take a lifetime of induction to get at any one natural body. "Essential" definitions are not an easy deductive climb down the Porphyrian tree, but a laborious refinement through more and more explicit knowledge of properties, which is never exhaustive.

As we clarify our ideas from the general notion of being down to the individual, we discover that differences can be of many kinds, some more essential than others. In this sense scientific induction is a controlled abstraction, one which might take a million-dollar research grant and the combined efforts of a laboratory team working over many years to complete. It refines the insight a child or an Archimedes might have had. For this reason there is really no contradiction between the simple perception of a table as a solid physical object and a physicist's conception of it as a mass of whirling atomic particles with great spaces in between, even when reduced to mathematical functions between certain physical constants having no counterpart in ordinary perception. Both are correct and form a continuity, as Eddington shows in *The Nature of the Physical World*.

It is clear that Einstein did not one day just come up with $e = MC^2$ out of nowhere; the notion arose out of much previously acquired sense data and current theory. But he and many scientists report that when "the light dawns" there is no orderly rational deduction, only an insight or intuitive hunch. It has been suggested by some that the superiority of man over the computer probably lies in this intuitive function of intellection. The computer may come up with a vastly greater number of possible hypotheses or chess moves, but man seems better able to suspect which will be the more fruitful. (The more intuitive functions of intellect are often ascribed to women, but any sex difference here is debatable and at most a matter of degree; there are intuitive men and rational women.)

Our ordinary ways of speaking manifest this noncategorical, existential grasp of reality which is so important in human knowledge. Language is not merely to state facts, to give names to all things as if by some Adam. Grammar is not language, says Wittgenstein; and one might add, logic is not thinking. Besides structure and referents, there is the intent of the speaker to communicate something. If I say, "Damn you!" this is no objective proposition reducible to definition of terms. It is subjective, personal—but intensely meaningful and quite communicable. A lover does not speak in syllogisms, but he may very well resort to poetry to express his thoughts. Marcel uses drama as a vehicle to portray his philosophical notions in existential concreteness. The "I-thou" relationships so important in personal encounter are not universal concepts and cannot be communicated in univocal terms or rational arguments.

This intellectual but nonrational meaning is not disembodied from the whole perceptual and imaginal experience in and through which it is apprehended. And our first- and second-person forms of speaking bring out perhaps best of all the intimate interdependence between word and concept, precisely because of the phenomenological experience which is communicated—something more than a mere association or stimulus-response behavioral connection. The very groping and inadequate manner of our speaking brings out the intuitive, "ineffable" nature of the understanding involved, as Kwant shows in his *The Phenomenology of Language,* by examples of humor, children's play, colors, sex, and religion wherein this type of awareness is had before the person has a word to express it (1965, pp. 18, 29, 32, 36, 199, etc.). The account in Helen Keller's autobiography of her great discovery that thought could be symbolized by a word seems to bear this out. Scientists and inventors report that they had the idea before they ever had words or even formulas for it. Artists and mystics struggle to put into words the insights they grasp so vividly. Value judgments are often hard to explain in words, yet we are quite confident that they are more than animal reactions, that they are based on understanding if not on reason.

Conscience   The mention of value judgments brings us to an intellectual function often misunderstood. We shall see that scholastic philosophy followed Aristotle in rejecting Plato's theory of innate ideas. It would be surprising, then, if the Christian concept of conscience implied that we are born with a ready-made set of ethical conclusions. We are born only with the power of reaching such conclusions, once we have experienced facts from which they can be known. As a parallel, we are not born with the concepts of "whole" and "part" but only with the power of recognizing their relation; once we understand what the concepts really mean, we cannot judge otherwise than that the whole is greater than the part. So we are not born with the ideas of "murder" and "bad" but only with an intellect whose nature is such that it joins these two concepts, once learned, in the appropriate judgment. Judging is an act; what is inborn is the ability to judge. Conscience is simply the functioning of the intellect in making moral judgments.

The problem arises when cultural anthropology reveals that moral judgments vary around the world. Primitive tribes may find cannibalism or torture of prisoners quite in accord with their conscience. Yet we should not be surprised that human intellects do not always function correctly and uniformly: errors and conceptions based on diverse cultural viewpoints are to be expected. If we make errors in something as cold and objective as arithmetic, it is surely not surprising that all human beings do not judge alike on moral matters, in which emotional and social pressures can be so strong. When the chief, the priest-shaman, parents, and peers all agree, it is very hard to think otherwise. Most of us warp our moral judgments a little when we are emotionally involved, e.g., when angered over the rape of a little sister. An added reason for erroneous conscience is the variety of customs and cultures which influence the experiences from which we derive our concepts. Even a properly functioning machine will not give correct answers if fed with faulty data.

Emotion, self-interest, and cultural diversity do not alter the nature of the intellect with which we are born, but they can and do interfere with the intellectual function which we call conscience, affecting either the process itself or the ideas with which it works. But since the object of intellect is the being of things, the intellect is able to judge moral issues and even correct its own errors by adverting to whether an act is in conformity with nature, independently of customs or mores. Because of this ability, conscience differs from Freud's superego, to which it is sometimes compared; for the latter is largely the irrational and unconscious influence of habits acquired from parental admonition and social approval during childhood, rather than intellect judging on the basis of the nature of things. (The strength of such influence is not denied, only its identity with conscience.)

Set   An important factor in reasoning is that of *set*, which we mentioned among the subjective factors in perception in Chapter 5. The course of our thinking can be determined ahead of time. Given the numbers 2 and 3, we can instantaneously give an answer, but whether it is 5, 6, or 1 depends upon whether we have previously set ourselves to add, multiply, or subtract.

Intellectual memory   We shall see that knowledge does not consist in a purely passive reception of forms, as in wax or modeling clay. It is only when the knowing power vitally reacts to the impression received and entertains it in consciousness that we have that intentional union which is the act of knowing. But when this ceases, does the knowing power return to its original state of pure potentiality? The answer to this is suggested by the fact that the next time the intellect wishes to have this knowledge it need not start from zero and go through the whole process again. To say nothing of the enormous funds of knowledge stored in the minds of certain geniuses, we have all had the experience of recalling things of which we have not been conscious for years, without having to learn them again. Unlike the Freshman trying to juggle the fruits of his last cramming period, the experienced college student does not expect to carry all his knowledge around in a state of actual consciousness. He knows that if he has learned his material well he can recall it as needed from its state of habitual knowledge.

   This capacity to retain intellectual knowledge parallels the functions of imagination and memory at the sensory level. Once the knowing power has been actuated by an impression, it is evidently capable of retaining this impression and reviving it for future use. Theoretically, it would seem that any impression ever received would be capable of recall if only the right stimulus were hit upon. This seems to be confirmed by the use of hypnosis and sodium Pentothal to recall stored experiences beyond the reach of ordinary means.

   This *habitual knowledge* is halfway between actual knowing and mere ability to acquire knowledge. This is the state of habit which will be discussed in Chapter 12. We obviously are not always aware of all the things we know, so these forms, whether sensible or intelligible, are not evoking cognitive reaction. But they are in the knowing power, which therefore need not receive the impression anew but only reactivate what has been there all along. The adequate stimulus seems to be some act of knowing or appetition which is associated with—or symbolic of, or motivationally related to—the original impression. Thus the familiar word "tree" causes me to have the idea, without needing to see or even imagine a tree. Precisely how the knowing power selects this particular stored impression to be reactivated into awareness, rather than some other, is a difficult question. Neurophysiology of the cerebral cortex offers little help, and philosophers can only emphasize the substantial unity of all man's powers in the one person.

OBJECT OF INTELLECTION

It seems the only way we can designate the object of intellection is to say that it includes all beings, actual and potential. We can think about objects which are material and those which are spiritual; we can think about incidentals, essentials, principles, relationships, and even negations. We can talk about the existential order of real beings, or we can understand and compute the area of a hypothetical non-existent triangle, or consider other purely logical entities which have no existence outside our own mind. Since these beings do not have a common nature, they can be designated only by the broadest and most analogical term: they are all beings.

The magnificent scope of human intellection covering this all-inclusive range of objects is truly breathtaking. Meaning is discoverable throughout the universe. Wisdom seeks to understand man and all things in relation to Supreme Being. Analogy does not weaken intelligibility but enriches and orders our knowledge by unifying it under the broad concepts of being (see Olgiati, 1925; Rousselot, 1935; and Sertillanges, 1956).

Proper object of intellect

Here we must distinguish between the object of intellect as such, common to all intellects, and that which is proper and specific to man's intellect.

COMMON OBJECT OF ALL INTELLECTS Any intellect, be it man's, God's, or an angel's, can know an object only insofar as it is being or has relation to existence. We know it *as being*.

This concept is perhaps best understood by considering the opposite: what is absolutely impossible is also unintelligible. Try to get a good, clear idea of what a square circle is. There is no intelligible essence here which I can conceive as having a relation to existence, either actual or potential. In general metaphysics or the philosophy of being it is stated that being as related to intellect is said to have ontological truth. Hence the object of any intellect is *being* as intelligible, or being as true. Whatever is intelligible is known precisely as being. (Truth as truth is the proper object of the judgment and hence is not the proper object of intellect as such.) We might define intellect as the ability to know being as being.

PROPER OBJECT OF THE HUMAN INTELLECT   The proper object of a power is that toward which it is primarily and essentially ordered and in relation to which it knows all other objects. The power of sight knows extension and shape only by way of its proper object, color. What is the proper object of the human intellect precisely as human? Now what is distinctive of the human intellect in this life, as opposed to other intellects, is the fact that it must get its knowledge from sensory experience. Yet we know not merely the sensory qualities but the very being of sensible things. Hence the proper object of the human intellect, as human, is the *abstracted being-what-it-is of sensible things.* This does not mean that man has full or adequate knowledge of essences—this would take prodigious research, as we saw above. Whatever limited knowledge of further essential properties we may acquire, the first thing we know about anything is being, the difference between existence and nonexistence. It is proper to man's intellect to know this aspect of being from and in *sensed* objects.

INTELLECTUAL KNOWLEDGE OF PARTICULARS   We say the "abstracted being" or whatness is not the individual, sensible being but its universal nature. For example, when I sense the particular qualities of some object which I understand to be an apple, the universalized concept "apple" is not directly concerned with the fact that this particular object happens to be red, soft, and sweet. The universal concept "apple" could apply with equal meaning to an object which, to the senses, is different, i.e., to an object which is green, hard, and sour. The intelligible whatness of a sensible thing is restricted to a singular, material object by a complex act of intellect and senses which combines their activities into a unified act of knowing.

We have seen that the idea itself represents what a thing is. This idea is consciously neither universal nor particular. We may reflexly advert to its universality, or we may recognize its applicability to a particular instance. But since what is represented in my concept is equally applicable to any individual in that class, the idea of *this* particular individual can be obtained only by relating the concept to a sensory experience which localizes it in time and space. This is necessary because of the abstractive nature of human intellection, not because the singular is in itself absolutely unintelligible; otherwise we would have to say that God could not know the singular.

Suprasensible being, abstract and spiritual realities, are not the proper object of the human intellect because its knowledge is derived from sensory experience and mediated through sensory images and symbols. Hence we know these immaterial realities only by analogy with material things. Our knowledge of the spiritual is at best indirect and imperfect. We can abstract out such concepts as cause and substance, negating the imperfections and limitations of materiality. Our inability to form proper ideas of immaterial reality is not because of a lack of intelligibility there. As being, immaterial reality is intelligible in itself, but not readily accessible to the human intellect which in this life must know in and through the senses.

This is the correct interpretation of the old adage, "There is nothing in the intellect which was not previously *in some way* in the senses." Even spiritual realities are knowable by the human intellect only because the foundations for such concepts existed already in what is in the senses and could be derived from sense knowledge by a process of reasoning and analogy.

CAUSE OF IDEAS

To explain the origin of ideas has been one of the central problems of philosophy throughout its long history. From the time of the ancient Greeks there have been three main traditions with regard to this problem. The first is known as *sensism*, empiricism, or positivism. This solution is to deny one of the elements, i.e., intellection. There is no problem of explaining the origin of intellectual knowledge from sensation if there is only sensory knowledge. This solution will be discussed in the following chapter.

The other horn of the dilemma was taken by Plato, Berkeley, and others who were so impressed by the evidence *for* the spiritual nature of ideas that they neglected the role of sense. This is called *idealism*, exaggerated intellectualism, or conceptualism, and has appeared in one form or another in almost every century. It does great violence to man's nature by divorcing intellect from body, thus splitting man into two beings. From exaggerated intellectualism flows the exaggerated dualism which has plagued philosophy and psychology especially since the time of Descartes. Aligned with this position are *ontologism*, which explains our knowledge as a direct intuition of God, and *innatism*, which says that ideals are innate (inborn). The men who take these positions seem all to have been impressed that the abstract and universal cannot come from what is singular and material, so they denied the other element of the problem.

As a biologist, Aristotle was too empirical to accept the idealism of his master Plato; but the evidence for the spiritual nature of our thought processes convinced him that the sensism of Democritus was not the answer either. Instead of trying to minimize either line of evidence, Aristotle boldy seized both horns of the dilemma and solved the problem by proposing that man can derive ideas from sense experience by his own action. Thus ideas are neither innate nor sensory. In this solution he has been followed by early philosophers, by the whole stream of scholastic philosophy from the Middle Ages to the present, by many existentialists, and by other followers of moderate realism.

This view, which does not deny either the nature of intellection nor its roots in sense knowledge, seems to be confirmed by our everyday experience. Every student is all too well aware of how right Shakespeare was in saying that "Knowledge maketh a bloody entrance," and we might long for the ease of inborn knowledge. Learning would be unnecessary and psychotherapy impossible if our ideas were all innate. We always begin by examining sensible reality, even in building up our most abstract theories. We communicate such abstractions by means of sensory symbols and try to picture them to ourselves in concrete images. We always develop ideas of material objects prior to those of the spiritual realm, which are then built upon analogy with what we know first. People who were born blind and subsequently have gained their sight through an operation describe how they build up ideas from sensory experience.

POWER OF ABSTRACTION   At birth the intellect is like an erased blackboard (John Locke's *tabula rasa*), or one upon which nothing has ever been written. Man can know, but he needs data from the senses. By observing trees I do not build up the concept of a bicycle. On the other hand, it seems that the senses alone could not account for our intellectual knowledge of either trees or bicycles. Man must have the ability to abstract ideas from sense experience. To this ability the scholastic philosophers gave the name *agent intellect,* which is misleading because it is not some separate power of knowing, nor an observable agent. Man is the agent who abstracts. This seems the most satisfactory solution proposed so far to the problem of the origin of ideas, in terms of analysis of the causality involved rather than in terms of psychology. It is a complex process involving the whole man as knower, with close interrelationship of intellect and sense experience.[1]

Since it is man's nature to have ideas, it is clear that the agent intellect is not God or something supernatural. Thinking is not a continuous succession of miracles but something within man's power.

Because of a different interpretation of a difficult and ambiguous passage in Aristotle (*De Anima,* III, 5, 430a 17), some Arabian philosophers thought that there was only one agent intellect, a separate spiritual substance, for all men. This theory seems to deny the control each man has over his acts of abstracting and understanding, and to contradict other evidence which points to the conclusion that each man has his own power of thought independently.[2]

ESP   At this point the question of ESP, or extrasensory perception, arises. Can we acquire or communicate ideas without going through the ordinary channels of sensory perception? This is still an open question, with perhaps

[1] *Phantasm* is a word used in scholastic philosophy to refer to any sensory knowledge from which the intellect can abstract an idea. It does not have any specific reference to fantasy. Phantasm is conceived of in this theory as the subordinate and instrumental efficient cause of the idea, the principal efficient cause being the agent intellect.

The instrumental causality here seems to be of a unique kind. It is natural, not artificial; conjoined, not separate from the principal cause. Aquinas calls sense knowledge a "quasi-instrument" (*Quodl.* 8, q. 2, art. 3), and elsewhere speaks with similar caution (*Q. Un. De Anima,* art. 5 ad 8um; *Truth,* q. 10, art. 6 ad 8um). See my *Man and His Nature* for further explanation and sources.

[2] Cf. "Introduction" to Aristotle, *De Anima,* trans. K. Foster & S. Humphries (New Haven, Conn.: Yale University Press, 1951), pp. 18–24.

the majority of experimental psychologists still maintaining that ESP is not a proved fact, and that apparent instances can be explained away as the results of secondary perceptual cues, suggestion, coincidence, or mere variations from statistical probability. Even those who claim that ESP is established fact do not pretend to have an explanation as to how it would work.

Although ESP is an activity apparently different from the ordinary way in which our minds are observed to operate, the notion contains nothing contradictory to the immaterial nature of the intellect itself. J. B. Rhine of Duke University claims that his researches on ESP give basis for a proof of the spiritual nature. We prefer to base our case for spirituality on less contestable evidence, but would welcome the confirmation from this source if it is established. If proved, it would cause no embarrassment to those who hold the essentially immaterial nature of the intellect; it would only prove an exception to the ordinary way in which our intellects operate. Its establishment would be most embarrassing to those whose philosophy does not admit reality beyond the material. The same might be said of whatever new fields of psychic awareness are developed by LSD and other "mind-expanding" drugs.

Mind

The word "mind," with its adjective "mental," is a very ambiguous term and the source of many difficulties in both philosophy and psychology. Webster's dictionary gives eight primary and five secondary meanings, or a total of thirteen different meanings, for the word. We can distinguish at least four distinct meanings which the word might have:

1. *Activity.* Mind may mean consciousness, the sum or stream of psychological activities going on, awareness, or experience. This is the meaning intended when one says, "What is on your mind?" i.e., what is in your consciousness or awareness? When used this way, the phrase "mind and body" refers to mental and physical processes, considering strictly the realm of operation, not substance.

2. *Habits.* But mind can also refer not to the actual contents of consciousness at any given time but to the habits which perfect our abilities, even though we may not be acting upon them. Thus if I say, "I know his mind on the question," I am not referring to what he may actually be thinking, since he may be asleep and not thinking at all. I refer rather to his habitual attitude about the matter, viz., the habits which dispose him to think about it in a certain way if he were to think about the topic.

3. *Powers.* The word mind can also mean not act, nor habit, but the sheer ability to perform psychological operations. Thus when one says, "He has a sharp mind," one is referring to his ability to reason. Mind in this sense can refer to any or all of our mental powers but especially to the power of understanding, or intellect.

4. *Soul.* The word mind has even been extended into the realm of substance and is sometimes used as synonymous with the ultimate formal principle of mental operations, viz., the soul. The use of the word in this sense usually suggests a gross dualism and is better avoided. As we shall see, the concept of the soul as form is quite different from the Cartesian idea of mind as substance.

Because of the frequent mention of the term *unconscious* in modern psychology, it is well to note here that only the first meaning (1) above pertains to the realm of consciousness. The other three meanings can be learned only from inference, not from direct conscious experience. Consequently the term unconscious could rightly include all three of the latter. However this term usually refers only to (2), the habits which modify our operations in subtle and powerful ways often quite unknown to us. Besides the unrecognized influence of habits, the term unconscious also covers many pertinent facts of physiology.[3]

Since the term mind is so ambiguous, we generally avoid it in this treatise. Its adjective, mental, will be used only in a general way to refer to all knowing and wanting experiences.

DO WE KNOW REALITY?

Epistemology is that branch of philosophy which deals with questions such as, "Can we know anything for sure?" "Do we know things as they really are?" "Can we know anything at all?" and, "Is there anything 'out there' to know?" These problems preoccupied a great proportion of philosophical discussion from the seventeenth through the nineteenth centuries, in both Europe and America. Some have mistrusted the senses, felt that all physical appearances are illusory, and that only the intellect is to be trusted. Others argued that if you start inside the mind you can never logically get out of it, since you have no way of verifying whether your knowledge corresponds to reality if you know only your knowledge and not reality. This line of thought led either to a mistrust of intellect and total reliance on the senses, or to a skepticism which doubted that we can know anything at all. The latter was in a way more logical, for in order to verify either intellectual or sensory knowledge you have to use the very power you are questioning, and hence argue in a circle. The conceptualists or idealists decided that there is no reality, only mind; or at least if something is real, we can never know anything about it for certain.

Twentieth-century philosophy has largely abandoned preoccupation with these extreme solutions to the problem of knowledge. We saw earlier that its critics pointed out how positivism violates its own principle of empirical verification on three counts: acceptance of reports from others, prediction of future events in scientific laws, and the nonempirical character of the doctrine of positivism itself. Pragmatic, existential, and phenomenological philosophers have each in his own way pointed out the falsity of the subject-object dichotomy which traps the knower inside his own mind like a fly in a bottle, and puts reality "out there" as if the knower and the act of knowing were not

---

[3] See James E. Royce, S.J., *Personality and Mental Health* (Milwaukee: Bruce, 1964), pp. 178–185, and the references on pp. 186–187, for a fuller discussion of the unconscious. "Subconscious" is perhaps best used to refer to states of marginal or subliminal consciousness.

also reality. The subject is not outside the totality or Gestalt, but is a part of it, indeed at the very center of it. They have shown that the unique, primary relationship that constitutes the knowing experience is so immediate and irreducible that it finds proof unnecessary. Not proof but direct examination, a simple regard for the fact of being aware at all, reveals that even the denial or doubt of existence implies its recognition. For I cannot doubt without existing, and I cannot know my own existence except in contrast to others, to not-me. Any act of knowing is shown to imply being-as-known-to-me, even the simple "Here I am!"

The question now is rather how much and how well I know. Besides the extreme epistemological positions of the past centuries, three general lines of theory might be proposed as to our knowledge. The first might be called the *copy theory*. In this naïve approach, knowledge is an exact representation of the object as it is. Now we have already seen that our knowledge of things is never complete or perfect, that what we know becomes data for more and more refined knowledge of essential properties or characteristics. The whole problem of scientific induction is involved here. But in any case human knowledge remains imperfect and hence never exhaustively commensurate with its object. In addition, this theory runs into great difficulties when faced with the facts of illusion, ambiguity, distortion, emotional and other subjective factors, even delusion.

At the opposite extreme, and perhaps out of despair with the copy theory, is the supercautious position of *operationism*, which makes no attempt at knowledge as representative of reality. It is content to describe the operations by which we arrive at a piece of knowledge instead of the knowledge itself. Besides the contradiction involved in assuming that we know the operations (which are part of reality), we saw toward the end of Chapter 2 the difficulties which have led to the abandonment of extreme operationism even by many of its leaders. It has the obvious disadvantage of never telling us anything about either knowledge itself or its real object, but only about our own methodological procedures.

The third, *moderate realism*, holds that we can have a true, though limited and imperfect, knowledge of things as they are. At least I know that the store-window dummy is a being, even if I am temporarily in error in thinking it a man. Further data will settle the issue. The man in the street, even though sophisticated enough to know that the world is composed of atoms rather than of solid "stuff" as he sees it, is quite sure that there *is* a real world. The mathematician does not spend all day wondering if he can really trust his reasoning processes at all, though he is quite aware of the possibility of error in his calculations and is constantly checking to detect or prevent them. The scientist in his laboratory does not spend all day wondering whether there really is a test tube or whether it is just an illusion, though he knows illusions happen and is on his guard against them. We know that if we multiply 2 by 2 indefinitely, there is no likelihood that eventually the correct answer might be 5 instead of 4. We are equally sure that if we read this book until the end of the world it will not suddenly turn into a pumpkin.

These certainties about the reality of test tubes or the reliability of our reasoning are held in full view of the facts of ignorance and error and doubt. It is not naïve or blind, but pragmatic. It is reflected in the way we act and speak. We do not say, "Look at the percept of a man over there," but "Look at the man." We do not say that we dreamed about an image but about a dinosaur. We do not think about thoughts (except in philosophy or psychology) but about things and people. We don't converse with a subjective impression, but with a person. The experiments with the prism glasses which invert the retinal image and the pseudophone which reverses the right-left ear input again demonstrated that perception is not knowledge of sensations but of objects. The impressions are only means *by which* we know, not *that which* we know in direct experience. We don't see sensations but trees and houses. Hence there is no question of getting outside the mind, because knowledge starts there and within me simultaneously.

The moderate realists note that I never construct reality entirely out of my own mental fashioning. I see trees rather than ships in a forest (or find scientific theories converging) because things are what they are. *Why* does everything lend itself to a dialogue with man? Apparently because things contain within themselves the possibility of meaning. This is the fascination of scientific research, man reaching out to discover the intelligibility of the universe. The scientist would have no point in trying to discover laws in nature if there was no intelligible order there for him to discover. Of course there are hallucinations and delusions, but the very fact that we can discuss them means that we already know the difference between this kind of process and knowledge. We could not even ask the question as to whether all of reality was a dream unless we already knew from our own experience the difference between dream and reality.

Effect of subjective factors on perception

Gabriel Marcel compares sensory perception to receiving a guest into your house: he enters, but you are not purely passive as you act the gracious host. The facts of constancy, etc. in Chapter 5 show perception as a transactional encounter between knower and reality, in which each gives something of itself. There is constant activity, selection, interpretation on the part of the knower. That all or many of these subjective factors can influence and distort our impression of what we hear as well as what we see is well illustrated by the old parlor game in which a story is told to the first person in a circle, who whispers it to the second, who repeats it to the next in turn, all around the room, and then the story is told aloud by the last person; often it is an unrecognizable version of the original. This is not deliberate or conscious distortion, as you can know from your own experience.

Does the influence of these various perceptual factors help or hinder our perception of reality? Ordinarily the result is so satisfactory as to provide a useful guide to action; in fact, it is only because cues are so commonly dependable that we trust them on occasions when they should not be trusted and so sometimes are led to error. These factors tend to correct real discrepancies between stimulus received and object, and thus make us see things more nearly as they really are than as they might seem to be. Images on the retina are inverted, yet we see objects upright. Images move on the retina as we walk, yet we see buildings as standing still. Even when we try to fool the senses, as by wearing inverted prisms for glasses which turn images up the other way or by the pseudophone which reverses the input to the to ears, somehow our sensory apparatus adjusts to this reversal of stimulation and after a while we see and hear things in their right position. Morgan (1956, pp. 177–178) says,

> Our perceptions of objects correspond more closely to the true object, however, than to the sizes of images on the retina or to the sensory stimulus in general.
>
> As human beings, we enjoy several advantages from perceptual constancy. It would be exceedingly difficult to move about or operate in a world where sounds changed their location when we moved our heads, and where objects changed their shapes and sizes when we viewed them from different positions and distances. Imagine what it would be like if your friends and associates had a multitude of sizes and shapes that depended upon how far away they were and from what angle you viewed them. Or imagine how difficult it would be to live in our society if the colors of things varied markedly with changes in sunlight and weather. It would be impossible to identify anything by color or whiteness, since the color of an object would depend not only on what time of the day it was but also on such thing as cloudiness and shadows.

He concludes that though our eyes do sometimes trick us, they do so only in the line of duty. They operate in a way which is more than a matter of physical efficiency; they give us impressions of the outside world which are basically correct, even though they are by no means perfect.

The perceptual judgment

Man knows existence not as some abstract concept but embedded in the existing things he perceives through his senses. As we have seen, he is implicitly aware both of his own existence and that of objects distinct from himself in the very act of knowing at all. Even our most exalted metaphysical conceptions, such as that of being itself, are discovered by the experience of direct contact with physical objects through the senses. Thus intellection, the act of knowing being as such, combines with sense perception, the act of knowing material objects, to produce the distinctive act of human knowledge, the perceptual judgment.

It is this fact, the sensory-intellectual nature of human knowledge, which suggests an answer to the epistemological problems of the past few centuries.[4] We need not begin with a subjectivism which proceeds from subject to object. Nor need we subscribe to an Augustinian theory of illumination which would explain knowledge by some divine influence. Nor need we hold a naïve rationalism which begins with objects and tries to deduce man's knowledge of them. We can begin with the basic fact that if this man understands anything at all, the intellectivo-sensitive awareness involved in any full act of human knowledge immediately puts him in a unique subject-object relation which is not purely phenomenal because he is primarily aware of the object, not of his knowledge. This relation is in one sense subtle and almost defies analysis, but on the other hand is so immediate and direct that it needs none. It is the primary experience itself.

So true is this that if a person claimed he did not know what existence was, it would be impossible to explain it to him, for there is nothing more immediate to which it can be reduced. The basic distinction between knower and thing known is something which is absolutely irreducible to simpler terms. But it does not erect a barrier or false subject-object dichotomy, because of the total continuity stressed in earlier chapters. Nor does it lend any support to an exaggerated realism which imputes separate existence to ideas outside this

[4] Etienne Gilson, *Réalisme thomiste et critique de la connaissance* (Paris: Vrin, 1939), a work which unfortunately has not been translated. Chapters 7, 8, pp. 184–239, give the basic argument here, especially pp. 207–209. On the importance of this work, see Gerard Smith, S.J., "A Date in the History of Epistemology," *The Thomist* (Maritain volume), 1943, 5:246–255, in which he suggests that Gilson thereby puts an end to the epistemological haggling of the past three centuries.

continuum of man-in-the-world. "It would be a mistake to think that phenomenology does not defend a realistic awareness of reality just because it rejects representative realism," says Luijpen. The statement means little to an American student, but unfortunately, because of the neo-Hegelians, the term "realism" (even moderate) suggests to many current European philosophers either Platonic idealism or positivism, neither of which of course is intended by our use of the term.

Conclusion

From this analysis of human knowledge we can see how operations serve as a clue to the nature of a thing. An old axiom in philosophy says, "Whatever is received is received according to the manner or nature of the recipient." Now what is characteristic of human knowledge is precisely the fact that material being is known in a universal and immaterial way by abstraction from sense. This suggests that man must be constituted somehow of both material and immaterial principles, to make him capable of both aspects of this operation. The need for joint activity of intellect and sense in man's knowledge of particulars is a specific instance of how man's operations imply the kind of being he is. His manner of knowing particulars indicates both this admixture of the organic and the immaterial, and his unity as one knowing subject.

REVIEW QUESTIONS

1. If abstraction separates what is together in reality, is it not false knowledge?
2. Is any true science possible if there are no abstractions or universal ideas?
3. Until recently words like insight and intuition have been suspect. What reasons can you give for agreeing? What factors are behind the current tendency to accept them?
4. What does the proper object of our intellect suggest for the future of human knowledge?
5. In what way do you agree with the sensists?
6. In what way do you agree with the idealists?
7. Would evidence (if established) of learning during the latter months of pregnancy, indicating that the child is born with some ideas, support Plato against Aristotle?
8. What implications for the nature of man does the theory of innate ideas have?

9.   What implications for the nature of man do you see in the position of senso-intellectualism?

10. How do we intellectually know the past as past? How do we know singulars?

11. Compare the functions of conscience and of the cogitative sense. How are they similar? How do they differ? Does either involve innate knowledge?

12. "Unconscious" is an adjective. If a noun must be supplied, what do you suggest? If you suggest "mind," which meaning or meanings must the word have?

13   What is epistemology?

14. Can we know something with truth but not certitude?

15. Can we be certain of something and yet wrong? (Cf. question 3 on Chapter 5)

16. Discuss the relative advantages of starting epistemology with "Cogito, ergo sum," versus starting with the perceptual judgment.

17. If the epistemological problem is real, can it logically be answered?

FOR FURTHER READING

Kelly & Tallon: the selections from Descartes on pp. 42–46, and the chapters from Rahner and Aquinas.

Bernard Lonergan, in his penetrating book, *Insight,* delves into the the process of abstraction and the formation of human knowledge, with intuitive and post-Kantian overtones; see also the chapter "Metaphysics as Horizon" in his Collection. Geach's writings, especially *Mental Acts: Their Content and Their Objects,* show the inadequacy of defining abstraction as merely recognition of a common element in repeated experiences. Ernest Kapp includes the intuitive aspects in *The Greek Foundations of Traditional Logic.* Sebastian J. Day has a study entitled *Intuitive Cognition: A Key to the Significance of the Later Scholastics.* Also opposing excessive intellectualism is the article by Robert O. Johann, S.J., "The Return to Experience," *Rev. Metaphysics,* 1964, 17:319–339.

Practical applications of this chapter are given by A. D. Sertillanges in his book, *The Intellectual Life.* Also practical, at least in the sense of beautifully setting the material of this chapter into a total perspective, is chap. 13 in *The Spirit of Medieval Philosophy* by Etienne Gilson.

Psychological investigation of intellectual cognition has proliferated of late, much of it from a developmental standpoint. Representative are the writings of **Jean Piaget, T. V. Moore, Charles E. Osgood,** and **Jerome S. Bruner,** especially the latter's *Studies in Cognitive Growth.*

Epistemology, the study of whether we know reality, has its own vast literature. Perhaps one of the most useful statements of moderate realism is by **Kenneth T. Gallagher,** *The Philosophy of Knowledge.* Also helpful are **Frederick D. Wilhelmsen,** *Man's Knowledge of Reality* (especially chap. 3), **L. M. Regis,** *Epistemology,* and **Reginald F. O'Neill,** *Theories of Knowledge.* Another view is given by **John Dewey** in *The Quest for Certainty.*

Because the trustworthiness of our knowing process is a question that has largely arisen in the past few centuries, it probably can best be understood in historical context. One of the most enlightening books on the subject, and one that is highly recommended, is **E. Gilson's** *Unity of Philosophical Experience;* read at least parts III and IV.

7 LANGUAGE AND MEANING

Man is a symbolic animal.   Cassirer

Man has traditionally been defined as a rational animal. Now a definition proves nothing; it just formulates the result of investigation. Moreover, we find many instances in which man is not nearly so "rational" as he would like to think himself. Yet his achievements in literature, art, poetry, engineering, science, government, and other areas of civilization clearly mark him off from the other animals, even from those among whom some apparent similarities to human traits have been found. The difference between intellectual and sensory knowledge is further suggested by the fact that a moron can store up a great fund of useless factual information, while an intellectual genius may not even know his own telephone number or may be ignorant of the facts of history. Mere sensory knowledge is not necessarily wisdom.

IS MEANING SENSORY?

These facts pose a most fundamental question: is the difference between intellectual and sensory knowledge merely a matter of degree, or are they of really different kinds? Upon the answer to this question depends our solution to many crucial problems affecting law, society, and our own destiny. Man's responsibility as a free agent, the spiritual and immortal dimensions of the person, human rights and dignity—all hinge to some extent on the immaterial nature of intellectual operations.

Since even the most ardent materialist would hardly insist that he has never had an idea or that he cannot think, the problem is to analyze what thinking is. Is an idea the same kind of knowing as an image? Is thinking a matter of muscle twitches in the throat or neurological activity in the brain? Do computers think? What is the meaning of "meaning"?

To sharpen the issue we should make clear that to claim that man is rational is not to deny the sensory, animal aspects of his nature, nor the fact that he often acts in a very irrational way. Infancy and early childhood, severe mental disorder, and the spontaneous actions of normal adults give ample evidence that much of our activity is animal. Since "He who proves too much proves nothing," we do not appeal to the intellect when animal activities will explain behavior.

Some ambiguous terms

Again, we must avoid the ambiguity which has accrued to many terms in current psychology because of the philosophical backgrounds of the people using them. Such terms as intelligence, meaning, insight, trial and error, and learning are all analogical and can be applied to the operations of both the internal senses and the intellect. Spearman (1950, p. 67) went so far as to say that the term intelligence had become so vague as to lose all usefulness. Even the term concept formation is now used to refer to the association of images of a general type with certain words or arbitrary symbols, which is within the power of at least the higher brute animals. For example, a rat can be conditioned to associate food with a square figure rather than with a circular one. Similarly, the term problem solving can refer to a great variety of activities, some involving intellect and some explainable by perceptual awareness of a total pattern of concrete relations. Thus the ape that piles crates on top of one another to get at the banana, and the cat which associates certain movements with release from the puzzle box, show awareness of concrete relations but not necessarily of abstract principles (see the Appendix).

Philosophers have inked tons of paper in discussions of the meaning of "meaning." We can say that the rat learned that a square "means" food and a circle "means" a punishing shock. In this case a concrete sensory association is rather obviously there, but the question is open as to how much understanding is involved. We say that the sign "means" smoking is not allowed, but we do not impute to the sign any ability to understand and communicate its meaning in the same way that we imply when we ask another person, "What do you mean?" With Shakespeare we could say that there are

> *Tongues in trees,*
> *Books in the running brooks,*
> *Sermons in stones,*

and meaning everywhere. But it is obviously there for you only if you understand, and to the extent that you understand. To say that a poem has no meaning may be an admission that its meaning is too deep for you to grasp. That piece of ultramodern music may be for me a jumble of sounds, but to you it conveys much. Yet we reach for the dictionary to look up the meaning of an unfamiliar word, confident that all meaning is not totally relative and that the word has some standard meaning or meanings which are understood in pretty much the same way by all who use the language correctly. We shall return to this when we discuss the relations between language and thought.

But "thought" is itself an ambiguous term. When you say, "I was thinking of a nice blue lake with a sandy beach and green wooded shores," you are not reporting any great intellectual activity, but just daydreams, which are largely sense images. On the other hand when we "think a problem through," we are reasoning, trying to understand. But what do we mean when we call computers "thinking machines"? They certainly give us the answers to problems. And the steps are so involved that instead of patterning the computer after his own thought processes, man is now studying how the computer solves problems, in a search for clues as to how he himself thinks.

Lastly, we must note that when we ask whether meaning (understanding) can be reduced to sense knowledge, we immediately find that "sense" is ambiguous, too. So far we have used sense and sensory to convey an organic awareness of material objects with and through their sensible qualities, as described in Chapters 4 and 5. "Sense" refers to something that belongs to the realm of physical and animal matter, material. But we also use expressions such as, "It doesn't make sense," and, "What is the sense of that word?" where obviously we do not refer to sensory knowledge but to intelligibility, understandable meaning. (If the latter expression seems a bit like going in circles, it is because we are here wrestling with one of those irreducible, fundamental notions that philosophers must examine.)

Sensism

This theory on the nature of understanding has had its ardent proponents down through the ages. Sensism is a philosophy which reduces all thinking processes to the sensory. Note that a sensist is not merely one who asserts the existence of sense knowledge; rather, he is one who denies that there is any other kind of knowledge beyond the sensory. Democritus tried to explain cognition by describing it as a tiny image caused by a stream of particles emanating from material objects. This materialistic view has been revived in various forms over the centuries: by the associationists (who attempt to explain thinking as the association of sense images), the empiricists, the positivists, and such modern psychologists as the behaviorists, some structuralists (Titchener and his followers), and many Gestaltists, not to mention most current British and American philosophers.

Considerable evidence can be given in support of this position. Democritus could point to the fact that when clothes are drying in the yard water is being carried off into the air in tiny droplets not always visible. The success of computers in solving problems seems to favor a mechanical explanation of thought. Much of thinking seems to be the manipulation of models or symbols. We always seem to be talking to ourselves when we think, signaling to ourselves about new responses to our environment. This is true even of our most abstract and lofty thinking. Moreover, delicate instruments can detect slight movements in the muscles of the throat and vocal cords (subvocal speech) during thought which indicate that we are talking to ourselves even when this is not audible. Perhaps most impressive evidence is that from the development of language which indicates that we learn meanings of words pretty much by a conditioned-response type of process in which our language community reinforces the right association for each word. For instance, I soon learn that if I say, "Salt, please," I do not have the meat passed to me. B. F. Skinner, in his book *Verbal Behavior*, seems able to explain all language as the result of such conditioning, without any recourse to inner meaning. In the Rice symposium he said, "I find it useful to think of my inner processes as no different from those of a white rat."

Intellectualism

On the other side are those who claim that understanding involves operations of a distinctively different nature, going beyond sensory experience. For them, intellectual processes do not possess any material qualities, such as color, shape, sound, or extension, which we discovered even in the operations of the internal senses. They hold intellection to be free of the limitations of matter, universal, capable of perfect reflection on itself, able to deal with immaterial or spiritual objects and values, giving man superiority over the other animals, and making him able to design and program computers.

While we are unwilling to subscribe to any exaggerated intellectualism which would neglect the importance of sense experience and the role of body in knowing, it seems unlikely that so many philosophers would have stressed the immaterial nature of intellection if the evidence were wholly to be discounted. Twentieth-century American students are often under the impression that a philosophy of materialism dominates the major portion of human thought, opposed only by a religious minority. Now truth is not decided by majority vote, nor does the philosopher argue from the weight of authority. But it is well to correct this impression by pointing out that the spiritual nature of the intellect is upheld by philosophers of widely different schools of thought, varied cultures, and all degrees of faith: pagan Greeks like Plato and Aristotle, Arabians like Averroës, most Oriental philosophers, divergent and even opposed European philosophers like Descartes, Kant, Hegel, Spinoza, and Bergson, and contemporary American psychologists and philosophers scattered across the country. Although these Americans are certainly a minority in this country, it is probably true that the majority of philosophers, except in our particular culture, oppose the materialistic view.

After decades of either ignoring intellectual processes entirely or reducing them to sensory and even behavioral responses, American psychology in the second half of this century has taken a renewed interest in the subject. Value judgments and thinking began to be studied as psychological facts, followed by "cognitive" theories of personality, a personal construct theory of personality (Geo. Kelly), studies in "cognitive dissonance" (L. Festinger), semantic differential (Osgood), and intense study of the development of "cognition" (as opposed to mere sense knowledge) by Piaget, Werner, Vygotsky, and especially Jerome Bruner and his associates at Harvard. ". . . to learn the senses or semantic markers of words is to learn the constraints on their conceptual range—an intellectual task, not a perceptual one" (Bruner, 1966, p. 32).

Cantril was one of the first contemporary psychologists to state this position frankly; in *The "Why" of Man's Experience* (1950b) he used terms such as "immaterial" and "freedom of choice" which had been taboo during the behavioristic era. Symonds (1951, 1956) noted that the swing in emphasis is away from purely emotional factors in adjustment, toward rational control. The work of Spearman, Thurstone, and Guilford on factorial analysis constantly comes back to the notion of intellect as distinct but not separate, whether it be called G, super-G, or a second-order factor. (See Gannon, *Psychology: The Unity of Human Behavior,* 1954, pp. 347–362, for a full discussion of this, and for other examples from modern psychology.)

L. Terman, father of intelligence testing in the United States, toward the end of a long career stated that in his opinion intelligence could still best be defined as "the ability to do abstract thinking." There is experimental evidence that knowledge of concrete facts in "pupil-oriented" learning may actually hinder problem solving if abstract principles are neglected. Abraham Maslow, Gardner Murphy, David McClelland, and others have recently emphasized that maturity is characterized by goal seeking and by other activities which are rational rather than emotional, or at any rate are distinct from animal activity and mere need reduction. Hilgard, in his *Theories of Learning* (1956), indicates the swing back toward values, and the responsibility of those who speak vaguely of intervening variables to face the question of their precise nature:

> *An important aspect of motivation long neglected in learning*
> *theories . . . is that motives are organized in some sort of*
> *hierarchy within the individual, resulting in a value-system expressed*
> *in behavior. (p. 469) Stimulus-response psychologists . . . have*
> *assigned as little as possible to ideation, but they have*
> *usually recognized that some behavior is controlled by ideas . . .*
> *Tolman, in Behavioristic spirit, makes of ideation a "mere*
> *behavior-feint at running-back-and-forth" without specifying the*
> *precise nature of the feint. (p. 476)*

Faced with this divergence of views, we can only examine the evidence as best we can. The history of the problem suggests that maybe both lines of evidence are well founded in fact, and perhaps the choice is not exclusively one or the other but some combination. Analysis of our own experience is paramount, but it needs to be checked against that of others. One rather public, universal, and accessible way to do that is through analysis of the way in which we use ordinary language.

CONCEPTUAL LANGUAGE

Since the use of conceptual language is often asserted to be a characteristic difference between men and the other animals, it is important to analyze the relation of language to thought. Whether or not animals communicate, with each other or with man, is a false issue. One reindeer communicates a sense of danger to the whole herd; one bee informs the others of the location of a find of sugar. The dog indicates to his master that he is hungry and to the delivery boy that he is angry. But all these manifestations are by natural signs and always communicating concrete sensory messages. The same is true when the dog "understands" a verbal command, as is clear from the fact that he will do the same thing in response to a meaningless word that *sounds* very similar, but he fails to recognize a synonym where meaning is identical but sensory experience differs. Parrots and certain animals have all the mechanical equipment for language; the difference must be in whether they have anything to say, not in whether they can talk.

What we mean by conceptual language is a system of arbitrary symbols which can be the outward expression of ideas or concepts. Language may have its origin in natural signs, such as gestures or mimicry of certain sounds that suggest objects or movements. But it is not true language until these signs become conventional and are recognized as signs. No sensory power can recognize an arbitrary relationship as such. Bees and parrots do not discuss the functions of language, nor use metaphor. This is important, because a figure of speech always involves the separation of the sign from its natural or concrete significance. It requires the recognition of sign as symbol, not merely as significant. It goes beyond mimicry and concrete association to meaning, in the strict sense of that term. For example, the difference between animal communication and true language could be illustrated by the fact that a lower animal such as an ape could learn to drive a tractor by imitation or by conditioning, whereas a man could read the instruction book (symbols) and go out and drive the tractor.

What we are exploring here is what some philosophers have described by the difference between natural signs and arbitrary signs. A natural sign like an arrow or hand motion "up" conveys concrete, sensory "meaning" at the animal level. But the *word* which might differ in every language of the world, is significant only if I know the conventional symbolism of that language. Since an animal can associate a concrete response with any given word, the real problem is the nature of the meaning associated with it. Obviously a word, or for that matter an image or natural sign as in hieroglyphics or Indian sign language, may be a *symbol* for a universal idea (concept). The question is whether the word symbol *is* the idea, or whether its meaning is the understanding it triggers.

Here "ordinary-language" philosophy seems to join forces with phenomenology in furnishing data about our knowing experience which has some universal validity. Suppose a little boy is looking out in the pasture at a horse, and he asks, "Mommy, what's that?" She answers, "A horse, sonny." Has she given him the idea of horse? He does not understand what a horse is any better now than before he asked. The only thing he knows now that he did not know before his question is the word for it. Suppose she had answered, "That's a fire engine." Would he know any less about what a horse is? No, he would only be confused about the name, and of course would have a difficult time getting along in our society if she continued his "education" in this fashion. But his concept of horse would be unchanged.

Again, if I say, "What is a triangle?" or "What is justice?" you may answer, "Well, I don't know whether I can formulate a nicely worded definition right off, but I can try; I certainly know what a triangle is, and have a pretty good idea of what justice is." You have the idea, the understanding of what the word means. On the other hand, suppose I ask, "What is a blitri, or a xad?" Your answer can only be, "I haven't any idea, I don't know." You hear the word, or could see the symbol, but it conveys no meaning to you; you do not understand because these words have no meaning. You understand quite well that to be a triangle is not the same as to be justice, because you have at least some general understanding of the nature or essential properties of each.

Words and ideas

We rarely think without speaking to ourselves, though we would probably be less willing to admit that we occasionally speak without thinking. But these are matters of concomitance, not identity. Regardless of whether one occurs without the other or whether they are always simultaneous, the question is whether language is automatically meaningful, i.e., whether there is a direct and necessary connection between the word and its meaning, or whether meaning is an intervening variable between language and reality. By "intervening" we cannot mean in some sort of time sequence, for we have seen they are usually simultaneous. Nor do we mean some meaning disembodied from all expression in human language, for in practical experience our ideas just do not occur that way.

Nominalism was a theory which held that only the word is truly universal. Confusing concept with image, the nominalists felt that the concept was never the same and the word is a convenient catchall applying to objects which always differ in reality. In effect, nominalists deny that we have true universal ideas; the universal representation is simply the name (*nomen*) of the object. For them thinking becomes merely the manipulation of symbols. Language *constitutes* thought; it is not simply the vehicle for expressing it.

In reaction to nominalism some scholastics exaggerated the distinction between word and concept, divorcing them unrealistically. Modern philosophers have stressed that even if they are distinct, thought exists intimately bound up in a context of sensory and language experience.

Language is at once of tremendous importance as the means of communicating thought and of relative insignificance compared with thought itself. The extent to which we can use our thinking process is almost entirely dependent upon the degree to which we can express or record our thoughts for ourselves or others. Yet the language in which we do so is a purely arbitrary, conventional set of symbols with no value in themselves, whose whole meaning is the concept or idea we have associated with them. Exceptions are a few onomatopoetic words like "whoosh" and "boom," where the form of the symbol itself expresses the idea. Except for the musical pleasure of the sounds, the most sublime literature of a completely foreign language has no more meaning for us than the babble of an idiot. A truth is equally true regardless of what language it is expressed in or whether we have an expression for it at all. Yet it is undeniable that the language in which we formulate our ideas to ourselves, or through which others communicate their ideas to us, has an important and subtle influence on the way we think as well as on the content of our thought.

This view of the relation between language and thought fits with the work of Benjamin Whorf on comparative languages. Eskimos were found to have many different words for different kinds of snow but only one word for many objects for which we have separate terms. Whorf showed that these differences in language largely reflect the different ways in which people conceive of reality. The structure of a language parallels the pattern of the people's thinking. Few would deny Whorf's conclusion that the structure of language influences the manner of thinking; most would assert that many of the facts are equally well explained by the theory that the manner of conceiving reality influences the structure of language. No doubt Whorf is partially correct in that there is a mutual influence between thought and language, so that to some extent the way we talk does shape our thinking. The work of Whorf, Piaget, Vygotsky, Bruner, and others all shows that in their development language and thought constantly interact, apparently in both directions.

The relationships between word-symbol, object, and idea are subject to other interpretations. One theory is that there is a natural or magical relation between the word and the object. Some psychoanalytic psychologists have made much of this theory, and there is some evidence in certain instances of such a relation. It is not surprising that symbols and their objects can be very intimately related, especially in childhood and among primitive peoples. But analysis of conventional language among adults, especially those who can use several languages, shows the inadequacy of this view as a comprehensive theory.

Behavioral psychologists have been inclined to explain the relation of symbol and object by saying that they produce a common response. The psychologists correctly infer that thought is a mediation process between symbol and response, but the issue is confused because the word "meaning" is applied to various types of response, some of which involve thought and some of which do not. Thus the sound of the dinner bell "means" food for both dog and man by concrete association of images; but whereas man can understand this meaning independently of any behavioral response, the dog apparently can not. Osgood's work on semantic differentials as measures of the difference between denotation and connotation proves, or at least confirms, the distinction between thought and both its symbols and responses. The fact that his work could hardly apply to brute animals is suggestive of a radical difference between them and man.

In the 1920s the behaviorists tried to reduce thinking to *subvocal speech*, viz., to electrically measurable muscular contractions in the throat which are the beginnings of the formation of words which would express thought. There is no need to deny the existence of these action currents or "implicit speech" any more than to deny the evidence from the EEG (electroencephalograph) for brain waves during thought. But their existence does not prove whether they are cause or effect. The real question is whether these physical activities constitute the essence of thought, or are merely its concomitants. Every car makes noise, but this does not prove that the noise moves the car.

We may have a very clear idea for which there is no word in our vocabulary, as Helen Keller's autobiography or a simple experiment shows. It is not the theoretical impossibility of this situation which prompts the teacher to refuse an answer such as "I know it, but I can't express it," but only the practical consideration that knowledge which cannot be expressed is of little use to the student and impossible for the teacher to grade. The parrot, on the other hand, has many words but lacks the corresponding ideas.

We can have many words for a single idea, or many ideas may be expressed by a single word; both these situations would be impossible if the word was the idea. Thus the words *horse, pferd, caballo,* and *equus* look and sound quite different, yet they represent but one idea, not four. Conversely, the word "bat" can have a great variety of unconnected meanings, from a flying animal to an instrument for hitting a baseball, which shows that the ideas must be different from the word which stands for them. Again, we do not logically group bat, hat, and cat together. We conclude that there is little doubt that language and thought are closely related but not identical.

NATURE OF IDEAS

How well we know is always a question, but at least it seems that I can know very clearly that a horse is not a steam engine, or that the sum of the angles of a triangle always equals 180°. We must see if we are able to ascribe any material, sensible qualities to our awareness of either of these assertions. We may have images of horses and steam engines, or red-white-and-blue triangles, but do these constitute our intellectual understanding of the propositions?

The question is whether this act of awareness itself is material or spiritual, i.e., whether it has those characteristics of sensory knowledge previously described or whether it is totally devoid of them. Let us return to the idea of horse. My knowledge of horses is largely derived from sensory perception of horses and is usually accompanied by some image of a horse. But does my understanding of what a horse is consist of either of these? If the horse I see is brown, or the image I have is neutral gray, this does not mean that I understand either brown or gray to pertain to the essential nature of horse. To be a horse is not to be brown or gray, since it can be white or black. Yet all are equally horses, and my concept applies equally well to each of them. It is universal.

Similarly, when I asked what a triangle is, the diagram from a page of your old geometry textbook may have arisen as a visual image. It is black, obtuse, small. Is this your concept of triangle? If so, then you would not understand that a large, red, equilateral three-sided figure is also triangular. You discover that your concept has no particular color, size, or even shape (i.e., acute, obtuse, equilateral). You just know what a triangle is. We seem to be catching ourselves in the process of having an experience which is not limited by physical qualities, time, or space. Note that we do not say there is a triangle "out there" which is immaterial, nonphysical. What exist in reality are triangular objects, and a perfect mathematical triangle is only a mental construct. The point is that your act of understanding is immaterial, even though the triangular objects you see or imagine are quite material. Obviously a tree in the forest is not a mental construct; but my concept of the nature of tree has no material qualities. It applies equally well to all trees, whereas any sensory representation I have can not.

Here the sensist would point out that I can have an image of a .22

bullet which applies equally well to every bullet in the box. Therefore my universal idea of a .22 bullet could be a sensory image, with its material qualities. But is this really my understanding of what a .22 bullet is? Suppose some of the bullets in the box happened to be of a different color. My general image would no longer apply to all, but I would still say they are .22 bullets, since they will fit my gun and perform exactly the same functions as those of the other color. Why? What I think about their nature has not changed essentially because of the change in the sensible quality of color. For that matter, my concept of bullet applies equally well also to a .38 or a .45, although I can get no sense image which will fit perfectly all of these.

Interestingly enough, my sensory experiences may actually become more sharp as my ideas become more vague, and vice versa. My images of cow versus horse are clear; my ideas on the difference are hazy. But my idea of mammal versus nonmammal is clear, whereas the images become vague and inadequate here. Understanding is different from picturing.

The unpicturable nature of an idea means not only the lack of *visible* qualities, but of *any* material qualities. We cannot *see* sounds or odors, but this does not make them immaterial. I can hear or imagine (auditory image) a particular tune, but the idea of opera or ballad has no melody and cannot be heard any more than seen. The universal concept of symphony applies to all symphonies; the sensible sound of Beethoven's Ninth does not.

Note, too, that the difference between sense and intellect is not a matter of whether the object is absent or present, real or unreal. I can understand (have an idea of) a present horse, a horse I rode last summer, or a hypothetical flying horse. At the same time the understanding would be accompanied by percept, memory, and image respectively, but the question is whether these latter sensory accompaniments are the same kind of experience as my concept of horse.

Universal does not mean common to all men, but common to all objects of that class. If only one man existed, his concept of horse would still apply to all horses. The question here is not whether all men have at least the same general idea of what a horse is. Certainly their understanding varies from the profound knowledge of the expert to the naïve impression of the little boy. But here the fact of communication is pertinent evidence. In spite of difficulties, we do communicate. However different our understanding may be in profundity, when I say, "I rode a horse today," you do not think I rode an elephant. You know what I mean. Again, although ideas of their nature are universal, since they ignore the particular qualities and present only the common, the idea of a unique being would still be immaterial.

Thus my concept of "the first President of the United States" is not shaped or colored like George Washington, even though it has him as its only referent.

Intellection

We have been proceeding inductively, working from the way we speak and think rather than from any definition of rationality or intellect. The nature of understanding now seems to be coming clear.

The range of things we can understand, at least imperfectly, seems vast and even unlimited. I can ignore sensible qualities and just be aware of what is essential, as in the concept of tree or triangle. Or I can be aware of just one essential property, as that the angles of a triangle always equal 180°. Or I can focus intellectually on some purely incidental feature of a given class, as that all the horses on this ranch belong to its owner. In none of these cases does my understanding consist of sensible qualities. The idea in each case has no color, shape, size, or sound. Of course, the words by which I might express the idea have sound, but they would be meaningless babble if the hearer did not understand, i.e., if they were not symbols for the idea. Even the concept of color is itself colorless. If it were any one color, it could not apply to all colors. My understanding of the term when I say, "Color is not shape," does not involve sensory awareness of all the colors of the spectrum, or of any color at all.

We have seen that the object of a universal idea can be either concrete, like trees, or abstract, as in the case of mental constructs like justice, energy, triangularity. These latter have foundation in reality and are not airy nothings conjured up entirely in the mind: to demand racial justice is to demand something real, not a pure mental fiction.

In fact, although the consideration of abstract and spiritual objects might seem at first glance like the most impelling evidence for the immaterial nature of intellectual activity, some argue that the evidence from our understanding of concrete material objects like horses and trees is even more conclusive. It meets the sensist on his own grounds, where the data might seem most to favor his position, as in the general image of the .22 bullet. For even here the evidence seems to point to intellectual experiences which are unaccountable in sensory terms. An eminent psychologist puts it well:

> Thinking may deal with contents and relationships not perceptible. *A second difference between perception and thinking is that thinking goes beyond perception by dealing with relationships that cannot be perceived, that lie outside the field of perception*

entirely. A relationship like the square root of minus one is commonly symbolized by the small letter "i." This letter can, of course, be perceived, but the thought content involved is beyond perception. A concept like "justice" is too abstract to be perceived, even though it, too, may be symbolized by something perceptible, e.g., a blind goddess holding a pair of scales and a sword.

Perception, then, does not tell the whole story of thinking, even though there is an intimacy between thinking and perception. Thinking may conflict with and correct perception; it may deal with contents that are not perceptible at all.

Because he can think, man has opened before him vast possibilities that perception and habit alone would never have yielded. Through thought man can transcend space and time and pry into the mysteries of a universe measured in millions of light years. He can depart from reality into a fanciful world of his own making; he can become a creator as well as a discoverer. Because he can use and understand symbols (words, formulas, etc.), he can treasure up knowledge from the past. The monuments of ancient and contemporary civilizations—old aqueducts and modern hydroelectric dams, medieval cathedrals and modern skyscrapers, great libraries and museums—are at the same time monuments to man as a thinker (Hilgard, 1953, pp. 327–328).

JUDGMENT AND ANALOGY   If one says, "No man is a stone," it is easy to have a sensory image of a man and a stone and even of the word symbols "no" and "is." But the understanding of the fact that a man is not a stone has itself no material qualities knowable in a sensory way. This is especially clear if we consider the truth of a necessary judgment: the necessity is clearly grasped but impossible to reduce to sensory content. Even our judgment that the half-immersed oar is not bent is not expressed in a sensory way: we *know* it is straight, but we do not *see* it as straight. I know intellectually that the railroad tracks remain parallel, yet they continue to seem to converge in the distance.

The unpicturable nature of our intellectual judgments is strikingly illustrated by the analysis of understanding an analogy, which involves the ability to abstract out the similarity between two different relations. If the poet uses a metaphor like "smiling meadow," I can appreciate this only by recognizing that the arrangement of flowers on the meadow is somehow similar to the arrangement of muscles on a smiling face; a process which seems quite different from seeing either one. Perhaps for this reason small children are unable to think in analogy, or appreciate satire. Alfred Binet, the founder of intelligence testing, experimented with thought processes involving analogy and the reconciliation of opposites. He came to the conclusion that these thought experiences are irreducible to sense. This is all the more significant because he began his investigations as a convinced sensist.

THE "IMAGELESS-THOUGHT" CONTROVERSY   A similar case, where psychologists reversed their sensist preconceptions in the face of what they discovered in their laboratories, is the history of the Würzburg school, which around the turn of the century engaged in a controversy with Titchener of Cornell over the question of whether we always "think in images."

The crucial meaning of the expression "imageless thought" is *thought which is not image,* i.e., is not reducible to sensory experience, regardless of whether it may be *derived from* sense or *accompanied by* sense. The experimental evidence was that imageless thought in this meaning of the term does occur.[1] Not only K. Bühler, Külpe, and the other members of the Würzburg school, but also Alfred Binet and others in France, Watt and Spearman in England, R. S. Woodworth, Betts, and many others in this country, all agreed on the evidence. Their conclusion would seem to be the more objective because all these men started with a theoretical bias against this interpretation of the facts discovered. Titchener, who takes the contrary position, very frankly admits approaching the facts with a preconceived bias in favor of his interpretation. His Cornell observers were constantly running into the same facts upon which the Würzburg people base their claims; the argument depends wholly on the interpretation of the facts or the value placed on them as scientific evidence.

Titchener at best offered only negative evidence, inability to discover thought beyond images. Actually, it was his restricted descriptions of consciousness that brought introspection into disrepute and precipitated behaviorism. He attempted to avoid recognizing the suprasensory nature of an idea by reporting that it was a "grey patch of fog in the northeast corner of consciousness" or by reducing meaning to "the blue-grey tip of a scoop" and saying that this image not only accompanied the thought but actually constituted the thought itself. Since others could have exactly the same thought without these images, it is clear that the imagery he reported was not the thought. When Morgan (1956, p. 139) says that the controversy showed that thought is not conscious, what he really means is that thought is not sensory. If you look for material pictures, you will never discover that you have an idea; but you are quite *conscious* of "what a triangle is." Your idea is a conscious act, but not one of *sensory* consciousness.

Some proponents of imageless thought actually claimed evidence for thoughts existing without any accompanying image. While not going this far, the assertion of the difference between thought and image is based on positive evidence, not on negative (absence of imagery). Thought is more than some unknown intervening variable between stimulus and response. Ideas can be analyzed, discussed, communicated, and compared, as well as contrasted with object, word, and percept or image. They are not mystical, mythical, or supernatural, but part of the everyday experience of one whose nature includes the ability to think.

OTHER ARGUMENTS

We have ended the investigation of our thought processes with an account of the Würzburg controversy for whatever added light it throws from another source on this important question. Skinner's analysis of verbal behavior seems to impress more people today. In this sense the debate still goes on, and it is up to each one to decide. We list some other arguments for intellection, the value of which the student must likewise assess for himself.

[1] See the Readings at the end of this chapter.

SELF-REFLECTION   One reason offered for the immateriality of the intellect is the fact that it is able to reflect or bend back perfectly upon itself. I can think about my thinking. No extended material being can bend back perfectly upon itself but only upon some other part or power, at best; for instance, the central sense can know the activity of the special senses. But the intellect can know itself and its own act by a process of proper and perfect reflection which is beyond the limitations of material being.

Teilhard de Chardin seems to feel that this argument is particularly impressive: "Only man knows that he knows."

UNLIMITED CAPACITY   Some argue from the fact that sense is limited to a proper object which restricts it to the world of sensible qualities and material objects, whereas our understanding does not seem thus limited, as we have seen. The proper object of intellection seems to be meaning wherever found in the whole realm of being. The argument can hardly claim that man actually knows everything by the mere fact that he is intellectual. But it does seem to claim a certain infinity for the scope of our intellectual activities. This would have to be understood not as actual infinity but rather as potential, i.e., we are subjectively finite but the object of intellection is unlimited, being anything which is intelligible.

This unlimited capacity of the intellect seems further confirmed by the fact that there is no limit to the amount of knowledge we can acquire: our intellect never becomes full like a box. If sound becomes too loud, it becomes painful; if light becomes too intense, we cannot bear it. But no one complains of understanding too clearly, nor does the learned man complain of knowing too much—rather, he is especially aware of how much more he wants to know. Another way of seeing how intellect goes beyond sense is to imagine a square, hexagon, octagon, etc., until imagination finally is incapable of getting clear pictures. But we are still quite capable of *understanding* clearly the difference between a polygon of 3,897 sides as opposed to one of 3,896 sides. Sensory perception could not distinguish a polygon of 3 million sides from a circle, yet intellection clearly knows the difference.

VOLUNTARY ATTENTION   A case for the immateriality of intellection has been made from the fact that we can voluntarily direct our attention, within limits, to what we will. It is argued that attention of this kind' must be suprasensuous in character, since any purely sensory process is determined by the causal stimulus and follows the material conditions of organic functioning. Voluntary attention, being self-initiated and self-controlled, enjoys a certain independence from physical stimuli and organic factors.

This is illustrated by what Piaget calls the *reversibility* of thought. I can easily *understand* the alphabet as the same sequence of letters starting from either end, ABC . . . or ZYX. . . . But I find it almost impossible to reverse the chain of sensory symbols and recite them backwards, without considerable new learning. Thought is free from sequences in time and space; I can arbitrarily view relationships from opposite approaches, choose alternative correct solutions to the same problem, substitute algebraic for arithmetical symbols for the same content, or substitute different contents for the same set of symbols, as I choose. Sensory knowledge manifests less of this openness to choice.

SUPERIORITY OF MAN   A pragmatic argument for the existence of the intellectual order of knowledge is that we cannot account for man's superiority by any appeal to the sensory order. Brute animals can surpass man in any category of sense experience. The superiority must come from some other source, it is claimed.

There are instances in which human beings have been gravely deficient in the realm of the senses and yet have achieved remarkable superiority. The case of Helen Keller comes to mind, and there are many other similar examples of handicapped persons. A man completely paralyzed can still manage to communicate thought somehow, whereas the most glib parrot never does (Mowrer, 1954, p. 675). People surpass animals that are far better endowed. Monkeys are far more agile and can manipulate better than many cripples; man's superiority can hardly be explained purely because he has an apposable thumb. Attempts to explain human personality, responsibility, and dignity by appeals to a more refined nervous system or a more conducive environment do not seem to square with these facts. (See the Appendix.)

Computers   Man is also compared with the machine. We now have computers which calculate much faster and more accurately than a staff of mathematicians, and which have far better memories. Yet the men who work with the computer do not talk of its superiority but rather of its stupidity: the machine "knows" only what it is programmed to perform; it is helpless without a man to feed information in and interpret what is taken out. Such machines can be "taught" to play chess so well that they can beat good players, but only because the mechanical brain has a statistical advantage in running through many possible moves[2] and has been programmed by a good chess player. And it cannot design either games or machines, unless programmed to do so.

Even more interesting is the relation of computers to language. They can be programmed to translate, and to write "poetry" as well as carry on an apparent conversation. Since the computer can be programmed to store and recall data according to any scheme, these functions are largely a matter of statistical frequency in the occurrence of word sequences. Somewhat like the parrot that learns to associate certain stock phrases with questions or situations that recur frequently so as to utter an appropriate, "Goodbye," when people leave or reply correctly when asked, "What's your name?" the computer can reproduce words and phrases in accordance with their usual frequency in spoken or written English. The resulting sequence sounds like composition or conversation. Using the same techniques and adding the equivalent for each word in another language, translation of literal statements becomes possible.

[2] For example, Alex Bernstein, "A Chess Playing Program for the IBM 704," *Chess Review*, July, 1958, pp. 208–209, shows how the machine can have available seven plausible first moves and seven possible responses to each up to the fourth move, totaling 2,800 positions it can run through with electronic speed and accuracy. See K. Sayre, *Recognition: A Study in the Philosophy of Artificial Intelligence.*

The basic problem to be faced is whether the computer really understands. Scriven[3] compares it to a man blind from birth in contrast with one who has lost his sight. The latter really knows what "red" is, but the former can learn the appropriate language games so well that one would hardly know he has not had the primary experience. One indication of understanding is the use of metaphor. The story that a computer translated "out of sight, out of mind" as "blind idiot" may be apocryphal, but it illustrates the basic problem of recognizing meanings as opposed to mere storage of mechanical sequences and equivalents. To appreciate the comparison implied in an expression like "smiling meadow" one has to be able to do more than come up with an equivalent like "grinning valley." A blind Venetian is different from a Venetian blind, and "hunting dógs" (an occupation) is different from "húnting dogs" (a class or breed). The computer could sort out "fountain pen" from "playpen" by frequency occurrence data, but to grasp that "the pen is mightier than the sword" requires understanding. Adding a randomizer circuit seems to make it creative, though the quality of the resulting literary product is open to question. Mere novelty of order due to random occurrence may sound like poetry to one who pays no attention to meaning, but in itself does not constitute any poetic message or insight. Again there is always the question of consciousness in the sense of self-reflective awareness; does the computer have a sense of personal worth? Equally disputable are the questions of whether the computer can achieve highly abstract notions like the theory of relativity, or make value judgments.

Those who minimize the difference between man and computer counter that people, too, have to be "programmed"—that we all learn by a constant process of adaptation to our environment and especially of reinforcement by our language community. As to creation of the aesthetic in the poetry or music the computer composes, they point out that the kaleidoscope mechanically combines particles into new patterns which are pleasing; they argue that beauty is all the more feasible when we add to randomness the advantage of "memory" circuits which can store sequences from great poems or operas. The computer handles arbitrary symbols with ease, i.e., it can "learn" arbitrary meanings. It even seems to show emotion at times, being cooperative or balky. Lastly, if imitation is the sincerest flattery, the computer fans can draw comfort from the fact that man is now studying its electronic processes in order to understand man's own brain circuitry better. Will computers eventually take over?

[3] Michael Scriven, "The Compleat Robot: A prolegomena to Androidology," in Sidney Hook (Ed.) *Dimensions of Mind* (New York: Collier, 1961), pp. 113–133. See also his *Primary Philosophy* (New York: McGraw-Hill, 1966).

Disproportion of thought and brain If the brain secretes thought as the liver secretes bile, as was once thought, one would expect some direct one-to-one ratio in increase of size or complexity of the brain as it acquires more thoughts. But in spite of tremendous progress regarding the role of the RNA molecule in the process of storing sensory data, all attempts to establish such a ratio between brain and understanding have proved fruitless. Size of brain, either absolute or relative to the body, does not correlate with intelligence. The value of fish as a "brain food" because of its chemical content has long been disproved, as has phrenology, which tries to correlate mental powers with "bumps" on the head. In spite of rather accurate localization of centers in the brain for the various sensory and motor processes, all attempts to localize thought have failed, except the vague designation of "association areas" which are apparently the organs of the internal senses so closely associated with understanding. Much is known now about feedback and learning circuits in the cortex, as well as about the biochemistry involved. Philosophers ask whether thought consists in these activities, or whether they are just the organic aspects of the sensory experiences involved with intellection. (See Chapter 8.)

Measurement of intelligence

The question must be raised as to whether the fact that intelligence can be measured quantitatively according to IQ, or intelligence quotient, serves as evidence that intellection is material. Granted the disputes about the reliability and validity of such testing, quantity or extension is the hallmark of matter; mathematical measurability would seem incompatible with what is more than matter. Let us first review some definitions.

Intellect is the power or ability to think and refers simply to the fact that man is able to do so. It is not strictly correct to say that the intellect knows; rather, man knows by means of his intellect.

Thinking, or intellection, is the act of this power and includes ideas, judgments, and reasoning. These are the operations for which the intellect is the basic natural ability.

Intelligence is the degree to which intellect is operative. Thus defined it differs from intellect because it refers to the amount of measurable operation we can expect from this potency. But we say operative, not operating, since a man is equally intelligent whether he is thinking at the moment or not. Intelligence thus differs from both root potentiality and actual operation. Intellect is a qualitative term, describing the kind of being man is. Intelligence is a quantitative term, expressing the degree to which he can exercise this ability.

Since a power is known by its act, there is no difficulty in expressing mathematically the external effects of its operation. The psychologist does not pretend to measure intellect directly, but only its functioning in comparison with the performance of others of the same age or other grouping. This relative performance can be expressed quantitatively without implying extension in the intellect itself.

By contrast, when we say that all men are created equal we obviously do not refer to degree of intelligence, any more than to amount of musical talent or color of eyes; we mean that they are qualitatively similar; they have the same basic powers and rational nature, which gives them equal rights before the law.

The inheritance of IQ is explainable because of the dependence of thought upon sense. Any direct influence of parental intellect on that of the child through heredity is impossible, if procreation is a biological process and intellection is immaterial. (Expressions such as "cultural heritage" refer to environment, not heredity.) But the parents' genes carry determiners for a brain and nervous system somehow similar to their own, causing the child's intellect to have similar sensory equipment with which to work. Greater perfection of nervous system means better perceptions, memories, and images for the intellect to abstract and manipulate. The extent of correlation between parental and child intelligence is for the psychologist to measure; they certainly do not correspond perfectly. Even if they did, it would not be wholly a matter of heredity; psychologists are busy now trying to assess the relative influence of parental environment, as well as non-hereditary biological factors such as faulty embryological development.

REVIEW QUESTIONS

1. If language is automatically meaningful, what is meaning in that case?
2. If meaning is an intervening variable between object and word, can it be mere sensory association?
3. If everyone associated the same image with the word horse, would this prove that the meaning was the image?
4. Suppose sensism is right. What are the philosophical and political consequences if followed up rigidly?
5. List all the ways in which a concept differs from an image or perception.
6. Is there a difference between asking if computers think and if they understand? Explain.
7. Suppose we train an animal to find a piece of food under a card with a Roman numeral I on it. Then suppose we train the animal

to look first under card I, *then* under card II if the food is not under card I. Then we train the animal to look under the card numbered III if he does not find the food under card II or I. Does this require intellectual knowledge? Does it require a concept of number?

8. In what way would an argument based on concrete universal ideas be even more telling against the sensists than the more obvious argument from abstract ideas?

9. Is the difference between intellect and sense a matter of distinction or of separation?

10. Show how the difference in meanings of "imageless thought" is pertinent to the above question.

11. Show how the facts of brain waves and subvocal speech also exemplify the same problem as in question 9.

12. Would it be impossible for man to perceive reality through his senses as if he were an animal without intellect? Could he understand reality intellectually as if he had no senses?

13. Explain the difference between intellect and intelligence.

14. Does IQ express absolute measurement of intellectual operation or comparison relative to others?

15. Answer the following:

   a. We prove the immateriality of the intellect from its object, since every power is specified by its object. But I can have intellectual knowledge of a tree, which is a material object. Therefore the intellect is material.

   b. If all ideas are universal, man could not have any intellectual knowledge of singulars. But we do know singulars. Therefore ideas are not universal.

   c. I know the essence of trees only by examining trees. But this is a sensory experience. Therefore my knowledge of essences is sensory.

   d. Abstraction is just a special type of attention. But animals can direct their attention to one thing or another. Therefore abstraction could be just a sensory process.

   e. All ideas are derived directly or indirectly from sense experience. Therefore sensism is right.

   f. The proper object of the human intellect is the being of material objects. But God is not a material object. Therefore no human knowledge of God is possible.

   g. All thinking involves motor activity. But motor activity is organic. Therefore thought is organic.

FOR FURTHER READING

Kelly & Tallon: the chapters from **Locke** and **Hume,** and the selections from **Kant,** on pp. 68–79, and **Peters,** on pp. 236–238. Also the chapter from **Jaspers,** mentioned after Chapter 2.

Of the various authors mentioned in the chapter, **Whorf** is perhaps one of the more stimulating. See *Language, Thought, and Reality: Selected Writings of Benjamin Lee Whorf,* edited by **John B. Carroll. C. F. Hockett's** "The Origin of Speech," in *Scientific American* for September, 1960, lists the features which distinguish human speech from all other communication systems, whether animals or machines, and also confronts us with our real ignorance as to how speech began. **George A. Miller** of Harvard enjoyably presents, **"Some Preliminaries to Psycholinguistics,"** in *American Psychologist,* 1965, 20:15–20. See also Kolers (1968).

Gilbert Ryle and others present readable lectures on language analysis in *The Revolution in Philosophy.* A good collection of primary sources is *Classics of Analytic Philosophy,* edited by **Robert R. Ammerman.** In the second edition of *Language, Truth and Logic* (1946), **A. J. Ayer** in the Introduction modifies his extreme earlier position. **G. J. Warnock's** *English Philosophy since 1900* and **Maxwell J. Charlesworth's** *Philosophy and Linguistic Analysis* are very useful secondary sources. Like them, **Frederick Copleston's** *Contemporary Philosophy* is both historical and evaluative.

B. F. Skinner's *Verbal Behavior* makes a strong case for the reductionist position, as does **Rudolf Carnap's** "Psychology in Physical Language," in *Logical Positivism,* edited by **A. J. Ayer.** A good collection from original sources is that edited by **F. J. McGuigan,** *Thinking: Studies of Covert Language Processes.* Two other useful collections of psychological writings on the subject are those edited by **Robert J. C. Harper** and others, *The Cognitive Processes: Readings,* and by **H. J. Klausmeier** and **C. W. Harris,** *Analyses of Concept Learning.* Other psychological works of interest are:

Gannon, Timothy J. *Psychology: The Unity of Human Behavior.* Chap. 13.
Gendlin, Eugene T. *Experiencing and the Creation of Meaning.*
Harmon, Francis L. *Principles of Psychology.* (Rev. ed.) Chap. 12.
Lindworsky, Johannes, S.J. *Experimental Psychology.* Pp. 250–270.
Michotte, Albert. *The Perception of Causality.*
Royce, Joseph R. (Ed.) *Psychology and the Symbol.*

Spearman, Charles. *The Nature of "Intelligence" and the Principles of Cognition.*

The "imageless-thought" controversy

SENSIST

Chapin, Mary V., & Washburn, Margaret Floy. "A Study of the Images Representing the Concept of Meaning," *Amer. J. Psychol.*, 1912, 23:109–114.

Titchener, Edward B. "Description versus Statement of Meaning," *Amer. J. Psychol.*, 1912, 23:164–182, and the following books by him: *Experimental Psychology*, Part I, *Qualitative Experiments; Lectures on the Experimental Psychology of the Thought Processes; Systematic Psychology: Prolegomena;* and *A Text-book of Psychology.*

Wundt, Wilhelm. *Introduction to Psychology.*

INTELLECTUALIST

Binet, Alfred. *L'Étude expérimentale de l'intelligence.*

Binet, Alfred, & Simon, Th. "Langage et pensé," *Anneé psychol.*, 1908, 14:284–339.

Gruender, Hubert, S.J. *Problems of Psychology*, chaps. 1 and 2, and *Experimental Psychology*, chaps. 14, 15, and 16 (pp. 301–395). He gives a very full analysis of the arguments and counterarguments of Titchener and his opponents.

Moore, Thomas Verner. "Image and Meaning in Memory and Perception," *Psychol. Monogr.*, 1919, 27(119):67–296.

Moore, Thomas Verner. "The Process of Abstraction," *Univ. Calif. Publ. Psychol.*, 1910, I:73–197. Perhaps the most valuable source in English on the Würzburg school, based on original German sources and firsthand laboratory experimentation. Unfortunately out of print, it remains a most valuable historical record, even if Moore's own experiments were later criticized as involving not abstraction but intellectual memory associated with images (Sister M. Coady, 1932).

Moore, Thomas Verner. "The Temporal Relations of Meaning and Imagery," *Psychol. Rev.*, 1915, 22:177–225.

Woodworth, Robert S. "Non-sensory Components of Sense Perception," in *Psychological Issues.* Pp. 80–88.

Woodworth, Robert S. "A Revision of Imageless Thought," *Psychol. Rev.*, 1915, 22:1–27.

The chapters in Gannon and Harmon noted above contain copious references to experimental psychologists, of the Würzburg school and otherwise, whose data favor the intellectualist position.

8　THE NATURE OF KNOWLEDGE

Consciousness is not a thing.　Merleau-Ponty

 We have described the facts of human knowledge and analyzed the distinction between the two different kinds of knowledge in man, sensory and intellectual. This description, though less technical than a psychological analysis, has had much in common with it. But philosophy is not content merely to describe these processes; it tries to understand their nature. What does it mean to know?

The nature of knowledge is elusive partly because it is so close to us. We describe it largely in terms of what we know and how we know, without directing our attention to the nature of knowledge itself. Another difficulty is that there is nothing simpler and more immediate to which we can reduce knowledge, or in terms of which we can understand it. Either I have had the experience of knowing or I have not. Any communication, explanation, or attempt to understand already presupposes the experience under investigation. Nevertheless the philosopher cannot be content with a merely behavioral or operational description but must seek to understand the nature of knowing.

UNION OF KNOWER AND OBJECT

When we enter the realm of knowledge we must be prepared to deal with a new order of things, a unique reality to which there is no precise equivalent in the world of physical reality. The first thing that we notice about cognition, or knowledge, is a certain openness, the ability to acquire somehow the attributes of a being other than oneself. This other may be a real object or merely a fanciful image or abstraction, but in any case it is something outside the nature of the knower. The knower is not limited simply to what he is.

Intentional being and intentional union   But how does the knower add this *other* to his own being? Now we must first distinguish knowing from wanting in that the latter is a tendency toward actual physical union with the object, in order to enjoy it or possess it. Cognitive union is different. Instead of tending to go out toward physical union with the object, cognitive union receives the object into the knower. But since the object continues to exist physically in the same way after it is known, it must be received into the knower and have existence there in another manner than that of physical or natural existence in reality. This existence of the object in the knower, as other than the knower, is called intentional being.

The word intentional is perhaps unfortunate because it suggests purpose or resolve. Originally the word did not have this meaning and could perhaps better be translated as "attentional." It is the kind of being that the object has in me when I direct my attention toward it so that it exists in my consciousness. "Representative" might do, except that it suggests that I know primarily the representation rather than the object. As we have seen, my concept of a horse does not look like a horse; we must not think of knowledge as pictures. It simply means that "what a horse is" somehow is now within me.

F. Romero, probably the greatest philosopher of Latin America, dwells a great deal on this capacity for intentional union as an outstanding characteristic of man. In a metaphor, which of course cannot be taken literally, he describes intentionality as "a living mirror capable of rearranging its images according to its own criteria and reacting to them in diverse ways" (*Theory of Man*, 1964, p. 68).

KNOWING INVOLVES IMMATERIALITY

Physical change   It will help to understand the nature of this intentional existence which the object has in me if we contrast it with physical change. Suppose I take a cube of wax and impress it with the seal of the State of Washington, which happens to have the face of George Washington on it. The wax loses its form as cube and acquires the form of George Washington's face. In a sense it has become George Washington, so that we can point to the wax and say, "Look, there is George Washington." But we would not even suggest that the wax becomes aware or knows what George Washington looks like. The change has been a purely physical one: the loss of one accidental form or shape and the acquisition of another. The subject (wax) has become the object (Washington), but physically, not intentionally or attentionally. Take another example of material change. When a cow eats hay or a plant takes in other materials and makes them into its own substance, there is also a loss of form. This time the loss is in the object, not in the subject. The hay loses its form and is now united with the form of the cow (see Chapter 15). Again, there is no awareness on the part of the cow in this action as such. The ingested matter now exists within the cow physically, not representatively.

Intentional change   Let us now see what happens when the cow *sees* the hay. The hay keeps its form, the cow keeps its form. Neither is physically changed, but the hay begins also to exist in the cow intentionally. The cow, without losing its form, acquires the form of hay, but without the matter of the hay.

What is characteristic of cognitive union is that the knower acquires the form of the object without its matter. Instead of the loss of form there is an enrichment of form. When I know something, that object begins to have intentional being in me so that in a sense I have "become" that object without ceasing to be myself.

Form without matter   We say that the knower becomes the thing known, not physically but intentionally. The reason is that "to become" means to come into being in a new way, and the knower acquires a new mode of being whenever he takes on this additional new form. For this reason Aristotle says that by the intellect man can become all things. So Walt Whitman says,

> There was a child went forth every day
> And the first object he look'd upon, that object he became.

And Virgil makes all that Aeneas saw and ventured become a part of him.

"Form" of course is a term with many meanings. The form of the wax or seal is physical shape; as a sensed quality it is intentional form within the knower. The meaning or intelligibility we discover even in material things suggests that there is more than crude matter there. If beings are understandable at all, it is because intelligible form is in things, not in Plato's separate "world of Ideas." As we shall see, this form is what makes a thing to be what it is; matter is undifferentiated except by the form with which it is united. If union with a form is what makes something become what it is physically, the philosopher says that union with intentional forms makes the knower "become" other things intentionally.

It is thus clear that the hallmark of knowing is a certain freedom from the limitation of matter. Matter of itself is limited to only one form at a time. The knower must be able to possess not only his own form but other forms also. These forms must be capable of existing in the knower intentionally, without ceasing to exist physically in the object known. For this reason we speak of a "well-*inform*ed man," because he contains many forms besides his own, or much *inform*ation. Similarly, we define truth as the con*form*ity of knower and object, because the knower has acquired the same form as the thing known.

Degrees of immateriality

Although some sort of immateriality is necessary for all knowing, the different kinds of knowledge will demand different degrees of independence from matter. Knowledge is an analogous term; it has partly the same meaning and partly different meanings when applied to different kinds of knowers. Some are impatient with such gradations and would like to simplify reality to the point of saying that it is either material or immaterial. But the philosopher must take things as he finds them, not impose upon them his own scheme of things. It will help to distinguish three senses of the term immateriality as related to knowledge.

1. The lowest degree of immateriality is that found in sensory knowledge: form without matter but with material qualities. As we saw above, the animal is not limited like the wax to a purely passive reception of form in a physical way but is capable of entertaining the intentional forms of other beings along with its own. But the object of sensory knowledge always exists in the knower clothed with the sensible qualities of a concrete individual thing. This retention of the sensible qualities is true of any sensory knowledge, be it percept, image, sense memory, or instinctive estimate.

These sensible qualities are accidental forms and although they exist in the knower without the matter of the object known, being material they must exist in some matter, for material qualities cannot exist outside a material substance. This substance is probably the cerebral cortex of the brain. When I say that I have a lake in mind, I do not have water on the brain. But if this is a sensory image, I do see the lake as a certain size, shape, color, and from a certain direction. Because this lowest degree of intentional being is but one step removed from the limitations of matter and is still bound up with these material qualities, we refer to it as "quasi-immaterial," meaning to a degree or "sort of" immaterial.

2. The second degree of immateriality is that proper to human intellection: spiritual, but related to matter. When the cow *sees* the hay, the cow has the form of hay with a particular set of material qualities of size, shape, color, etc. When man *understands* hay, he has the form of the hay, regardless of the appearance of any individual sample. Here he has acquired the form of hay without its material qualities, the conditions of matter. Note

that we only say that the intellectual knowledge itself has no material qualities; being human knowledge, it may be accompanied by the material qualities in the senses. "Without material qualities or the conditions of matter" refers to the intrinsic nature of thought itself, regardless of its sensory concomitants and origins. For this reason intellection is called *strictly immaterial* or *spiritual* because matter does not enter into its internal constitution. It is said to be *intrinsically* independent of matter.

But although human intellection has this intrinsic or essential independence of matter, all our ideas in this life must be derived in some way from sensory experience. The senses are extrinsic to the intellect itself and its operations, though intrinsic to man. Hence we say that the intellect has only *extrinsic* dependence on matter. This is in contrast to sensory knowledge with its material qualities which demand intrinsic dependence on matter, since matter enters into the very nature of the process.

Spiritual, therefore, means strictly immaterial or intrinsically independent of matter. It may or may not involve extrinsic dependence on matter: this is the difference between the second and the third degrees of immateriality. Spiritual does not mean supernatural. If it is part of man's nature to think, then such power is not above man's nature. The use of the term "spiritual life" is misleading when applied to the supernatural life of grace, because any truly intellectual operation is spiritual, even though very secular.

3. Immateriality can also be *absolute:* intrinsic independence of matter without even extrinsic dependence on matter. This is the manner of operation in the case of God and the angels, since their intellects do not even need to abstract knowledge from sensory experience.

The mention of God and angels at this point should not be misunderstood. They are introduced purely for the purpose of contrast with man's intellect, not as a proof of anything. Although some ancient pagan philosophers seem to have concluded by natural reason alone that pure created spirits exist, we might grant that certain knowledge about the angels can be learned only in theology. Since they are introduced here only for purposes of explanation and not as the premise of a proof, we can leave the question of their existence open and simply say that if there are such things as angels their intellects would differ from man's, inasmuch as their manner of cognition is absolutely immaterial. In dealing with analogical notions such as knowledge, life, being, substance, and so forth, it is often useful to orient the reader by seeing how they apply over a wide range of instances.

From this we can get a better appreciation of precisely what the adjective "rational" means when applied to the human intellect. We usually think of man's rationality as putting him at the top of the visible universe, and so it does. But in the realm of intellect, a rational intellect is the lowest and most imperfect type. God knows by means of one infinite and exhaustive act of knowledge; the angels, by intuitive judgments. Man's rational intellect must get its knowledge piecemeal through the process of abstraction from sense experience, then laboriously combining and distinguishing these ideas in judgments and reasoning.

Defining knowledge

Cognition might thus be summarily described as immaterial union with the form of an object. More fully, it is the act by which the knower becomes the known object intentionally by possessing, in addition to his own form, that of the object, but without its matter. This intentional being of the object in the knower is not to be taken too lightly. The poorest art student looking at a cheap copy may really know and thus possess, or become intentionally, a masterpiece much more fully than the millionaire who possesses the original canvas in his safe. Using the other meaning of the word intentional, if I am resolved to commit murder, I am already guilty of committing murder, not physically but intentionally. For just as a block of marble becomes the statue by taking on the form of the statue, so I become that which I know when I take on its form.

It will be noted that we say cognition may be "described" rather than "defined," for it should be clear by now that knowledge cannot be strictly defined for many reasons. Being an analogous term, it does not admit of a univocal definition. There are degrees and kinds of knowledge. Secondly, definition requires genus and species, and knowledge fits under no genus which is common to knowledge and other things. Lastly, definition should be in terms of what is better known than the defined; but knowledge is the most basic and immediate experience we can have, so there is nothing simpler or more fundamental to which we can reduce it. It is a unique type of being, not explainable in terms of any other type of being. Hence all attempts to define knowledge in terms of behavioral response miss its unique essential nature.

IS KNOWLEDGE MERELY PHYSIOLOGICAL?

There is still controversy as to whether both sensory and intellectual awareness are distinctly psychological in quality, or whether they can be completely reduced to biochemical or physiological elements. Since the reductionist view is frequently and well stated in positivist and scientific literature,[1] only the case for the immateriality of these intentional forms will be presented here. Although their production may require an organ (the word means "instrument" in Greek) in the case of the sense, the distinctively psychological nature of these processes can be argued both deductively and empirically.

Worthy of note here are the contemporary uses of the term "intentional" as presence, participation, dialogue, existential being-in-the-world. Inspired by Husserl and Heidegger, these forms of expression all seem to suggest the nonmaterial. Reduction of course in phe-

---

[1] For example, the excellent statement by Francis O. Schmitt, "The Physical Basis of Life and Learning," *Science,* 1965, 149:931–936.

nomenology means something utterly different from reduction to the material level.

Since the knowing power is in itself indifferent to objects and undetermined, something must determine it. This determination must be of the same order as the power of which it becomes a form. Since any knowledge demands a certain degree of immateriality, it is clear that the form which determines even a sense power cannot be merely physiological.

Empirically, the immateriality of intentional forms would seem to be confirmed by evidence from physiology and experimental psychology. Illusion, ambiguity, constancy, and other perceptual phenomena described in Chapter 5 show instances in which stimulus or physiological activity remains constant and the psychological or conscious response varies, or vice versa. Blindness induced by hypnosis or emotional shock leaves the optic nerve intact. Another confirmation would seem to be the case of excessive physical stimulation of the physiological organ, which may produce less or even no psychic activity instead of more, as would be expected if psychic and physiological were identical. The same conclusion is suggested by the abandonment of the theory of specific nerve energies for the different types of sensation. Nerve energies certainly do not explain everything: compare hypnotically induced color blindness with that due to a physiological defect. The testing and training of pilots as well as the correction of certain visual defects indicate that what and how we see appears to be as much a matter of perceptual habits as of physiological functioning. In all these examples there is a discrepancy between the physiological pattern and the resulting conscious impression which is incompatible with any theory which would identify them.

> Current texts in psychology are frank in admitting that in spite of extensive experimentation we still have no factual basis for claiming to explain psychic activity in physiological terms. Substitution of "central" or cerebral theories for peripheral does not alter the basic issue. After decades of talking about engrams or memory traces in the brain, we now admit that we have no factual evidence of their existence or nature.[2] Such theories seem incompatible with the facts of habit formation, to say nothing of either the extreme case of the hysterical blindness produced by a single traumatic experience, or the ordinary instance of a lifelong recollection from a single perception. We have no evidence that such single events wear a groove or alter a nerve.

[2] David Wechsler, "Engrams, Memory Storage, and Mnemomic Coding," *Amer. Psychologist*, 1963, 18:149–153. Also K. S. Lashley, "In Search of the Engram," in F. Beach, D. O. Hebb, and others (eds.) *The Neuropsychology of Lashley* (New York: McGraw-Hill, 1960), pp. 478–505.

Research on the biochemistry of learning, especially that on the RNA molecule (ribonucleic acid), has shifted the search. But philosophers argue that this new research is still concerned only with the physiological basis of knowledge rather than with its essential nature. The physicist Michael Polanyi has suggested that it is never possible to reduce to the terms of physical science man's personal knowledge, his deepest life concerns, his inner apprehension of reality. The eminent neurophysiologist Sir Charles Sherrington repeatedly notes in chaps. 9 to 11 of his *Man on His Nature* that mind is irreducible to biochemistry or neurology. Even a physiologically oriented psychologist such as Hebb confesses:

> *Until neurological theory is much more adequate, the psychologist has to take it with a grain of salt. But we must go further. It seems that some aspects of behavior can never be dealt with in neurological terms alone. . . . Psychology cannot become a branch of physiology. . . .*
> *It seems on occasion to be thought that the neurological entity is somehow more substantial, more "real," than psychological entities; that the study of nerve impulses is a more scientific affair than the study of anxiety or motivation. This is entirely mistaken (1958, pp. 262–264).*

Psychologists have long since ceased to speak of the conditioned reflex in connection with most learning, and prefer the broader term conditioned response. The breakdown of attempts to explain learning as any process of connections in the nervous system really begins with the report of Karl S. Lashley on the results of his fifteen years of attempts to do just this. He systematically cut out every part of the cerebral cortex of white rats, without eliminating the possibility of learning. As an eminent neurophysiologist, he was elected president of the American Psychological Association in 1929, when behaviorism was perhaps at its peak in American psychology. In his presidential address to the Ninth International Congress of Psychology in December of that year, he said that it had been characteristic of American psychology to "explain psychological processes and functions in terms of correlated neural anatomy. In reading this, I have been impressed chiefly by its futility. The chapter on the nervous system seems to provide an excuse for pictures in an otherwise dry and monotonous text. That it has any other function is not clear. . . ." (1930, 37:1). Although Halstead (1947) and others have corrected Lashley's work, showing that there is even less correlation between amount of brain damage and mental functions in human beings than Lashley found in his rats, Lashley's frank confession tells the story graphically:

> *I began life as an ardent advocate of muscle-twitch psychology. I became glib in formulating all problems of psychology in terms of stimulus-response and in explaining all things as conditioned reflexes. . . . I embarked enthusiastically upon a program of experiments to prove. . . . and the result is as though I had maliciously planned an attack upon the whole system. . . . the conditioned reflex turned out not to be a reflex (1931, 5:14).*

Decades later, Hilgard in his classic *Theories of Learning* made a careful review of the experimental work aimed at explaining learning in terms of physiology and concluded that such experiments "have not led to any significant generalizations about the precise mechanisms of learning" and "new interest in neuro-physiological theories of learning also has thus far led to little that is of genuine explanatory value" (1956, p. 453). Physiological theories not only do not explain, he goes on, but they are not even established. "Despite all the attention commonly given to simple conditioning in learning theory, the evidence for it is very fragmentary" (p. 462). "There is some concealing of ignorance in attributing specific stimulus-response bases for psychological functions such as drives, sets, images, and thoughts. If we are critical about accepting the results of experiments, then stomach contractions are *not* the basis of appetite, eye movements are *not* the cause of the Muller-Lyer illusion, kinesthetic cues are *not* the preferred ones in maze learning, tongue movements are *not* the basis for thinking. The burden of proof is on those who believe otherwise" (p. 477).

Lashley's work is of course crude in comparison with current brain physiology. But although we understand today much better the biological basis for learning, the lesson from history can be ignored only at a great price. The organic basis need no more be the essence of knowing than the foundation is the house.

Thought and the brain

The above argument against crass materialism applies even to animal or sensory knowledge, which is only quasi-immaterial. Being spiritual, intellectual knowledge is even more impossible to explain in terms of brain function.

There is obviously some dependence of thought upon the nervous system, since all our knowledge is derived in some way from the senses and they are organic. The fact that understanding requires to be fed by sense does not prove that understanding itself is sensory any more than the fact that an automobile needs gasoline proves that the automobile is the fuel. The dependence is real but it is extrinsic and instrumental. If I continuously knock the brush out of the painter's hand, he does not get much painting done. The brush is not the painter, only an instrument. There is a real dependence, but that the brush is only extrinsic is clear from the fact that the artist can get another brush or even finish the painting with his finger. Contrast this extrinsic interference with the essential change which takes place if I alter the intrinsic nature of the painter by killing him.

Such seems to be the relation between brain and intellection. Brain waves, cortical circuits, and biochemical changes certainly indicate a real connection between thought and brain activity. It is the precise nature of this connection which requires close philosophical scrutiny. Brain waves may tell us how a man is thinking, but they never tell us what he is thinking. They give no clue as to the content of thought, but simply some indication of its emotional and imaginal mode. One confirmation of this seems to be the fact that there are two times when the brain wave pattern is strikingly similar: when there is no thought going on at all and when one is indulging in pure abstract thought. These two states are poles apart at the level of thought itself, but at the sensory level could easily have the same physiological pattern of low imagery and emotion.

Particularly fascinating here is the history of the association of mental dysfunction with brain injury. It was the evidence with regard to this association which apparently impressed such originally materialistic philosophers as Bergson, Driesch, C. E. M. Joad, and others with the inadequacy of materialism. T. V. Moore, M.D., in his *Cognitive Psychology* (pp. 45–73) tells how the medical literature successively abandoned attempts to locate intelligence as a function of the right hemisphere, left hemisphere, frontal lobes, or any other part of the brain when war injuries or brain tumor operations showed that these parts could be removed and the person still think. Loss of speech and memory are connected with brain injury according to complex patterns involving degree of abstractness or concreteness of thought in a way hardly explainable if thought is a physiological mechanism.

Leaving aside psychogenic or purely mental disorder, the abnormal psychology of even brain-injured patients shows clearly that their mental symptoms cannot be explained purely in terms of the area or amount of brain damage.[3] The discrepancy between brain lesions and impairment of mental performance is too great to square with the theory that the brain is the principal cause of thought, rather than an extrinsic instrument. Though slight damage in a certain area may cause death or paralysis, the medical literature attests to many cases of continued rationality in spite of very wide destruction of cortical areas. Brain injury may interfere with mental functioning, but some thinking can take place as long as there is any nervous tissue left which can provide sensory materials upon which the intellect could work. Brain cannot be the proper and immediate organ of intellect, but is the organ of intellect only indirectly, through the mediation of sense.

Such facts are quite compatible with the explanation proposed here of an essential or intrinsic dependence upon matter for sensory and vegetative activities, but only an extrinsic and instrumental relation to the processes of thought. Conversely, a materialistic philosophy seems hard pressed to explain cases where thinking continues in spite of widespread destruction of large masses of the brain. Note that we adduce these cases not as the principal evidence for the spirituality of the intellect, but rather to point up the inadequacy of the materialistic theory.

The question of mental fatigue would seem to be best explained in this way also. The weariness of the individual doing continuous mental work has been shown experimentally to be muscular fatigue, which in turn can affect activity measured in time and errors, but there is no evidence that the intellect itself wearies like the muscles. We seem to tire readily when studying metaphysics because of the strain involved in trying to picture the unpicturable, to conjure up helpful concrete images for abstract ideas and universal principles such as potency and act, which cannot be pictured. This shows a real, even if extrinsic, dependence of intellect upon the internal senses whose organ is the brain.

Recall what was said previously about the meaning of rational as opposed to other kinds of intellect. Aristotle compares our human intellect in its present state with the night owl. Just as this bird cannot bear direct

---

[3] N. Cameron devotes chap. 21 of his *Personality Development and Psychopathology* (Boston: Houghton Mifflin, 1963) to a detailed elaboration of this statement, although his background is medical and behavioristic. See also the articles by G. H. Estabrooks and Alwin Dressler in the General Bibliography.

sunlight, so our human intellect receives the light of pure intelligibility only when softened by reflection through matter. He stresses the intimate relationship between intellect and sense organs, and even mentions a correlation between intelligence and sensitivity to pressure and pain which has been verified experimentally in modern times. (Slavin, 1936, pp. 129–131, and references therein.)

It is really incorrect to talk about intrinsic and extrinsic dependence, as if there were questions of dependence of one thing upon another thing. Man is only one thing. Aristotle preferred to talk about a substantial form which was human but virtually animal and vegetative, so that these various powers were encompassed in the same nature. Brain may be extrinsic to thought, but it is intrinsic to man. (See footnote 1 in Chapter 6 on the unique, natural, conjoined instrumentality of sense knowledge.)

THE CAUSES OF KNOWLEDGE

Is knowing active or passive? Knowledge is the act of possessing another by having its intentional form. It is not in itself change, although we compared intentional with physical change to try to understand its nature. But it is clear that we can pass from a state of not-knowing to a state of knowing, a change which must be explained. The following analysis holds for both sensory and intellectual cognition.

Does knowing change its object (active), or is the knowing subject changed by the object (passive)? Let us return to our examples. If the cow eats the hay, the object, hay, is changed. But if the cow sees the hay, there is no change in the hay—only in the cow. An object is no different for having been known. The change is in the cow as it passes from the state of potentially knowing to a state of actually knowing. From this it seems clear that the intentional change involved in becoming a knower is *essentially passive*, the knowing subject being acted upon by the object. Grammar could play us false here: "see" is an active verb, but the cow is not acting on the hay.

But is knowledge therefore *purely* passive? The wax and the modeling clay are capable only of purely passive reception of forms. An object such as a seal impresses its form upon them, but they do not know; their reception is purely passive. Even the photographic film, which might be said in some way to react to the impression, is really only passive; we do not say that the camera knows. Knowledge is a characteristic of living things which have the power to react to the impression of forms in such a way that they are able to entertain these forms precisely as other, in contrast to their own. "Con" in the word "consciousness" means "with," and it is this relationship of knower getting together "with" object known which is distinctive of knowledge. It is the difference between the purely passive possession of form by the wax and the copenetration of being by which a knower is capable of soaring beyond the limitation of matter to only one form. Intentional change is thus essentially passive, but also *vitally reactive* and therefore not purely passive.

Two Causes. Knowledge is thus both active and passive. If it were purely passive, then the wax or modeling clay would know. If it were essentially active, then knowledge would create its object and we would have no way of telling whether things were real or the product of our knowing processes.

The answer to the question of what causes knowledge can be brought out by asking the trite old question, "If a tree falls in a forest and there is no man or animal around to hear it, is there a sound?" The answer, of course, is to define the word "sound." If by sound you mean the purely objective physical stimulus for hearing, its presence could easily be verified with a tape recorder and it is absurd to imagine the laws of physics do not operate simply because we are not there to observe the results. But if by sound you mean auditory sensation, it is equally obvious that there is none unless there is a being present equipped with the power of experiencing such sensation.

Knowledge, then, is the joint product of two causes: the object and the knowing power. Without an object impressing it, the knowing power would remain in sheer potency to know. Without this peculiar potency to receive it, the impression would never result in this knowledge.

Intentional form

The student must be very clear that the intentional form is not some image or picture which we know. It is simply a means or intermediary by which we know objects. It is the actuation of the cognitive power whereby its indeterminacy is removed and by which we are made to be actually aware of this rather than of that. The object needs to be able to be present in the knower in a manner proportionate to the degree of immateriality involved in knowledge. But since no material object can be immaterial in its physical being, it needs this intentional form to give it immaterial existence in the knowing power.[4]

Knowledge is not an action, in the sense of something which produces an effect. It is essentially the act or state of intentional union.

[4] In scholastic philosophy, the technical term for this intentional form was *species*. The term was perhaps unfortunate, for it is not to be confused with species in logic which is a division of genus, nor with species as in zoology where it means a class of animals.

It is not representation, nor similitude, but simultaneous possession of one's own form as well as another's form without its matter. To make cognition consist essentially of representation is to raise the old question of how do we know that the representation conforms to reality if we know only the representation, not the thing.

SUMMARY OF KNOWING PROCESS

The forming of an idea is usually instantaneous. Only by analysis and reasoning do we discover that several powers are operative in the process, whereas the product is a matter of clear experience and was examined in Chapter 7 when we contrasted idea with sense knowledge. Without suggesting that there is any actual separation or even time interval between the parts of the process, we may recapitulate the various stages in the formation of an idea.

We start with an object, since even imaginary beings like the flying horse have their foundation in our sensory experience of birds and horses. The object impresses itself through a medium physically upon the receptor organ and brain. This physiological activity is the means or instrument by which the object actuates the sensory power. The sense power vitally reacts, uniting with the object intentionally. The object is now present in the knower as form without matter, but with material qualities, and hence in only a quasi-immaterial state. Man, by the joint activity of intellect and this sensory representation, can then receive the intelligible form in a strictly immaterial or spiritual way, without indivdual material qualities. Since knowledge does not consist in a purely passive reception of forms, the intellect vitally reacts and produces the idea, notion, understanding, or concept. Lastly, unless the object which started the whole process was a spoken, written, or imagined word symbol, language completes the process by hanging a tag or label on the finished product, so that we now have a means of expressing our idea in conventional terms. Without understanding (idea), the word would be useless because meaningless.

When knowing ceases, the intentional forms are usually stored in the knowing power as habitual knowledge. Under proper stimulation, as we have seen, they can again actuate the power and result in consciousness.

REVIEW QUESTIONS

1. Is knowledge a univocal or analogous term? Explain.
2. Why is the analysis of knowledge difficult?
3. Can knowledge be defined simply as response to stimulus? Why?

4. "Scientists cannot tell whether certain organisms have sensation or not. Hence they could be either plant or animal. But if they could be either, then there is no real difference." Evaluate this argument.

5. Can the difference between physical union and intentional union be explained in terms common to both? to some other union?

6. Why does all awareness involve *some* immateriality? Explain what you mean by this immateriality.

7. Describe fully the precise degree of immateriality proper to sense knowledge.

8. *a.* Define "spiritual."
   b. Describe precisely what spiritual means in the case of human intellection.

9. If all cognition involves immateriality, then how can we say in Chapter 7 that intellect differs from sense by being immaterial?

10. What do you mean by "rational" intellect as opposed to other intellects? What practical import does this distinction have for education?

11. Is knowing active or passive? Explain.

12. What would be the epistemological consequence of saying that knowledge is purely active?

13. Is there any contradiction in saying that knowledge entails vital activity and yet is essentially passive?

14. Show how the facts of illusion, ambiguity, and constancy indicate that cognition is not merely a physical and physiological process.

15. Will the psychological nature of sensory knowledge be disproved by more fruitful research on central (or cerebral) factors in the brain? Why?

16. Is matter extrinsic to thought? to man? to sense knowledge?

17. If the intellect is spiritual, explain how brain injury can interfere with thought.

18. If heredity is biological and thought is immaterial, how can you explain that there is some real correlation between IQ of parents and children? Is it simply a matter of parental environment?

19. Explain the entire process of getting an idea, naming all the steps.

20. Do these steps indicate a sequence in time?

FOR FURTHER READING

Kelly & Tallon: the selection from **Peters,** pp. 232–236, presents a contemporary reinterpretation, including a reaction to the notion of "intentionality." The student may wish to discuss whether Peters improves upon the traditional concept. The selection from **Karl Rahner,** assigned to Chapter 6 above, could be reread at this point with profit.

We have mentioned **Francisco Romero,** *Theory of Man.* Since other contemporary philosophers rarely treat the question in metaphysical depth, we simply list here some of the better modern presentations of the views expressed in this chapter:

Gilson, Etienne. *The Spirit of Medieval Philosophy.* Chap. 12.

Olgiati, Francesco. *The Key to the Study of St. Thomas.* Chaps. II, V.

Renard, Henri, S.J. "The Problem of Knowledge in General," *The Modern Schoolman,* 1946, 24:1–11. (Chap. IV in his book, *The Philosophy of Man,* 1956.)

Sertillanges, A. D., O.P. *Foundations of Thomistic Philosophy.* Chap. II.

Wilhelmsen, Frederick S. *Man's Knowledge of Reality.*

Brain and thought

The strictly materialist view is less common now among philosophers. Besides the article by **Schmitt** in *Science,* 1965, 149:931–936, a representative statement might be that of **Thomas K. Landauer,** "Two Hypotheses Concerning the Biochemical Basis of Memory," *Psychol. Rev.* 1964, 71:167–179. We list, as less well known, some who oppose:

Bergson, Henri. *Matter and Memory.*

Cameron, Norman. *The Psychology of Behavior Disorders,* chap. 17; *Personality Development and Psychopathology,* Chap. 21.

Estabrooks, G. H. "Your Brain," *Scientific American,* 1936, 155:20–22.

Goldstein, Kurt. *Human Nature in the Light of Psychopathology.* Chaps. 2 and 3, especially p. 60, where the author insists that abstract and concrete mental processes differ in kind, not merely in degree.

Hilgard, Ernest R. *Theories of Learning.* (2d ed.) Pp. 452–485.

Joad, C. E. M. *How Our Minds Work.*

Lashley, Karl S. "Basic Neural Mechanisms in Behavior," *Psychol. Rev.,* 1930, 37:1–24.

Lashley, Karl S. *Brain Mechanisms and Intelligence.*

Moore, Thomas Verner. *Cognitive Psychology.* Since, like Cameron, he is both a psychiatrist (M.D.) and a psychologist (Ph.D.), Dom Moore is able to give much fascinating medical and experimental data, which refutes a purely materialistic explanation of cognition. Pp. 45–73, 513–525.

Sherrington, Charles. *Man on His Nature.* New York: Cambridge, 1940. Chaps. 9, 10, and 11. Unfortunately ends in dualism.

Solomon, Harry C., Cobb, Stanley, & Penfield, Wilder (eds.) *The Brain and Human Behavior.*

III
HUMAN DYNAMICS

9 EMOTION

Man is the anxiety-avoiding animal. Becker

 Although we have stressed the role of body in human knowing, the consideration of the difference between sensory and intellectual cognition may have tended to make us lose sight of the continuity man has with the animals lower on the evolutionary scale. Man may be a peculiar kind of animal, the kind that understands, but he is nevertheless an animal. As we observed about blue and green blending into one another in the spectrum so that even the person with normal color vision has difficulty pinpointing the dividing line, so in the concrete the difference between man and other animals is not always so sharp as it might seem. Some apes are more "intelligent" than idiot men, and bees or ants appear to be better community organizers than our politicians. One area which exemplifies this continuity is emotion.

We noted earlier that words like conscious and experience refer to more than knowing activities: they also include the whole range of man's *dynamic* interrelationship with the world. Experimental psychologists have shown that when presented with words such as pretty, ugly, love, hate, people may react by mere recognition of cognitive meaning or they may experience genuine feeling, an emotional arousal. This affective or emotional meaning can be distinguished from the former even physiologically.

Knowing versus wanting

When studying knowledge in Part II, we made practically no mention of the use of that knowledge. But to be aware of a situation is a different kind of activity from being inclined to do something about it. The difference between knowledge and dynamics, between knowing and wanting, seems a fairly obvious fact of experience. I may see a boat, or daydream about it, or understand what it means; but whether I want it or not, get emotionally excited about it, choose to buy or steal it—these represent a different kind of conscious activity.

Appetition (or appetency) is the name traditionally given to this tending. Modern psychology uses a great variety of terms to describe this activity: motivation, drive, conation, dynamics. Since the tending may be either toward or away from the object known, paired terms are sometimes used, such as attraction-aversion or approach-avoidance. None of these terms is perfectly satisfactory because the notion is analogous rather than univocal and refers to many different types of dynamic activity.

Again we must be careful not to separate in our thinking what is together in reality. Man is a cognitive-affective unity, and the above does not mean to imply any separation of knowledge and dynamics. Quite the contrary: our reactions to our environment are largely stimulated by some kind of knowledge, so that knowing and striving are inseparable and mutually complementary. We merely stress that man the person *does* things in the world, he does not just speculate. He makes dynamic responses to his environment. And he does not make them mechanically, in a coldly unemotional way. Love or anger will drive him to action he would never attain by mere theoretical knowledge, no matter how clear or lofty.

Emotion is good

Emotion is an important part of human activity. Man's actual achievements are ordinarily in direct proportion to the extent that he is emotionally involved. How we feel is of primary importance in what we actually do, though our feelings cannot be relied upon to indicate what we should do.

Contrary to the stand of puritanism by whatever name, it is a fact that feelings are an integral part of human nature. Man is not an angel, and his rational operations cannot be studied in isolation from his animal drives and affections. These may need to be controlled, but they cannot be eliminated or ignored.

Jansenistic and puritanical thought have for the last several centuries taught or implied that emotion is somehow bad. "Don't be so emotional" or "It's just an emotional affair" are typical expressions which oppose feelings to reason. We go beyond this and practically identify sin with the movements of our animal tendencies. When the gospel speaks of "a woman who was a sinner," everybody just assumes her sin involved an abuse of the body. We misinterpret St. Paul's remark that "the flesh lusteth against the spirit" if we think he meant by flesh only bodily passion; flesh for St. Paul meant not a part of man but the whole man insofar as he might rebel against the action of grace and misdirect his freedom toward a false good.[1] Some have even thought that the original sin was a sexual act, which seems rather farfetched since the pair were married and had been told to "increase and multiply."

G. K. Chesterton, on the other hand, was fond of pointing out that the body cannot sin, since sin is an act of rebellious choice and hence necessarily stems from the spiritual part of man. We might prefer to say that it is the person who rebels, and the person who experiences passion, but at least it is clear that it is not the feeling itself which is bad but only the abuse we might make of it. We have seen that every object is apprehended in a sensitive-intellective way by man; it follows that our cravings are likewise both animal and spiritual all at once. It is not the "lower" in man that is dangerous, but his "higher" powers which make him capable of abuse and rebellion. If we are to believe the scriptures, the first sin was by a brilliant angel with no body to abuse: it was a purely spiritual sin of pride, as was basically the original sin (disobedience) of early man.

Anxiety and care

Although they gave full account of the influence of emotion in their ethical treatises, the scholastics' philosophy of man tended to spend little time on emotion. Many contemporary philosophers concentrate heavily on it. And while they give full measure to those emotional drives which we have in common with other animals, such as sex and power, they are particularly concerned with those which are peculiar to man. F. Romero and Max Scheler, in particular, develop philosophies of values and more personalized philosophies of man because

[1] Karl Rahner, S.J., "Current Conception of Concupiscentia," in *Theological Investigations*, vol. I (Baltimore: Helicon, 1964), pp. 352–354. See James E. Royce, S.J., "How Puritanism Persists," *Insight*, 1963, vol. 1, no. 3, pp. 3–6.

of the place they give to specifically human feelings. Kierkegaard speaks much of *angst,* the anxiety which is so dominant in the present human situation and which reflects the fact that man is an animal that can *care.*

Man cares a great deal: he is anxious about love, about honesty and justice, about beauty. His anxiety shows itself in a great variety of ways, from increased dependence on tranquilizers to various sorts of protest. Tension, anxiety, concern, value feeling characterize modern man. He is conscious of being mortal, sexed, social, finite. Being sexed and social has led to wide study of group dynamics, social perception, and social conditioning. Being finite and mortal makes him aware of the paradox, the absurd, the personal.

The person is always unique and hence never fits into scientific generalizations and universal concepts. Reality is full of paradoxes, apparent contradictions which defy neat categorization. Whether the universe is absurd depends, of course, on one's overall perspective on life's meaning. One is tempted to think sometimes that the preoccupation of some existentialists with this theme is little more than a morose reaction to what has always been the toughest problem in philosophy, the problem of evil in the world. But in any case anxiety is the source of much unrest and mental disorder, and is part of the human condition.

Nevertheless man's emotional nature makes him more interesting as a person, richer in his appreciation of beauty, warmer in his interpersonal relations. The humor in the current jokes about two tape recorders talking to each other stems from the lack of the "I-thou" relation of personal dialogue. Man communicates not only ideas but feelings. He loves not as one angel might love another angel, but as a being with warm blood in his veins. Human sex is not just a biological act of union but a whole lifetime of attitudes and feelings toward others. Man knows that there can be sex without love, and love without sex. His emotions run a wide range of objects and intensity, but they are all part of what makes this person his unique self.

AFFECTIVE STATES

Affective states is the general term used to comprise this intriguing area of dynamics. It includes the following:

Feeling: the most elemental states of pleasure or displeasure.

Mood: an affective state more acute and more prolonged, but still rather vague. "He is in a good mood today."

Sentiment: a group of emotional tendencies concerning some object or person. More specific in its object and associations than feeling or mood, it is like them in being less intense and longer lasting than emotion. Patriotism would be an example, or friendship.

Emotion: a spontaneous, intense feeling state, aroused by a meaningful stimulus and characterized by peculiar bodily changes. It is more complex and more intense than any of the afore-mentioned, as well as more specific in its relation to the meaning of the situation. It is therefore more involved with perception, and in addition has a characteristic bodily resonance. Fear, love, anger, and hatred are typical examples.

Temperament: one's habitual emotional disposition—as opposed to the actual emotion. "She has a placid temperament," and, "He has a violent temper," may both be correct, even if she is angry at the moment and he is not.

Although these are all complex processes involving cognitive, dynamic, and physiological activity, they are primarily activities of our sensory drives. Psychologists once distinguished more sharply between the mild feeling states of pleasantness and unpleasantness and the intense state of emotion, but the tendency now is to consider them a continuum ranging in intensity and specificity, without attempting to delineate the precise point at which the feeling becomes so intense and meaningful as to be called an emotion. They are called affective states because they refer to the way in which some stimulus affects us, i.e., how it makes us feel.

Nature of emotion

We all know from direct experience what it means to be angry or afraid, joyous or hating. It is not so easy to analyze the nature of these states, especially because while we are experiencing them we are in no mood for analysis. Emotion is also difficult to grasp or define because it is a highly complex activity. Yet an understanding of its nature is important not only as a basis for any intelligent discussion of its development and control, but also because it is a good indicator of the kind of being man is.

Although centered in intense movements of the sensory tendencies, emotion involves practically all of man: sensory knowledge and especially imagination, intellection and some spontaneous volition, and striking physiological changes. In general, it is more complex and more intense than feelings or moods, and has a more direct relation to a meaningful stimulus situation. Another very important difference is the characteristic bodily resonance, a set of physiological changes peculiar to emotion.

Of course, when we actually have an emotion we are not aware of all of this complexity; we only feel very strongly in a certain way. Nevertheless, upon analyzing emotion, we can distinguish three elements: (1) the apprehension of the stimulus, (2) an affective response, and (3) bodily resonance reinforcing this response.

1. *Meaningful stimulus.* It is not enough that I see a situation or hear a word to be aroused emotionally. Whether I so react depends on whether I recognize the situation as pleasant, desirable, or threatening to me. A meaningless stimulation would cause no emotion. The object may be present or absent, remembered or imagined. But it must be not only perceived but also appraised as affecting me personally in some way.

It is important to note that I need not be conscious of the connection between the stimulus and the emotion, or know why it has this emotional meaning for me. Abnormal emotional states are often due to a failure of the individual to recognize the emotional meaning which a situation or object has acquired for him.

The manner in which the meaning is grasped serves to distinguish a truly human emotion from a purely animal one. In an analogous sense we can say the lamb fears the lion, or a dog loves its master; but the fear and love here result from mere sensory awareness, whether it be an instinctive appraisal by inner estimative power or the result of stored-up associations in imagination and memory. In contrast, a love proper to a human being should include some intellectual appreciation of the goodness of the beloved, and even my fear of a tiger may involve some rational as well as sensory knowledge, although in neither case is the emotion a purely Platonic affair existing only at the rational level.

2. *Affective response.* The heart of emotion is the impulsive, almost explosive response or tendency, especially at the animal or sensory level. It is an affective or feeling state, not a cognitive act.

It is with this connotation in mind that the medieval philosophers called emotion by the name of passion. Now *passio* has some six different meanings in medieval philosophy, whereas in modern English the word passion or passionate is often restricted to just one appetitive response, that of carnal love. This is unfortunate, because puritanical thinking then goes on to imply that all emotion is bad. It is also unfortunate because passion might suggest passivity, although the adjective passionate does not imply this.

One notable characteristic of emotion is the fact that it is spontaneous. This does not mean inborn, for we have already noted that the power of a stimulus to elicit an emotional response is largely acquired through previous learning experience. Spontaneous is the opposite of deliberate, and refers to the automaticity which is proper both to our sense drives and to the autonomic division of the nervous system which enters so intimately into emotional response. Even the volition which may be involved in a truly human emotion is not the deliberate act of choice, but the first spontaneous tending of the will which usually precedes (and sometimes overrules[2]) the act of free choice.

This spontaneity means that emotions are not subject to our control directly, but only indirectly. Aristotle (*Pol.* I, 5, 1254b2) distinguishes between those acts over which we have despotic or dictatorial power and

---

[2] Aquinas, S. T., Ia, IIae, qq. 8–16; or *C. G.*, IV, 19.

those acts over which we have only political or persuasive power. Spontaneous tendencies and autonomic responses obviously fall in the latter class. Emotions are to be distinguished from emotional *behavior*, the external behavior which may be dictated by emotion: this is usually within our direct or despotic control. Thus I am usually able to refrain by direct control from hitting someone, but the fact that I feel like hitting him is not so easily handled.

3. *Body resonance.* Certain notable physiological changes are characteristic of emotion. They constitute an integral part of emotion, being closely bound up with any intense activity of our animal appetites. At least a general pattern of organic activity is characteristic: heartbeat, blood coagulative power, perspiration, digestive processes, and adrenal secretion all undergo marked changes commonly recognized as integral to emotional experience.

These mobilize the body for the action or protection usually called for in an emotional situation. We say usually, for although in other animals emotion prompted by the unreasoned estimate of a situation may be an adequate guide for action, in human beings action depends also on reasoned evaluation of the goal. Since this goal may be a distant one and the means to it unpleasant, emotion may hinder rather than help.

Note that *awareness* of these physiological changes may or may not accompany the emotional experience; this is irrelevant to the nature of emotion itself.

Facial changes and other external expressions of emotion are likewise of little import. For one thing, they are more separable from emotion. Moreover, they lack the spontaneity which typifies emotional response. A good poker player can control the emotion on his face because this is a matter of voluntary musculature; but he can do little, except indirectly, about the autonomic physiological changes which we have enumerated and which the polygraph or so-called lie detector measures. The latter, incidentally, does not measure truth and falsity, but simply the spontaneous physiological aspects of embarrassment which are beyond our control.

Divisions of emotion

There are many different divisions of emotions. Perhaps the most obvious is that of pleasant and unpleasant, viz., those aroused by a desirable stimulus and those aroused by an undesirable one. This obviously is on a different axis from the division in terms of intensity or duration given above.

From Aristotle to John B. Watson and Sigmund Freud, various attempts have been made to reduce emotions to a certain basic few.[3] Psychologists have largely abandoned such attempts at identifying primary emotions and prefer a developmental approach, studying the gradual growth from the simplest excitement of the infant to the variegated shades of adult emotional response. The generalized excitement first observable in infants becomes differentiated fairly early into fear, rage, and love. Later we can observe desire, joy, hatred, sorrow,

[3] Among them Descartes, *Traité de l'ame*, and Spinoza, *Ethics*, Books III and IV.

hope, despair, courage, and still later further refinements. Love, in the general sense of a tendency to seek the good and avoid what threatens its loss, may be said to be primary.

Medieval philosophers generally held that sensory drive itself is twofold: concupiscible and irascible. The distinction is based on whether the good desired (or evil to be avoided) is considered simple to attain (or avoid) or as involving some difficulty. Concupiscible, or pleasure-pain, drive refers to unqualified attraction and avoidance: desire, joy, aversion, sorrow. Irascible, or aggressive, drive is aroused when there is some threat or difficulty in the attainment or avoidance of the object. Thus hope, despair, courage, fear, and anger would be considered activities of the irascible drives.

This distinction seems to have some foundation. First, there is the fact that these two tendencies can oppose one another. We know that hunger or sex desire (concupiscible) can be diminished or temporarily wiped out by anger or fear (irascible). This fact has recently been used by a Dutch psychiatrist[4] to explain repression: pleasure drive is overcome by fear or strengthened by boldness, rather than by volitional control. This would explain the irrational and unconscious nature of anxiety and other neuroses, which are then due largely to habits of the irascible drives. Secondly, one can also see some vague parallel between this distinction and the mutually antagonistic activities of the two divisions of the autonomic nervous system. Concupiscible appetite seems to involve the parasympathetic (craniosacral) functions which mediate routine behavior. Irascible partakes more of the sympathetic (thoracolumbar) division and adrenal glands which activate the body to an emergency state. However, oversimplification here is dangerous since both divisions of the autonomic, as well as the central nervous system, are involved in many emotional states.

Psychologists and physiologists have tried for many years to distinguish emotions on the basis of different bodily reactions. External reactions, such as facial expression and gestures, seem to be largely stylized by convention. Even parents were unable to tell from observing silent motion pictures of their own infant whether the child was joyful or sad. The internal physiological changes, which are really the more important aspect of the bodily reaction, likewise fail as an adequate basis for distinguishing emotions. Blood pressure and pulse rate may go up equally high without telling us whether the presence of a newcomer arouses love or fear. Since the discovery of norepinephrine (another secretion of the adrenal medulla), some success has been attained in distinguishing physiologically between fear and anger; and specific activation centers have been localized in the limbic system (in the lower midbrain) for some emotions.

Organic nature of emotion

Of course we are not aware of any of this when we are angry or afraid. We must still depend largely on our conscious experience of the dynamic impulse itself to determine whether we love or hate a person, whether we are happy or sad at a bit of news. Yet it is clear from all

[4] A. Terruwe, 1958. Michael Stock presents another view in *The Thomist*, 1961, 24:544–579.

the above that emotion is by no means purely immaterial. This should be equally obvious from the fact that knowledge and dynamic response have to be at a corresponding level, and we have already seen that sensory knowledge is at best only quasi-immaterial. Emotion especially is very important in modern psychosomatic medicine, which is the study of those physical ills and symptoms due largely to psychological and especially emotional causes. But a clear grasp of the organic nature of sensory impulse itself precludes any possibility of separating psyche from soma as if they were two different beings. The psychic and somatic aspects of emotional experience do not constitute the acts of two separate beings, since they constitute one affective experience.

Emotion thus illustrates the unity of man, and prevents us from thinking of matter and spirit as two separate beings somehow hooked together. All the processes connected with knowing and wanting involve physiological functioning in one way or another, using the nervous system as organ and connector. Endocrine glands and body structure exert important influence on human activity and must be considered if we are to have a complete knowledge of man's nature. Man is animal and even vegetable in his activities, while not ceasing to be one.

The philosopher must consider the physiological side of man so that he will know when a biological explanation is sufficient and will not appeal unnecessarily to more exalted interpretations. Likewise, he should be aware of the limitations of organism: we have to know when a phenomenon like creative artistry or heroic altruism can not be accounted for in terms of biological factors alone.

REVIEW QUESTIONS

1. "If there were no animals, man would be defined as a rational vegetable." Do you agree? Where would the contents of this chapter fit?
2. Man has been said to be the only being that blushes. Why? Why not say, "the only animal"?
3. William James said that emotion is the awareness of the bodily changes; John Watson said that emotion *is* the bodily changes. What reasons can you give for disagreeing with both?
4. What is the connection between puritanism and the notion that the emotions are tendencies toward evil?
5. Why is immaturity often characterized as a predominantly emotional condition?
6. Distinguish feeling as used in this chapter from feeling as a tactual sensation.

7. What is the relation between temperament and emotion?
8. What reasons can you give why the classification of emotions must take into account subjective factors?
9. Why is the way one defines emotion an index to one's concept of the nature of man?
10. Is there any contradiction in saying emotion is spontaneous and yet is largely developed? Explain.
11. Which of the three elements of emotion is involved when we say that a truly human emotion should have a rational aspect?
12. What is meant by saying that emotion is more adrenal than cortical?

FOR FURTHER READING

Kelly & Tallon: the selections from Plato on pp. 1–6, from Augustine on pp. 24–26, and the chapter from John Stuart Mill (in which he attacks Calvinism).

Jean-Paul Sartre gives an existentialist view in *The Emotions: Outline of a Theory.* In chap. 6 of *Language, Truth, and Logic,* the analytic philosopher A. J. Ayer proposes an emotive theory of ethics, in which moral statements are not propositions which are either true or false.

The physiology of emotion makes surprisingly fascinating reading in the semipopular writings of researchers such as Walter B. Cannon, *The Wisdom of the Body,* and *Bodily Changes in Pain, Hunger, Fear and Rage,* and of experts on psychosomatic medicine such as Walter C. Alvarez and H. Flanders Dunbar. Psychologists have of course written copiously about emotion. We list some works of general interest:

Arnold, Magda B. *Emotion and Personality.* A solid treatise in two volumes.

Arnold, Magda B., & Gasson, J. A. "Feelings and Emotions as Dynamic Factors in Personality Integration," in M. B. Arnold & J. A. Gasson (Eds.) *The Human Person.*

Eymieu, Antonin, S.J. *Le Gouvernement de soi-même.* Vol. I, *Les Grandes lois.* Unfortunately, the four volumes of this intriguing French Jesuit were never translated.

Kenny, A. *Action, Emotion and Free Will.*

Michotte, Albert E. "The Emotions Regarded as Functional Connections," in Martin L. Reymert (Ed.) *Feelings and Emotions.*

Moore, Thomas Verner. *The Driving Forces of Human Nature and Their Adjustment.* Pp. 107–164.

Royce, James E., S.J. *Personality and Mental Health.* (Rev. ed.) Pp. 63–70.

10 FROM MOTIVATION TO ACTION

It is a general rule that human motives can never be fully explained on the basis of physiological influences alone. Hilgard

Why man acts has always been of great concern to the student of human nature, whether philosopher or psychologist. We are rarely satisfied with knowing merely what man does, without knowing why he does it. Dynamics are so central in the study of human personality that when contemporary psychology speaks of theories of personality it usually means theories of motivation.

Men have proposed many different theories of motivation to explain human conduct. As in most complex problems which the human mind attacks, there is a grain of truth in every one, for each discovers some one facet of the total picture. They are usually correct in what they assert, and wrong in their denial of other aspects of reality. Thus they are not so much errors as part truths.

Hedonism is the theory which holds that all human activity is governed by sensory pleasure. It ignores activity prompted by utility, generosity, and many needs of both self and species, as well as higher goals and motivations. The *extreme voluntarist* view would tend to exaggerate the role of choice to the neglect of other motivating and even determining factors. It claims that all man's activity is voluntary, whereas a great deal of it may be reflex, instinctive, governed by sensory attraction or unconscious motivating factors. Those versed in clinical or depth psychology are likely to stress very much *unconscious motivation,* and certainly we are unaware of many of the influences within us. The S-R, or stimulus-response, formula of classic *behaviorism* would ignore our mental experiences and pattern all human activity after the simple reflex. As an exclusive view, it has long since succumbed to the criticisms of psychologists. The *instinct* theory suffered a similar fate as an exclusive view, since to claim that the sources of all activity are innate is to ignore the importance of learning or conditioning, as well as other factors.

In view of all this difference of opinion, we need to explore our experiences and the data from science with an open mind, trying to cover at least in a broad way the entire field of human dynamics. We have already entered this area with our consideration of emotion, and must now achieve perspective by considering its full scope. A study of human dynamics or motivated processes reveals a wide range, from organic drives to self-directed activity.

MOTIVES AND MOTIVATING FACTORS

Motive, from the Latin word for "move," means whatever moves one to act. The term was restricted by the medieval philosophers to a reason for action of which one is aware at the rational level, an intellectually known good serving as the object of the will. Modern psychology has considerably broadened the meaning of this term and brought it back closer to the original Latin root. We think it practical to conform more to this current usage and use the term motive to refer to any specific goal or object which, on a conscious level, directs conduct, regardless of whether it is sensory or rational. Thus used, the term is more or less synonymous with incentive, and runs through a wide range of psychological dynamics.

Although inseparable, knowing and tending are distinct activities, since they have different proper objects. The object of the former is the being as knowable, whereas that of the latter is the being as good or desirable.

Knowledge, whether sensory perception, image, or idea, is not precisely a motive until it serves as a stimulating force to our dynamic powers. Knowledge is not virtue, principles are not character, daydreams are not meritorious, temptation is not sin. It is only when these things lead to action or at least to deliberate resolve or intention that they merit praise or blame.

One reason why there is confusion in modern psychological discussion of motivation is that everyday terms are frequently taken over without distinguishing between final and efficient causality. Strictly speaking, the terms motive, incentive, goal, purpose, stimulus, and even need, all refer to the realm of final cause. Drive, urge, impulse, desire, emotion, and choice refer to appetitive responses with regard to such motives and are in the realm of efficient causality. Knowledge gives us the goal, and appetite gives the inclination towards it.

The concept of final cause is established elsewhere, in general metaphysics. ("Final" here does not mean last or ultimate, but purpose or goal.) "How can a thing act as a cause when it does not even exist?" is a question which only serves to bring out the difference between efficient and final causality. The objection stems from a univocal identification of the term cause with efficient cause. If the final cause or goal exists only in the mind of the one desiring it, it can hardly exert efficient causality. It is the nature of a final cause to "cause" precisely by being desirable, by attracting, by stimulating the efficient cause to take means to make it become a reality.

The study of final causes is called teleology, from the Greek *telos* meaning "end" or "goal." Because psychology around the beginning of this century was anxious to attain scientific status by patterning itself after classic physics, which ignored finality, psychologists once tended to decry teleology. But motivation is impossible to ignore in studying the determinants of human behavior, so the notion crept back in. At first it was controversial, but opposition to teleology has now waned (Hall & Lindzey, 1957, p. 539).

Motivating factors is a term sometimes used to designate other influences which initiate or sustain activity and which are not incentives or motives even in the broadened sense used above. These include needs and drives, physiological conditions of the organism, the unconscious influence of previous experience, and a host of other factors which may be only vaguely conscious or completely beyond our awareness. Motive refers to the object of a power; motivating factors can refer to the power, its natural tendency to action, habits which can modify its action, and even the appetitive act itself. Modern psychologists often use the word motive as a general term referring to both motives and motivating factors: anything which contributes toward need-satisfying and goal-seeking behavior, including the avoidance of undesirable objects.

A *need* is a lack of something either suitable or necessary: food, information, social acceptance. *Drive* is a tension or tendency to act caused by an unfilled need: hunger for food, curiosity for knowledge, loneliness for acceptance. The philosopher need not be concerned that modern psychologists are not wholly consistent in their use of these terms.[1] Philosophically, a need is an objective fact, the actual lack. The drive is an appetitive state consequent upon that need. It is usually rather indeterminate until directed by a specific incentive or goal. Thus the drive of hunger may be a vague

[1] For further clarification see the discussion of needs and drives in James E. Royce, S.J., *Personality and Mental Health* (Milwaukee: Bruce, 1964), pp. 23–29.

craving which causes Junior to wander aimlessly in the general direction of the kitchen, but action becomes specific once the cookie jar comes into view.

Motivated activities

Impulse is a tendency we experience, in the presence of actual opportunity, to exercise any one of our human abilities. Here the motive is present and activity is called for at once upon its apprehension. The incentive or deterrent may be instinctual, learned, or intellectual, but in any case it calls for indeliberate and immediate response, which makes control difficult. Impulse differs from reflex in being conscious, less mechanical, more complex, and more dynamic. It differs from drive in being called forth by a specific incentive.

There is no point in trying to enumerate or classify our impulses; we have as many impulses as there are things we can feel impelled to do. This view also obviates useless attempts to name "instincts," as if such a set of entities existed. Evidence merely indicates that some tendencies are unlearned, that often there is at least a partially instinctive impulse impelling us to exercise our natural abilities.

Desire is a similar tendency, but regarding an *absent* object or situation. (The word "appetite" is often used in common speech to refer to this act, instead of in the traditional sense of any tendency.) Again, desire may involve our lowest animal needs or our highest human aspirations. We may define desire as a craving we experience to seek or produce a situation in which impulsive tendencies may be satisfied or natural wants supplied.

Such desires may have *goals* which are clearly defined, or vague. They may be necessary, or mere "wants" acquired beyond nature's demands. They may be insightful, or without an understanding of their true motivation ("repressed"). Normal desires are usually more controllable than impulses, and less dependent on the present situation or organic conditions. They are modifiable by education and training, as opposed to impulse which is usually modified only by satisfaction or by the passage of time.

Affective states are more general in their reference to action, but powerfully dynamic. They include feeling, mood, sentiment, and emotion, all defined in the previous chapter.

Choice has as its stimulus a motive in the sense of an intellectually known good. The object may be only apparently good, or it may be seen as "good to avoid." It may be material or immaterial, means or end, fleeting or habitual. The motive can be an attitude, a principle, an ideal, or some sentiment based more on feeling than on intellect and perhaps involving bias or prejudice.

Motivation is complex All these motivated tendencies except the last, choice, may be either sensory or rational or both. Usually in the human adult there is such a combination and mixture of the sensory and rational in motivation that it is practically impossible to identify a given tendency as purely animal or purely rational. We must turn to infants, the mentally abnormal, or brute animals to find clear-cut cases of unmixed sensory appetency. And even the act of choice, although elicited by awareness of an intellectually known good, usually occurs with an admixture of sensory motivation. As in the case of knowledge, we distinguish for purposes of study what is not separate in reality.

DOES MAN HAVE A WILL?

We noted at the beginning of this chapter the divergence of opinion between philosophers who exaggerate the role of will and those who deny it entirely. While postponing to the following chapter the controversy as to whether man is capable of self-determination or free choice, we shall try in this chapter to clarify what the word "will" means and see if our experience warrants use of the term at all. This is especially true because of a tendency to caricature the will as a "little man in the head" which chooses.

Suppose the sight of some luscious strawberries stimulates a strong tendency of my sensory appetite, while at the same time my intellectual awareness that I am allergic and they will make me sick evokes a rational tendency to avoid them. Again, a fireman, motivated by principle, may go into danger, though his senses elicit only repugnance. The sight of a mountain stream may evoke thirst, regardless of whether I really need water just then or not. Or, I may know intellectually that an unpleasant medication may save my life, even though I feel a sensory revulsion toward it. All these experiences seem to point rather clearly to a distinction between tendencies stimulated by sensory knowledge and those stimulated by intellectual knowledge. Not that sense and intellect always evoke contrary appetition: my intellect may tell me that this pleasant-tasting food is also nourishing, or that the intelligent thing to do is to avoid this painful object.

The important fact is that we can be motivated both by non-sensory stimuli such as honor, freedom, or rights, and by intellectual knowledge even of sensory objects, as when food is desired precisely because of its nutritional value, i.e., known through universal principles. Thus we see evidence of an intellectual dimension of human appetition, which may be either antagonistic or complementary to sense drives.

If we analyze the moral content of our ordinary speech we see again that values not within the grasp of sensory perception play a large role in our motivations. We do things "out of duty" or "because I felt I ought to" or "because it's the right thing to do." Justice, charity, principle, obligation, generosity, etc., frequently appear in our manner of speaking. Unless language is meaningless and communication impossible, there must be some existential foundation for these expressions. Current psychology is witnessing a rebirth of interest in values and value-oriented behaviors.

Implicit in these facts is the notion that if man experiences these activities, he has the ability to do so. The ability or power may not always be in operation, and may be a capacity for many different acts. But the evidence seems clear that man has such an ability. It is to this ability of rational appetition that we give the name *will*. It is a power whose act is called volition, just as intellect is a power whose act is understanding.[2] Neither is a separate substance but only an ability of man. Hence it is not correct to say, "The will chooses," but rather, "Man chooses by means of his will."

Nature of volition

Volition may be defined as a conscious tendency regarding an intellectually known object. *Voluntary* is the general adjective applied to all activity involving attraction-aversion tendencies resulting from intellectual awareness.

Volition, conation, or will-activity can be of many different kinds. It may be the simple tending of any appetitive power toward an object known as good; this simple tending which is the first act of the will is not free but spontaneous. Volition is desire if it regards an object absent or not possessed; it is called enjoyment or complacency if the object is already present and possessed. (Note that the names of some of these states of will are taken from their accompanying emotions.) Volition is called intention if it regards the goal or end, resolution if it regards means, and interest if it is a general disposition to direct activity toward a specific goal. It is choice if it involves selection between various motives. Thus choice is seen to be only one of many acts of the will.

Far from being an uncaused act, choice is seen always to involve two causes: efficient and final. The will itself is an ability by which the human being (the ego or self) exerts efficient causality; but being an appetite, of its very nature it demands also a final cause or purpose for which to act. It is of the nature of the will to act because of a motive.

Motive may be defined here as an object intellectually known as good, serving to attract the will. This is motive in the strict sense of the word, not motivating factors such as organic drives, habitual tendencies, or sensory attraction. The prime importance of motive as

---

[2] Factor analysis by R. B. Cattell reveals the existence of a β factor which seems to be will, just as Spearman's G appears to be general intelligence or intellect (Gannon, 1954, pp. 402–403). Snider (1954) also found evidence for the existence of will, using a different mathematical technique.

a key to understanding the operation of the will is brought out by Lindworsky (1929), and by studies of communist brainwashing.[3] Without intellectual convictions there can be no decisiveness of will. Only by understanding the role of motive in the will-act can one avoid needless misunderstanding when we come to the question of free choice.

Object of volition

The object of volition can be any being, since every being has some ontological good. This good may be material (physical) or spiritual, particular or universal. Thus the motive may be the good of a dinner, a particular right, the democratic ideal of justice for all, or God Himself. It may be a pleasurable good such as smoking, a useful good such as coffee to keep me awake while studying, or it may be good sought for its own proper and intrinsic worth.

The proper object of volition is always some intellectually known aspect of goodness. The object of volition is goodness in general, regardless of how it is realized in the particular good. It may be only negative, in that the object is "good to avoid." It may be only an apparent good, not a true or moral good: a person's motive for murder can only be that it seemed "good" to him at the time, even though murder in itself may be bad. As long as it is true that this being contains at least apparent goodness, it can be presented to the will under its proper object of goodness in general.

It is quite clear from the foregoing that the will is never free with regard to goodness in general, since its very nature is to tend toward the good. It is naturally determined to seek the good. Even the person who wants to be miserable is not seeking misery precisely insofar as it is not good, but because he mistakenly looks upon it as a means to

---

[3] A. D. Biderman and H. Zimmer, *The Manipulation of Human Behavior* (New York: Wiley, 1961). One authoritative nontechnical report on the subject of brainwashing is that by Maj. William E. Mayer, "Why Did Many GI Captives Cave In?" *U.S. News and World Report*, Feb. 24, 1956, pp. 56–72. An Army psychiatrist, Major Mayer spent four years interviewing brainwashed Americans from the Korean conflict. His report emphasizes that there was no question of physical torture, but rather points to serious weaknesses in Americans' character and shortcomings in their education. His whole report accords well with the teaching here on choice and the importance of motives. A similar view using different sources is presented by Eugene Kinkead, "A Reporter at Large: The Study of Something New in History," *The New Yorker*, Oct. 26, 1957, pp. 102–153. Like Mayer, he points out that steadfast choice requires intellectual convictions about the truths of democracy and "... adherence to religious beliefs. Many of the men said that in prison camps these intangibles were of greater help to them than anything else. Now, much more than in the past, such things bulk large in Army training" (p. 152).

happiness. Similarly, the suicide does not seek nonbeing as such, but rather avoidance of trouble, and this nonbeing appears to him as being-without-trouble. Self-destructive behavior is really a misguided attempt at self-perfective activity.

THE WILL AND OTHER POWERS

Volitions are activities taking place in the will itself. They may be of many kinds, such as desire, complacency, choice. It is with these acts of the will itself that we are primarily concerned in philosophy.

Voluntary acts are commanded by the will but executed by some power other than the will. Thus if I choose to lift a 300-pound weight, I do not choose with my muscles nor lift with my will. Moreover, the will may command but the muscles be unable to obey. The execution is clearly a matter of physics and only my intention is a matter of choice. The will may command acts of almost any of our other operative powers: I may voluntarily conjure up certain images in my imagination, direct the attention of my special senses, willingly think about a certain topic, or move this pencil about the table. All these are voluntary acts if done under the command of the will. As in the case of the 300-pound weight, the command is not always obeyed. I may choose to entertain only certain images, but be disappointed in the execution of this resolve because of the spontaneous activity of imagination not under my control.

This distinction between choice and execution is strikingly illustrated by some work in experimental neurosurgery done by Wilder Penfield at McGill University in Montreal. Keeping the patient conscious and using only a local anesthetic to enter the cranium, the surgeon was able to stimulate directly the motor centers of the cortex. Thus by touching a certain point he would cause the patient's left foot to rise. The patient, being fully conscious, was then instructed not to raise his foot. In spite of his best efforts, the foot would come up. But his insistence that he did not want it to brought out clearly the distinction between the voluntary choice and the involuntary movement. No stimulus made him *want* to.

The words "voluntary" and "willingly" are often used in popular speech as synonymous with "free." Actually, some volitions elicited in the will are quite spontaneous and not free, though technically voluntary. Again, an act which is the result of a previous choice or voluntary habit may be called a voluntary act to the extent that it flows from the will, even though it is not free at the time. For example, the driver may not be actually choosing to speed at the moment of a crash, yet his fatal speed may be voluntary in virtue of a prior decision to speed or a culpable habit of speeding.

Voluntary acts must therefore be distinguished into those that are *actually* voluntary, *virtually* voluntary, and *habitually* voluntary. The first are those in which the operative power executes a choice under the present influence of an actual volition. For example, I choose to pick up this pencil and do so while choosing. An act is virtually voluntary if it happens in virtue of a previous act of choice which has ceased to exist in the will at the time it is being executed. For instance, if I am walking downtown to buy some shoes, my walking shows the influence of the previous decision, even though I may have long since ceased to be actually choosing to purchase shoes and am now thinking about something else entirely. Lastly, my motive may be habitual, and I may perform an act without any new act of choice, but it will still be a voluntary act to the extent that the habit was built up voluntarily.

Failure to make these necessary distinctions accounts for much of the confusion which arose over early attempts to study freedom of choice in the experimental psychology laboratory. Experimenters looked in vain for an act of choice during the experiment, but there was none. The choice was made at the time the person agreed to do the experiment or accepted the instructions;[4] what happened during the experiment followed in virtue of this previous choice and did not involve a new act of the will. A great deal of what is discussed under the term "set" belongs in the category of the virtual or habitual voluntary.

Voluntary control

The will can normally exercise some control over other activities, depending on their nature. The vegetative processes can be influenced only indirectly; e.g., growth by regulating the intake of food, or heartbeat by controlling physical or emotional stimuli. Sensory and rational cognitive powers naturally tend to their acts, but I can decide to look or not to look, to think of this or of that. This voluntary attention becomes the key to what control we have over the sense appetites, which are quite spontaneous, as we saw when discussing emotion. I cannot control the fact that a certain object evokes desire, but I can usually conjure up other images, or direct my attention to opposing motives and thereby dominate its attraction.

Lastly, over voluntary musculature I normally have direct control, so that I can move my hand at will. This seems to be accomplished largely by the will's control over the imagination, wherein my decision is translated into motor images which being sensory have a neurologi-

---

[4] Orne (1962) and Milgram (1964) stress this in discussing the social and ethical implications of psychological experimentation.

cal basis, apparently in the motor centers of the cerebral cortex. (See the section on neurology in the next chapter, p. 184.)

Action of other powers on will   Since the nature of the will as an appetite means that it can be influenced only through final causality (motive), there is no question of any efficient cause (except God) moving the will. The question is whether other powers can influence the will through motivation, and how.

The influence of the intellect is plainly paramount. But since the rational intellect is so intimately bound up with sensory knowledge, it is not surprising that imagination and the other senses can thus indirectly affect the will by vivid presentation of attractive goods. Moreover, we stressed in Chapter 5 how subjective factors can distort or enhance perception and imagination. Drive and emotion can shift our attention to other aspects of a situation, as when hunger causes one to consider only the desirability of stealing, or pride gives us a false picture of our own importance as a motive. Since intellect originally sees the situation as a mixture of conflicting aspects, a person can usually determine whether or not he has allowed emotion so to channel his thought, which is why we speak of a man *yielding* to temptation.

S-R FORMULA IS ANALOGOUS

The dictum of some psychologists that "all behavior is a matter of stimulus and response" is perfectly acceptable to the philosopher who is accustomed to thinking in analogy. The stimulus-response formula can include many different kinds of stimuli and hence a corresponding number of different responses. Beyond the tap of a rubber hammer on the patellar tendon giving a simple reflex, the stimulus can be anything from a sensory awareness eliciting a sense drive up to a sublime ideal or principle apprehended in the intellect and eliciting a response such as choice.

Throughout this range of variety in response runs the basic principle that these activities do not "just happen" but are always the result of some cause. But cause is an analogous term. Let us survey briefly the different kinds of causality involved here. Perhaps it is not too foreign to the mind of Teilhard de Chardin to suggest that in man we can discover recapitulation of the entire phylogeny, an epitome of the continuity which he saw in an ascending scale throughout the entire universe.

Ordered operation supposes a goal; goals suggest ontological good, that which has value in itself and is perfective of that which seeks it. Therefore operation in some way involves tendency toward the good. The perfection of this tending will be measured by the value or excellence of the good itself and the perfection of the manner in which it is sought. The most imperfect kind of seeking is that in which there is no awareness on the part of the seeker, and the highest is that in which there is fullest knowledge of the excellence of the good in itself as well as of its perfectiveness to the seeker. Thus we have in nature a hierarchy of tendencies with their corresponding objects or goods.

The appetition which we have been considering is sometimes called elicited, to distinguish it from what philosophers call natural appetite. If I let go of this piece of chalk, it "tends" toward the center of the earth; but no one would imagine that this tending is the result of any knowledge or conscious desire on the part of the chalk. Its tending toward the center of the earth is called natural appetition, by an analogous use of the term. Chemical affinity, magnetism, the natural tendency of the eye to see or the stomach to digest, are called natural appetites because these inclinations are not elicited or evoked by any knowledge. Much of what falls under the psychological term "need" is a matter of natural appetite. With all due respect to Teilhard, most of us find little evidence for his assumption of an infinitesimal degree of consciousness below the animal level (except of course the potency of matter to become animal). The atom has its chemical affinities and the plant its thermotropisms and selective osmosis. To say that a plant "loves" water is a very broad analogy, because it is hardly aware that water is good for it, much less aware of the excellence of water in itself.

The more perfect form of tending is that in which the seeker is aware of the object, and experiences a conscious tendency, such as happens in sensory appetition. At this level man and the other animals may be aware of the object and *that* it is good, but the precise reason *why* it is good is not recognized. Highest on the scale is conation, or volition, in which the knower is not only aware of the object but intellectually aware of its goodness and why it is perfective of the seeker.

As we ascend this scale of tendential forces in nature, we see an increasing disproportion between stimulus and response. At the lowest level of physical causality, there is a direct proportion between the efficient cause exerted and the magnitude of the effect. In the realm of living things we see that at the vegetative or physiological level a very slight stimulus can produce a remarkably powerful and complex effect, as in the case of fertilization or reflex response to a stimulus. Ascending still higher on the scale, we see that there is an even greater disparity between the external stimulus and the end result, still more being due to the activity of the organism. Thus, the slightest menacing gesture on the part of the postman or even his mere appearance may throw the watchdog who has been kicked by him into violent defensive reaction. Still higher is the case in which the simple word or sentence may set in motion the whole machinery of human warfare, and lastly there is the instance where the activity seems initiated entirely within the man himself or at least is under his control.

These facts have led some investigators to worry about whether there is some violation of the law of cause and effect in higher human activity. Actually, there is no question of this but simply of a shift in proportion between the causality exercised by the stimulus and that exercised by the responding organism. Moreover, such activity involves not only greater efficient causality on the part of the agent rather than the stimulus, but also and especially a higher degree of participation by him in the final causality involved. We have seen that the nature of knowledge is such that it makes the knower capable of possessing the object known somehow within himself; this makes it possible for the goodness or perfectiveness of the object to exercise a higher degree of final causality. There is no violation of the principle of causality, but simply a shift from outside forces to the agent himself.

REVIEW QUESTIONS

1. Distinguish between knowing and dynamic activities, giving examples.
2. V. Frankl says that lack of meaning in life can cause neurosis. Is this the same as having no value system? i.e., can one have a set of values and have life still lack meaning for him?
3. At the turn of the century scientific psychology tended to reject teleology. We have noted that recently this rejection has been withdrawn. What reasons can you give for this?
4. *a.* Why is the notion of an unmotivated volition absurd?
    b. Does this mean that we are always aware of the specific motive for our actions?
5. Distinguish several different meanings of the word motive.
6. "All man's activity is a matter of stimulus and response." List at least four different kinds of response and their corresponding stimuli which this statement must include to be true.
7. How do you know that you have a will? Is it a "thing"?
8. Is a commanded act voluntary? Is it a volition?
9. Is every volition a choice?
10. In cognition, we find cooperation between the sensory and intellectual levels; is this always true in appetition?
11. Is man the only irrational animal? Explain.
12. "Harry was so drunk he didn't know what he was doing, so he was not responsible." Was he? Why? Was he free? Can one be responsible for an act even though not free at the time? How?

13. "I just can't help disliking spinach; it nauseates me, in spite of myself. Obviously I have no free choice about it." Discuss.

FOR FURTHER READING

Kelly & Tallon: the chapter from **Schopenhauer,** and the selections from **Teilhard de Chardin** on pp. 140–144, and from **Luijpen** on pp. 271–173 and 281–291.

Freidrich Nietzsche fathered much of modern thought on motivation with his concepts of Will to Power and of the Superman, influencing such diverse thinkers as Alfred Adler of Vienna and Adolf Hitler. Among his most famous works is *Thus Spake Zarathustra.*

Vernon J. Bourke's critical *Will in Western Thought* shows how will has been differently understood over the centuries. **Charles DeKonninck's** *The Hollow Universe* and **Bernard Wuellner,** S.J., in *A Christian Philosophy of Life* explore widely in human values. **Etienne Gilson,** in chaps. 6, 14, and 15 of *The Spirit of Medieval Philosophy,* writes beautifully on the dynamic relation of man to his world.

Teilhard de Chardin, in *The Future of Man* and *The Divine Milieu,* opens up vistas of man's potentiality, also discussed by **Frank T. Severin** in, "The Humanistic Psychology of Teilhard de Chardin" (pp. 151–158 of *Challenges of Humanistic Psychology,* edited by **J. F. T. Bugental**), and, "Teilhard's Methodology for the Study of Cosmic Psychology," *Catholic Psychol. Record,* 1967, 5:1–7.

Psychologists of course devote much space to motivation. **Rollo May,** in *Existence: A New Dimension in Psychiatry and Psychology,* has collected representative thought connecting the existentialist movement to psychotherapy. The two works in English of **Johannes Lindworsky,** S.J., show a great experimental psychologist at work applying his results to practical living: *The Training of the Will* and *The Psychology of Asceticism.* Again one regrets that volumes 3 and 4 of *Le Gouvernement de soi-même* by **Antonin Eymieu,** S.J., have not been translated: *L'Art de vouloir* and *La Loi de la vie.* The annual *Nebraska Symposium on Motivation* (Lincoln, Nebr.: University of Nebraska Press) is a handy source of current psychological thinking, as are the writings of **A. H. Maslow, Joseph Nuttin, David C. Mc-Clelland,** and **T. V. Moore** (see pp. 231–250 of Moore's *The Driving Forces of Human Nature and Their Adjustment*).

11 SELF-DETERMINATION AND ITS LIMITS

Those who maintain a deterministic theory of mental activities must do so as the outcome of their study of the mind itself and not with the idea that they are thereby making it more conformable with our experimental knowledge of the laws of inorganic nature. Eddington

Is man the hopeless and helpless victim of forces that surround him? The tail wagged by heredity, or the mirror of environment? This problem is one of the most crucial in all philosophy. Either man is to some extent the master of his own destiny, or he is a mere chip being tossed about on life's ocean. Either he is a responsible agent with the corresponding rights and duties, or our entire system of law must be reexamined. Because it is the crucial question with regard to the determinants of human behavior, it is of paramount interest to philosopher, psychologist, sociologist, and political theorist. Perhaps here more than on any other question the interests of philosophy and psychology overlap.

THREE VIEWS

Because one finds some psychologists stating flatly that there is no such "thing" as "free will" while other psychologists speak quite frankly of free choice and self-determination, one suspects immediately that the issue may be clouded by unfortunate historical developments and lack of agreement on the meaning of terms. We must be careful to dissect out the true issue and get at facts rather than mere words. Scholastic philosophers were probably overly suspicious of the new science of psychology and its talk of stimulus-response and unconscious motivation. Scientific psychologists were equally suspicious of talk about independence of motives and freedom from the laws of physical causality. Perhaps we can set the stage for an intelligent evaluation of the problem by first considering two extreme theoretical positions.

Exaggerated indeterminism

Perhaps the worst enemies of free choice are those who insist too much on it—not the determinists but the exaggerated indeterminists, the adherents of the theory of unmotivated behavior. Though they would deny it formally, there have been men who talked as if they held that *all* men's actions are free, ignoring the fact that in one's ordinary waking day one may be carried along for some time by the force of habit, organic drives, natural preference, sensory attraction, and other determinants, without making an act of choice every minute.

Again, there are those who seem to hold that at least in those deliberate acts which are free, *all* the motives are known to us. Now even in these acts, a certain portion of the motives are unknown to us, though we may be vaguely conscious of the influence they exert. We are not always so free as we think. This is not entirely the discovery of modern depth psychology. The Fathers of the Desert and medieval writers on asceticism certainly acknowledged the powerful pull which subconscious motivation and the lower appetites can have on the will, and were amazingly aware of the subtleties of compensation and rationalization. Tanquerey (n. 781) speaks of "a sort of psychological determinism." Ignoring such facts, the exaggerated indeterminists were unable to defend free choice intelligently. To exaggerate the extent of our liberty is to make the doctrine untenable. It is to wield the battle-ax so strenuously that one cuts his own throat.

Moreover, we have already seen that in some senses the will is naturally determined. Its nature is to tend toward the good in general, and it cannot be indifferent with regard to goodness itself. When we are presented with a good simply, without any alternatives (even the alternative of rejecting it), we have no choice, and are not responsible.

The term "free will" has unfortunately come to mean this exaggerated indeterminism in the minds of many writers. They rightly criticize the tendency to ignore the important influence of factors which limit freedom: emotion, habit, the natural preference which comes from spontaneous likes and dislikes, external stimuli, organic drives, and physiological conditions.

Another misconception which might be listed under this heading is that which makes the will out to be some supernatural force. Thus, we read in a discussion of the determinants of human behavior the misleading aside that "some believe in a causal sequence with an intervening supernatural power." The question here is whether choice making is a natural ability of man, whether a naturalistic conception is possible in which these acts are as much a matter of observation as any other psychological phenomena. Any appeal to an intervening supernatural power takes us outside the realm of both philosophy and science. Even though one's philosophy may leave open the possibility of the supernatural, we are concerned here precisely with the nature of man as revealed by analysis of his operations and abilities.

Lastly and most important, "free will" symbolizes to many the doctrine of unmotivated and therefore uncaused behavior. This misinterpretation is illustrated, for instance, by the insistence that "psychological events have a cause. This statement may be made for all the sciences. It is called universal determinism.... Freedom of action in the sense of causelessness is an empty concept.... Uncaused action is a notion of the unthinking man.... There are as many varieties of beliefs in uncaused action as there are pickles. All are unscientific.... Every event has a cause."[1] Freud advocates a universal psychic determinism whose theme is that nothing "just happens" without a cause (e.g., 1901, p. 254).

A professional psychologist, testifying in a United States district court, was reported as making the statement, "Free will is an arbitrary sudden explosion *without cause*" (*Amer. Psychologist*, 1964, p. 843, italics mine). A survey on free will in the light of experimental psychology and modern science is summed up by R. Piret:[2]

> *From a general review of experimental works on the will, the author*
> *concludes that there is such a thing as physical freedom and moral*
> *liberty (freedom of low instincts and inferior tendencies), also*
> *psychological freedom (freedom of choice conditioned by motives*
> *and drives); but there is no metaphysical liberty or free will, that is to*

[1] Douglas Fryer & Edwin Henry, *An Outline of General Psychology*, 3d ed. (New York: Barnes & Noble, 1950), p. 10.
[2] N. Braunshausen, "Le Libre-arbitre à la lumière de la psychologie expérimentale et de la science moderne," *Rev. sci. pédag.*, 1947, 9:38–46 (*Psychol. Abstr.*, 1950, 24:1032). E. Hartmann (1966, p. 521) makes free will "an exception to the laws of nature implying that certain actions are initiated *ex nihilo*. . . ."

say choice independent of motives and drives. Will is, therefore, not independent of all causality. It is determinism that is right.

The inference in the last two sentences will be examined shortly.

If we are to understand why some psychologists object so strongly to the word "will," it is important to realize that for some it has come to have this meaning of a magic, supernatural "thing" contrary to the laws of causality. Otherwise it would seem ridiculous, for instance, that Boring, Langfeld, and Weld (1948, p. 50) can spend pages describing human activity involving choice, decisions, and self-determination, and end with the statement that "there is a 'willing' but not a 'will.' " They do not mean to imply that man performs certain activities but does not have the power of doing so.

Early experimenters asked the subject to choose between two colored liquids "for no reason." It is no wonder that D. O. Hebb states (1958, p. 63) that "free will for many workers meant that voluntary behavior was not subject to scientific law, not determined by cause and effect." Now it is preposterous to imagine that scholastic philosophers, who have been the principal systematic proponents of the doctrine of free choice, could have held action without cause or motive as a legitimate meaning of free will. If for no other reason, they could hardly deny the principle of causality here when they based their whole case for the existence of God upon it. One will look in vain for any assertion of uncaused activity among the scholastics.[3] There is some question about Leibniz.

It even seems doubtful if any respectable proponent of free choice actually held for action without motive. We have already seen that the very nature of the will demands motive as a necessary condition for its operation. This motive is a final cause, and the will itself is not some mysterious entity but simply the ability or power man has to exercise efficient causality in response to such motivation. Thus, rather than a lack of causality, there is an abundance of it in the act of choice.

Determinism

Determinism, too, is an ambiguous word. As opposed to the above-mentioned doctrine of uncaused behavior, determinism may mean simply the assertion that every event has a cause. With this interpreta-

---

[3] D. O. Hebb, in a personal communication to the author, states that in the passage cited he "had in mind members of the English neurological school, who seem never to have recovered from the philosophy of the nineteenth century." These can hardly be considered representative exponents of the doctrine of free choice.

tion few would quarrel. The validity of the principle of causality is established elsewhere. Even those scientists whose positivistic philosophy might lead them to consider causality a mere assumption do in actual practice base their scientific logic at least reductively on causality. Every activity of a creature demands a cause, either inside or outside himself. On this most philosophers and scientists agree. Unfortunately confusion here has sometimes allowed the word determinism to mean "lawful" or "predictable" or even "intelligible."

Determinism, however, usually means a denial that man has the power of self-determination or free choice. It means that all of his activity is determined by forces either outside or within himself over which he has no control. In brief, it holds not only that all human behavior requires an adequate cause but that every cause is a necessitating cause. According to this view, motives do not merely attract, they determine. It is not I who determine whether or not I yield to the attraction of this or that motive. Motivating forces not only influence us, they force us. Determinism denies that I (the ego or self) may be the efficient cause which selects or determines whether or not I yield to the attraction of this or that motive. Determinism takes several different forms.

1. *Physical determinism.* The first type of determinism claims that the only cause for activity is a physical stimulus evoking a physical and automatic response. This notion appears in certain mechanistic philosophies and in the reflexology of early behaviorism, with its simple S-R formula. This would reduce psychology to physics or physiology.

2. *Psychological determinism.* Psychologists have long recognized that except in the case of the simple reflex there are "intervening variables" between stimulus and response. Hence the formula S-O-R, where O stands for something within the organism besides the stimulus which must be taken into account to explain a response. Psychic determinism says these intervening variables (images, thoughts, feelings, dispositions, and habits) wholly determine the course of our action. According to this theory, if one knew all the previous and present mental states, conscious and unconscious influences, one could predict with infallible certainty any behavior. One form of psychic determinism says that behavior is totally determined by motor images. Another form stresses unconscious motivating factors. According to this, we have the illusion of freedom but we are actually determined by forces of which we are unaware. Lastly, the most subtle form of psychic determinism is that which asserts that man always chooses what appears to be the greater good. This is ambiguous, for it may

be simply another way of saying that the object of the will is good; we would never choose anything precisely because it is non-good or less good. The real question is not whether this appears to be a greater good, but whether it is a necessitating good. Otherwise the theory is simply a reassertion of the primacy of motives in volition, a commonplace in all theory of training, education, and psychotherapy.

3. *Environmental determinism* is a combination of these first two types. It explains all behavior as conditioned responses, not in the old behavioristic reflex sense but according to the principles of operant conditioning whereby our social environment by selective reinforcement wholly determines how we react.

4. *Theological determinism.* This view holds that God's cooperation determines the will-act.

Moderate indeterminism or limited self-determination

Faced with the dilemma of having only exaggerated indeterminism and determinism as alternatives, which side would one take? This seems to have been the situation for the psychologist of the early twentieth century. Knowing no third possibility, and rightly insisting on the necessity of a cause for every act, rejection of exaggerated indeterminism and acceptance of determinism seemed to be the only course holding scientific respectability. Unfortunately, this position not only missed the possibility of a third alternative in this false dilemma, but erroneously equated the first alternative with free will. And if there is no alternative, "It is determinism that is right."

The third theory is called moderate indeterminism to distinguish it from the other two possibilities. It is called the doctrine of free choice rather than free will, since it is the act of choice which is free; still better, *man* is free in his act of choice. It is called self-determination because, in contrast to the theory of uncaused act, it insists that the self is a true cause, while in contrast to the determinists, it insists that under proper conditions man determines his own choice rather than being determined wholly by other internal or external influences.

Moderate indeterminism recognizes the influence of motives, but they do not always determine. There must be adequate motive, but not every sufficient cause is a necessitating cause. I am the cause which determines which motive shall prevail. The question is not whether motives attract, or whether one motive is greater or weaker than another, but whether the motive necessitates me. In other words, do I have to do something just because I have sufficient reason for doing it? Recognizing the importance of both heredity and environment, moderate indeterminism holds that we can still determine to some extent what we do with heredity and how we react to environment. The adequate cause of human behavior must include the entire phenomenological field of the behaving organism, including the agent himself.[4]

Thus the dilemma of having to choose one or the other of the first two doctrines proposed above turns out to be false; there is this third alternative. We shall see later that this view is being adopted more and more by recent psychologists, as well stated by Combs and Snygg:

> *This gives us a view of man neither so completely responsible for his behavior as the first view we have cited above, nor on the other hand so willy-nilly at the mercy of his environment as the second would lead us to believe. He is part controlled by and in part controlling of his destiny. It provides us with an understanding of man deeply and intimately affected by his environment but capable also of molding and shaping his destiny in important ways. Such a view fits more closely our own experience and is an understanding broadly significant in helping us find solutions to some of our great social problems (1959, p. 310).*

In summary, moderate indeterminism states that we must have an adequate cause, both final (motive) and efficient (ability to choose). It states that choice is always limited by the limitations of our knowledge, because of the need for motivation. The execution of choice is always limited by the laws of physics. Having cleared the ground of misunderstandings, we are now in a position to state the meaning of free choice and examine the arguments for and against it.

NATURE AND KINDS OF FREEDOM

Necessity

Freedom is the opposite of necessity. *Necessity* means that a being must be what it is and cannot be otherwise. Necessity is sometimes divided into antecedent and consequent. Consequent necessity is really just another way of saying that you cannot turn time backwards, or a restatement of the principle of noncontradiction. Once I have chosen, it is necessarily true as an historical fact that I have chosen. I may change my mind, but this is another choice, and does not alter the fact that the previous choice was made. This need not concern us here. Antecedent necessity is what must be eliminated if we are to establish freedom of choice.

[4] C. M. Louttit, *Psychol. Bull.*, 1950, 47:170–171.

Antecedent or predetermining necessity is subdivided into extrinsic and intrinsic. *Extrinsic* necessity, or coercion, is that imposed by an efficient cause. For instance, if the hammer drives the nail with sufficient force, it necessarily goes into the wood. Antecedent extrinsic necessity, or coercion, is the opposite of spontaneity. An action is spontaneous if it flows from the agent without being forced by an external efficient cause or constrained by external forces. The growth of organisms and the movement of animals illustrate this spontaneity, which is freedom only in an improper sense.

Instrinsic antecedent necessity means that something in the internal nature of a thing makes it act one way rather than another. This necessity may be metaphysical or absolute, as that a triangle must necessarily have three sides, or it may be physical or relative, as that acorns produce oak trees and not pine trees. Again, the mere lack of intrinsic necessity is not freedom in the full sense, but only contingence or passive possibility, since these terms do not exclude extrinsic necessity. Movement of subatomic particles or falling bodies may be contingent, but it is not free of extrinsic determination. Mere passive possibility is again freedom only improperly, as when we say that the billiard ball is free to move either right or left. What we mean is that it is free to *be* moved, and this is a far cry from the active power of self-determination. It implies lack of act. The difference might be summed up by saying that it is a matter of "not able to do" rather than "able not to do."

Freedom

Freedom of choice   Freedom in the proper sense means a lack of both extrinsic and intrinsic antecedent necessity. It means first that will enjoys the spontaneity of any elicited appetite, which cannot be coerced against its inclination by any external efficient cause. This does not mean that the will-act lacks cause, but simply that the will as an active operative power is the efficient cause of the act. As such, it is the property of a being in act, since whatever moves is moved by something in act. It is not a mere passive possibility for being moved.

Freedom of choice also means lack of intrinsic necessity. Besides not being subject to external coercion, in the act of choice the will is not necessitated by anything within itself. This is the opposite of psychological determinism. It means that choice is based upon indifferent motives, goods apprehended as adequate but nonnecessary final causes for action. Here again freedom does not consist in a lack of motives, but in a lack of necessity. It does not mean lack of influences, but only that these influences do not force me.

But we must be careful not to define freedom only in a negative fashion, as if it were merely a lack of something. Free choice is self-in-action, a positive force rather than a mere absence of forces. Rather than lack of determination, it is self-determination. It is a positive power of selection between influences rather than the absence of all influences. Putting it metaphysically, freedom is the property of a being *in act*. Since whatever moves must be moved by something in act, self-determination demands that the self be in act to the extent that it determines its own conduct.

This is all-important because a common objection against free choice is based on the fact that we are not always aware of all of the in-fluences at work upon us at a given time. The implication is that if we knew this or that unconscious or organic motivating factor, our conduct would be explainable by that cause and free choice would be negated. Actually, free choice means conscious self-determination along with unconscious determinants, not in their absence. The question is not whether there may be influence of unconscious motives, childhood experiences long since forgotten, social conditioning, habit, organic factors, etc.,[5] but whether such influence is always *necessitating*. In other words, whether there is not merely evidence for their existence, but also evidence against the activity of the person as agent. (See pp. 175–177 on unconscious motivation.)

Freedom of choice, then, means self-determination in act, that I myself have dominion over my own choice. This means that when confronted with a good seen as contingent or indifferent, and all other necessary conditions for action are fulfilled, I can determine whether or not I yield to the attraction of this motive. I am not determined by intrinsic or extrinsic necessity. (The expression "I am determined" is ambiguous, since it can mean either that I am necessitated by certain influences or that I have chosen firmly and intend to carry through.)

Other kinds of freedom Freedom of choice, or psychological free-dom, as just defined must be clearly distinguished from other kinds of freedom which are not the issue. (1) Physical freedom would mean immunity from the laws of physics. In the execution of his commanded voluntary act, man is obviously not free in this sense, as in the case of the 300-pound weight. A man bound in iron chains is not free to move about. (2) Moral freedom would mean that man was not under the obligation of moral law. Freedom of choice is neatly distinguished from this concept by the phrase, "I can, but I may not." (3) Political or social freedom refers to conditions within the framework of society in

[5] Largely ignored by the followers of exaggerated indeterminism.

which we can exercise our human rights such as free speech, conscience, or property ownership.

Lastly, freedom of choice must be distinguished from unlimited alternatives. If I am free to choose to go to Chicago or not, I may choose to go by bus, plane, or train. But if there is only one way to get to Chicago, I have no freedom between alternative means. Here choice of the end is necessarily bound up with this unique means, which I can reject by rejecting the end. It is irrelevant whether or not I am correct in seeing this as the only means: it is clear that I can only choose between known alternatives, so that the extent of my choice depends on my actual thinking, regardless of its correctness. The question is not whether man makes choices sometimes out of stupidity or limited knowledge, but whether he makes them at all.

The choice of specifying between moral good and evil is by no means essential to the notion of freedom; our examples have not involved moral choices. It is even a defect of freedom, or at least an imperfect freedom. Better than none at all, it puts man at the top of the visible universe, but places him at the lowest level of will, just as his rational intellect is lowest among intellects. Far from being the essence of freedom, to be faced with the need to choose between good and sin is an unfortunate consequence of our present condition, in which we are not free from the attractions of false goods and the danger of inordinate factors swaying our judgment. True freedom means self-determination and mastery of one's acts, whereas this freedom always involves the possibility of acting contrary to reason and yielding to the attraction of false goods. (God, and those souls and angels who enjoy the beatific vision, theologians tell us, are free from this dangerous kind of freedom.)[6]

Limits of freedom

Moderate indeterminism does not claim that man is free in all his acts, nor fully free even in his choices. We have already had occasion to note the limitations on free choice which arise from biochemical factors such as hormones and other organic influences, from ignorance or limited knowledge, error, unconscious childhood influences, and conditioning. Further limitations of free choice will be better understood if we consider four possible situations in which a good is presented by the intellect as an object for the will (see Figure 2).

[6] Jacques Maritain, *Freedom in the Modern World* (New York: Scribner, 1936), develops this thought, at first shocking to the novice philosopher with limited ideas of freedom.

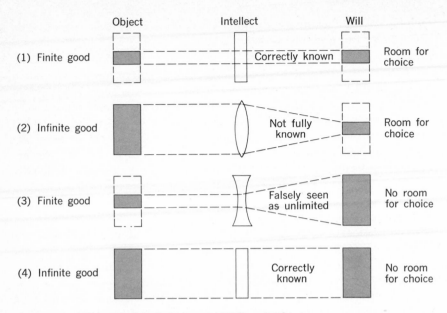

Figure 2 *Four Possible Relations of Will and Object*

1. If any finite or limited good is presented by the intellect to the will correctly, this good obviously does not occupy the entire scope of the will, whose capacity extends to the universal good or good in general. Just as the object of the intellect is being as knowable, and the intellect is not limited to any particular truth, so the will has as its object being as desirable, and is not limited to any particular good. Nothing less than an infinite good can fill the entire horizon, so to speak, of will-activity. Any other good always has an aspect of nongood which leaves open the possibility that the will may divert the attention of the intellect to some other good, or at least to the possibility that there are other goods and hence that this particular one is not necessary. Psychologists describe this as the approach-avoidance situation (to which the others are reducible), where it is seen that neither alternative is necessitating (K. Lewin). Therefore the presentation of any particular good by the intellect always leaves room in the will for choice, for the intellect can always advert to the limitations of this good and consider the possibility of not choosing it. The function of the intellect is to discern truth; if one sees some finite good as unlimited in goodness and in no way rejectable, the intellect is not telling the truth about that object.

2. The second possibility is when Goodness Itself is known, but in the indirect and imperfect way which we have described as natural

for the rational intellect which must operate through sense. I may know *that* God is infinitely good, but in this life I do not see him *as* infinitely good. God as known in this life does not fill the whole horizon and leaves open the possibility of diverting our attention to some good incompatible with His friendship. This makes a choice possible and explains how sin can happen.

Sin is possible ultimately because the created intellect is objectively infinite, subjectively finite: capable of knowing God, but incapable (unaided by a supernatural gift) of knowing Him adequately. Without the objective capacity, there would be no sin but only ignorance or error; without the subjective limitations, we would not be left open to choices contrary to our best knowledge. Sin is an act of the whole man, not just of his will. The words "Ye shall be as Gods" and the name of Lucifer's conqueror Michael (which means "Who is like to God?") suggest that the sins of the angels and our first parents were due to their ability to conceive and therefore "become" God (intentionally). The angels sinned before they had the beatific vision.

3. A third possibility is that some finite good may be falsely seen by the intellect as unlimited, and hence filling the entire scope of the will. This would leave no room for choice. If something so distorts the picture that I cannot conceive of this good as rejectable in any way, and cannot even consider the possibility of rejecting it, I am not free. This could happen when the intellect is clouded by strong emotion, sleep, alcohol or other drugs, certain mental disorders, brain injury, or perhaps sheer distraction or inadvertence. In any of these cases (though not always, e.g., not in every strong emotion) it may be that there are not two alternatives. The object is seen as unqualified good, with no room for any other consideration. In such a case there is no free choice.

It is obvious, however, that the intellect here is not functioning in accordance with its nature, which is to tell the truth about this object and present it to the will as finite, limited, and therefore rejectable. The will is not free because the intellect is impeded from doing its job. No deliberation between alternatives is possible, or at least freedom is diminished to the extent that such deliberation is impeded.

4. Lastly, we have the case of the beatific vision, in which the theologians tell us that the infinite goodness of God is known directly and intuitively as infinite. Here again there is no choice, for the scope of the will is completely occupied by the infinite object which fills its entire range. It cannot direct the attention of the intellect to any aspect of nongood. Freedom is the power of choosing between *eligible* goods: in the beatific vision one still has this power, but God is seen in such a way that nothing incompatible with His friendship is seen as

an eligible good. Sin is impossible to such beings, not because they lack self-mastery, but because they know too much. Put technically, all this means that we have freedom with regard to contingent means toward an end, but not with regard to happiness or the perfect good. Toward the latter I have freedom only as long as I can abstain from considering it and consequently cease to will it.

Deliberation

From this it is clear that deliberation is a necessary prelude to choice. In the first presentation of any object to the will as good, before there is any question of whether or not it is limited and therefore rejectable, the natural and spontaneous inclination of the will is toward that good. But as a matter of fact we do not always choose everything which occurs to us. Normally, we can consider the possibility of an alternative, at least the alternative of rejecting it. In the third case given above, where various factors eliminated this possibility, it was because the intellect was not functioning properly. Hence a drug which "destroys free choice" really only eliminates the necessary condition for the exercise of choice, by interfering with the intellect's ability to consider alternatives.

The process may become extremely complex and involved, or on the other hand may not explicitly take even the complete form we have depicted in our analysis. Deliberation may demand in some instances no more than intuitive judgment, with implicit alternatives.

Speculative and practical judgments   We must distinguish between judgments in the speculative order, where the intellect can sometimes achieve necessary truth, and practical judgments about a particular action. Once I understand that two plus two equal four, or that murder is wrong, I cannot judge otherwise. The intellect is forced by the evidence of the truth. But this is speculative; in the practical order, my intellect can never tell me that it is necessarily true that I must *say* two plus two equal four at this time, nor that I cannot murder this man. As long as I can see some aspect of goodness in the act, I can choose to say that two plus two equal five, or commit murder. The truth of the speculative judgments may be necessary, but when I get right down to the last practical judgment of what I am going to do here and now, the intellect can see alternative aspects of goodness and hence can only judge that this course of action is good but not necessary. ("Practical" here does not refer to practicality or feasibility, but merely to consent or the decision to put an idea into practice.) I see the murder as morally bad, and at the same time as a useful or pleasurable good. Both judgments are true, neither necessitates the will to act. My decision to murder does not make it morally good, but only that-good-which-I-choose.

Roles of intellect and will

Choice is seen as an activity of *man,* utilizing the powers both of intellect and will. Freedom resides formally in the act of choice, but we have seen that its foundation is in the unlimited scope of the intellect.[7] When functioning in accordance with its nature, it presents indifferent practical judgments which leave the will undetermined, and free to determine selectively which motive shall prevail.

The intellect is not free, but necessarily knows what it knows. If it knows correctly, it knows the truth about finite goods. If an object is good, it is choosable; if it is finite, it is nonnecessary and rejectable. If the intellect sees the situation as it is, it is not free to judge otherwise, but its judgment leaves the will free.

In any case, the mutually complementary roles of intellect and will escape the charge of mutual causality sometimes brought: "The intellect causes the will to act and the will causes the intellect, so there is a vicious circle." The answer lies in the different kinds of causality exerted. It is true that the intellect causes the will to move by presenting motives or eligible goods. This is the realm of final causality. On the other hand, when these eligible goods are not seen as necessary, the will determines the intellect to the ultimate practical judgment that this one is to be chosen. This is the realm of efficient causality. The will directs the intellect, so to speak, to focus upon this aspect of goodness rather than that. Two efficient causes mutually causing each other would be a vicious circle; but this is not the present case. That would be as if one cripple said to another cripple, "You carry me and I'll carry you." The present situation could be compared to that in which a blind man says to the cripple, "I'll carry you and you tell me where to go." In this case each is a cause of the action, but in different ways: one providing the motion efficiently, the other supplying the goal or final cause.

The will cannot act until the intellect presents motives, but if it presents conflicting motives it leaves the will free to choose between them. The intellect can judge that "this is good to do," or, "I *could* do this," but with regard to a finite good this judgment is always indifferent or

---

[7] "Beings are free to the extent that, by their intellectuality, they escape from the determinism of matter," is Lottin's conclusion (1929, p. 159). Again we insist that most difficulties in this matter stem from letting our imaginations make intellect and will out to be little persons rather than mere abilities of the same man.

changeable by the will. Put differently, about a particular contingent good I never have absolute certainty, but only opinion. The intellect can never say absolutely, "I *will* do this," regarding any good in this life, for there is always the possibility of doing something else or not acting at all. Yet in these cases man does make a choice. The person by his will actively settles this indifference.

Deliberation is thus a necessary but not sufficient condition for choice. The elements of the deliberation may be the result of previous determining factors, but when the intellect sees no necessity in the alternatives, the deliberation cannot determine the decision.

SELF-DETERMINATION: PRO AND CON

Having cleared the ground of some false issues and gained some understanding of the processes involved, we are now in a position to examine the arguments which are proposed regarding man's ability to determine his own choices. The history of the problem is as old as human thought, and perhaps first appears in discussions over fate. Zeno's slave argued, "Master, according to thy teachings it was determined that I would steal from thee, and thou should not beat me for that for which I am not responsible." Zeno replied, "It is also determined that I will beat thee." Oriental philosophies are often tinged with varying degrees of fatalism, though they usually do not avow rank determinism. In the patristic period and the Middle Ages the question was tied up with the problem of evil, and especially after Calvin with the problem of predestination. Descartes held free choice, but only because the body could not interfere with the soul in this respect—a reason hardly acceptable to modern philosophers and psychologists alike, with their recognition of the unity of man and the importance of organic, animal factors. Locke also thought man free, but one wonders how well this view could be defended on the premises of his sensism. Kant held freedom at least as a postulate of practical reason, but seemed to despair of philosophical proof.

Coming to the modern era, materialists such as B. Russell and positivists such as R. Carnap have presented strong determinist positions. The linguistic analysts, at least of the older school, dissect uses of words like "choose" and "decide" and "free" to the point of explaining away free choice as mere verbal misuse. Most psychoanalysts follow Freud when he states, "I have already taken the liberty of pointing out to you that there is within you a deeply rooted belief in psychic freedom and choice, that this belief is quite unscientific and that it must give ground before the claims of a determinism which governs even mental life" (1916, p. 106). Most psychologists feel uneasy about the question because it seems to disturb their conception of science as able to predict and control.

Some argue that this alleged freedom would be inimical to morality, education, and the purposes of religion since man would be free to disregard all such training. Conversely, some determinists argue that their position is not a denial of moral obligation: the good swimmer is obligated to save the drowing man, even the determinist being called upon to do something here. An amoeba or even a computer seems to make choices; man is just more complex than the amoeba and more emotional than the computer. The apparent freedom we experience is just an illusion; ignorant of the true causes of our behavior, we flatter ourselves that we have some control over nature.

We have noted that the exaggerated indeterminists took the opposite side so strenuously that their position was quite vulnerable to the determinist arguments. The existentialists talk a great deal about freedom, but they irritate the scientifically trained empiricist because they rarely get down to detailed arguments or evidence in support of it. They rather seem just to assume it, and then proceed to examine its implications for man, praise it, even complain about it. They might answer the empiricist that the examination of what is implicit in man's free choices constitutes the best proof, but one wonders if this satisfies him. Some existentialists are inclined to exaggerate freedom and to ignore its limitations.

But overlooking the flamboyancy of expression, what is Sartre trying to express when he says, "Man is freedom"? He surely does not mean to equate the whole of man with free choice. Rather, he seems to be making the point that freedom is the most characteristic feature of man, the aspect which is most distinctive about him, and especially that it is the one fact which gives man value as a person, as opposed to mere things. Many existentialist and humanistic philosophers would agree.

Other contemporary philosophers in their own ways seem to tend in this direction. John Dewey, so deep in the bloodstream of American thinking, shows a recurrent emphasis on self-realization, the human control of fate. William James energetically asserted free choice. Michael Scriven has been giving increasing attention to the problem in recent writings, and will be cited later in this chapter.

Moderate indeterminism has perennially had its proponents, of varied backgrounds. Outside the historical stream of scholasticism —itself composed of quite divergent views, such as those put forth by Plato, Aristotle, Augustine, Aquinas, and Scotus, all of whom held for freedom—many other philosophers and schools have maintained a doctrine of free choice. In this century these include C. E. M. Joad,

Henri Bergson, John Wild, some of the recent "ordinary-language" analysts, physicist-philosophers such as Compton, Eddington, Planck, and M. Polanyi, and those who represent the recent humanistic trend in psychology. An examination of three survey textbooks in philosophy taken at random reveals each devoting considerable space to the question, presenting arguments and citing numerous philosophers.[8]

P. Sorokin[9] of Harvard found that down through the centuries human thinking has dipped into determinism periodically but has always returned to the conviction that man has free choice. From history the environmental determinists would find it hard to explain how man could have been "conditioned" by Western culture to deny freedom—one is tempted to suggest that determinism could arise only because man freely chose to deny that he can freely choose. In contrast to the preoccupation with the abnormal in modern drama, Shakespeare's plays, with their shrewd insight into the subtleties of human emotion and mixed motivations, dramatize consistently the common human persuasion that the normal man is the protagonist on life's stage who ultimately determines his own destiny: "The fault, dear Brutus, is not in our stars but in ourselves, that we are underlings."

From this melange of opinions we select three main areas in which the controversy over free choice has centered, and examine the arguments.

Direct experience

The phenomenologists examine in detail our actual experiences in making a choice, and recent language philosophers analyze our ordinary expressions of this experience. Freedom itself of course is a property and not directly observable; nor is the ability we call will. But the act of choice seems to be as much a matter of phenomenological observation as any other psychological fact. Choices and decisions are as much a part of everyday experience as perceptions, images, or understanding. Whatever metaphysical implications are involved in the

[8] John Hospers, *An Introduction to Philosophical Analysis* (Englewood Cliffs, N.J.: Prentice-Hall, 1953), pp. 262–281. Excellent on the distinction between being caused and being compelled. Harold T. Titus, *Living Issues in Philosophy* (New York: American Book, 1953), pp. 172–189, presents the case for freedom. Philip Wheelwright, *The Way of Philosophy* (New York: Odyssey, 1954), pp. 299–321, gives both sides. Of the many sources noted in the three textbooks, none is scholastic.
[9] *Social and Cultural Dynamics* (New York: American Book, 1937–1941), vol. II, pp. 339–349.

explanation of choice, the fact seems inescapable.[10] The capacity for freedom may be a matter of inference, but the experience of choice is an empirical datum to be observed and analyzed; the only alternative is the theory that this experience is a universal mass illusion, which in turn would be something which would have to be explained.

Before choice, I am conscious of the alternatives before me, and that I see them as nonnecessitating. The whole process of deliberation is nonsense if the decision is already determined. As we saw, deliberation is a necessary but not a necessitating condition for choice. The man or self and the alternatives are caused by previous events, but none of these determine what he will do here and now; that is to be determined by his decision.

During choice, I am conscious that I actively determine the course to be taken. This experience of the actual domination we exercise over the act of choice has been called by psychologists "the active interposition of the ego." Although not open to quantitative measurement, what we experience here is not a mere lack of necessitation or an ignorance of motivating factors, but a positive exertion of influence on the part of the person. This is perhaps the only instance in which we really have direct experience of causality. In other instances causality may seem obvious, as when the hammer strikes a nail, but this is really only inference in comparison with the observation we have of ourselves when we settle an issue between conflicting motives. Recall the Montreal experiment related above where the patient reported the clear opposition between his choice and the movement of his foot under cortical stimulation.

After choice, we experience remorse, self-approval, and other evidences of a sense of responsibility. We are clearly aware of the difference between hitting a person accidentally and deliberately. No matter how sorry we feel over the former, we do not feel responsible or guilty, as we would in the latter instance. We are quite conscious of whether or not the act flowed from a deliberate choice on our part, and this is reflected in such expressions as "I decided," "I made up my mind," "I made a choice," or "I yielded."

Unconscious motivation This phenomenological approach faces its greatest difficulties from the facts which indicate that our conscious experience is not always reliable. We have discussed this controversy at the end of Chapter 2, but must consider the special applicability here

[10] Nicholas Hobbs, "Science and Ethical Behavior," *Amer. Psychologist,* 1959, 5:221–223; P. Mullahy, *Psychiatry,* 1949, 12:379–386.

of the influence of unconscious motives which make consciousness of freedom possibly a mere illusion. The unconscious is a bedrock principle of all psychoanalytic and other theories of abnormal psychology and psychotherapy, and the facts are undeniable. Full of pride in our intellect, we invent rational explanations for many actions which stem from baser motivation. The man who, under the influence of posthypnotic suggestion, picks up a chair and puts it in the middle of the table will explain, when asked why he did so, that he wanted to see something on the floor, and so moved the chair out of the way, being entirely unaware of the unconscious influence under which he acted. Thus it may be that we only think we are acting freely. The argument against free choice based on unconscious motivation arises most often from three sources: depth psychology or psychiatry, hypnosis, and subliminal motivation.

Regarding the first, it might be useful to recall what was said earlier about choice as a positive causing rather than a mere lack of other causes. Establishment of free choice does not depend on the complete enumeration of all causal influences. Even the most astute psychiatrist might be unable to render account of all his likes and dislikes, his habits, organic tensions, memories, and vague desires. Free choice is not a denial that these things exist; it is a positive causal influence in addition. It is not necessary for the normal person to know all the various factors that might be impelling him in order for him to behave himself. I may not know why I feel like hitting the person, but normally I can choose not to hit him. The attraction is there, but I determine whether or not I yield to its influence, regardless of whether I understand it. I may resist the inclination in spite of not knowing its origin, its precise object, or its connection with previous experience. Otherwise the simplest act of self-control would demand a complete psychiatric history.[11]

HYPNOSIS AND SUGGESTION   A vast amount of experimentation with hypnotism over nearly a century has shown that it is a natural phenomenon: unusual, but not very mysterious or even abnormal. It seems to be largely a matter of narrowed attention plus heightened suggestibility, both of which are possible to all men in some degree. Consequently the power of the hypnotist over his subject differs only in degree and circumstance from the power of any persuader, salesman, or seducer. We all have varying degrees of sales resistance, and some are far more able to dominate than others. Does this contradict free choice?

Before hypnosis the subject is usually free to choose whether or not he

[11] Cf. Charles Odier, "Les Deux sources, consciente et inconsciente, de la vie morale," *Cahiers de philosophie,* November, 1943–February, 1947 (Neuchatel: Éditions de la Baconniere).

will consent to it. We say "usually," for the same limitations of free choice which we have laid down earlier apply here. One may be tricked into it without knowing what is involved, or be otherwise unable to deliberate because of distraction or other factors. Here the person cannot choose, because he does not know; it is not the will but his knowledge that is affected.

During the hypnotic state, the person's knowledge is limited to what the hypnotist directs his attention toward. Under hypnosis a person will do many silly or embarrassing things which he would not do otherwise. Deliberation is interfered with and hence the necessary conditions for choice. Acts may be virtually voluntary to the extent that he vaguely foresaw and consented to them when he agreed to undergo hypnosis. Habitual convictions may be strong enough to control important conduct, as shown by the fact that usually the suggestion to do something contrary to his moral principles will shock the subject out of the hypnotic state. For example, in hypnotic experiments using a rubber dagger, an adult will stab someone under the suggestion of hate. Given a real dagger, he will ordinarily wake up (the intended victim is protected by invisible plate glass). But if the person has weak moral convictions and is vulnerable to nonhypnotic persuasion or seduction anyway, he is understandably liable to act on immoral hypnotic suggestion. Similar results have been obtained for posthypnotic suggestion.

After hypnosis, the rationalization with which he defends his obedience to the posthypnotic suggestion indicates that the subject is not aware of what was told him under hypnosis. Knowledge is thus limited and freedom to that extent diminished. For example, the person will act on a given signal after waking, when told that he would forget the instructions and only remember to act on signal, as in the case of the man moving the chair. But as we said about unconscious motivation in general, it normally leaves the person relatively free to resist the influence even without understanding it. He may feel uncomfortable and mystified by these impulses, but usually he can control them. He is in ignorance or error only as to *why* he feels impelled to act, but not about *what* he does. Hence if he has clear convictions about the object of his impulse he may resist it; if it is a nonmoral issue, like moving the chair, the suggestion may cause him to see it only as desirable.

The facts of hypnosis are thus seen to be quite compatible with moderate indeterminism. Although "cures" obtained by it are usually too superficial and transient for it to have much value as therapy, hypnosis is often useful in psychiatric diagnosis, in psychological research, and as anaesthetic. In the hands of a skilled and competent professional man it is quite legitimate. As parlor or vaudeville entertainment, or in the hands of the amateur or less conscientious, it is dangerous and unethical.

SUBLIMINAL MOTIVATION   This is advertising which uses devices to impress the public without their being aware of it, such as flashes so quick as to be below the threshold (limen) of consciousness. "Motivation research" attempts to discover and appeal to the public's unconscious desires. The question here is akin to that of hypnosis. Psychologists dispute the effectiveness of these means, and we incline to agree with Edgar H. Schein of M.I.T. that they leave free choice intact to the same degree as those other "techniques which have always been used implicitly by the competent manipulators, and which the man in the street has always been able to resist by an act of reason—if he chose to do so."[12]

Freedom from internal necessity

Other philosophers reason from the relation between motives and volition. (That the will is not subject to coercion by an external, efficient cause is hardly disputed. The only thing which can move the will to act is a motive, and motive is not an efficient cause. The real problem is the elimination of psychological or internal determinism, whereby the very motives which the intellect presents to the will would necessitate it.) Since human activity is always response to a stimulus, they examine the nature of the stimuli which cognition presents here. In other words, the will is determined only to the extent that the intellect determines it.

Being naturally determined toward the good in general, the first tendency of volition regarding an object seen simply as good without qualification is a spontaneous inclination which is not free. For example, if brain injury or intoxication so limits one's cognitive functioning that he can only consider that this object is good to have, without being able even to consider the possibility of rejecting it, he is obviously not free with regard to it. He has no alternatives.

The question is whether I ordinarily see objects in this way. Finite goods are seen as not good in every respect, and therefore as rejectable. Since the intellect is capable of knowing the universal good, it recognizes any particular good as contingent or nonnecessitating. I may have adequate reason for doing something, but this reason (even God himself as now known) does not tell me that I cannot do otherwise. Therefore I am free to determine whether or not I shall act because of this motive. The judgment, "This is good to do," is not synonymous with the judgment, "I must do it." If all motives were necessitating, two absurd consequences seem to follow. First, I would have to yield to every motive, choose every good that occurs to me, which is hardly in accord with my experience. Secondly, when the two motives are contradictory, I would have to choose both of them, which is impossible.

This indifferent or undetermined judgment regarding elegible goods is sometimes called changeable, but this is misleading. It suggests that the judgment is a determining motive right now, but that upon further information the judgment might change. This theory does not escape

---

[12] "The Id as Salesman," review of Vance Packard's *The Hidden Persuaders* (New York: McKay, 1957), *Contemp. Psychol.*, 1957, 2:308–309.

psychological determinism, for it could be argued that the further information then determines. Rather, right here and now with the information available I know that this good is nonnecessary, and that another alternative is possible. Again, the judgment is not free, since the intellect cannot help but know what it knows. But what it knows in this instance is that this act is choosable but rejectable; therefore the ultimate practical judgment to choose or reject it is determinable by the will. A more subtle complication of this argument is the following.

Greater seeming good always prevails Jonathan Edwards, a colonial American writer, claimed that man is not free because he always chooses what appears to be the greater good. This is ambiguous, and could mean nothing more than that the object of the will is good: we never choose something precisely because it is *less* good. It also emphasizes the importance of motive in choice. But it is a tricky form of psychological determinism when it implies that the greater good determines choice.

The ambiguity is unmasked when we grant that the "greater" good always wins if by that is meant the good contained in the ultimate practical judgment. But just what makes this judgment to be the ultimate? A finite good is seen as contingent or indifferent, be it greater, lesser, or equal to any other good. The will efficiently makes the intellect decide that this is to be chosen. It is irrelevant to freedom whether deliberation compares it to any other good or not: either this good is necessary or it is contingent. The question is not whether it seems greater, but whether I *must* choose it. The burden of the proof is on those who assert such necessity. "Greater" is not synonymous with "necessary."

Suppose I am thirsty, have only one dime, and am confronted with a vending machine which will dispense either a large glass of milk or a small glass of orange juice. Which is greater? Under the aspect of quantity, the milk is. But since I prefer the taste of orange, this becomes the greater good under the aspect of quality. Each aspect is a good falling within the object of the will. Each is plainly superior in its own category. If intellect were restricted to only one aspect of goodness, there would be no choice. But when I see each has objectively greater good, only by active interposition of the will can I make one the greater subjective good by determining which aspect of goodness will prevail. The point is that I am not necessitated by the preferable taste of the orange any more than by the larger quantity of the milk; as a matter of fact, I can put my dime in my pocket and choose to remain thirsty.

The false assumption behind this objection to free choice is that any finite good can somehow of itself become so great as to exclude the possibility of rejecting it. We have seen that certain factors can cause this, but only by eliminating the proper conditions for normal functioning of the intellect. The objection also falsely assumes that the attraction of motives renders choice impossible, or that it can occur only when goods are objectively equal. The facts are all to the contrary, for we act against natural attractions, and choose in spite of rarely, if ever, encountering objectively equal motives. As long as there is an adequate cause (reason) for acting, I can choose it, regardless of whether it is greater, less, or equal. I *make* it seem greater by voluntarily directing my attention to the aspect of good which I choose.

What is this "greater good" which always prevails? There are five possibilities. Is it always sensory good? Then all men are hedonists, and nobody acts for motives which are intellectual, much less noble. Is it always rational good? Then no man yields to his passions, and there is no vice in the world. Is it always habitual inclination? Then no reform and no tragic fall are possible. Is it always natural preference or *indeliberate* inclination? Then no heroes, no asceticism, no responsibility for good or evil. Or is it *deliberate* inclination? Then it is because of choice. Jonathan Edwards's dictum is thus either contrary to the facts or redundant. Actually, we all find ourselves at times acting contrary to sensory attraction, and confess having acted contrary to what we know was rational. We act against our old habits, and against our natural preferences. If the good contained in the ultimate practical judgment seems greater, it is only because "we ourselves by our own wilful act inclined the beam" of judgment, as William James puts it.[13]

Moral and legal obligation

A third argument given by some philosophers is that those who admit moral obligation or legal responsibility must logically hold that man is not completely the victim of determining forces. If a person cannot do otherwise, it is absurd to hold him responsible for what happens. Obligation involves both the possibility of my doing something and the fact that I am not forced to do it. Our entire legal system and administration of justice rest on this foundation. There would be no point in an elaborate trial to ascertain whether or not the alleged murderer was sane unless there was a difference between the normal

[13] *Principles of Psychology* (1896), vol. II, p. 534.

man who can exercise free choice and the person in whom some abnormality prevents this. The same argument holds for the notion of merit and reward. Why praise a man for doing something unless he could have done otherwise?

It is true that criminologists are rightly more concerned with cure than with punishment, and tend to emphasize the various influences which caused him to be the kind of person who would commit a criminal act. But emphasis on rehabilitation does not deny responsibility. After a period of extreme "can't-help-it" theorizing in the 1920s and 1930s, the pendulum has swung back to a middle position among experts on crime and juvenile delinquency, partly because of evidence from the perpetrators themselves, who insist that no person or thing made them do anything they did not choose to do.

Moberly[14] says Christianity agrees with psychology in concern for the subjective factors in crime, in distinguishing guilt feelings from guilt, and in the primacy of treatment over punishment. But if no adults were responsible persons, who would treat or legislate? If we assume that only a few are responsible, then society should be a vast mental hospital, a slave society where the majority were wards (nonresponsible) of the few (responsible). The law must assume that most people are responsible; it can afford to make special cases of the pathological, but they must remain the exception.

It is interesting to note that for centuries only the moralists considered factors which diminish freedom, and therefore guilt. Civil law looked only at the objective act, and took a "guilty-or-not-guilty" attitude. Canon 2196 distinguishes the quality (abnormality) of an act from quantity or degree of guilt. Although progress was gradual in developing the doctrine, the basic idea of diminished imputability was always clear in Christian thinking, and received early and thorough refinement.[15] Civil law is still wrestling with the problem, partly because of the differences of terminology between the legal and psychiatric professions, and the narrowness of the 1843 M'Naghten rule ("know right from wrong and the consequences of his acts"), which set a legal precedent that is only slowly being modified. Meanwhile, psychiatrists frankly state that a person may be quite responsible and free even though there are psychiatric considerations in the case.

The Durham rule of 1954 makes irresponsibility for a criminal act depend on whether it was the product of mental disorder or defect; this ruling was further clarified by the Carter decision in 1957 as meaning that the mental disorder or defect was decisive or critical in bringing about the act. It seemed to have psychiatric advantages but has not been widely accepted by the bar and courts. The biggest problem in all this is that there is no sharp line between the all-white of sanity and the all-black of total irresponsibility. They blend into one another through imperceptible shades of gray between the theoretical extremes.

[14] Sir Walter Moberly, *Responsibility: The Concept in Psychology, in the Law, and in the Christian Faith* (Greenwich, Conn.: Seabury Press, 1956).
[15] Alan Edward McCoy, O.F.M., *Force and Fear in Relation to Delictual Imputability and Penal Responsibility* (Washington: The Catholic University of America Press, 1944). Cf. Boganelli, 1937.

Opponents of this argument from moral and legal responsibility point out that it is only valid against those who admit such an obligation. They claim that the sense of obligation or "ought" is just an illusion, like freedom itself. We are conditioned by society to feel responsible. The debate then shifts to the explanation of this near-universal illusion.

SELF-DETERMINATION AND SCIENCE

Science in its quest for laws finds the notion of free choice difficult to fit into its ordinary framework of thinking. We have already shown at some length that this objection is baseless if it implies lack of causality. We have also noted that the execution of acts commanded by the will is strictly under the laws of physics.

Choice is not contrary to the law of conservation of energy, for it does not create energy but merely directs it in this direction rather than that. The will is inorganic, but whatever energy is needed for the organic activities connected with volition is supplied by the body. An automobile obeys physical laws, but this does not mean that no driver directs its activity. This "law" is now being questioned and called a theory by physicists themselves. But there is really no need at all to discuss a metaphysical problem at the level of physical theory. The will-act is qualitative, and does not change the quantity of matter or energy.

But "man is part of nature, and must follow nature's laws." True, but what is the nature of man? The objection betrays a preconceived assumption as to the nature of the will-act. It is certainly caused, for volition is in the realm of being, and the principle of causality is a law of being. Volition is outside the realm of man's physical being, though not beyond his conscious being. It is not outside man, but if man's nature is partly spiritual then it need not be supernatural. An astronomer would be laughed at who explained the earth's rotation around the sun as due to the earth's "desire" to go around the sun; but to apply this analogy to self-determination as explaining choice behavior is to miss the difference in nature between man and earth.

PREDICTION Some are concerned about the fact that choice introduces a factor which they cannot include in a formula. Others ask whether the desire to predict and control is more basic to science than the desire to understand. The student must decide whether determinism is a conclusion from experimental facts. Granted that "all behavior is a matter of stimulus and response," it remains to be seen whether an experiment could be designed which would demonstrate the impossibility that one type of response is a free choice whose stimulus is the indifferent or nonnecessitating judgment we discussed above.

Heisenberg's principle of indeterminancy or uncertainty showed that physical science itself could not always hope to predict. Failing to distinguish between active indifference and passive contingent possibility, some rashly hailed this as evidence for freedom. Mere lack of predictability is not itself a positive power of self-determination. Variability does not choose. More correctly, Nobel prize-winning physicist A. H. Compton (1935, 1957) pointed out that although this principle indicates chance rather than free self-determination, it at least opened the way to the establishment of free choice by knocking the scientific props from under theoretical opposition to it. Eddington in the passage quoted at the head of this chapter asserts that physics has no objection to free choice. Max Planck (1959, p. 63) says,

> It is a dangerous act of self-delusion if one attempts to get rid of an
> unpleasant moral obligation by claiming that human action is
> the inevitable result of an inexorable law of nature. The human
> being who looks upon his own future as already determined
> by fate . . . only acknowledges a lack of will power to
> struggle and win through.

Compton notes that man can predict his own behavior better than the physicist can predict physical events, and Rogers (1964) showed that inner, subjective events can be more lawful and predictable than external behavior; he got higher correlation coefficients than we often get on rats.

The question then is the kind of lawfulness. Chance is not choice. The path of the falling leaf is unpredictable only because of our ignorance of all the physical forces at work on it, not because it has the power of self-determination; it exerts no positive causal force of its own. M. Scriven (1965, 1966) has rightly insisted that prediction and explanation are not synonyms. Even if we cannot predict with absolute certainty what choice Joe will make, we can explain his choice in terms of quite adequate causal determiners, including unconscious factors, conscious motivation, and his own active self-determination as a part cause. Even if I cannot predict what I shall choose for dinner tonight, that does not mean it is not under my control. I am the cause of the final choice, within the limits of the alternatives. If to choose is a unique type of response with its own behavioral laws, it is equally true that all human behaviors are a different type of response than those of mere physics. Yet prediction is possible even here within the range of statistical probability familiar to social scientists.

Paradoxically, "One may predict and logically systematize compulsive (neurotic) behavior, whereas the mentally healthy man is more spontaneous, free, and creative in his personal behavior—hence, in detail, less predictable or logically organizable. A science of clinical psychology seems more realizable (as to detailed prediction) than a science of the general healthy personality!"[16] Statistical predictability of the normal is actually possible to a high degree of accuracy, in spite of free choice. The reason for this is the fact that human nature is basically the same for everyone, and the same motives are going to appeal in about the same proportion to most people, in spite of the individual differences. These predictions apply to averages, not individuals. They do not *cause* anyone to choose, but simply indicate how many will probably choose because of the same mo-

[16] Carlton W. Berenda, "Is Clinical Psychology a Science?" *Amer. Psychologist,* 1957, 12:725–729. Cf. C. E. Moustakas (Ed.), *The Self* (New York: Harper, 1956).

tives. Psychologists are used to the concept of probable error,[17] and know that the formula for an individual would have to be n-dimensional, a most complex calculus of possibilities.[18]

NEUROLOGY Perhaps the most genuine problem facing science here is to identify the precise manner by which volition is translated into action. We have already seen clear evidence that volition is not neurological, but the bridge between the two is baffling. The world-famous neurologist Sir Charles Sherrington (1940) seems to contradict himself on this point, for in chap. 7 he equates cause with physical cause, then spends much of chaps. 9, 10, and 11 showing that mind is irreducible to physics or biology, that brain and mind are "phenomena of two different categories" (p. 318). Experiments show that will can evoke action in a muscle fatigued by electrical stimuli, while an electrical stimulus can move a muscle fatigued by wilful action. Eddington came closer to the real issue when he utilized the concept of indeterminacy in cortical nerve cells, and Eccles proposes a plausible neurological theory of how volition might influence action when he suggests that minute but not random influences could take advantage of indeterminacy in the cortex, showing how Eddington's worry about the amount of influence was needless if you consider the synaptic knob rather than the whole neuron.[19]

The philosopher is indebted for such details to the scientist. Motor images are sensory, and therefore have a material component proper to animal nature. Being quasi-immaterial, they share with will the realm of psychic reality. Thus the level of sense is the natural intermediary between the spiritual will and nerve action, since it has both psychic and physical components. This is especially significant when we remember that these are not two separate beings, since man is a substantial unit. But the matter remains somewhat mysterious.

The tendency of thought to express itself spontaneously in action has caused some psychologists to mistake muscular contraction in the right forearm for the act of choice itself, just as the subvocal speech movements in the throat were taken for the thought process of which they are the incipient expression. "I choose this one" would quite naturally be accompanied or followed by such infinitesimal arm movement, but this does not prove that the choice and the movement are identical. These hardly perceptible movements sometimes account for the success of the "mind reader" who finds hidden objects in a room, and they also explain the Ouija board, on which people unwittingly betray their thoughts or wishes. Actually, motor images are not the initiators of all action, but they can be the sense-level intermediary between choice and its execution through voluntary muscles.

CONTEMPORARY PSYCHOLOGY Although choice is predominantly a philosophical question, psychologists have always discussed the determinants of behavior and hence have a legitimate interest in the problem. During the first half of the twentieth century, psychology manifested an understandable

[17] Edward G. Boring, *A History of Experimental Psychology* (1950), p. 467, describes McDougall's position on freedom in this way.
[18] Leona B. Tyler, "Toward a Workable Psychology of Individuality," *Amer. Psychologist*, 1959, 14:75–81.
[19] John C. Eccles, *The Neurophysiological Basis of Mind* (Fair Lawn, N.J.: Oxford, 1953), pp. 272–279.

anxiety to be a "grown-up" science and was very defensive in its avoidance of any term which might seem to smack of "uncaused activity," a meaning which had been erroneously attached to the term free will. Moreover, since freedom is a property and a reasoned concept, it is not directly observable. It would seem that freedom, at least in this sense, is beyond the methods of experimental psychology.[20]

But the intervening variables between stimulus and response merited increasing use of such terms as "cortical control" or "ability of man to direct his drives" or "selective inhibition and facilitation" or "choice behavior" or "self-in-action" or the "active interposition of the ego." Finally in 1950 Hadley Cantril of Princeton, then president of the Eastern Psychological Association, came out with an unabashed use of the term "free choice," and claimed that the scientific basis for a code of responsibility lies there. Since then, there has been an ever-increasing chorus of outstanding psychologists advocating the theory of free choice. Gardner Murphy, director of research at the Menninger Foundation, demonstrated how, by exercise of intelligence and conscious choice, man can actually transcend his biological and cultural inheritances and open the way for a free expression of his virtually unlimited potentialities (*Human Potentialities*, 1958). Edwin G. Boring of Harvard satirized the psychologist who would deny it (1954, p. x; 1957, p. 191).

Nondirective and existential therapies threw the responsibility squarely on the patient, implying that he had the power of free choice. When the psychiatrist helps the patient to face reality and understand his motivations, he considers the cooperation of the patient as free, not forced; were it forced, the psychiatrist would still claim that freedom for himself which he denies his patient. D. B. Klein (1951, pp. 142, 143) points out the inconsistency between theory and practice among those who still deny free choice verbally:

> *As a matter of fact, even the staunchest psychiatric advocates of determinism are not hesitant to use the concept of freedom in their professional work. . . .*
> *What is more, even an ultradeterministic psychiatrist wants to be left free to choose the course of action he deems best for his patients, and sees no incongruity in talking about his responsibility for their welfare. In his professional role he wants to be regarded as a free agent capable of making free choices, and willing to assume responsibility for what he prescribes.*

Speaking of the developing child, Stone and Church state that "he develops a species of *self-determination* (it is no longer fashionable to speak of a free will) and becomes able to accept or refuse the choices offered to

---

[20] John W. Stafford, C.S.V., "Freedom in Experimental Psychology," *Proc. Amer. Catholic phil. Ass.*, 1940, 16:148–153; Louis J. A. Mercier, "Freedom of the Will and Psychology," *New Scholasticism*, 1944, 18:252–261; H. Gruender, S.J., *Experimental Psychology*, 1932, p. 434ff. On the other hand, Ach, Michotte, Lindworsky, Prüm, Aveling, McCarthy, Barrett, and others in their laboratory experiments seem to have reached conclusions favoring free choice (cf. Lindworsky, 1929, pp. 32–38; Gannon, 1954, pp. 399–403). At least it is not quantitatively measurable: cf. Raphael C. McCarthy, S.J., *The Measurement of Conation* (Chicago: Loyola University Press, 1926).

him. . . . He becomes, within certain obvious limits, the master of his own destiny." (1957, p. 337. Italics and parentheses theirs.) Experiments receiving favorable review show the superiority of higher values as motives, of conscious ego over unconscious drives (e.g., using hypnosis), and of ego as power able to transform past experience rather than being a mere product of it.[21] Though still a minority, the list could go on: Gordon W. Allport, David Ausubel, Abraham H. Maslow, J. McVicker Hunt. The director of the psychological clinic at Harvard, Robert W. White (1952, pp. 364–365), states well the position of moderate indeterminism in a modern context:

> *Thus far the scientific study of man has unwittingly contributed*
> *to the trend toward apprehension and uncertainty. All three*
> *views of man—the social, the biological, and the psychodynamic—*
> *display that one-sided determinism which selectively views the*
> *person as the hapless product of forces. . . . But equally we*
> *have insisted that some attempt should be made to examine the*
> *gap in the scientific account so that natural growth and the*
> *activity of the person can be put back into the story. . . . precisely*
> *here lie the very facts about human nature that offer man the*
> *hope of influencing his own destiny. . . . Even though he be*
> *a nexus of biological, psychodynamic, social and cultural forces, a*
> *person serves to some extent as a transforming and redistributing*
> *center, responding selectively to create a new synthesis. Under*
> *reasonably favorable circumstances personality tends to continue*
> *its growth, strengthen its individuality, and assert its power to*
> *change the surrounding world.*

The controversy is by no means dead. Volleys from both sides appear in psychological journals (e.g., Chein and Immergluck, 1967). Leon Festinger's theory of cognitive dissonance has inspired a number of experimenters (e.g., Brehm & Cohen, Weick, Deutsch) who report on the importance of a person's perception that he is responsible for a decision. The followers of B. F. Skinner usually maintain a staunchly determinist position, although Skinner himself points out that it is we who choose whether to enter the utopian society of his *Walden Two*, and that it is we who can determine the goals toward which we wish to set up schedules of reinforcement.

OTHER PROBLEMS

Infinite series "If I am not determined (necessitated) to choose A rather than B, then I need a third motive C for choosing between them. But if this determines me to choose, I am not free; if it doesn't, then I cannot choose and need a further determiner D, etc." This argument is essentially the same as that which says, "If the will is

[21] David C. McClelland, "Conscience and the Will Rediscovered," review of Karl Mierke's *Wille und Leistung* (Göttingen: Verlag für Psychologie, 1955), *Contemp. Psychol.*, 1957, 2:177–179.

not determined to choose, then it has no adequate reason for choosing, and therefore it would never choose."

The facts provide the best answer here. We do choose, and without an infinite series of motives. We do not even need a third motive: since either A or B is good, I have adequate reason for choosing one (final cause) and efficient cause (will). The argument implies that volition needs a motive for itself, other than the object. But tendency is movement and it therefore indicates an imperfection: will-act is not an end, but motion toward an end. Another fallacy implied is that every sufficient motive is a necessitating one.

Theological determinism "God surely knows what I am going to do, and must cooperate if I am to do it. But God's cooperation is irresistible, and to do otherwise than what He foresees would make the divine knowledge false, which cannot be. Therefore I am not free." This objection really belongs to the philosophy of God (theodicy) or to theology. Briefly, we must distinguish the facts from the explanation of the facts.

The *facts* are clear enough: God has the perfection of freedom, and can confer that perfection on man; if He does so, He sees perfectly all that this involves. Note the word *sees:* There is no time in God, and to speak of *fore*knowledge here is anthropomorphism (projecting human qualities on Him). It is not of the nature of knowledge to cause its object; the essence of knowledge is conformity between knower and object, however achieved. The fact that I see a man sit down does not make him sit. What does God see? He sees me choose freely, since that is the nature He has given me. If it is true that I freely choose A, He knows this. Hence it is nonsense to talk as if I would cross God up if I choose B, for that too is included in His eternal knowledge. He does not guess or predict; He knows.

As for His cooperation, it does not derogate from His omnipotence that creatures exercise their own efficient causality. The fact that He cooperates with the will does not force our choices any more than His cooperation with our intellect means that He thinks our thoughts: He is the ultimate cause of both, the proximate cause of neither. God does not have to share with any creatures the perfection of freedom; but once He does, He cannot contradict Himself by not leaving them free. (This is not because of any lack in God, who can do any*thing;* a contradiction is *non*being, *no*thing.) "Just as by moving natural causes He does not prevent their acts from being natural, so by moving voluntary causes He does not prevent them from being voluntary, but rather is the cause of this very freedom in them, for He operates in each thing according to its proper nature."[22] In fact, "it would be more repugnant to the divine movement if the will were moved of necessity, which is not in accordance with its nature, than for it to be moved freely in accordance with its nature."[23]

The *explanation* of just how God knows and cooperates with man's free choice constitutes one of the knottiest problems in philosophy. St. Thomas, in the two passages just quoted, seems to go as far as the human mind can go with certainty. His followers divided into two main camps for several centuries in attempts to probe further the workings of divine knowledge and cooperation. Both sides agree on the facts stated above. One group, predominantly Dominicans following Banez, O.P., emphasizes the supreme dominion of God and proposes a theory of predetermining decrees to safeguard it. The other group, predominantly Jesuits following Molina, S.J., emphasizes the freedom of man and proposes a special theory of divine knowledge. Both seem to follow St. Thomas in principle,[24] while going beyond him in their theories. The controversy has largely died, perhaps because of a growing suspicion on both sides that neither theory is adequate and that a new approach is possible even within the framework of Thomism (Lonergan[25]). After all, if God's knowledge and action are identical with His infinite essence, they are beyond complete and adequate comprehension by our minds.

Since the question involves the supernatural aid of grace as well as the natural cooperation of God with creatures, the problem pertains also to theology, but the principles are the same. The question of whether original sin robbed man of freedom of choice is purely theological. The burden of positive proof is on those who assert that revelation teaches it has.

REVIEW QUESTIONS

1. An American philosopher states, "I am a determinist. I believe that all behavior is determined by external and internal causes. I can control some of the internal causes, but there is no such thing as free will" (Madden, 1962, pp. 107–108). Does he hold self-determination?

---

[22] S. T., Ia, 83, 1 ad 3um.
[23] S. T., Ia IIae, 10, 4 ad 1um.
[24] William R. O'Connor, "Molina and Banez as Interpreters of St. Thomas Aquinas," *The New Scholasticism*, 1947, 21:243–259.
[25] Bernard Lonergan, S.J., "St. Thomas' Thought on Gratia Operans," *Theol. Stud.*, 1941, 2:289–324; 1942, 3:69–88, 375–402, 533–578. Pages 387–402 and 541–553 are especially good on the basic problem and the facts.

2. Does Zeno's reply to the slave defend determinism at the cost of making the beating irrational?

3. Does the quotation from Freud shown on page 172 contain a contradiction? Was he concerned with free choice, or with uncaused act?

4. A psychologist defines freedom as "the ability to control the variables of which one's behavior is a function." (Dalton, 1961, p. 369) Is this compatible with self-determination? Can we control *all* the variables?

5. Another psychologist says that the question of determinism versus freedom takes the form of asking such questions as, "Is he free to perform at a Phi Beta Kappa level in an hour exam if his intelligence is that of an idiot?" (Sanford, 1961, p. 17) Do you agree?

6. Man is determined to be what he is by all his causes. Does it follow that his behavior is determined?

7. Choice is a type of response less predictable than some other behaviors. Is unpredictability a proof of freedom? Is it a proof that choice follows no causal laws?

8. Eric Fromm (*Man for Himself*, 1947, pp. 231–235) seems to consider moderate indeterminism, reject it, then follow it in practice. Is this what he actually does? If so, how would you explain his position?

9. Do I need explicit consciousness of my freedom in order to make a free choice? Implicit?

10. Must choice always be between moral good and evil?

11. The foundation for free choice is said to be in the nature of the intellect. Why?

12. If sensism were true, could determinism be false? Why?

13. Does strong emotion always eliminate free choice? Can it?

14. Do habits eliminate free choice? Do they diminish it?

15. Analyze the argument for human freedom given by Nobel prize-winner Lecomte du Noüy in *Human Destiny* (New York: Longmans, 1947), pp. 47–51. Does it prove freedom of choice? What is the key point of his argument?

16. Why does the proof from indifferent judgments eliminate the need to consider whether the object of choice is a *greater* good?

17. If I am not determined (necessitated) to choose A rather than B, then I need a third motive C for choosing between them. If this determines me to choose, I am not free; if it doesn't, then I cannot choose and need a further determiner D, etc.

18. The will-act of its very nature must follow upon intellection. But the intellect is not free; it necessarily knows what it knows. Therefore the will cannot be free either.

19. The will always tends toward its object under some aspect of goodness. Therefore there is no such thing as crime, only ignorance or error.
20. Scientists can predict how many people will commit suicide in New York next year. Therefore determinism is right.
21. One "proof" of free choice is from consciousness. But consciousness often testifies falsely: a drunk or insane person might say he is conscious of being free, or of many other things which he isn't. Hence this argument is worthless.

FOR FURTHER READING

Kelly & Tallon: the chapters from **Sartre** and **Nietzsche**, and the selections from **Kant** on pp. 79–83 and from **Merleau-Ponty** on pp. 229–231.

   Mortimer J. Adler has reviewed through two large volumes *The Idea of Freedom* in all its ramifications and from all philosophical viewpoints. Two smaller collections are those edited by **Sidney Hook,** *Determinism and Freedom in the Age of Modern Science,* and by **Bernard Berofsky,** *Free Will and Determinism.*

   Bernard Lonergan has a profound discussion on "The Notion of Freedom," on pp. 607–655 of his book, *Insight.* Other current views are by **A. I. Melden,** *Free Action;* **Paul Ricoeur,** one of the leading French philosophers of the day, *Freedom and Nature;* **Stuart Hampshire,** an ordinary-language philosopher, *Freedom of the Individual;* and the analytic philosopher **Michael Scriven's** chapter on "Responsibility," in his *Primary Philosophy,* pp. 198–228. **Theodosius Dobzhansky** is a great biologist who has written a book on *The Biological Basis of Freedom.*

   C. E. M. Joad is a recent British philosopher whose book *Guide to Philosophy* has an interesting section on free choice on pp. 229–250. The book of **Paul Weiss** titled *Man's Freedom* might be termed a moderate existentialist view, in contrast to the views of Sartre and others on freedom. **Henri Bergson** is one of the great philosophers of the century; he wrote *Time and Free Will.* **C. S. Lewis** is an Oxford don with an easy style who concerns himself with the problem in *The Abolition of Man.* **Austin M. Farrer** has some interesting insights in *The Freedom of the Will,* and on pp. 106–229 of his *Finite and Infinite.* Lastly, **Michael Maher, S.J.,** gives a most thorough explanation of will and choice through chaps. 18 and 19 of his *Psychology,* really a philosophy book.

Raymond L. Erickson discusses the relations of free choice and the problem of criminal responsibility, including the question of whether penal law is a deterrent to others, in **"Psychiatry and the Law: An Attempt at Synthesis,"** *Duke Law J.,* 1961, 30–73. This is a vast area and no attempt will be made to suggest other readings.

The psychological literature on freedom versus determinism is almost interminable. **Timothy J. Gannon** in chap. 14 of his *Psychology: The Unity of Human Behavior* gives an excellent explanation of choice in the light of scientific psychology. **Joseph Nuttin,** in the chapter on **"The Nature of Free Activity"** of his *Psychology, Morality and Education,* shows how the psychological evidence against extreme indeterminism does not invalidate self-determination. **T. V. Moore** is a psychiatrist who does the same in chap. 27 of his *The Driving Forces of Human Nature and Their Adjustment. The Training of the Will,* pp. 25–153, by **J. Lindworsky** is a classic treatise. But perhaps the most useful source is *The Human Person,* edited by **Magda Arnold** and **John Gasson:** articles on free choice from the view point of psychotherapy by **Noël Mailloux** on pp. 264–280, from that of psychometrics by **L. Snider** on pp. 222–263, and by **M. Arnold** on **"Unconcious Determinants"** on pp. 19–22.

Most of the items mentioned in the preceding paragraph contain ample references. A collection giving both sides of the debate is that edited by **Samuel Z. Klausner,** *The Quest for Self-control.* Both sides are also presented by **R. R. Holt** and others in **"Ego Autonomy Reevaluated,"** *Int. J. Psychiat.,* 1967, 3:481–536. A most interesting diagnosis of the ambivalence of scientific psychology over the problem is **David Bakan's "The Mystery-Mastery Complex,"** which appeared in *Amer. Psychologist* in 1965 and as a chapter in his book, *On Method.*

12 ABILITIES AND HABITS

Man is a bundle of habits.   James

So far we have seen that man is equipped to relate cognitively and dynamically to his environment in a meaningful way. As we shall see, the notion of relating is at the heart of the concept of person. Meaning is everywhere, and it is up to man to discover it and determine within limits what relation he will have to his universe. We must examine in this brief chapter the nature of his cognitive and dynamic powers, and the habits he builds up in them as he learns through life's experiences.

ABILITIES OR OPERATIVE POWERS[1]

Why bother with powers at all? Why not simply consider man and his operations? This may be satisfactory at the level of science, but the philosopher must ask some questions which take us deeper. Can man be the immediate principle of his operations? It seems not; the proper act of being is to exist, not to digest or think. Again, if there are only being and activity, does one being cease to

[1] This section may be taken up immediately after Chapter 4.

differ from another when activities cease? Then there is no difference between man and brute animal when man is not actually thinking or willing. A sleeping man or an infant would have no rights. Again, if being is the sole principle of operation, how can the same man have different *kinds* of operations simultaneously? These activities can even be in opposition, so that we seem to have a nature in conflict with itself. What happens to the unity of man? He would seem to be as many beings as he has activities, or kinds of activity.

The existence of operative powers

Let us begin with the fact that man is not always doing all the things he can do: I am not hearing, thinking, choosing, remembering every second of my whole life. Right now I am thinking, not sleeping. Am I the kind of being that can sleep? And when asleep am I the kind of being that can think? I seem to be the same person, and it seems doubtful that my nature changes every time activities begin and cease. Is one a thinker only when thinking? Then a corporation could not hire an applicant for his high intelligence unless he were actually thinking. One can contract for so much to be done, but ordinarily one hires a person, not an activity. That person is then the employee of that corporation for eight hours a day even though he is not actually thinking every minute of that time.

What is our nature when powers are not operating? We know powers from acts, so it is true that if we had no evidence, even inferential, of activity, we could conclude nothing about a nature. (Nature usually refers to a being considered precisely as the source or subject of activities or operations.) But it is often obvious that we have the power even when it is not in act. When sound asleep we are still the kind of being that can think; the mere act of awakening does not change our nature and give us a power that we did not possess. Similarly, the drunk or abnormal person is still basically rational, in the sense that he possesses the root power of thinking even though he does not have the exercise of the power at that time. Sobering up or medical treatment cannot change the nature so as to give it a power which it did not have; we do not pump intelligence through a hypodermic syringe or a pair of electrodes. The proof is that no amount of such treatment will make rational a being whose nature was not such to begin with, as evidenced by giving electroshock, insulin, thyroxin, or gultamic acid to a dog or a monkey. Again, the infant manifests no thought, but it is unlikely that mere growth or the passage of time changes his nature and gives him a new power; maturation is only a condition for its exercise, providing the necessary materials for thought. Were not his basic potentialities determinate, we would never know whether to expect this infant to mature into a monkey, or this kitten to grow up a mathematician. Certain powers are properties of the nature of each being. This notion is important to ethics, when discussing rights of the mentally ill, the unborn baby, etc.

Accidents We saw at the end of Chapter 4 that an ability or power does not exist as a separate thing. It simply means that this thing (man) is the kind of being that can do certain activities. The fact that these activities can come and go while the man remains intact implies a distinction between the activity and the man. Traditionally in philosophy the activity is called accident, and the man substance. Accident here does not mean something which happens unintentionally, but rather that which has no existence of itself and whose only existence is that of the being in which it inheres. Thus there is no red or round except the round red apple, the red paint, the round ball. "To be" is analogous. To be paint or apple is to have one's own existence; to be red or round is to exist in a certain way. Red and round can be said to "be" only because they exist in something (substance) which is red or round.

This rather obvious distinction has become badly confused, especially since Berkeley and Kant, but the idea is simple enough. Changing the shape of the wax from sphere to cube does not change it from wax to some other kind of being; we say it is accidentally but not substantially changed. If I buy a bucket of red paint, I do not buy a bucket of accident; I buy a bucket of liquid substance with some quality inherent in it which we designate as red. Substance is not to be thought of as some *noumenon,* or unknown, lurking behind the accidents. I know substance when I know accidents, to the extent that the kind of being is implied in the properties I observe. Whatever I know about the substance of either wall or paint is what I know in their qualities which I can see, feel, or otherwise test; and what I know about man's substance is that I know he is the kind of being that can see and get angry and think and choose.

Nature of an operative power

A problem arises at this point. Accidents can come and go, while the beings remain, as in the wax. If operative powers are not substances, they must be accidents. Can they come and go? Would I still be a man if I no longer even had the power of thinking or choosing, i.e., if I were not the kind of being that *can* think, regardless of whether I am actually thinking?

To answer this we must recall that there are two kinds of accidents: proper and contingent. *Proper* accidents or properties are accidents which always and naturally inhere in this being and make it to be this kind of being; e.g., matter is always quantified, so quantity is a property of matter. *Contingent* accidents are those which can come and go without causing substantial change. An idea, an image, the act of running are all contingent accidents: they come and go without changing our nature. But intellect, imagination, and being radically the kind of thing that can run are all properties of human nature, inseparable from it. If one lacks such basic powers, one is just not the kind of being we call man. The paralyzed man may not walk now, but he once did, or at least is the kind of being which could, if not impeded by abnormal circumstances; we would never say this of a desk or a tree. Why do we not refer to this table as "deaf"? It certainly cannot hear, but the term is inappropriate because hearing is not proper to the nature of a table to begin with.

This notion of property answers a question raised at the beginning of this chapter. Can one say that man differs only accidentally from the brute animals, since intellect and will are accidents? Not if we realize that we differentiate one essence from another precisely by their properties. We do not know essences directly. But when certain properties manifest that man is in a different category of being, we say he differs essentially.

Operative potencies are thus in the realm of accidents, the peculiar and special kind of accident we call properties. Accidental does not necessarily mean unimportant or incidental: it means inherence in substance as opposed to separate existence. These powers are an intimate part of our nature, but they are not substances. It is for this reason that we avoid the older term "faculty," which has come to connote a little entity in man, a *homunculus* or little man in the head who sees or chooses. (This is an unfortunate caricature of the original idea. Faculty comes from *facio*, meaning "I do," and suggests action, not substance.)[2]

We have seen that a knowing power is not purely passive, an inert receiver of impressions. It is actively passive, or reactive. A percept, or idea, is not a dead picture, but a vital operation, an act. We saw that will is the ability of man to exercise efficient causality in a most intimate way. This helps us to understand substance not as a mere substratum, on which hang accidents like clothes on a store-window dummy, but as a dynamic reality operating through its powers which are simply qualities that make it the kind of being that can so act.

This very dynamic character of the abilities of man is at once in accord with the best in modern psychology and opposed to the mechanical, sub-

[2] Cf. J. Cardinal Mercier, *The Origins of Contemporary Psychology*, 2d ed. (London: R. & T. Washbourne, 1918), pp. 224–246.

stantive conception implied by the old faculty psychologists. Even Freud's id, ego, superego, and censor, though usually classed as highly dynamic concepts, smack more of the eighteenth- and nineteenth-century philosophers. "Self-actualization," "functional autonomy," and "operant learning" are all more intelligible against the philosophical framework of these immanently active, fecund principles of operation. "Every doer is perfected by doing" is an old philosophical adage reflected in progressive education and dynamic theories of personality development. And this is not determined wholly by random contact with environment or mere need to maintain the status quo, but by the whole scope of our unrealized potentialities—by man's nature, if you will, but an open-end nature endowed with objectively unlimited capacities and goals as broad and deep as all being.

It is sometimes objected that the power of reproduction could never cause a new substance, since cause and effect must be proportionate. But powers do not act by themselves, because they do not exist by themselves. It is substance that causes other substance. It does so in the only way a created substance can act, viz., through the quasi-instrumentality of its power of reproduction. Only that Being which is its own "to be" can have its power of acting identical with Itself.

It is not difficult to conclude that man's powers are distinct from his substance (but not separate from it). The proper act of a substance is to exist. But existence is not the same as operation. Man does not "do" a man; he "is" a man, and does other things. If to be a man is the act of his substance, to operate must be the act of some other potency.

Again, were my substance identical with my potency for operation, then logically whenever I was in act (existing) I would be doing all the things I can do, which is absurd. My substance can be in act while I am also in potency to other acts: therefore I have other potencies besides my essential potency to be. These other potencies are my operative powers.

POTENCY IN ORDER OF OPERATION   This argument seems to lead to a serious difficulty. Operative powers were said to be in potency, not in act, when a man was not exercising them. But above it was asserted that he still had such powers, i.e., was still the kind of being that could do these acts. This would argue that the powers were still in act, viz., the act of existing. Now they cannot be both in potency and in act at the same time. Are they actual or potential?

To answer this we must recall that potency and act are analogous concepts. They correspond only in the same order: something may be in potency in one order, and in act in another. The operative powers are actual in the order of existence, i.e., insofar as they are accidental forms or perfections of an existing substance. But they are only in potency in the order of operation until they begin to function. Your great-grandson's intellect is now in potency in the order of existence; when he is first born it will be in existential act, but in operative potency until he begins to understand.

Powers and the unity of man

The notion of power as property helps solve the problem mentioned in Chapter 2 about the unity and diversity of man. It is the one person who acts, by means of many operative powers. Man is one substance or supposit. Substance considered as the source of activity is called nature, which therefore includes those essential properties which make it capable of its various activities. But no multiplicity of accidents can multiply substance, for accidents are qualities having no being except through inherence. Therefore man's nature remains one being. I may be a hearer, a sleeper, a thinker—but I am not three beings, nor a different being during each activity.

The fact that the various powers are distinct from one another explains how man is capable of different and even conflicting activities. Since they are all accidents of the same substance, this conflict is all within the same person: there would be no true internal conflict if Joe's emotions were at odds with Pete's intellect! Activities so diverse and even opposed stem from different proximate principles of operation ultimately rooted in the same man.

Though relatively simple to enumerate, man's powers are exceedingly complex in their interaction and combined multiple activities, as both the psychologist in his perception experiments and the psychiatrist in his office find when they try to isolate and disentangle them. Similarly, in the philosophical sense there is no such power as "speech" because speech involves complex activity of many powers at once.

The notion of powers helps us to understand individual differences as being in the powers rather than merely activities or in substances. If in activity, men would not differ when asleep; if in substance, there would still be the question of how these substances differ. It also explains how man can share some aspects of his nature with brute animals and even with the vegetative level, since he has powers of all three kinds. Again, the activities of the different powers are related to different organs of the body, as we have seen. Diversity of organic structure and function thus corresponds to differences of powers, leaving man's substance as one.

Modern psychology, understandably afraid of the word "faculty" because of its connotation, just as it was of the term "free will" for similar reasons, nonetheless has provided interesting confirmation for the basic concept of operative potencies. Psychological testing has revealed that man's activities are not only intermittent but fall into different categories. Each different way of acting stems from some general tendency to act in this way. These tendencies seem to be inborn, but are developed and individualized by actual experience. Although capable of great modification by environmental influence, these tendencies to action seem to vary innately among individuals, usually in a bell-curve distribution.

Now all these facts about natural tendencies or abilities in man coincide with the notion of operative potencies or powers. The difference is only in terminology, and in the technological manner by which the facts were acquired. Mention has already been made of the evidence from factor analysis by Spearman, Cattell, and others for intellect and will as distinct powers. The work of Thurstone seems also to verify, through factor analysis of test results, the notion of diverse powers.[3] We listed many different operations of intellect; this allows for the special or subgroup activities under the general heading of intelligence. To a lesser degree visual perception also involves diverse kinds of experiences, yet we logically group them as stemming basically from the same power. Always we must remember the inter-relatedness of all man's powers, though distinct, as mere abilities of the same one man. Their distinction, and ultimate unity in man, ac-count for the fact that factor analysis shows that no two human abilities are perfectly correlated or perfectly uncorrelated. Both the unity of man and the complexity of his operations are rooted in the fact that his several powers are but accidents of one substance.

> The student would do well to remember that schematic charts such as Figure 3 are simply attempts to indicate in orderly fashion the facts of human behavior and experience. They do not presume to prove anything. Other schemes may be used to portray alternative descriptions of the same facts; e.g., the Freudian categories id, ego, and superego emphasize com-plex activity rather than basic powers. The chart does not pretend to indi-cate the interrelation and organization of the various acts listed. But it does suggest that a great deal of man's psychic structure is unconscious and that much of it is animal. Emotion is not listed, since we saw that it is a complex activity involving practically all man's powers. Moreover, these charts avoid completely the question of man's being: all these operations and powers imply a substance in which they inhere.

HABITS

Emphasis on the rational nature of man may be a necessary antidote to the materialistic philosophy which threatened to dominate our Western culture a few decades ago, but the student is in danger of getting the impression that man consists of a reason and a will some-how stuck onto a substance, like arms on a crude scarecrow—and forming just about as much in the way of a person. Our description of the dynamic nature of operative power sets the stage for our agreeing that in practice man comes much closer to being a "bundle of habits," as James put it.

As a matter of philosophical fact (and philosophy is much more factual than some realize), after infancy man's intellect and will by

[3] L. L. Thurstone, *Vectors of Mind* (Chicago: University of Chicago Press, 1935), pp. 45–53.

	Knowledge			Dynamics	
POWERS	Habits	Acts	POWERS	Habits	Acts
INTELLECT	Science Wisdom Prudence	Ideas Judgment Reasoning	WILL	Virtues and Vices	Rational desire Complacency Choice
IMAGINATION etc.	Habitual associations	Images	SENSORY APPETITIVE POWERS	Emotional habits	Sense desires Feelings
SENSE OF SIGHT etc.	Perceptual habits	Seeing			Impulses Drives
NUTRITION: Metabolism GROWTH: Cell proliferation etc.					

Note: Only what is in *italic* is conscious; all else is unconscious. POWERS are in capital letters. Enumeration of powers is not complete, e.g., one example each is given of internal sense power and special sense. Observe the relatively large proportion devoted to the level of sensory or animal life.

Figure 3   *Powers, Habits, and Acts*

no means always pass directly from a state of pure operative potency to a state of act. Without going as far as psychological determinism, we must admit that a very large part of the activity of these powers is determined by the complex systems of habits which have been built up in them. This is a great advantage: it would be an intolerable burden if we had to start from scratch each time to think through our reasons for acting and to make a new choice. Habits, born of previous conviction and choice, rid us of much routine decision making. This frees us for more creative achievement. More than that, we are carried through many difficult or tempting situations by the force of good habits, where otherwise weakness might cause us to abandon principle. The long-time member of Alcoholics Anonymous rejects a proffered drink automatically; habit is now his friend, and prevents each situation from being a crisis.

Nature of habits

But what is a habit? Most students will offer a definition which makes habit a repetition of acts. But if habit consists of acts, then no act means no habit. Suppose Professor Jones is asleep, and not even dreaming. Can I say he is a good man? That he knows a lot of chemistry? He is not doing any good acts, nor exercising any actual knowledge of chemistry. What reality in him justifies my attributing goodness and knowledge to him, even when asleep? Certainly it is not his acts, for he is not performing any. Is it his *power* of performing such acts? Then how does the professor differ from his grandson, who also has the powers of intellect and will? Both possess intellect, the potency for knowing chemistry; yet nobody attributes knowledge of chemistry to his grandson.

Comparing the two, sleeping professor and grandson, we can see no difference: both possess intellect, and neither is displaying actual knowledge of chemistry. Wake up the professor and ask questions about chemistry of each. Immediately we observe a difference in performance. The grandson may have only the potency for acquiring chemical knowledge, but the professor answers our questions with ease, without needing to acquire the answers because he somehow already possesses them. How? Not in act, for he is not always thinking of all the chemistry he knows. Not purely in potency, for he differs from his grandson precisely in not having to acquire the knowledge. But since potencies are known by their acts, it is clear from the ease of his performance that the professor's powers are not pure potency for learning chemistry, starting at zero, but powers already well disposed to think about chemistry with great facility. He has habitual knowledge. Similarly, his will is disposed to good acts, so that we call him a good man; for virtue is nothing more or less than a good habit of the will.

We may summarize our findings by defining habit as *an acquired quality of an operative power which disposes that power to act with facility in a certain way.*

Potency or act?   The question of whether habit is potency or act is somewhat similar to the question we raised about the powers themselves. The difference in this case is that here we are dealing with an additional perfection of the power, ordered not merely to operation but to facilitated operation. In the order of existence, habit is act; it is a quality, an actual form perfecting and disposing a power. But in the order of operation it is still potency, ordered to facilitated operation as act. This semiactualization places habit in a unique position midway between potency and act. But the philosopher must take reality as he finds it, even if it does not fit his neat preconceived categories.

Varieties of habit

Aquinas usually preferred to restrict the term habit to the rational level. But even he, Aristotle, and their most ardent followers are seen at times to use the word habit in a broader sense, to include habitual knowledge and the dispositions of other powers. Such a manner of speaking is certainly much more in accord with modern English usage. Language being conventional, it seems practical to use the term habit in conformity with this broader meaning. The philosopher should feel at home with analogy, and this seems to be an analogy of proper proportionality. Granted the different degrees of indeterminacy, the definition still fits if we take into account the natures of the various operative potencies.

By whatever name, the facts are there. Facility in thinking is admittedly different from thought content, but retained knowledge seems also to verify the definition of habit, even if in an analogous sense. The senses, at least the internal senses, do seem to acquire modifications which dispose them as subjects of *improved* action, rather than merely directing them to determinate objects. Recall the experiment of wearing inverted prisms for glasses, and the superior perceptions of the experienced woodsman. These and other lines of evidence point to perceptual habits in a true sense of the word, yet their development is not due to influence from the rational level. The wearer of the prisms does not reason intellectually to the position of things; he acquires a perceptual habit of seeing them aright. Again, the dog learns to avoid the hot radiator grill through his own sad experience, and the cat improves her skill and accuracy in jumping by practice—both without the influence of a trainer. For these reasons, we disagree with Aquinas.

HABIT IN ANY POWER To others, habit suggests activities at the very opposite end of the scale from rational: an automatism like scratching one's head, or alcoholism. We would like to emphasize the broad range of its application, and speak of habits as perfections of *any* of man's operative powers. Thus we have traits and skills or habits of acting, emotional complexes or habits of feeling, perceptual habits, association of images or habits of the imagination, retained or habitual knowledge both sensory and rational, attitudes and understanding or habits of thinking, and character or habits of will. We need only to remember that the term is analogous and depends on the power to be perfected. Throughout the whole scale of human activity, habit is an important medium between stimulus and response. Along with native equipment and self-determination, habits constitute the "O" in the S-O-R formula of psychology (stimulus-organism-response).

GROUPS AND SYSTEMS OF HABITS Rarely does a habit exist in reality as an isolated perfection. Usually, habits are combined in varying degrees of complexity. The good mechanic has motor dexterity, facility in picturing spatial relations, the urge to have things work right, and understanding of the principles of machinery—all so closely interwoven that it is difficult, if not impossible, to isolate the function of each in a given act. Smoking or drug addiction may involve appetitive habits, association of images, attitudinal thinking, motor habits, and physiological modification in organic tissues. These are not only habit systems but systems of systems, piling up and interacting. In the well-adjusted personality or virtuous man these habit systems are integrated and in an orderly, hierarchical fashion related to one another and the good of the whole man.

HABITS AND PSYCHOLOGY

Personality is largely a matter of habits. Mere possession of basic potencies makes one a person, but how experience habituates these powers and how they are now disposed to act tells what kind of personality one has. Again, we judge personality not by what one happens to do at the moment, but by what is characteristic or typical because flowing from the more or less stable dispositions we call habits. They are always with one, awake or asleep, acting or not. Their all-pervasive influence on behavior is powerful, subtle, and often unconscious.

Habits and free choice As mentioned previously, habits diminish freedom of choice by disposing the will to act in a certain way and thus removing some of its original indeterminacy. But habits do not determine, because as qualities of a power they belong to the realm of potency, leaving us free to determine whether we will bridge the gap from potency to act.

Figure 4

Referring to Figure 4, we may consider schematically the will without any habits at 0, or zero on the scale of act. Perfected by a good habit, it would be at H, still short of act but further along than originally and hence able to reach A with greater ease than before. Thus the good man finds it easy to perform good acts. (If habit placed it already at A, the will would be determined; but being in potency at H it still can determine whether or not to traverse the remaining distance $H \rightarrow A$.) He is free to perform bad acts, as sad experience shows. Only to do so he must act against the disposition of his good habit, i.e., travel the whole distance $H \rightarrow B$. Conversely, the bad man can do a good act, since his bad habit still leaves him in potency; but he in turn must act against the disposition of habit and travel from BH to A.

This explanation leaves intact both freedom of choice and the value of character training.[4] It also gives sound philosophical basis for the practice

[4] See J. Lindworsky, S.J., *The Training of the Will* (Milwaukee: Bruce, 1929), a classic treatise on motivation and free choice; and A. Eymieu, S.J., *Le Gouvernement de soi-même* (Paris: Perrin, 1935), especially vol. III. *L'Art de vouloir*.

of psychotherapy, and especially for the client-centered and existential therapies of Carl Rogers, L. Binswanger, Rollo May, Viktor Frankl, F. J. Buytendijk, and others which throw the responsibility on the client and enlist the cooperation of his free choice, while recognizing that his personality problems are largely a matter of faulty adjustive habits developed over the years. It is precisely because it happens at the level of habit formation, and therefore unconsciously in great part, that the way in which emotion can distort the operation of our natural powers is so baffling. These are the dynamisms that Freud and others try to describe and explain.

ABNORMAL STATES   Although habits normally diminish but do not destroy freedom of choice, in certain pathological cases the force of habit may be so strong and so irrational that for practical purposes we may say that the person is not free. This of course is abnormal and does not change our concept of man's essential nature. But it does constitute a difficult problem in both ethics and law.[5]

NATURE OF WILL-HABITS   Since the nature of the will is to act because of motives, "disposed to act in a certain way" in the case of will-habits means "disposed to act because of certain motives." Hence there is no question of training the will like a muscle, which acts regardless of the value of what it lifts. Lindworsky (1929) refuted the muscle-training theory of will by experiments showing that it can be habituated only by being disposed to respond habitually to certain values as effective motives. This position seems to be confirmed by Knight Dunlap (1932), whose "beta hypothesis," or negative practice, advocated breaking habits by doing the very action not wanted, showing that the will does not gain strength from mere exercise but that the reason or motive for its action is cardinal. Experiments on transfer of habits of neatness, with and without stress on the *value* of neatness, lead to the same conclusion.

Character is a set of will-habits by which one is disposed to act according to principles. It is built up by choices for good motives, and seems to provide a middle ground between "situation ethics" and traditional stress on rules. Choice in a situation shapes more than the situation; it shapes the person. Both the situationists and the rule-moralists concentrate on isolated actions rather than on people. Character is both individual and general, subjective and objective; it looks to the concrete without getting lost in immediacy. It stresses that moral goodness is primarily a goodness of persons, and this is a matter of habitual dispositions that have to be worked at to be acquired (Johann, 1967).

Acquisition of habits

Our definition says only that habits are acquired; it does not state how. Since the philosopher is only interested in the nature of habits, he can rightly leave the conditions of their acquisition to the psychologists, whose investigations on the topic fill volumes.

Although repetition in some form is the usual way of acquiring habits, repetition is by no means necessary to the nature of habit itself.

[5] Cf. James E. Royce, S.J., *Personality and Mental Health*, rev. ed. (Milwaukee: Bruce, 1964), pp. 249–254.

It is enough that habit be acquired, regardless of how. Sometimes a single act can engender a habit. One clear explanation may cause me to understand something in geometry, let us say. There is no need for repetition: I have the idea, and twenty years later could use it with ease even though I have never thought about it since that day in high school. Obviously I was not born with knowledge of geometry or of anything else. It was acquired, but not by repetition. This way of acquiring knowledge holds chiefly for simple ideas which appeal directly to understanding; most knowledge is made habitual only by repeated use. Again, one intense emotional experience may implant a habit: a single great fright in childhood, for example, may leave a habitual emotional revulsion for similar objects. The child need not repeat the frightening experience many times to acquire this emotional habit. (Supernatural virtues are acquired and fit the definition of habit, but they are infused and belong to the order of grace, not to philosophy or psychology.)

Habits and learning

The term *learning* likewise has been broadened so as to include the whole range of human activity. Rather than the mere acquisition of knowledge, learning or conditioning has come to refer to any change in mode of response acquired through experience, and the result of this change is called habit. Thus we have not only learning of school subjects, but emotional learning, volitional learning, perceptual learning, sensorimotor learning, etc.

We must keep in mind the analogical kinds of knowledge and the complexity of human activity involving the simultaneous and interrelated operations of many powers. We must also distinguish between the process and the product: the learned response is not always the learning response. Even insight may involve some residue of habit formation, though not in the process. Association, conditioning, trial and error, and insightful understanding may in practice all shade into one another in varying degrees.

Experimental psychology has yielded a prodigious amount of literature on the topic of learning. A welter of theories are still being tested in the laboratory and debated by their proponents. Pavlov's conditioning seemed to provide Watson with the answer as to how learning takes place; subsequent events have shown that it raises more questions than it answers. Rather than explaining, it needs to be explained. Patched up as it now is with drives, sets, secondary reinforcement, operant behavior, it has lost its original physiological meaning and approaches more and more the notion of habit formation.

TRANFER   A similar situation appears when one surveys the transfer-of-training controversy. Much of the difficulty arose from the absurd connotations of the eighteenth-century "faculty" theory. Conversely, the opposing theory of identical elements suggests a post-Cartesian concept of knowledge as atoms in a mental chemistry. As the muddy water has gradually settled and the facts are seen in clearer perspective, neither position is entirely vindicated, but the compromise position of modified transfer is strikingly in tune with the notion of operative power as a vital, fecund potency perfectible by habit. As in the cases of conscious experience, free choice, operative powers, teleology, and other concepts rejected in earlier phases of modern psychology, the trend of scientific thought has come full circle on this point. The swing is attested by J. P. Guilford:

> A general theory to be seriously tested is that some primary abilities can be improved with practice of various kinds and that positive transfer effects will be evident in tasks depending on those abilities. At the present time some experiments are going on of this type. . . . In one sense, these investigations have returned to the idea of formal discipline. The new aspect of the disciplinary approach is that the presumed functions that are being "exercised" have been indicated by empirical research (1950, p. 449).

The facts of abnormal psychology give additional confirmation that our abilities can be trained. In cases of brain injury and hysteria, it is reported that the patient suffered total loss of mental content, sometimes not even being able to understand any language or recall any previous event. Yet the ability of these patients to reason and acquire knowledge was not that of an infant with corresponding lack of knowledge, but that of a mature adult with well-developed powers. The capacity for learning is evidently something other than the act of knowing or the acquired knowledge, and is perfected by previous use.

Conclusion   Though we stretch the application of the term habit into conformity with modern usage, we have by no means abandoned thereby the richness of the traditional philosophical conception. Our concept of habit as perfectant of an operative power is dynamic. It connotes more than a mere automatic routine of semiconscious repetition or neurological conditioning. Rather, it tells of a vital growth of originally indeterminate potencies. This is not organic or physical growth, but metaphysical growth in the order of potency for operation. Like the current renewed interest in motivation and existential relations, it implies finality: the developed ordering of all our powers toward their proper objects, for the good of the whole person.

REVIEW QUESTIONS

1. At birth, is the child's intellect in potency or in act? (Distinguish.)
2. If "faculties" destroy man's unity, the notion of ability or operative power saves it. Explain why.
3. Power must belong to either the realm of substance or that of

accident. But if power is substantial, man is many beings and his unity is destroyed; if not, then it is just accidental whether man has an intellect or not. Solve this dilemma.

4. What justification is there for saying that our picture of man is both more complex and more unified than that of the faculty theorists of a few centuries ago?

5. "All men are created equal." In what sense is this true? in what sense not? Show how the notion of operative power is necessary for a correct interpretation.

6. Is habit properly defined as a repetition of acts? Discuss (four reasons).

7. Can you define habit without the notion of operative power?

8. Is habit the same as trait?

9. Why do habits belong to the realm of the unconscious?

10. Why does not our definition of habit say anything about *how* habit is acquired?

11. Do you prefer the strict Thomistic tradition which confines the term habit to the rational level, or the text's conformity with modern usage? Why?

12. If habit were act, what would the possession of will-habit do to freedom of choice?

13. Do you think that recent psychological theory on learning is approaching or departing from the concept of habit?

14. Are habits proper or contingent accidents? Why?

15. "Learning consists in the establishment of functional connections between nerve cells in the cerebral cortex." Evaluate this statement now, in the light of the pertinent section of Chapter 8.

16. "If the will is free, then all education, training, and psychotherapy are in vain, since free will could go contrary to them. Either they are useless, or the will is not free." Is this reasoning correct?

Alburey Castell asks the following three questions. Answer each of them in terms of the power-habit-activity distinction.

17. If education is conditioning, does the student or the teacher deserve the grade?

18. Make a tape recording of a person reasoning aloud. Play the tape back. Did it do any learning?

19. "Learning is modification of behavior." Why not, "Modification of behavior is evidence of learning"?

FOR FURTHER READING

Abilities

First we list some philosophical treatises:

Adler, Mortimer J. *What Man Has Made of Man.* Pp. 79–81; Note 46, p. 205.

Allers, Rudolf. "Functions, Factors, and Faculties," *The Thomist,* 1944, 7:323–362.

Hart, Charles A. *The Thomistic Concept of Mental Faculty.*

Klubertanz, George P., S.J. "The Unity of Human Operation," *The Modern Schoolman,* 1950, 27:75–103.

Pegis, Anton C. "St. Thomas and the Unity of Man," in J. A. McWilliams, S.J. (Ed.) *Progress in Philosophy.* Pp. 153–173.

Second, some interesting items are listed showing how the facts from psychological testing, factor analysis, and other data of modern scientific psychology confirm the concept of abilities once it is properly distinguished from the "faculty" notion of the eighteenth and nineteenth centuries:

Allport, Gordon W. "Traits Revisited," *Amer. Psychologist,* 1966, 21:1–10.

Brennan, Robert E. *Thomistic Psychology.* Chap. 9, especially pp. 250–257.

Moore, Thomas Verner. *Cognitive Psychology.* The chapter on transfer, Pp. 473–493.

Murphy, Gardner. *Human Potentialities.*

Spearman, Charles. *Psychology down the Ages.* Vol. I, chap. 11. See also his *The Abilities of Man* and his *Human Ability.*

Habits

William James wrote a classic description of habits in the first volume of his *Principles of Psychology,* pp. 104–127, though it lacks metaphysical depth. See also his *Talks to Teachers.* Less well known but invaluable are the writings of a brilliant young Mexican Jesuit whose promising career was cut short by an untimely death, **Jaimie Casteillo: *A Humane Psychology of Education,*** and his articles **"The Psychology of Habit in St. Thomas,"** *The Modern Schoolman,* 1936, 14:8–12, and **"The Psychology of Intellectual and Moral Habits,"** *Jesuit Educ. Quart.,* 1941, 4:59–70.

Jacques Maritain in *Art and Scholasticism* has some valuable insights in chap. IV. A. D. Sertillanges points up the value of intellectual habits in *The Intellectual Life*. Lastly, the metaphysical paradox of habit is discussed by **Vernon J. Bourke** in, **"The Role of Habitus in the Thomistic Metaphysics of Potency and Act,"** in **R. Brennan** (Ed.) *Essay in Thomism*, pp. 103–109.

On the nature of learning, it is most interesting to see **Mary Helen Mayer** describe a "we-learn-by-doing" theory which sounds like the progressive education of the thirties and discover it to be *The Philosophy of Teaching of St. Thomas Aquinas.* **Charles Spearman** in his usual fascinating way traces the concept of learning in *Psychology down the Ages*, vol. II, pp. 236–237. The psychologist **Horace B. English** gives important background in *The Historical Roots of Learning Theory.* **Knight Dunlap** explains his paradoxical "negative learning" in *Habits: Their Making and Unmaking.* And **O. H. Mowrer** states his now-famous dual theory in **"On the Dual Nature of Learning: A Reinterpretation of 'Conditioning' and 'Problem-solving',"** *Harvard educ. Rev.*, 1947, 17:102–148. The readings on **"Brain and Thought"** at the end of Chapter 8 list useful items on the nature of learning as more than merely neurological connections.

IV
THE WHOLE PERSON

13 MAN AS PERSON

Man is a social animal.   Spinoza

 We have completed our survey of man's activities, but who is he? This man we have been analyzing is not some abstract universal; no such man exists. It has been said that we know more about man today than ever before, yet never has man appeared so mysterious as now (Heidegger). Apparently the more we know about him, the more we realize how impenetrable is the uniqueness of each person.

Far from concluding our analysis with some pat paradigm of human nature, the analysis itself revealed aspects of man which make him mysterious and incomprehensible. By his intellect he has capacity for unlimited meaning. In his choices he is free for infinite variation. These characteristics show an openness to *being*: not merely to knowing and choosing things, but to becoming by his own acts what he is to be. A person is a person-to-be-achieved; integration of the personality is a lifelong self-constituting process. Man's complex nature is not fixed, static, universal. He is an individual, not merely evolving but developing himself by his own active encounter with the rest of being.

The reason why man is mysterious is that his nature is a bundle of paradoxes. He is individual yet social, unified yet diversified, complete and yet incomplete, incommunicable (subjective) yet communicating objectively, self-contained yet transcending himself. He is a person with his own rights and in his own right, yet responsible for and to others. He finds meaning through cognition, yet he is fully understood only when he defines the meaning of a situation by his action.

It is this paradoxical and mysterious aspect of man which makes him the fascinating object of study by poet and dramatist, philosopher and psychologist. If it is a platitude that Shakespeare is the greatest psychologist of all time, this is only because he saw and delighted in the paradoxes, and dramatized the mystery without trying to dissolve it entirely. And herein lies the danger of the excessive psychologizing which has become a favorite indoor sport: we tend to treat persons as objects, to reduce them to logical or language games. Now scientific psychology is a very legitimate and laudable pursuit; we eagerly and rightly seek to discover the laws of human behavior. The depersonalization of man is something else; much amateur psychologizing is really an attack on the value of persons. Man may be the object of scientific study, but a person is not a thing. Civilizations begin to totter when men begin to use people as things.

Modern philosophers revolt against this tendency. One way of revolting is by analyzing the implication of first- and second-person expressions in ordinary language, as opposed to third-person speech. Martin Buber is the most prominent in this revolt, with his stress on the I-thou relation. The old introspectionism was first-person centered, and behaviorism spoke always in the third person. But a "you" can talk back, can refuse or cooperate freely. Alburey Castell describes person as "one who can reason and be reasoned with," a subject as well as an object. He notes that if you deny this, logically you can not agree or disagree with him because only subjects can dialogue. We can observe a statue all day without communicating with it, but to gaze into someone's eyes is an intensely interpersonal experience. We look for understanding, for response that is deliberate and uncoerced. This expectation contains implicit evidence about the nature of person. The very fact that we refer to a person as "you" in a dialogue implies an entirely different relation than when we refer to a thing as "it." Person is an "I" which immediately strikes up a "thou" relation.

Person as relation

It is precisely this notion of relation to others that seems to lie at the heart of personality. "Here I am!" is useless until there is a potential hearer, another person to whom I can relate in some way, if only by contrast that I am not he. I am myself, not somebody else, whatever else I may know about me. I may be uncertain of my identity, but the very fact that I say, "Here I am," means that I recognize myself not only as existing but as having some identity, however vague, which sets me apart from and yet puts me in relation to others.

This intersubjectivity, this relation between persons as subjects and not mere objects, seems to be a basic given in much of contemporary philosophy. Man has tired of a post-Copernican world which substituted one universe structure for an earlier one, but robbed man of his personhood. Once again people are important. The organization man in the gray flannel suit is now a sign of rebellion instead of something that conforms.

If we say, "He has a lot of personality," we mean that he has qualities which enable him to relate well and readily to other people, to draw them out. If we say, "He is a great person," we mean that he has qualities of distinctiveness which make him stand out as an individual. In such expressions lie clues to the basic concept of person. Implied here is that to be a person is to be one's own distinctive self, and also to be one who relates well to others. Even if we refer, by analogy, to a dog or cat as having "a lot of personality" we seem to mean something of these same qualities of distinctiveness and relating to others, if only by attracting attention. Obviously a human personality whose values lay only or primarily in attention-getting would be shallow; sooner or later the personality does not wear well if its chief function is to call attention to self. One must be related in ways that bring out the best in others, radiate truly great human qualities on one's fellowman, exhibit a goodness which is truly loving and lovable.

All this suggests that there is a social dimension of man which perhaps has not been sufficiently emphasized in the foregoing chapters. True, we did stress that perception is influenced by how others see things, that meaning develops in the context of a particular language community, that conscience is formed to some extent in the light of local customs and social acceptance, that freedom implies responsibility.

To be responsible one must be responsible to someone, to another person or persons. Self and other are not entirely separable. One of the paradoxes of man is that he is a complete being in himself and that at the same time he yearns for completion by relating to others. There is something about this self which needs others, not in the sense of immature or neurotic dependency, but for perfect self-fulfillment and realization of all the potential within oneself. Knowledge is like joy: we want to share it with others, feeling an urge at times to tell even a total stranger rather than keep something to oneself. Choice nearly always is exercised in a social context, with some sense of the repercussions of our act on others.

An indication of this profoundly social aspect of human nature is the phenomenon of loneliness. Why should it occur at all? If one is getting along all right, busy and achieving goals, should not this be enough? For some it seems to be: the prospector or trapper in the wilderness, the recluse in his isolated cave or cabin. But even here we call "normal" the sense of loneliness the former occasionally feels and his eagerness to make human contact when opportunity offers, and "abnormal" the escapist or antisocial tendencies of the latter. The man who "has everything" discovers that money cannot buy love. The couple who truly have each other find there is much truth in the old saying that shared joys are doubled and shared troubles are cut in half. Another example of man's capacity for relating to others as persons is the discrepancy between masturbation or mere selfish exploitation of another and genuine sexual relationship as a commitment.

Person and personality

The topic of personality fills whole libraries of psychology books and journals, but we must confine ourselves here to examining its philosophical basis in person. *Persona* comes from *per + sonare*, "to sound through," and had its origin in the masks worn by actors in the ancient Greek theater to identify the various characters. But this approach leads to stereotypes, not to individuals. Moreover, it is more suggestive of the kind of personality one *has*, rather than of what it means to *be* a person at all.

We say someone is "quite a person" if he has original ideas and strong convictions. We feel this even more if he displays great courage and forcefulness in carrying out his convictions and achieving his goals. The powers of understanding and choice behavior thus seem to characterize person. A bulldozer may be more powerful, but we do not think of it as a person because it has neither convictions nor courage. A computer may be more "brilliant," but again we do not speak to it as to a person because its computations and choices lack the self-actualizing qualities we ascribe to persons. Neither computer nor bulldozer shows any evidence of a sense of self-identity, any relation to others in a personal way.

The fact that man is the kind of being which has these abilities makes him a person. The extent to which he actualizes these potentialities, and the manner in which he stabilizes this actualization through habits, are what make up his personality. If these powers and habits are highly developed and harmoniously integrated, we attribute a high measure of personality. But the mere possession of the root potentialities at all constitutes one a person. Their actualization may depend on circumstances quite incidental to a person's basic nature. Thus the wolf children of India, the wild boy of Aveyron studied by Itard, the born deaf who cannot speak, the child victim of sensory or cultural deprivation, the demented patient before his memory and skills are restored by shock therapy—all have the basic powers of a human person, but their "personality" is largely negated by extraneous (though important) factors. The partial or total loss of the exercise of these potentialities in psychosis or senility, though practically erasing the psychological personality, does not remove the right to life as a person. Similarly, the courts have often declared the unborn child, before he has exercised his powers of understanding or relating to others through choice, to be a person which has the right, for example, to inherit. In all these cases the essential abilities which make a person may be dormant, but there is at least indirect evidence that they could be operative under normal circumstances. As we saw in the previous chapter, merely making a power operative is quite different from giving something a power it does not have. And inability to exercise a power is different from not having the power, as illustrated by our not calling the table "deaf."

ENDURING PERSONAL IDENTITY

William James is often portrayed as proposing a theory which would make the ultimate subject of our mental processes the stream of consciousness itself. In this hypothesis ideas would be activities without an agent, thoughts without a thinker. Actually, James seems rather to have been reacting against the notion of mind as a static mosaic or mechanical association of ideas and images; he was concerned with the dynamic continuity and flow of mental processes. He speaks of a "brand" or "familiarity mark" and admits that the crux of the question is whether there is someone to recognize and claim the brand: "the only point that is obscure is the act of appropriation itself" (1896, I:340). "If there is nobody to do the appropriating, I have no basis for asserting that these thoughts are all mine" (p. 344).

An enduring sense of personal identity seems to be a common human experience, expressed in our everyday talk. Each man has a historicity, a unique place in the time flow. You and I are the same persons who met five years ago in New Jersey. When a man says, "I wasn't myself today," he is not stating he is a different person, but merely that today's actions and feelings were not part of his usual personality pattern.

The very expression implies a recognition of his identity, for if he were not the same person it would be pointless to remark that he is not acting as the same.

We do not have to change pronouns when we change verbs: The "I" is the same in "I went" and "I go" and "I shall go." When a man hears the clock strike twelve, he cannot recognize it as the twelfth stroke unless he is the same listener. If the listener changes with the listening, then the second listener could not recognize the second stroke as *second* (Castell).

The metabolic cycle replaces all of the matter in our bodies regularly—every seven years, it used to be said, but science and the monthly food bill tell us it is much sooner than that. Why am I still the same person? There must be some permanent element in man's nature which remains through all these changes. I am still responsible for acts committed when every molecule of matter was different. My lawyer could hardly get me off a murder charge on the grounds that I am not now the same person because my matter has been replaced since I committed the act. Chaucer or Dante might take twenty years to complete a masterwork; a scientist may pursue one line of research for even longer. We have seen in Chapter 11 that man is conscious of himself as the source of his own acts. Even the denial of this is an act of which he is the source.

Our distinction between person and personality helps us see how the abnormalities of amnesia and multiple personality do not invalidate this position, which is further confirmed by psychoanalytic and other studies of personality development from infancy through adulthood. The same person (being) may have different sets of habit systems and associations (personality) at least potentially identifiable by this person as his own. We say "at least potentially identifiable" because actual recall and recognition may involve all degrees of difficulty, from a simple absentmindedness or normal forgetting up to those abnormal states in which the different streams of experience and habits can be linked only by the use of extraordinary means such as hypnosis or sodium Pentothal. It now seems theoretically possible to recall any conscious experience we have ever had, given the right stimulus. If so, there must be an abiding subsistent self through all the interchanges of matter.

The subsistent self

The "self" here is not a mental construct, but a living organism, a person. When I say that I cut myself shaving this morning, I do not mean that I cut a mental construct. Likewise, if you hit *me*, that "I" who got hit is not some "ego" of Freudian theory. We are talking here not about one's self-concept or self-image but about the existing reality. And this reality is the same referent when we say, "I understand," or, "I choose," or, "I run."

Most philosophers put self in the realm of substance. The nonphilosopher is inclined to think of substance as synonymous with material substance, as when he speaks of a solid floor as substantial. But substance is opposed to accident, and means simply that which exists in itself, not in another by inherence. Substance may be either spiritual or material. God and angels (presuming they exist) are spiritual substances. They exist in themselves, not as accidents of something else. No number of accidents would add up to a substance. Accidents may be material, e.g., size, shape, and quantity. Or they may be spiritual, such as ideas and volition. They can never exist by themselves; they are always the shape or idea of something. Powers, habits, and activities all require a subject in which they inhere.

The logical positivists who deny substance are understandably reacting against the deductive essentialism of the rationalistic age which preceded them. But positivism is not the only alternative, as is clear even historically from the rise of existentialism and other realistic philosophies, and from the fact that several of the leaders of logical positivism in America have abandoned that position. Most of the difficulties of the positivists here stem from a faulty concept of substance passed down from Locke and Hume, and the confusion of the proper realms of science and philosophy. Substance is not a static, unknowable substratum. It is existing reality, dynamic and changing, knowable in our immediate experience.

The spiritual self

Whereas Aristotle's soul is the result of deduction from various observable facts, the contemporary philosopher is more inclined to analyze what is present in consciousness prior to all philosophical inquiry, at least implicitly contained in the concrete, subjective, immediate experience. The phenomenologists "have induced us to re-examine experience and be prepared to find revealed there what we have heretofore consciously or unconsciously avoided seeing" (J. Q. Lauer, 1965, p. 185). Thus Husserl sees, in interpersonal relations, evidence of Begeistung—"spiritualization."

So far we have surveyed man's activities and have seen that some of them lack material qualities, the physical properties of a being extended in space. An idea, a judgment, an act of choice, a perfect reflection, the permanent identity of the conscious ego, all show inextension. Matter excludes other matter from occupying the same space; these acts show a compenetration, a disregard for the limitations imposed by quantity, which can only be due to the fact that they are not spatial. My concept of a triangle cannot be measured. I can have larger and smaller images, but the idea of what a triangle is applies equally well to all triangles, large and small, which could not be possible if the idea had size itself. My idea of an elephant is no bigger than my idea of a flea, for neither is quantified. Ideas do not occupy space: not having parts, they cannot extend over quantified matter. Nor does a simple idea occupy many parts of the brain at once, for then we would have many ideas, not one of any one thing. A judgment means recognition of identity or nonidentity of two concepts; but if one concept is in one space, and the other in another part, I could never get the two together in a judgment. Implicit here is that the ultimate subject of such operations is itself in some aspect nonextended, spiritual.

Drawing on Scheler, Dilthey, Bergson, and others, the Spanish-American philosopher Francisco Romero makes "spirit" the key word in his *Theory of Man* (1964). Man shares with all animals the sex and power drives; what makes a man is intentionality, judgment, language, culture, community, and, above all, spirit. Mere intentionality to him is egoistic; but spirituality is oriented disinterestedly toward the other. Spirit in man is characterized for Romero by universality, freedom, historicity, responsibility, and transcendence. His transcendent or disinterested openness to other is peculiar to man.

Spiritual does not mean supernatural, much less divine. It is the nature of man to understand and choose. Immaterial does not mean unnatural, any more than metaphysical is the same as mystical or even mythical. Our thinking needs to be clear here, for not only do we naturally look for sensory images to accompany each concept; we also tend to think of real as synonymous with material.

The most powerful things in the world are things we cannot see or feel. Ideas start wars, and thinking can change a whole economy. Choices based on principle, or on love and hate, direct whatever is done by bulldozers or atom bombs. We yield to rights, or fight for them. None of these—idea, love, hate, principle, right—is something you can weigh or measure. The materialists themselves, by their elaborate hypotheses or appeals to unknown but discoverable intervening variables such as the Psi factor, simply confirm the assertion that man can soar beyond the confines of sensory observation. It may seem that excluding the spiritual is the easy way out, but it is no solution for the investigator who faces all the facts. Discovery of more and more of the laws of physiology will never explain spiritual operations (see pp. 122–127). Biochemistry is continually revealing more marvels which call for a life principle, but they afford no explanation of universal ideas and lofty choices. If it is of the very nature of matter that it should understand, we cannot explain why all material beings do not think; if it is not, then we cannot explain in material terms the beings that do. Thought and choice are irreducible to laws of physical nature; above but not contrary to such laws, they remain within the metaphysical laws of being and causality.

Spiritual life is thus part of man's nature, revealed in his immediate experience. Rather than opposed to his material life, it is precisely the means of man's greatest intimacy with the material. For by his understanding and creativity he gives meaning to the material universe of which he is a part, and through which he works out his destiny.

VALUE OF PERSONS

We have been interweaving the two threads of distinctive identity and social relation as the two dimensions of what it means to be a person. Intrinsic worth or value seems to stem from both. Man is important because of what he is, and because of the way he relates to others.

To be a person is to be the kind of being that is open to relation with others. Here we approach the most basic question, the reason why every person has intrinsic worth. Why are people important? Perhaps this notion of relating contains an answer. To be of worth or value means to be esteemed or deserving of esteem because of what one is. Paradoxically, it may be that man is important in himself because he is important to others, and vice versa. If one's own inherent qualities are such that he is good for others and brings out the best in them, he must be good in himself. Although a hypocrite or a fake may occasionally spark a response, in the long run his artificial qualities are unmasked. Only a person of genuine worth evokes a consistent response in others.

The truth in this last sentence enables us to avoid a purely utilitarian theory of personal worth. One is not of value merely because he is good for others. Things, too, can be useful; they are not persons. Rather, he is good for others because he is good himself. When doctors and emergency vehicles and other means are called upon to save a human life, it is not because there is expectation of reward or profit for the rescuers; it is because of a conviction that a human being is worth keeping alive. The value of human life is measured not in productivity but in the potential of each person to become whatever he may make himself. Yet in the process he both uses others and is useful to others. He completes his own nature both by what he gives to others and by what he gets from them. His relations with others are largely due to what he is, and what he is develops to some extent from his past relations with others.

This is not mere conformism or social vanity. Even a sense of "ought" or obligation which stems from one's own self-respect is based on responsibility to one's sense of worth as a person. When Shakespeare says,

> This above all, to thine own self be true,
> And it must follow, as the night the day,
> Thou canst not then be false to any man.

he appeals to a feeling deep in the heart of every human being, a feeling of intrinsic dignity often obscured by slavery, neglect, war, and poverty, but still there. Your norm is not to be like everybody else, but to be the best *you* that you can be. The pervert and the alcoholic are abnormal not because they are unlike everybody else, but because they are not living up to the potentialities of their own selves. And this self is one who wants to be able to hold his head high in the world of his fellows, whether or not they appreciate him for his true worth. In fact, the very reason why he is an alcoholic or a pervert may well be a sense of inadequacy in living up to his potential for achievement or for normal sexual relations. It may be an escape from that self to which he feels unable to be true.

Person, then, is an individual subsistent being which is intellectual and responsible. We say that a person has rights which are inalienable, which our Constitution protects but does not bestow, and hence which no government can take away. A philosopher must ask, whence come these rights? If the answer is that they are inherent in man's nature, one immediately wants to know why this is so. If the answer is that man is capable of understanding the meaning of his actions and responsible for choosing accordingly, we may still be unsatisfied and ask why these qualities give man rights which are truly inalienable.

It is here that we return to the notion of relation as fundamental to the concept of person. We have seen that a person has a certain enduring identity and at least limited autonomy. He may not remember who he is, or others may not recognize him, but he is still the same person. He does not exist as another being when memory fails or appearances change. Hence he still has the same fundamental relationships to others: he is still his father's son, for example. This relation remains unalterable even by the death of either or both. Moreover, as we have hinted and shall see later, this person or self has aspects of immortality, a destiny beyond the grave. It is these relations, and especially man's transcendental relation to his Creator, which no government, however totalitarian, can touch. Man has a destiny for God and the right to pursue that relationship without interference, granted that proper pursuit includes due respect for the rights of others. This is not a theological argument, but one which can be established by reason in philosophy. (There is a theological parallel to this consideration of person as relation, viz., that in the Trinity the precise formality which makes the divine Persons distinct within the same absolute nature is their relation to one another.)

Related to all beings

If we recall the analogy of being, we can envision man as person standing in a hierarchy of relations with all the rest of being. To the physical universe he is related as master, to predict and control through scientific understanding and make it serve his pursuit of other goals. To his fellowman he is related as brother, as fellow voyager on life's sea, engaged in cooperative pursuit of mutual goods. To himself he is an identical subject, the author of his own activities, with a sense of his own history, responsibility, and destiny. Lastly, he is related to Supreme Being in ways which manifest themselves in the diverse phenomena of religion as human experience. This last relation takes us beyond the philosophy of man, but the phenomena themselves are a matter of anthropological and psychological fact so widespread that they must be included as data in any investigation of man.

His relations to the rest of being demand both integrity and integration: he must be himself, and he must be organized harmoniously in all his diverse aspects. Moreover, he is constantly adjusting to a changing universe, so that his integration is not a static mosaic but "an orderly series of dynamic processes, which allow me to adapt myself to the ceaseless changes of cosmic formations" (Strasser, 1962). A perfect person would be in well-ordered relationships with all of reality, habitually able to respond to each being in proper proportion, with due regard to the rest and to his own nature. Man of course can only approach such perfection in this life. And no one man can encompass all possible relations, whether of knowledge or dominance or aesthetic appreciation. One mark of greatness is the ability to accept one's limitations while striving to maximize one's potentialities to the fullest. Each achieves his own degree of integration, his unique set of relations with the rest of all beings—inadequate, but precious because his own.

We have seen how man is open to the true and the good as we examined his capacities as knower and lover. In the facts of human communication we saw that man's understanding has social implications, for this presupposes understanding in both parties; in other words, symbols connote meaning which can be shared. In contrast to the disintegration of the demented, the immoral, or the disorganized, we saw that person implies integration or organizational unity. This leads to another aspect of man: he is open to beauty.

Man sees meaning in the universe, but it is not merely intellectual. The symmetry and order and grace he observes in a rose or a galaxy of stars is more than just intelligible; it is enjoyable. The symbols he uses to communicate meaning to others are not mere intellectual tools, but pleasurable ones also. He uses poetry and drama, painting and sculpture, music, all the various art and literary forms to express meaning in ways that are truly beautiful. In both nature and art we see unity in diversity, harmony and rhythm in the concrete, the splendor of order manifesting the truth and goodness and unity of material things, and symbolizing thereby man's search for Truth, Goodness, Beauty Itself.

REVIEW QUESTIONS

1. What is the difference between personality in psychology and person in philosophy?
2. Romero says that just as rationalism taught us little about rationality, so the spiritual tradition has taught us little about spirit. Do you agree? Is current personalistic philosophy filling the gap? (See the Readings for this chapter.)
3. Many Americans thought from the title of Erich Fromm's *The Art of Loving* that it was a sex manual. Does this inference indicate a philosophy of person? Describe it.
4. If we speak of an object as a subject, we personify it. If we speak of a subject as an object, do we "thingify" him?
5. Philosophically, what does it mean to say that one is a beautiful person?
6. What is the connection between integration of personality and a total view of reality?
7. In a humanism or humanitarian philosophy, is the concept of person different than in a theistic philosophy?
8. Can you have a philosophy of art without a philosophy of person? Why?
9. Is your own philosophy of person optimistic or pessimistic? Why?
10. What would a person be if the universe lacked all meaning?
11. If you make self an activity rather than an agent, what happens to the concept of person?

FOR FURTHER READING

Kelly & Tallon: the chapters from **Berdyaev, Scheler, Buber,** and **Maritain.** Also the chapters from **Marcel** and **Schutz,** mentioned after Chapter 1.

Personalistic philosophy has taken a leading place in the past decade or so, thanks partly to the writings of **Marcel, Sartre, Buber, Paul Tillich,** and **Dietrich von Hildebrand,** among others. See **Emmanuel Mounier's** *Existentialist Philosophies,* and his *The Character of Man.* Of special note are **Paul Tournier,** *The Meaning of Persons;* **Jacques Maritain,** *True Humanism;* **Paul Weiss,** *Nature and Man;* **Jean Mouroux,** *The Meaning of Man;* and of course the monumental *The Phenomenon of Man* by **Pierre Teilhard de Chardin.** Etienne Gilson has chapters on "Christian Personalism" and "Christian Anthropology" in *The Spirit of Medieval Philosophy.*

J. Itard, *The Wild Boy of Aveyron,* and **J. A. Singh & R. M. Zingg,** *Wolf Children and Feral Man,* both treat of children raised in non-human environment, and cause one to appreciate the question of what man would be without society. A further step is the current emphasis on love, as reflected in such widely read books as **Erich Fromm's** *The Art of Loving* and **Robert O. Johann's** *The Meaning of Love.* Others in this area include **C. S. Lewis,** *Four Loves;* **Jean Guitton,** *Essay On Human Love;* **Ignace Lepp,** *The Psychology of Loving;* and **Michael J. Faraon, O.P.,** *The Metaphysical and Psychological Principles of Love.*

In quite another vein are the writings of the language philosophers such as **Gilbert Ryle** (e.g., pp. 195–198 of his *The Concept of Mind*); **A. J. Ayer** (pp. 208–226 of his *The Problem of Knowledge*); and **Peter F. Strawson** (pp. 81–113 of his *Individuals*). Their approach is opposed by recent philosophers such as **Alburey Castell,** *The Self in Philosophy,* **F. Romero, C. E. M. Joad, John Wild,** and **Henri Bergson.** Psychotherapists such as **V. Frankl, L. Binswanger, Rollo May, Gordon Allport, Igor Caruso,** and **Jos. Nuttin** reflect an existential influence, which is profoundly explored by the philosopher **Herbert Fingarette** in *The Self in Transformation: Psychoanalysis, Philosophy and the Life of the Spirit.* See also Rollo May, *Psychology and the Human Dilemma.*

On conformity verses individuality, besides the writings of **David Riesman, Wm. Whyte's** *The Organization Man,* and **Paul Tillich's** *The Courage to Be,* see the list on pp. 56–57 of **James E. Royce, S.J.,** *Personality and Mental Health* (Rev. ed.), and the discussion on the meaning of normalcy on pp. 47–54 of the same.

14 MAN A LIVING BEING

Every organism is a melody that sings itself. Uexkull

 In Chapter 2 we asked some questions which could be answered only after we had examined the full panoply of man's activities, for we said that we can know a being only in its operations. We are at last in a position to make explicit from this evidence the nature of man as a living being.

"Life" is an abstract term. The existential approach of Aquinas was more concrete; he frequently states that "to live" is simply the "to be" of living things. Life, for him, is the very being of a living thing. To ask the nature of human life is to bring us to the fulfillment of our investigation: it is to ask what sort of being man is.

Is life equivalent to the operations of a living thing? (Life operations are called vital operations, since *vital* in Latin means "of or pertaining to life." Unfortunately the word vital in English often connotes "necessary for life" and suggests only a certain few physiological operations such as heartbeat and respiration.) We have already seen that man is not always acting in all the ways he can. Moreover, all these activities must be the operations of some thing which operates: one cannot conceive of just activity with nothing acting. Operations come and go, begin and cease, while man remains. What man *is* must be something other than what he does.

What, then, is the nature of this being which performs vital or life operations? Is it essentially of a different kind from nonliving being? This question will be the burden of the present chapter.

UNITY OF HUMAN ORGANISM

First we must ask the question whether man is a being at all, or merely a conglomeration of many beings. It would be fruitless to look for a principle of unity which makes man one being, if he were not first seen to be one.

Gardner Murphy (1949, pp. 444–445), states:

> But the most acute of all issues in contemporary psychology seems to be the issue of wholes and parts; the quest for patterned structure or for the definition and functional analysis of component elements. It is in a sense the old issue of Aristotle's forms versus Democritus's atoms, but it is stated today in terms of evolutionary holism, the indivisibility of the "living system," or in terms of laboratory analysis of behavior into identifiable and measurable units. There are so many facts that call for the one approach, so many that call for the other, that at first sight one might hesitate to make a final choice between them. . . .
>
> One may begin to suspect that the basic temperamental or emotional incompatibility of the promachine and antimachine theorists has changed rather little in recent decades. One might even point out that the issue drawn by La Mettrie two hundred years ago still stands approximately as he defined it. More and more technical research gives more and more weapons to each school. The history of biology and that of psychology give no reason for believing that the question of mechanism is soluble by the mere accumulation of more and more data . . . it cannot be resolved by any present type of evidence, or by any evidence of which we can conceive. . . .

This passage tells us that the question of the unity of man is perennial and acute. Murphy's further assertion, that the question is not to be answered by amassing more factual evidence, suggests that for a solution we look toward the methods of philosophy.

The evidence against unity

At first glance the evidence that man is not one being seems overwhelming. The philosopher, if he is honest, must take into account all the facts, or at least his explanation must be able to assimilate them. The facts pertinent here are gathered from many sources: our own experience, the clinical psychology of abnormal states, the biology of organism, biochemistry, and the arguments of some notable philosophers. Factual evidence which seems to indicate that man is not one being may be listed under the following headings.

1. *Parts.* Man has many operative parts: the eye is not the hand. Are they both man? More important, biology tells us that man is composed of many individuals cells and that growth takes place by division and multiplication of these cells. The theory has been proposed that man is simply a colony of cells, which are individuals much like the bees or ants which constitute the colony of insects.

2. *Chemical elements.* Moreover, spectroscopic analysis reveals properties of many different elements within the living body.

3. *Particles.* The nature of neural activity indicates electrochemical activities involving a flow of electrons, and perhaps of atoms in the case of other changes in the body.

4. *Fragmentary life.* Besides the well-known experiment in which Alexis Carrel kept a piece of chicken heart alive for years after the chicken had been dead, there is much evidence of various kinds of tissues being capable of separate existence as in skin grafts and organ transplants.

5. *Multiple personality.* Clinical psychology tells us of many cases where the person had two or even three "personalities," now Dr. Jekyll and and Mr. Hyde, or three different "faces of Eve." This is in addition to the splitting of personality manifested in schizophrenia, and the conflicts we all feel within ourselves at times.

The conclusion is summed up in the philosophical position called *mechanism,* which says that man is just a physicochemical machine, a conglomeration of many parts which are really separate beings working together in close cooperation. In this context the soul, if such there be, is a "ghost in the machine" or supernatural entity over and above the nature of the organism—a construct which the mechanist rightly rejects.

The evidence for unity

Other philosophers, usually called *vitalists,* point to evidence that a unified living organism differs from a beehive or a machine. The parts and activities are primarily and directly ordered to a common end which is intrinsic, not something outside themselves; and they are ordered to this common end intrinsically, i.e., by the nature of the being itself.

PRIMARILY AND DIRECTLY A part may act secondarily for itself without destroying substantial unity; thus the heart also supplies itself with blood. But the primary purpose of the heart is to pump blood for the whole body, not merely for itself. Conversely, all the bees or ants share indirectly in the good of the whole colony. But the parts of man work primarily and directly for the good of the whole man; and this can only happen if man is a unit.

INTRINSIC END Nutrition, growth, scar tissue are all aimed at the good of the organism itself. If several men join to push a truck, or even to form a business corporation, this common end does not make them one (except metaphorically) because the end is outside themselves. The key to the unity of a living thing is *intrinsic* finality. The proper end of the business itself is extrinsic to the members; only as a means does it relate to their own good. Similarly, the parts of a machine work for a common end, but it is an end outside the machine: garments are extrinsic to the sewing machine.

INTRINSICALLY ORDERED But take the case of an automatic oiling device, or the voltage regulator on your automobile: does not this work for the good of the whole? And is not the good to which it is ordered intrinsic to the machine? Yes, but this does not prove that the parts of the machine constitute a substantial unit rather than a mere aggregate. The reason is that these devices are so designed by an extrinsic agent: they show no intrinsic finality. Contrast the autonomic or endocrine systems of the human body: it is their self-organizing and self-regulating aspects which point to the unity of a living thing. The most marvelous feedback and self-correcting features of modern machines are but the products of the men who designed and built them; on this precise point they are essentially different from even simple organisms which develop and maintain themselves from within. Even the lowly amoeba is an organism in this sense (though not in biological terminology because it has only one cell).

Further evidence for the unity of man can be observed when we consider the dynamic unity of purpose between disparate functions. The circulatory, digestive, endocrine, and nervous systems not only maintain vegetative or biological life in themselves, each other, and throughout the body. They also develop and maintain the sense organs as instruments of conscious life. The fetus develops sense organs months before there is any question of using them. Of what use are eyes to a fetus? This shows an overall unity in organization from the beginning of development. And they are specifically *human* eyes and ears, not dog or "just-animal" eyes and ears. Fainting, blushing, hysterical paralysis, hypnotically induced body changes, and even psychosomatic disorders such as gastric ulcers from chronic worry—all point to the unified organization of man across all levels of operation.[1]

One must be careful here not to use an argument which will prove only that man is an intimately united number of substances. This type of argument occurs if one argues from the unity of the effect rather than from the unity of the operation. Thus when several people push a car, the effect is one: the motion of the car. But the operations are several: there are as many "pushings" as there are pushers. Man's unity is primarily that of intrinsic finality, not merely that these activities and parts are intricately connected. Even when they go awry and work against the good of the whole, as in the case of tumor or ulcers, this is an accidental disorder, the abuse of what normally works for the good of the whole.

Vitalist reply to difficulties

The application of these criteria to organisms below man is sometimes difficult. Sometimes it is hard to tell whether we have a cluster of individual organisms together, or a single organism. The fact that they are all alike often indicates a colony, as opposed to the different structure and functions of the cells of an organism. But as we said earlier about the distinction between plant and animal, or between animal and man, the mere fact that we

---

[1] Although commonly observable, the pertinent facts can be seen even more clearly in scientific investigation. The semipopular writings of doctors like Alexis Carrel (*Man the Unknown*), Sir Charles Sherrington (*Man on His Nature*), and Walter B. Cannon (*The Wisdom of the Body*) contain authentic and fascinating details.

find it hard to tell the difference in an individual case does not prove that there is no difference, any more than the fact that I could not tell counterfeit from real money means that they are of equal value. Again, there are cases of symbiosis, such as grafts on fruit trees, parasites, Siamese twins. Close association and even sharing of some parts may suggest unity, but usually these are distinct living beings, manifesting different kinds of operations.

The vitalists give the following answers to the five types of evidence mentioned above which seemed to point to the conclusion that man is not one. Here, the concern of the philosopher is not to question facts. Rather, it is the interpretation of the facts and the correctness of the ultimate conclusions drawn which fall within his competence.

1. *Parts.* Possession of parts of various kinds does not prove any more than that man is a complex organized being rather than a simple homogeneous one (similar throughout). In fact, their very heterogeneity (dissimilarity) argues against the cell-colony theory. But the basic question is whether these parts themselves act *as independent beings.* The vitalist says that they do not, but as parts of a unified whole, to whose good they are essentially subordinated and outside of which they have no existence, or have existence in an utterly different manner than when existing as parts. They do not operate for themselves, but for man.

2. *Chemical elements.* Here we must distinguish between chemical properties and substance in the philosophical sense. Certainly the elements which make up the body will produce their characteristic pattern of lines on the spectrograph, and some can be tagged and traced through the system. But do these chemical "substances" exhibit *all* and *only* the properties they have when not in the body? Nitrogen does not grow, water does not see and hear. They now do things that they were never capable of doing before. But this means they are a different kind of being. They are no longer nitrogen and water, but living human flesh. This is a different nature, even though some of the chemical properties may be retained. The nitrogen *was* nitrogen before becoming part of the body, and it will be nitrogen again when the body decomposes. Right now it is human, a part of man's body; it does not act as an independent being. This is clear from the demonstration of intrinsic finality above. Conversely, man does not act like a chemical element or an electric current. An essentially different operation shows a different kind of being; even though elements enter into the composition of man, they do so precisely by being changed into man.

This should cause no surprise. We have already remarked that heterogeneity of parts characterizes any complex organism. Tissue is of different kinds in different parts of the body, yet it is all human. So the elements retain some of their various properties, but this does not prevent their all being man. That man is not the same all over (homogeneous) is a commonly observable fact, not a discovery of modern chemistry. In man these chemical "substances" are not supposits, i.e., complete substantial units with their own proper acts of existing. Remember that in seeking to know whether these are beings or one being we are asking philosophical questions, and these cannot have chemical answers. The two approaches are not opposed, they are simply different.

3. *Particles.* The same reasoning as in (2) could apply to the evidence for subatomic particles like electrons. There is considerable evidence for their activity, and enough evidence to show that they behave differently

than when not in the human composite, for man does things that these particles by themselves do not. Again, we are speaking of what is demonstrable fact; in so far as this involves theoretical constructs, it belongs to the realm of scientific theory. Theories may change, and in any case are outside the realm of philosophy.

4. *Fragmentary life.* The key answer again is that we must not look merely to the fact that these parts are capable of being kept alive after separation: the question is whether they have independent existence *before* they are severed from the whole.

Even in the unified organism these parts exist in varying degrees of proximate potency to separate existence. Being already organized to that degree of perfection by its union with the organism, the matter is well disposed to operate as living when separated. It is not in mere potency to life, as food is before being digested and assimilated into human flesh. It is actually part of the one living being. Whether the part can live by itself depends on how nearly disposed its potency is to separate existence. This usually is a question of how complex the organism is.

In a simple one-celled organism mere division can result in two complete beings, yet nobody would argue that before the division it was two, except potentially. A worm is so simple in structure ("a digestive tract with a hole on each end") that again mere division can result in two worms: it is already disposed to such an actuality by its nature. A cutting or slip of a plant nearly contains the perfection of the whole plant, as all it lacks are roots. As functions and organs become more specialized, any part contains less of the whole, and its chances of independent survival diminish. Organs and tissues in test tubes can exist for any length of time only when the other functions of the total organism are somehow artificially supplied in the laboratory by the ingenuity of the scientist. They lack that self-organization and self-maintenance we noted in the total living thing. Hair and fingernails are said to grow for a while after death. The cells which produce them are so specialized that even though organized for that function and virtually independent for it, they cannot supply other vital operations and so eventually cease. But they are capable of that function at any time only because organized to that level by the total organism, which has the abilities for many different kinds of operation.

Thus man is seen to be actually one, but multiple by reason of his many parts. It is not surprising that some of these parts may have the potency for separate existence, but far from proving that they have independent being before separation, the evidence points to the conclusion that they have this potency only in virtue of their being parts of the whole. To be a "part" means to be "of the whole;" separated, it is no longer a part but a new but smaller whole with its own existence.

5. *Multiple personality.* We have already seen the answer to this when we distinguished between person and personality in the previous chapter. The person is the same, but the psychological personality may change, as first one and then another set of habitual associations and emotions is operating. Psychiatrists like Morton Prince and William McDougall who reported on some of the classic cases claim that the person would always recognize the underlying identity when cured, or under hypnosis, or at least on his death bed. In schizophrenic "splitting" of personality, or in other instances of personality conflict, thought and emotion do not correspond. Affect may be inappropriate, or lacking. Sense appetite may attract

one way, reason the other. Does this destroy the unity of the person? Quite the contrary: there would be no true internal conflict were these not all the operations of the same one man, as we noted in Chapter 12 when explaining the multiplicity of man's powers as properties of one being.

Phenomenology of self

Many contemporary philosophers tend to bypass the mechanist-vitalist controversy and work through an analysis of what is implicit in immediate experience. Are we not immediately conscious of the fact that it is the same self or "I" who has all these parts and does all these things? Here we must be careful lest a purely subjective phenomenological approach lead us back to the quibbles that flowed from an excessive introspectionism at the beginnnig of this century. But both philosophers and psychologists today are recognizing that even subjective experiences are communicable, without the preconceived structures of the introspectionists.

What does analysis of our ordinary language reveal about man's unity? We say "I think," and, "I run," without ever implying that I am a mind that understands and a body that runs. Rather, it is the same "I" who is the subject of both activities. Similarly, if we say, "John is intelligent," and, "John is fat," the referent in both propositions is the same visible mass of walking, talking protoplasm.

These and similar expressions indicate that man has direct though implicit evidence of himself as a single unit, in spite of the multiplicity of operations and parts which he observes in himself. I am aware of my own body, and have some idea of its parts and their locations. Now the important thing about this bit of evidence is that I know myself as myself, not as something other. I am quite clear that if someone steps on my toe he is stepping on me. In this sense I *am* a body, rather than *have* a body. I do not say that my eye sees, but that I see. When angry or afraid we may say that our stomach is in knots or our blood pressure is up, but we are very clear that this complex mass of feelings and activities is *mine*, not that some of them are part of something else.

Secondly, when I know anything else, in the very fact of knowing this other thing I am implicitly aware of myself as distinct from "other." This implicit awareness of self is, upon analysis, a clear indication of the unity that man has in opposition to all the rest of reality. Experiments which have attempted to isolate a man from all external stimulation by suspending him in a vat of water at body temperature and excluding all sights and sounds (stimulus deprivation) have brought out the fact that all awareness of other somehow involves awareness of self.

Finally, by explicit or conscious acts of self-reflection, I can be directly aware of myself as the single source and term of my own activities. This of course is a special type of self-awareness and different from the above.

NATURE OF LIFE

The upshot of all this seems to be that one act of existence, one "to be" or *esse*, is the ultimate source of both man's activities and his unity. He acts as one because he is one. What is the connection between being one and being alive? This will become apparent as we investigate further just what life is, and how a living being differs from nonliving things. We have already made considerable strides by analyzing man's intrinsic finality, his self-organization for the good of the whole. For our first naïve impression of the difference between living and nonliving objects has to do with whether they exhibit self-initiated activity. Thus if a thing is inert and moves only when moved from outside, we judge it is dead; primitive peoples may judge an automobile alive because it apparently moves itself.

Upon closer analysis, it is seen that the car does not truly move itself, for it depends upon designer, mechanic, and driver, and so is utterly different from a living thing which as we have seen is self-sufficient. Even its "self-starter" turns out not to be such in reality. More important, the "self" of the car is seen to be not one being, but an aggregate, a number of substances put in juxtaposition by an external agent and moving each other as distinct things. But for one thing to move another is not self-activity at all. On the other hand, some apparently inert glob of matter will upon further examination be found to exercise remarkable self-activity: it grows, nourishes, and repairs itself, and reproduces its kind. We say it is alive, whereas the automobile it is not.

Self-actualizing independence

Examining all things which are said to live in contrast with those which do not, we find one characteristic appearing throughout: a living being exhibits a certain independence or self-sufficiency in action. It is more a self-contained unit, less dependent upon outside help for preserving and exercising its nature. The most marvelous electronic computers not only do not grow by themselves, but they need a host of technicians swarming over them to keep them in operation. They cannot gather knowledge; it must be fed into them. They cannot understand or interpret their output; what they do must be programmed into them. In contrast, man grows, develops his mode of operation, maintains life, "becomes" the whole universe through his knowledge, and is a determining force in his environment—the source of all this activity is within, and he utilizes and transforms what he receives from outside with a power of self-actualization not found in nonliving things.

Vital activity thus is seen to be fundamentally *that by which the living thing perfects itself.* Some capacity for such operations seems to be found in all living beings, and none found in nonliving things.

Man's self-initiating and self-perfective activity

Let us now examine in greater detail the notion of life as we find it verified in the operations of the living things we know, especially man. The first two operations man shares with other spiritual beings; the last four with the organisms below him.

1. *Knowledge.* We have already seen that knowledge differs from just passively receiving an impression precisely in the power of the knower to enrich his own form by the addition of cognitive forms in act.

2. *Dynamics.* Likewise, man perfects himself by responding to stimuli in ways which show a lack of proportion between stimulus and response, indicating how in varying degrees he initiates the response from within.

3. *Nutrition.* The self-perfective nature of a living being is clearly illustrated by the manner in which we take food from the outside and transform it by our own digestive powers so that it is assimilated into living human flesh. Contrast this with the way in which crystals are said to "grow" by the mere accretion of more of the same from the outside, not by taking foreign matter and actively transforming it within themselves as living beings do by intussusception. We "feed" a car gasoline, but nothing comparable to nourishment takes place, for the gasoline never becomes automobile. Nourishment continues even after a thing reaches maturity and stops growing.

4. *Growth.* Perhaps the most fascinating evidence for both the unity and self-perfectiveness of the human organism comes from embryology, where we see a simple one-celled structure evolve and differentiate itself into two, then four cells, gradually into three general types of tissue, and eventually into the marvelous complexity of organs that make up the complete body. Who or what does it? No mother takes credit for the fashioning that goes on within her during those nine months. No anatomist would presume to construct a single organ like the cochlea of the ear, much less the interrelated regulatory system we call the endocrine glands. The nervous system alone comprises some twelve billion cells, all starting from one. And considering the permutations and combinations possible, it is statistically staggering that they should ever fit together correctly, not to mention in the majority of

cases. With so many trillions of chances of something going wrong, the fact that the human being ever comes out right attests to incredibly unified order. Here is internal finality at work, self-organization undeniable. Compare this process with the assembly line at the Ford plant where a car is "growing" as it moves along. How many external agents are at work, and how little does the car have to do with the whole process! Yet a fetus does not even take blood from the mother; it manufactures its own from materials it selects from the mother's bloodstream.

5. *Self-repair.* The pruning of vines and fruit trees, and the fact that some lower organisms will grow a whole new limb if one is amputated, are interesting illustrations of this power of living things, but they may cause us to overlook the importance of something so prosaic as the formation of scar tissue, without which all human recovery would be impossible and all surgery vain. As doctors never tire of reminding themselves, they do not "cure" anything really, but only help nature to help itself.[2] The surgeon does not join tissues; he puts them in close proximity in the hope that nature will take over and do what he cannot. But if you "injure" your car or a computer, you can expect no self-perfecting powers to work a repair. (The rust that forms after damage is not analogous to scar tissue. Just the opposite: it is decomposition rather than growth.)

This ability for self-repair in living things is sometimes called irritability, but the term seems unfortunate. The "irritability" of dynamite is not for the good of the dynamite, but destroys it. The compass needle is stimulated or irritated by a magnet, but this reaction does not have as its purpose the preservation and perfection of the compass itself, as self-repair has. The expression "adaptation to environment" is similar: thermostatic controls "adapt" furnaces to temperature changes, but the lack of intrinsic finality is soon apparent. There is nothing here comparable to the way a heart or a kidney, for example, will double its capacity to accommodate an increased demand.

6. *Reproduction.* Lastly, we have machines which make other machines, but we have no machine capable of reproducing itself, as human beings can, and as do other animals and plants. This indefinite reproduction of the species is one of the central marvels of the biological world, to which thousands of interesting phenomena pertain. Some are controversial and demand scientific investigation, but the one fact is clear. Nonliving substances may produce other nonliving substances, but only living things reproduce, i.e., make more of the same species, which in turn can reproduce themselves, and so on indefinitely.

[2] For these and similar reasons Herbert Ratner, M.D., pleads for medical schools to develop a philosophy of organism, in *Medicine* (Santa Barbara, Calif.: Center for Study of Democratic Institutions, 1962; condensed in *Saturday Review*, May 26, 1962).

An electronic computer might conceivably be programmed to produce other electronic computers so programmed, but besides their dependence on man not only in origin but also for repair, they would not in any true sense grow. Their production would be all by extrinsic accretion, not self-organization. They would also differ from living beings in the matter of nutrition, since man would have to supply materials. If this hypothetical self-reproducing "machine" were programmed to get its raw materials from, say, the atmosphere, in addition to having the power of true internal growth and self-repair, it would *be* a living thing. But could man make a living being? We must first ask what "makes" a living thing. That is the problem for our next chapter.[3]

"Living" is analogous

The term "living" covers a wide range of beings. Since to live is to be a certain way, the term must be analogous, as being itself is. Proportionately to the being of the thing and thus analogously, this self-activity will be found to exist in all living beings from God down to a fungus. (Extension of the term in metaphors like "living waters" is, of course, an extrinsic analogy.)

God is most independent and self-contained. Intellectual life displays more initiative than sensory life, and so the analogy runs down the hierarchy of living beings from the pure spirits through men and down to brutes and vegetation. The lowest plants are somewhat at the mercy of their surroundings, but even here we see vegetative life go on, adapt, and reproduce, while machinery obsolesces, mountains crumble, and that very symbol of stability, Gibraltar, is being slowly torn asunder by apparently feeble plant life.

Within these main categories we see degrees in the analogy; for instance, the genius with intuitive intellect is far less dependent upon outside help than the moron, and the circus monkey exhibits far more self-movement than the shellfish. Life is by no means a univocal term, but there is an analogy of proper proportionality between each living being and the degree or manner in which it has the characteristics. Man is our most direct and primary example; other kinds of beings up and down the scale are known only by analogy with our own life. But man is a good one to have to start with, since he combines immaterial and organic operations and thus partakes of the characteristics of both spiritual and material living beings.

[3] The actual question of synthesizing a living being will be discussed toward the end of Chapter 17.

Immanent action

Those familiar with textbooks in scholastic philosophy may be surprised that no mention is made of immanent action as a criterion of life. The reason is twofold. First, neither Aquinas nor Aristotle uses the notion of immanent action at any time in defining life. They often distinguish between immanent and transient action, but never as a means of dividing living beings from nonliving. The Greek equivalent of "immanent activity" does not even appear in the entire text of Aristotle's *De Anima*. Secondly, the use of this term creates unnecessary difficulties which arise purely from the terminology and otherwise present no philosophical problem. The usual solution is to broaden and distort the meaning of "immanent" until it means "independently self-perfective," as we have explained vital operations to be. But this is not what the word means, either in modern English, medieval Latin, or Aristotle's Greek. Immanent means "remaining within" and could apply to the activity of even nonliving beings which have motion within themselves, be they Aristotle's fire or the modern physicist's atom. It is the opposite of transient (that which acts on another), whether the agent be living or not.

The question is not whether the orbital movement of subatomic particles is immanent; the question is whether it is self-initiating and self-organizing. Actually, whatever causes the atom to be causes its subatomic particles to move. The movement depends on external causes for its origin, and the atom shows no signs of true growth, self-repair, or species reproduction. Any change tends to make it something *else*, instead of perfecting it in its own nature. Aristotle's physics was inadequate, but his definition of life in terms of *self-perfective* activity (rather than *immanent activity*) is open to no more difficulties from nuclear physics than from his own concept of fire.[4]

Some difficulties

1. Could it be argued that the movement of the animal is given it by its parents, just as the movement in the atom is given it by its external cause? They would thus be equally lacking in self-initiated activity.

Answer: The difference is that when the atom is formed it has this motion actually; it is formed as a moving substance. But when the animal is formed by its parents, it may have little activity at all; it is given not motion but a nature which can cause its own motion.

2. Does not a spring or a rubber band have self-action?

Answer: Not of its own nature, but only by reason of external agents: the manufacturer and the person who stretched it. Passive rather than active, it does not initiate the movement and exercises no control over it. Like electricity and unlike living beings, it depends wholly on external forces to cause its motion.

3. But is not the motion of self-initiated activity contrary to the principle

---

[4] *Physica*, VIII, 4, 254b7–256a3.
Curiously enough, Aquinas does not mention examples of immanent activity like cognition in explaining his definition of an active power. Perhaps it is because he took the definition bodily from the text of Aristotle as then known. See James E. Royce, S.J., "St. Thomas and the Definition of Active Potency," *The New Scholasticism*, 1960, 34(4):431–437.

of causality? To move or perfect oneself would seem to be pulling oneself up by his own bootstraps. After all, nothing gives what it hasn't got. If I already have the perfection, then I don't need so to perfect myself; if I do not, then I cannot give it to myself.

Answer: The budding philosopher who answered that the professor might not have a headache but still gave one to *him* was more accurate than perhaps he knew. The professor did not have the headache actually, but he did possess it virtually by possessing the power to give the student one. Recall our explanation of the very nature of an operative power. When not exercising the power, one has the formal perfection of this activity only in potency. But as an efficient (instrumental) cause the power actually exists. Answering another way, one might say that it is precisely in the possession of this unique kind of self-perfective power that living beings differ from nonliving, and any attempt to explain life by reducing it to nonlife is begging the question at issue. Even amoebae or animals in the one-cell stage have powers of self-movement which require a stimulus as part cause at most, being themselves the principal cause of their own action.

4. But "movement" seems hardly to apply to higher vital activities such as intellection.

Answer: Movement here is taken in a broad sense of any transition from potency to act, not mere locomotion.

5. But in contemplation of truth already acquired, there seems to be no movement even in this wider sense; certainly in the case of God's knowledge there is no transition at all from potency to act.

Answer: True, and we include under the terms operation or vital activities any such perfection, which is operation only in an analogous sense. The question is not of passage from potency to act, but independent self-sufficiency in having the perfection. And this is why our answer to question 3 above does not make all living beings independent of God, or self-sufficient in being. The difference between God and creature is one of dependence in being; the difference between living and nonliving is one of dependence in operation. God gives *being* to both dog and atom; but to the former He gives a nature capable of initiating its own activity; to the latter He gives only the activity which comes with the nature.

6. Certain seeds have been found fertile although kept for centuries, and frogs have likewise been kept in a state of suspended animation for alleged decades or more. Are they alive?

Answer: Remember that our definition speaks of being, not activity. The acid test is not whether the being is actually manifesting self-perfectivity, but whether it is the kind of being that can do so. Now the proof that these beings are capable of vital activities is the fact that they do grow when given an opportunity; mere opportunity will never evoke such activity in a rock or a machine. (There is some evidence that minute, infinitesimal activity may be going on in seeds, such as hardly measurable carbon dioxide exchange; this would not alter our position, which is based on kind of being, rather than on actual activity.)

REVIEW QUESTIONS

1. "Life is vital operations." Criticize on two counts.
2. What is the relation between the notion of life and the unity of man?

3. "You have to say either that an automobile is one since all parts work for a common purpose, or that man is not one since he is made up of various parts, chemical elements, and powers." Solve this dilemma.

4. "Chemical properties of the elements are manifested within the living organism; therefore the body is not one, but an aggregate of substances." Criticize.

5. Philosophy says man is one. Clinical psychology gives us cases of multiple personality. Do they therefore contradict?

6. Are living bodies essentially different from nonliving? Why?

7. Are living bodies essentially superior to nonliving? Why?

8. Is "life" a univocal or an analogous concept? Why?

9. What is the basic characteristic of all living beings?

10. Name four functions which distinguish organic life from all non-living beings.

FOR FURTHER READING

Kelly & Tallon: the selection from **Strasser** on pp. 254–264.

A good source is **R. Schubert-Soldern,** *Mechanism and Vitalism.* One of the best philosophical discussions on the unity of man is by **George P. Klubertanz,** S.J., in his *The Philosophy of Human Nature.* **Ralph S. Lillie** at the University of Chicago in 1945 was seeing some fascinating connections between science and philosophy, as in chap. 2 of his *General Biology and the Philosophy of Organism.*

The biochemistry of life is progressing so rapidly that it would be impossible to give current sources. Perhaps one of the best ways to keep abreast is through the articles appearing occasionally in *Scientific American.* There are many books, e.g., **William S. Beck,** *Modern Science and the Nature of Life.* Some other useful items are the following:

von Bertalanffy, L. *Problems of Life: An Evaluation of Modern Biological Thought.*

Driesch, Hans. *Mind and Body.*

Driesch, Hans. *The Science and Philosophy of the Organism.* 2 vols. Seems to make the soul an efficient rather than formal cause.

Gilby, Thomas, O.P. "Thought, Volition and the Organism," *The Thomist,* 1940, 2:1–13.

Gilby, Thomas, O.P. "Vienne and Vienna," *Thought,* 1946, 21:63–82.

Gill, Henry V., S.J. "Entropy, Life, and Evolution," in his *Fact and Fiction in Modern Science.*

Moore, Thomas Verner. *Cognitive Psychology.* Pp. 45–73, 86–89, 550–559. As physician, philosopher, and psychologist, Moore is always full of interesting insights.

du Noüy, Lecomte. *Human Destiny.*

Schrodinger, Erwin. *What Is Life?*

Sinnott, E. W. *Cell and Psyche: The Biology of Purpose.* Also his *The Bridge of Life,* and other works.

Windle, Sir Bertram C. A. *Vitalism and Scholasticism.*

Windle, Sir Bertram C. A. *What Is Life? A Study of Vitalism and Neovitalism.*

Detailed argument and documentation against defining life in terms of immanent activity are given in **James E. Royce, S.J., "Life and Living Beings,"** *The Modern Schoolman,* 1960, 37:213–232. **Aristotle** states his definition in his treatise *On the Soul,* I, 1 (412a, 14–15) and II, 2 (413a23 to 413b2); **Aquinas** in *Summa Theol.,* Ia, 18, 1–3; *Summa Contra Gent.,* I, 97–98.

15   MONISM, DUALISM, OR NEITHER?

To pursue the spiritual in isolation from matter is to play into the hands of the crudest kind of materialism.   Dewey

A fundamental contradiction now seems to rear its ugly head. We have seen evidence for the unity of man as a living being, yet we have spoken of the spiritual as well as the bodily life of man as a person. Which is man, one or two?

As in most problems which have occupied great minds, conflicting answers have been proposed. The most common are monism and dualism. Since each has been held by intelligent men, it behooves us to examine them for what truth they may contain. Yet they cannot both be right, and perhaps neither is satisfactory. Even this may suggest an answer for us.

Monism

From the Greek *monos*, meaning "one," this refers to any philosophy which teaches that there is *only one ultimate principle of reality* in the universe, and therefore in man. Monism may be either frank or disguised.

Frank monism may be either of two extremes: (1) Materialism holds that the only ultimate principle of reality in the universe is matter. This is not a mere assertion of the reality of matter, or most of us would be materialists. Rather, it is a denial of all else. It is a metaphysical position, not a scientific one, since pronouncements about the ultimate constituents of all being are beyond the scope of science. Some scientists hold this as their philosophy, many do not. (2) Idealism, or spiritualism, also holds for only one ultimate principle, but says that the only reality is mind or spirit. This is less common than its opposite in modern America. But many contemporary Oriental philosophies, some schools of Western thought in recent centuries, and a few sects in America today emphasize the reality of the spiritual to the exclusion of the material, which is considered unimportant or even nonexistent. Some religious groups hold this as their philosophy; many do not.

Disguised monism is a softened expression of one of the above extremes, usually materialistic, since men do not like to be crude about a position when there is conflicting evidence. Thus we have double-aspect theories, epiphenomenalism, and certain forms of parallelism. In all of these a subtle materialism is couched in terms which speak of the conflicting evidence as being like the concave and convex sides of the same curve. For them, brain and thought are "a matter of how you look at it."

Dualism

This holds that *man is two beings,* actually dual. If intelligent men have seen evidence which convinces them of the reality of matter, and others see equally impressive evidence for the reality of the spiritual, it is not surprising that still others should see good reason to accept both lines of evidence and reconcile them in some system which attempts to account for both instead of denying either. This has been done many times over the centuries in various ways, the most common being some form of either parallelism or interactionism.

Psychophysical parallelism says that man is two beings, only apparently united. Matter and spirit each function with varying degrees of independence of the other. Something is happening in the brain while thought goes on, but there may be no real connection. Certain forms of occasionalism also fit in this category.

Interactionism is by far the more common form of dualism. The union here is real, not merely apparent. This position says that man is two things, each acting on the other. In some books on psychosomatic medicine we have a "mind" which worries and a "body" which develops gastic ulcers, as if the psyche and the soma were two beings.

However poetically we may speak of the jockey and his horse becoming "as one" in a race, we are clear that they remain two separate beings. Whether or not Plato actually compared the union of body and soul to that of a horse and rider, he seems to have held the ultimate duality of human nature. With Aristotle's works lost, it is doubly understandable that early Christianity seized upon Platonic dualism. Not only was nothing better known, but Plato's notion lent itself readily to the antithesis between pagan debauchery and the salvation of one's soul with which the early Christians were concerned. This conviction was perpetuated by the ascetical writers for similar reasons, with strong influence from neo-Platonism. Loyola speaks of the soul as "imprisoned within the body."

Descartes imposed this dualism upon most of modern philosophy and psychology when he made man a body and a mind, hooked together at the pineal gland. This is probably the most fateful error in the history of philosophy, for no matter how intimate and intricate the interaction of mental and bodily processes, dualism of this sort destroys the unity of man.

Precisely here is the crux of the problem: dualism reconciles the two streams of evidence, for material and for spiritual reality in man, only to run afoul of the evidence that man is one being. Dualism is a most unacceptable term to most modern psychologists and biologists, because they are too much impressed with the unity of human nature. They are so determined to avoid dualism that they often prefer to adopt some disguised materialistic monism because they see no other answer, even though it means unsatisfactory explanation of the evidence for the immaterial.

Neither

Is there a way out of this dilemma? Apparently not, if we read the many books which present the above alternatives and then leave the student with the impression that they have exhausted the possibilities.[1]

Another alternative is that man is neither two beings, as dualism asserts, nor composed of only one principle, as the monists say. Rather, man is composed of two principles, but he is one being. This solution to the dilemma also seems to afford the best explanation to date for what happens at death. Is there a real change? Is a corpse a man? Does man have a vital principle which can transcend matter? To see how

[1] For example, Prof. W. E. Hocking of Harvard, *Types of Philosophy;* Edna Heidbreder, *Seven Psychologies;* H. Flanders Dunbar, *Mind and Body;* Gardner Murphy, *An Historical Introduction to Modern Psychology.*

this solution avoids dualism, one must understand the concept of formal cause.

FORMAL CAUSALITY

In the last chapter we satisfied ourselves that man is essentially different from nonliving things. As inquirers we want to know what this difference is. Science gives us many wonderful details. Physiologists describe how the endocrine glands normally maintain just the right balance of inflammatory and anti-inflammatory hormones in the bloodstream to enable the body to repair injury with maximum speed and minimum infection. Psychologists from Freud to Skinner have elaborate theories on the workings of human dynamics and the learning process. Embryologists tell us that during the nine months of fetal life the skin covering the young retina becomes transparent and transforms itself into cornea and lens because of a substance set free by the optic vesicle in the cerebrum. Excellent, and ingeniously discovered.

But the philosopher in his search for ultimates finds these less an explanation than something to be explained. *Why* should the optic vesicle secrete a substance just at that time with the property of rendering the skin translucid? And why should it act thus on just the skin over the future retina? Why is man the kind of being that is capable of operant conditioning or ego involvement, conformity or creativity? What makes him to *be* a man at all?

We say that a thing is the way it is be*cause* . . . and get many different answers, all true. The question "Why?" can be answered in as many different ways as there are kinds of cause. Some are easier to grasp than others. Cause in general is that which positively contributes to the being of the thing. Why is this statue what it is? Because the sculptor wanted money, or to honor Abraham Lincoln (final cause). Why? Because the sculptor made it that way (efficient cause). These two are obvious.

But there are other causes to account for why the statue is what it is, causes within the statue itself. Neither the sculptor's purpose (money) nor the sculptor himself and his instruments (efficient causes) enter into the internal constitution of the statue.[2]

Material But if we ask why the nose has this particular shape at the bridge, we might get the answer, be*cause* the marble at this point

[2] If we say the image did, we are still speaking of an extrinsic (exemplary) cause; for as a cognitive form it exists in the sculptor's mind, and acts as a cause by directing his efficient activity. It even existed before the statue, so it could not be inside the statue. It is also called *extrinsic* formal cause.

had a peculiar soft grain in it. This is the matter or *material* cause. It causes by giving itself to the effect, by allowing itself to be acted upon by the efficient cause in such a way that it can become this being. We ask why the statue is heavy, enduring, or beautifully colored, and again the cause of these properties is the marble itself, the material cause. It is passive, but important because its potency sets the limits of the finished product: even the greatest sculptor cannot make a statue with no material at all to work on, nor out of something which does not have the potency to become statue.

Formal Lastly, we may ask why this statue is what it is, i.e., a representation of Lincoln, and we will get the answer, be*cause* the marble has the form or figure of Lincoln. This answer does not deny that the sculptor made the statue, nor that he made it for the reason alleged. It points to what he produced in it, which makes it to be what it is, its *formal* cause.

Form is nothing more or less than the fact that the thing is the way it is: this kind of being, resulting from the adequate action of an efficient cause (or causes) upon a properly disposed material cause. It is not a thing separate from the being itself, like an extrinsic cause. Like a material cause, it causes not by doing anything, but just by being. Cause here is an analogous term. To cause by being desirable (final) is a different thing than to cause by mallet and chisel (efficient), and both are again different from intrinsic causes, which contribute to the existence of the statue internally, by giving themselves to constitute the very being of the thing.

Form is cause in a very analogous sense. Made present in matter by the efficient cause, it causes only by uniting with matter to form this being. Not being a thing, it does not come and go. It simply begins and ceases accordingly as the being is or is not this kind of being, just as the lap does not go anywhere when you stand up, nor the light when it goes out. To return to the comparison of the statue: when we say the sculptor "put" the form of Lincoln into the marble, we do not mean that he went out and got a form of Lincoln and somehow inserted it into the marble. No, he efficiently caused the marble to *be* this form. And when the statue crumbles into dust, we do not say that the form of Lincoln "went" anywhere, but simply that the marble ceases to be in this form. To ask whether the material being and its substantial form are one, says Aristotle, is as silly as to ask whether the wax and its shape are one.

To speak of internal cause as "it" is misleading, for that which has existence is neither the material cause nor the formal cause, but the composite being which results from matter being in this form. It even seems preferable to say *being*, rather than *having*, this form, because the latter suggests that matter is a thing which can have, and form something which can be had. Neither are things. The existing being is a thing; matter and form simply refer to the fact that this designated quantity of being (matter) is now existing as this kind (form) of being.[3] Again, it is better not to say that the form "makes" matter different; the being simply "is" of this kind.

Substantial form

So far, our example has been of shape or figure, an accidental form. This was only to set the stage. What we are really concerned with is substantial form—not the fact that the marble is this or that shape, but that the substance is marble at all[4] and not calcium chloride or U-235 or green cheese. Exactly the same reasoning applies, except that we move from the realm of accidental change to substantial change.

This is most clearly seen against the background of man's unity established in the previous chapter. Suppose a house collapses in a heap, or is exploded into bits (but not burned). It is no longer a house. But is there a substantial change? No, for the simple reason that the house was not *a* substance to begin with. The mass of rubble is still wood and plaster, steel and glass, exactly the same substances as before. The house was not one, but many beings, each with its substantial form. It is still the same beings now, arranged in a different accidental form or shape. Accidental means not having its own proper act of existence. The shape of the house had no existence other than the existences of the parts so arranged. The substantial forms of wood, glass, and the rest remain.

In contrast, examine a human corpse. The accidental forms of shape, size, structure, and arrangement of parts, color, and weight may all be exactly the same as they were in the living body. It looks more like a body than the ruins look like a house. But has there been a substantial change? Yes. This matter is no longer living human flesh. Regardless of accidental similarities, it is a different kind of being. There is no longer that by which it was human; there is only a heap of molecules temporarily arranged in the shape of a man. We say this matter has changed its substantial form.

[3] We shall see that there is a problem here when we discuss the spirituality and immortality of the human soul. But we elect to establish the notion of soul as organic form first, and face the apparent contradictions later.
[4] We prescind from the question of whether marble is a unified substance or an accidental aggregate of particles. The facts of substantial change and the unity of the living body are true in either case, so it need not concern us.

In the collapse of the house, wood remained wood, glass remained glass. In the death of the body, matter ceased to be human and became nonliving matter. When the carpenter builds the house, he changes wood into different sizes and shapes, and arranges an accidental unity with other substances, but he does not make wood into some unified, different kind of substance we call house. But when man eats food, he actually transforms water, carbohydrates, and other substances into his own substance, so that this same matter which formerly existed by the substantial forms of these molecules (or whatever physical unit is postulated) now ceases to be that kind of being and begins to exist by the substantial form which makes matter to be man.

This concept of form or formal cause is simple, yet absolutely fundamental to any understanding of man as a composite unit. Descartes admitted that his brilliant mathematical mind was unable to grasp the notion correctly ("a formis abhorreo"), and he spread the philosophical bassinet into which modern psychology was born with a tradition of univocal, efficient causality which made even good minds, thus culturally conditioned, practically unable to conceive formal causality.[5] It is the key to a conception of the ultimate nature of material beings called *hylomorphism*, from Greek words for matter and form.[6]

Matter and form

Matter is seen to be subject to change. At one time it is food on a plate, later it becomes man, still later it is so much fertilizer. (And since this can become plant and therefore food again, we call the process the metabolic or nitrogen cycle.) Matter is actually only one thing at any one time, but it is potentially many. When actually cabbage, it is potentially cow. When actually beef, it is potentially man. When actually man, it is potentially fertilizer (or tiger, if there are man-eating tigers about).

From this we conclude that any material being is a composite of two substantial principles: one which makes it actually what it is, one which makes it potentially other things. If there were no substantial potency, there would be no change. We would have to say that in digestion food was annihilated and more human flesh created, and that in death the matter of the living body was annihilated and the matter of the corpse created. The only alternative is to say that man has two constituitive principles, one by which he is actually man and the other by which he is potentially corpse. If both were actual, he would be two things at once; if they were both only

5 Karl Buhler, William James, and Harvey Carr are among the eminent psychologists who have said that the matter-and-form unity of scholastic philosophy is probably the best ultimate explanation of man, but that it was too difficult for them to think that way when not habituated to it from youth.

6 *Hyle-* would be more correct than *hylo-*, and *eidos* would be really more appropriate in this context than *morphe*. But the term hylomorphism has crystallized now. The adjective hylomorphic is perhaps best translated as simply matter-and-form theory, union, etc.

potential, he would not be what he is. There must be a principle (matter) common to man, food, and corpse; and a principle (form) specific to each.

These principles are not directly observable. They are the logical conclusion from the facts of change. But the process by which we arrive at them is a far simpler deduction from commonly observable facts than the findings of physics or chemistry. They are intelligible, but not picturable. Easily understood, they cause trouble if one attempts to imagine them. This chapter is a task for intellect, not sense perception. One must not imagine potency as a thing. It simply means the possibility of something to be or do. Here it means the possibility of a material being to become some other kind of material being, to change. Since the potential principle is not any kind of matter by itself, but is such only because it is united with this or that substantial form, it is called *prime* matter, first matter, or substantial potency. Since the form here is what determines this matter to be not merely in this shape or manner but this specific kind of being, it is called *substantial* form.

Prime matter has a relation to substantial form similar to that which second or informed matter (substance) has to accidental form. Thus the matter is actually marble because it has the substantial form[7] of marble. If we pour acid on it and make it something else, this is a change of substantial form. If we give it a different shape while it remains marble, this is a change of accidental form. Just as the marble cannot exist without being in some shape (perhaps irregular and nameless), so prime matter cannot exist without being some kind of matter.

Recent advances in chemistry and physics seem to confirm this notion, for it seems now that, theoretically, any material substance can become any other material substance, if we can just find the right way of changing it. "You can't make a silk purse out of a sow's ear" is an old adage aimed at emphasizing the impossibility of producing an effect which is not within the potentiality of the material cause. A sow's ear certainly does not seem very apt matter, and the task seems impossible until we learn a great deal more organic chemistry. But you *can* make a silk purse out of it now by feeding it to some silkworms or fertilizing their mulberry bushes with it!

Summary

Returning to the notion of death, we can exemplify four chief kinds of cause in this way. Why is John Jones dead? (1) Because Smith murdered him: efficient cause. (2) Because Smith wanted revenge: final cause. (3) Because Jones was the kind of being that could die: material cause. (4) Because his prime matter has ceased to be united with the human substantial form by which it was this organized whole: formal cause.

Each is a true and legitimate answer to the question. Each is different, for it points to a different kind of cause. Each exerts causality in a different way and is irreducible to any of the others. The same electricity will run a waffle iron and a radio, but no amount of current increase will give you music instead of waffles. No amount of final causality will make an efficient cause. Likewise, no amount of efficient causality will make a formal cause.

This is important, for the most common error here is to think of the soul

[7] Or forms (see footnote 4).

as an efficient cause, a gimmick or demiurge moving man from within. This is the error of certain vitalists, who oppose the mechanistic theory because of the manifest intrinsic teleology of the organism, yet attribute to the parts some kind of intelligence or otherwise make things out of what are only parts. The mechanists themselves, taking this view and thinking of the soul as an efficient cause or physical energy, are triumphant when investigation reveals no such entity. For this reason vitalism is a misleading term. It is nonmechanistic, but it is not always hylomorphic.

SOUL AS FORM

With our understanding of formal cause from the analysis of substantial change, we are now in a position to understand man's material and spiritual life as one unified being, without lapsing into the dualism which Gilbert Ryle rejects in his *The Concept of Mind* (1949). "With deliberate abusiveness" he calls dualism the "official doctrine" of body and soul. The word "dualism" is so firmly entrenched in the modern mind as meaning Platonic or Cartesian radical dualism that it should never be used for the alternative here proposed. At least a modifier like "moderate" or "hylomorphic" should indicate that we repudiate any splitting of man into two beings, the object of Ryle's scorn.

Prime matter and substantial form *are* living human flesh, not some other things. I am my body, rather than have a body. Similarly, I am my soul, rather than have a soul. Recall that life is not operations, but the very being of a living thing. We have seen that substantial form is simply the fact that this thing is the kind of being it is. *Soul* is the name for the substantial form of a living thing, especially the fact that a being is human.

We often use soul to mean person or self in ordinary language, as when we say, "I didn't see a soul around," or, "Don't tell a soul." This is illustrated by the Hebrew use of the word in expressions like, "I said to my soul," meaning, "I said to myself." The Hebrew *nepeš* meant soul or life or person, the "I," and was never used in contradistinction to body. (The notion of personal immortality comes clear only late in the Old Testament.) The Bible in describing the origin of man says that "man became a living soul," meaning person. Karl Jaspers uses soul to mean existence, Heidegger to mean the spiritual being of man. Strasser and Marcel refer to soul as ego source or primordial Ego. Contemporary philosophers refer to it as "a principle of subsistence transcendentally related with a principle of becoming." Though these latter expressions hardly seem easier to handle than the terms substantial form and prime matter, those who use them agree that soul is not merely a psychic structure of conscious elements; these conscious elements I *have*, not *am*.

How we know about soul

The combination of phenomenological-analytic and organic approaches used here may strike one as novel, and implements the plea in Chapter 2 for use of various methods in philosophy. These approaches also correct the notion that our knowledge of soul need derive from religion.

Organic approach For these reasons we have approached soul through a study of organism, even at the risk of making difficulties for the next chapter. To discard the soul is to say that matter of itself is capable of life. Then every material being should be alive, and the difference disappears. Body is not body simply because it is matter. Pinch my arm and you pinch me only because this matter is substantially one with the rest of me. Amputate the arm, and this matter ceases to be mine; you would not pinch *me* now if it is lying discarded in a corner of the surgery. It is no longer that composite of soul and prime matter that we call body.

Does the fact that the matter is organized explain life? Then all organized matter should be alive, and again, how account for the difference between man and a corpse? As we have seen, organized structure is precisely what needs to be explained, rather that being an explanation. For however much its structure may explain the activities of a machine, we can always fall back upon the machinist to explain the structure. But what explains the fact that a living body organizes its own structure by its own activity? Structure cannot explain itself, much less before it even exists, as in the one-cell stage from which we all start. But it contained within itself its own blueprint in the genes and chromosomes, you say, produced by its efficient cause. Very well, but blue print is not structure: it is precisely this ability of an organism to implement its own blueprints which points to its being a different kind of nature from nonliving things.

The difference between living body and corpse is not imaginary, but a real difference. Not accidental, but an essential difference. What makes the difference? It must be something real and essential. This essential difference is the soul. As a principle and not a being, it is not empirically observable. But it does not depend upon our reasoning for its existence: the difference between man and a corpse is a reality whether I am thinking about it or not.

Is it a difference in man's internal nature? The efficient cause made the living body different to begin with. But the difference is not merely extrinsic. Life is not a constant succession of activities imposed upon living beings from outside by their maker, like so many ventriloquists' dummies being operated by a supermanipulator. Their efficient cause, either Ultimate (God) or proximate (parents), actually gave them an internal nature capable of doing these activities themselves. The dummy's wit is not his own, but that of the ventriloquist. But my thoughts and choices and growth are mine, not God's or my parents'. The difference then is within me, intrinsic to my nature.

As part of human nature, the soul is not supernatural. One way it can be known is by faith or theology, but being a natural constituent it is also discoverable from facts and reasoning, just as the area of a triangle might be revealed by God and taken on faith, but can also be demonstrated by geometry. To many of us the first notion of the soul was a religious concept. This is legitimate, but not our only source of knowledge about the soul. Throughout this book we have been examining two basic pieces of commonly observable evidence: the fact of human knowledge and the fact of human death.

We point to an organism and say, "This man knows." What we point to is obviously material, yet we have seen that his knowledge is also immaterial. He must be a composite of both material and spiritual principles to account for this nature. Matter alone cannot know, any more than a dead eye can see. Spirit alone cannot see or feel. Idea, image, metabolism are all acts of the same agent. The two principles are distinct, but they are not separate. They form one being. Again, "This man dies." What happens is a substantial change. He ceases to be a knower, a dreamer, an organism. He has ceased to be a man.

Definition of soul   As usual, we have proceeded inductively, examining the facts and drawing what conclusions we could from them. We do not make up a definition out of our heads and then look for it to be verified in nature. We are now ready to formulate the results of our investigation in a definition. We have seen that the soul is simply the reality in man which makes him different from a corpse: the substantial form which unites with prime matter to form man. Soul is *the ultimate internal formal principle by which we live.* "By which"—not *that which* lives (the supposit, man), but *that by which* man is living. Man is the efficient cause of his activities, the soul is the formal cause of his being alive.

Psychosomatics: real or pseudo problem?

One can sympathize with the mental squirming of the author in the preface or introductory chapter of nearly any text in psychosomatic medicine. On the one hand, he is trying to impress upon his biologically oriented medical colleagues the reality and importance of the psychological as distinct from the physical. Worry and imagination *can* cause organic harm. On the other hand, he is trying desperately to avoid letting his insistence on the distinction leave him open to the charge of dualism.

To equate "mind" with soul, and "body" with matter, is to confuse the orders of substance and accident. This has been a favorite philosophical game since Descartes. Mind for him was substance, and ideas for those who came later were bits of this substance associated in various ways. Body was just matter, to be studied as a machine (see Figure 5). But can there be "just matter"? The physicist studies the properties of material beings and the laws of their operation, but as scientist he never tries to say what prime matter is. We have seen that matter is always some *kind* of matter, i.e., it is always united with some substantial form. If it is living matter, the name for this form is soul.

Psychologists studying the laws of behavior and experience again stop short of the ultimate nature of man. That is why it is absurd to criticize psychology for not treating of the soul. Scholastics who do so betray a Cartesian influence, forgetting the distinction between substance and accident. For the same reason, the old dichotomy between "physical" and "mental" is misleading and metaphysically incorrect. Much of the controversy about psychogenesis (the psychological rather than organic causation of mental illness) is a tempest in a post-Cartesian teapot: the whole man is the patient, a psychobiological unit. Water may be H_2O, but one does not ask whether a patient was scalded by the H or the O.

False dilemma "Mind" and "body" really refer to mental and bodily processes. These are operations, therefore in the realm of accident. Just

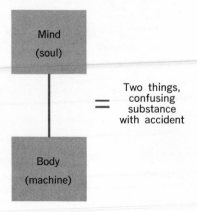

Figure 5 Dualism

because man has two (or ten) different sets of operations, is he two (or ten) beings? Soul and prime matter are substantial principles which constitute man, whatever powers or operations he may have. Both matter and soul are needed to have a man, before he can perform either mental or bodily operations.

Matter by itself cannot digest; a dead stomach does not develop ulcers. Only the composite of matter and soul can perform even "bodily" functions. So true is this that it is not correct to say "soul and body," for matter is not body until substantially informed by the soul. A body is composed of soul and prime matter; a corpse *was,* not *is,* a human body. Similarly, soul alone cannot see and feel, for these "mental" processes are organic and demand matter as a co-principle. Mind is not a substance, but is operations and habituated powers. These powers, habits, and acts all inhere in the substance of man without destroying his unity, for accidents do not multiply substance.

Figure 6 represents the hylomorphic view, first distinguishing (A) substantial principles on a diagonal axis, and (B) operative powers on the horizontal axis, then (C) combining the two diagrams below to give the total scheme. This composite diagram may appear complex,

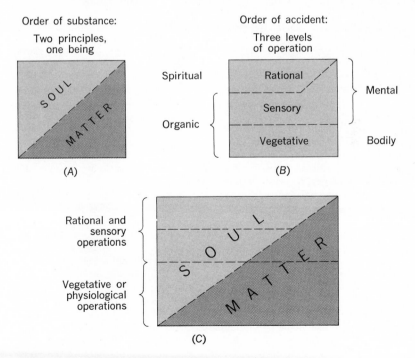

Figure 6   Hylomorphism

because it represents both accidental and substantial principles. But it will bear study, for it contains the solution to the pseudo problem. Note that "organic" and "mental" overlap at the level of sensory operations, for we have stressed the organic nature of perception and emotion. The diagonal line cuts across these, indicating that they demand both matter and soul (form) as substantial co-principles. Herein lies the philosophical explanation of hysterical paralysis, brain waves, psychosomatic illness, shock therapy for even psychic disorders, motor-image theories of volition, and a host of other facts which are otherwise puzzling. The dotted line dividing rational and sensory operation cuts upward at the point where matter intersects, to illustrate that matter does not enter intrinsically into the intellection and volition; but the diagonal continues, to indicate that matter does have a part (extrinsic) even here.

In this organically based view, soul is so intimate to man as substantial form that there is no question of his unity. The antithesis of psyche and soma becomes a pseudo problem. The student is not worried by apparent contradiction when he passes from elementary biology or psychology courses to psychopathology and psychosomatics, if his philosophical conception of man is that presented here.

PRESENCE OF SOUL IN BODY

If the soul is spiritual, how is it located in an extended body? This question implies that body is matter alone, missing the essential notion of soul as form. If soul is united to matter as act to potency, if it actualizes matter to form body, there is no question of body being a somatic container for some ghostlike psyche. It is just as correct to say that matter is in the soul as to say that soul is in matter. Each unites with the other to form man, even man's body. The soul is wherever man is, for that is what makes matter to be man. Being simple, it is wholly there wherever it is. When an arm is cut off, there is not less soul than before. The same soul is simply not united with as much matter. When a baby grows into a man, his soul is not bigger; it merely actualizes more matter.

But the soul does not actualize matter in exactly the same way throughout the body. Otherwise each part would be man, instead of just each part being human. Parts differ in structure and function. Thus the power of vision is in the eye, not the hand. We saw no difficulty in localizing the activity of the internal senses in the brain. A blow on the head which leaves one unconscious has not eliminated the soul, but suspended one organic activity. Again we emphasize that the soul is not an efficient cause. It is not an entity residing in the eye and looking through it. It is the form of the eye, making matter able to see; the composite does the seeing.

The soul as form is present only in those parts which are actually the unified substance of the living human body. It has no substantial union with food not yet assimilated, waste products not yet excreted, bacteria and other parasites, filling in the teeth, nor perhaps other apparent parts of the body.

INDIVISIBLE When discussing the unity of man in Chapter 14, we saw that an organism can be potentially many even though actually one. Now the soul is the principle of actual unity; matter is the principle of potential multiplicity. The soul therefore cannot be divided; it is simple and indivisible. Living bodies can be divided, not by dividing their souls but by dividing the composite in such a way that the matter after division is still organized at the level of perfection of a living body. Being thus organized means that it has the substantial form (not mere shape) of a living thing. The act of division was sufficient to produce matter having this form, since the matter was already living and virtually, though not actually, a separate being. This is also what happens when an embryo is divided at the one-cell stage and grows into two complete individuals. Human identical twins present a slightly special case, and will be noted in Chapter 17.

TRANSPLANTS These notions are useful in understanding the relation of soul to such phenomena as skin grafts and organ transplants. As long as it was an integral part of the donor's body, the tissue was informed by the donor's soul. Being virtually capable of separate vegetative existence by reason of such information, when severed it becomes actually living with its own vegetative form. It may continue to live by this form after being implanted, either indefinitely, like the graft on a fruit tree, or until such time as the receiver's body gradually replaces all the cells of the new tissue with its own cells. In the case of skin grafts between identical twins, the new part seems to become directly informed by the soul of the receiver, losing its own form at the time the graft is made.

INDIVIDUAL DIFFERENCES

A disputed question among scholastic philosophers is whether men differ only in their bodies, each having the same kind of soul, or whether human souls themselves differ from one another. This difference would be accidental, of course, for all are essentially human.

Some maintain that all individual differences are in the matter, every human soul being of the same kind and in itself of the same degree of perfection. This seems to suit a dualistic conception such as that of Plato, where soul is a separate entity.

Others hold that because of the intimate union of soul and matter there is a real though accidental difference in souls.[8] A soul is not just any human soul, but the unique form which unites with matter to form John Smith and no other. It corresponds to the perfection of the body, as act is limited by potency. While leaving it an open question, we note that this position is quite in accord with the interdependence of thought and brain described in Chapter 8. It also emphasizes the unity of man, wherein matter and soul are not separate but co-principles of one being.

THE SOUL AND VITAL OPERATIONS

The questions raised by heart transplants are not all new. Toward the end of World War II, a Russian soldier was pronounced dead by the attending

[8] Thomas Aquinas, *S. T.*, Ia, 85, 7; *C. G.*, II, 81; *In Sent.*, d. 32, q. 2, a. 3. Cf. Slavin (1936); Koren (1955), p. 258. On the unique pattern of endocrine functioning proper to each individual, and other evidence or physiological basis for innate differences, see the books by Roger J. Williams, *You Are Extraordinary* (New York: Random House, 1967), and *Biochemical Individuality* (New York: Wiley, 1956), and subsequent research on the DNA molecule.

surgeon. A team of progressive physicians went to work. Four and a half minutes later his heart began to beat. He breathed in three minutes, became conscious in an hour.[9] Many similar cases have been reported, and previous experiments had revived dogs which had been reported dead for as long as fifteen minutes. A letter to *Time* asked where his soul was during these four and a half minutes. To answer such a question, we must recall how we know there is a soul anywhere, at any time. We know it only if a being shows a capacity for vital operations. Suppose we give heart massage, artificial respiration, oxygen, blood transfusion, epinephrine injections, etc., to a corpse in the morgue. Nothing happens, because it is not the kind of being that can respond to such stimuli by spontaneous activity. The difference between the soldier and the corpse is that he could and did respond, and therefore had that within him by which he was alive. His soul is precisely that which makes him capable of so reacting. Since the soldier did so, the only answer is that his soul was right there within him, that he was alive.

The fact that the stimulation in this case was extraordinary is irrelevant. The amount of help from the outside needed by the living body is a matter of degree: we all depend upon certain things, such as oxygen, food, water. These do not give life, but are used by a living body. No amount of such stimulation will make a corpse live, for it cannot itself take and use them.

But did not the surgeon certify that the soldier was dead? As the doctor who edits *Time's* "Medicine" column said in a footnote, medical men have never defined death. Those who fail to distinguish between operation and operative potency are often oblivious to the difference between real and apparent death.[10] The above comparison with the corpse brings out that real death is a substantial change, while apparent death is a cessation of activities which are only accidents.

Just as life cannot be vital operations, so the soul cannot be the operations. Vital operations are the effect, not the cause, of man's life. They show that life is there, but they do not explain it. For instance, there is no doubt that the heart pumping blood is a part cause (efficient) of life activity. But what makes the heart live? What makes it to *be* the peculiar kind of thing which will pump, year in and year out, adapting itself to shifting demands and even doubling its size? Blood may be pumped mechanically, but the pump does not live. Why is this particular glob of matter a living organism, and not so much fertilizer (molecules) arranged in the shape of a heart? Only because it is united with a substantial form which is a principle of life: the soul.

BLOOD   Could the blood be the cause of life? Blood won't help a dead body, as we have seen. The heart must already be able to use blood. Blood is caused by living beings, not living beings by blood. Those who argue the blood is the soul because of a passage in the book of Leviticus (17:11) forget that this is symbolic; Moses was giving ritual, not teaching either

[9] "Medicine: 4½ Minutes of Death," *Time*, July 23, 1945, p. 75.
[10] For this reason, conditional administration of the last rites is permitted in cases of apparent death, on the possibility that real death has not yet occurred and the soul is still present. For the same reason, Christ delayed until Lazarus had been buried four days and putrefaction had set in, to ensure that His raising him would testify divine power.

science or philosophy. Such a position would create insurmountable difficulties. Would blood transfusion mean transfer of life, or that part of the donor's soul is now in someone else? If the soul is form, this would mean that part of the receiver actually is the donor, which is absurd. We can now completely replace all the blood of a dog or an Rh baby, and pump in a new supply. Have we made the dog a different living being, or the baby a different person? This would follow if blood is the soul or principle of life. And how explain that the corpse may be full of blood yet dead, while the dog can live?

ANIMAL AND VEGETABLE "SOULS" The implication that the dog also has a substantial form as principle of life brings up the question as to whether all living beings have souls. This causes no difficulty if we recall what we mean by soul and how we discover its existence. Since any living being must have a substantial form which makes it essentially different from the nonliving, it is clear that in this sense every live plant and animal has a soul.

This strikes the student as strange only because he is used to thinking of the term exclusively as applied to man's spiritual, immortal soul as known from religion. We have already laid the foundation for a distinction in kinds of soul when we drew its existence from vital operations. For just as man exhibits some operations which are immaterial and other organisms do not, so his ultimate formal principle of operation is immaterial whereas those of others are not. Likewise, a plant's substantial form is known to be inferior to that of the brute animal because the animal has sensory cognition and appetition, which plants lack. There are as many kinds of soul as there are kinds of living being, for soul is what makes the being live in this way. (The substantial form of a nonliving being has no special name.)

The whole function of the brute or plant soul is to unite with prime matter as a co-principle of material (or at best quasi-immaterial) operations. Such a soul is called a material form because it is a principle only of material operations and is wholly involved in matter. It is thus very different from the human soul which is also the ultimate principle of the strictly spiritual operations of intellection and volition. It is only to this latter form that we are used to attaching the term soul, but the language of philosophy need not disturb us if we are clear about the realities discussed. It is strictly a question of evidence: if a being exhibits no incontestable signs of immaterial operation, we do not assert it has a spiritual principle. The contrast will be clear from the next chapter, where only the human soul will be seen to be immortal. Meanwhile, the notion of an animal soul helps us grasp the concept of soul as substantial form.

THREE SOULS OR ONE? If soul is the ultimate formal principle of vital operations, and man has three kinds of vital activity, viz., vegetative, sensory, and rational, one might argue that by our line of reasoning he must have three souls: a vegetative soul, an animal soul, and a rational soul.

Once we understand soul as the formal cause of our being, to ask if man has three souls makes as little sense as asking if man has to have three sets of parents. Just as one act of efficient causality gave him being, so only one formal cause gives his substance this kind of being. Three or three hundred operations and powers would still be accidental forms; soul is substantial form. To have three souls or substantial forms would make him three substances or beings. It would mean the same substantial potency (prime matter) was actuated by three acts of the same order, which is absurd. By the same token, there is no need to postulate a third something as a bond between soul and matter, once we understand that they are related as act and potency. Man is vegetable, animal, and rational. But he is not actually a plant; he is a man, with vegetative powers.

Conclusion: unity in diversity

Whatever constitutes man must ultimately unite as co-principles to form one being. The common finality whereby the embryo grows eyes and ears long before it can see or hear shows that all is under the control of one organizing principle. The fact that it is the same ego or I who am the ultimate subject of operations at all three levels shows that I am one substance with many actions. They may inter-act and even conflict, but they are all mine. It is the same person who worries, gets ulcers, chooses, grows, and dies. This unity is especially evident from the nature of human knowledge: my sensory perception and my intellectual judgment are both mine, in the same consciousness. How can we compare an idea with an image, if it were one being who had the idea and another who had the image? The comparison is possible only because both terms of the comparison are my operations. The fact of human knowledge in this connection exhibits unity of diverse principles. Neither matter nor soul can have a perceptual judgment, only man can.

In the perceptual judgment, the intellectivo-sensitive act of know-ing which is peculiar to man alone, we seem to intuit implicitly the relation of the intellective soul to matter as actuated to be my living body. In knowing myself as subject I experience my most intimate contact with matter, while at the same time I am aware that this very experience somehow involves immateriality. Man is thus a unique system, an internal unified relationship of constituent parts. If man is evolving, the relation of matter and spirit maintains an isomorphic proportion as the universe and knowledge expand. For man's unity is seen as a dialogue between matter and spirit, between the universe and meaning.

REVIEW QUESTIONS

1. Discuss the meaning of the quotation from Dewey at the head of this chapter in the light of the history of dualism.
2. Discuss your answer to question 2 at the end of the last chapter in the light of hylomorphism.
3. Contemporary phenomenological philosophers explain man in terms of spiritual life plus organic life, without the notion of substantial form. Can you do so adequately?
4. Is the soul a cause of man or of man's vital operations? Explain.

5. Are there as many different kinds of souls as there are kinds of living beings?
6. Do a live man and a corpse have the same substantial form? the same accidental forms?
7. The soul is the principle of vital operations, and therefore prior to them; why is not this chapter prior to that on life activities?
8. Can the existence of soul be proved from the fact of substantial change occurring between living and nonliving things? Explain.
9. Can the existence of soul be proved from the fact of essential difference between living and nonliving things, even without the substantial change mentioned in the previous question? Explain.
10. Is it more correct to say that man is composed of body and soul, or that man's body is composed of soul and matter? Discuss.
11. Why were certain vitalists in error when they tried to discover scientific evidence of the soul as a cause or force in the organism?
12. If the soul were an efficient cause, not a formal one, how many beings would man be? Why?
13. Is it correct to call the soul supernatural or divine?
14. When we say, "Body acts on mind, mind acts on body," (*a*) Do the terms refer to the realm of substance or of operation? (*b*) Does the term body mean prime matter? Why? (*c*) Does the term mind mean soul? Why?
15. Is the so-called psychosomatic problem of interaction between body and mind a real problem or a pseudo problem to the dualist? Explain.
16. If there is no dualism, then what constitutes internal conflict?
17. Can this problem be solved without the distinction between substance and accident?
18. Does the theory of three souls (one for each level of operation) solve the problem?
19. Show how one's theory of knowledge determines one's notion of man's nature and unity.
20. When the finger is amputated, is the soul cut off? part of it?
21. Do you think that all human souls are alike, and individual differences are only in matter?

FOR FURTHER READING

Kelly & Tallon: the chapters from **Strasser** and **Aristotle,** and the selection from **Descartes,** pp. 46–48, from his *Discourse on Method.*

Descartes also states his position on body and soul in the sixth of his *Meditations on the First Philosophy,* and in his *Principles of Phi-*

losophy. Since his time the mind-body problem has been a favorite topic of discussion by philosophers. **Gilbert Ryle**, in his *The Concept of Mind* (1949), hoped to end the perennial dispute with his distinction between substantival and dispositional concepts; but as **Razel Abelson** points out in his chap. 29, "A Spade Is a Spade, So Mind Your Language," in *Dimensions of Mind*, edited by **Sidney Hook**, the distinction is good but not enough to solve the problem: we have both mental and physical dispositions, and we cannot ignore *person.* The first eleven chapters of the Hook symposium give a good sample of recent views on the mind-body problem. Slightly older is the symposium edited by **Herbert Feigl** and others, "Concepts, Theories, and the Mind-Body Problem," vol. 2 of *Minnesota Studies in the Philosophy of Science.*

In "Teilhard de Chardin and the Body-Soul Relation," Joseph **Donceel** puts the matter in a new light (*Thought*, 1965, 40:371–389). **D. H. Crowell** and **A. A. Dole** survey student thinking on the subject in "Animism and College Students" (*J. Educ. Res.*, 1957, 50:391–395). The phenomenologists rarely go into the problem in depth, but **Stephan Strasser** is one who attempts to do so in *The Soul in Metaphysical and Empirical Psychology.*

Ernan McMullin's symposium on *The Concept of Matter* shows how the modern trend is away from thinking about matter as in classic physics and post-Cartesian philosophy. The older concept of prime matter, rightly understood, might not be too foreign to the philosophical insights opened up by modern physics. See also **Peter Hoenen, S.J.**, *The Philosophical Nature of Physical Bodies* (1955), although some of his physical science is slightly outmoded now.

Michael Maher, again in his *Psychology*, has perhaps the most thorough treatment in English, chaps. 21–23 and 25–26 of the ninth edition. The medieval concept is explained well in the various writings of **Etienne Gilson**, and by **Anton Pegis** in *The Problem of the Soul in the Thirteenth Century.* Two medical histories of the problem are *Body and Mind*, by the British psychiatrist **William McDougall**, and *Mind and Body: Psychosomatic Pathology*, by **Pedro L. Entralgo.** Others who bring out the constant recurrence of the spiritual soul are **Pitirim Sorokin, Charles Spearman, Carl Jung, Hans Driesch, Richard Müller-Freienfels,** and the brain surgeon **Wilder Penfield.**

Aristotle states his notion in *On the Soul (De Anima)* I,3 and II,1–4. The position of **Aquinas** is set forth in his *Treatise on Man* (trans. by

James F. Anderson, paper), probably better than in most translations of his complete *On the Soul,* or in the *Summa Theol.* Ia, pp. 75–76. See also his *Commentary on Aristotle's De Anima* (trans. by K. Foster & S. Humphries as "Aristotle. *De Anima* in the version of William of Moerbeke and the commentary of St. Thomas Aquinas," with an introduction by Ivo Thomas, O.P.).

16   PERSONAL IMMORTALITY

*A person is not an embodied ego, but an ego
might be a disembodied person, retaining the logical
benefit of individuality from having been a person.*   Strawson

A most certain fact about man is that he is going to die. Heidegger calls man a being-unto-death, Camus makes this a central theme of his philosophy, and most existentialists are painfully aware of the mystery of man's historicity, caught in a fleeting moment of time between the finite and the infinite. Faced with his own limited being, man searches for Being while conscious of his own contingency. Is life absurd? Is life worthwhile? Where will it all end?

We pride ourselves on being reasonable, and have jokes about people who find themselves on trains or planes and don't know where they are going. Surely it is reasonable to expect a person to know whither he is headed, what direction or meaning there is to his going, even if he does not fully know what lies at the end of his journey. Even the vagrant hobo or wandering vacationer at least has some wants: survival, independence, recreation, or perhaps some other legitimate or intelligible goal.

The conviction of survival after death pervades the classic literatures of both Oriental and Western cultures, the teachings of all the major religions of the world, and the folklore of pagan primitives around the globe. As philosophers we cannot appeal to religious faith, but this widespread agreement itself suggests that we are here at grips with something very fundamental to man's nature and able to be deduced from commonly observable facts.

AGAINST IMMORTALITY

There are many who teach that death is the end of everything for a man. Some approach the problem with a preconceived materialism which does not allow for a spiritual survival after the death of the body. Some are dissuaded by the ineffectual attempts to establish a life beyond the grave made by those who appeal to spiritism, mediums, and séances, or other forms of occultism. Some univocally make life to be synonymous with organic life, adducing the incontestable but irrelevant argument that once a body is dead it is no longer alive. This misses the whole point that any life after death must be spiritual and hence not life in the biological sense. Others speak of immortality only in a metaphorical sense, as when poets say that someone will live forever in the admiration and memory of men. A few deny personal immortality by asserting that the soul comes back as another person or thing; this doctrine of transmigration of souls will be discussed later. Schopenhauer with his usual pessimism feels that "to desire immortality is to desire the perpetuation of a great mistake."

It seems incorrect to include the Buddhists among those who deny immortality, since the vast majority of them apparently understand nirvana to be not a return to absolute nothing, but an ecstatic state of peaceful contemplation, free of all passions. Kant, after rejecting the rational proofs for immortality, holds it as a postulate of practical reason; we prefer to base our position on more solid philosophical grounds than a blind *feeling* that the soul "just must be immortal."

Objections against immortality based on the positivist assumption that only what is observable and measurable is real are subject to the same criticisms under which positivism itself is now tottering. Science now deals in qualities as well as in quantities, and is more and more concerned with theories about things which cannot be directly observed. It is true that if you cut up a man, you will not find a soul. It is also true that if you cut into the man whose idea it is to deny the soul, you will not find an idea. Attempts to prove or disprove the soul by accurate weighing before and after death miss the point, as does photography at the moment of death.

Philosophical difficulties

More serious are the metaphysical arguments against immortality. No less a believer than Cardinal Cajetan said, "No philosopher has ever demonstrated that the soul of man is immortal, nor does there seem to be any demonstration of it. . . ."[1] He had in mind difficulties like the following: (1) The forms or souls of plants and brute animals cease when the plant or animal dies because such forms have no separate existence. But the generation of man is similar to the generation of animals, it is argued, and therefore their ends should be similar. (2) Again, man's soul is contingent being, not eternal or necessary. It once did not exist, so it seems logical that it should return to the nothing from which it came. (3) The operation proper to the rational soul of man is perceptual knowledge, understanding derived from sense. Now existence without operation is meaningless; if we cannot have our proper operation after the sense organs die, there is no point in asserting continued existence of the soul. (4) Most difficult is the fact that asserting the soul as capable of separate existence after death implies a separate existence now, making man two beings.

This last problem was never handled satisfactorily in Aristotle when he tries to reconcile hylomorphism with the evidence from the immateriality of intellection and volition that man's soul is spiritual. At the inorganic, plant, and animal levels, matter could not be without form, nor form without matter. The union was complementary and parallel, up to the point of the human form. Nobody likes to distort his own brain child, but acceptance of the facts forced Aristotle to make an exception of the human form, breaking the symmetry of his system. He concluded that, unlike other forms, man's soul is somehow separable. It is spiritual and immortal.[2] This statement, especially in his commentator Averroës, created such grave problems as that of the "separated intellect."

In the thirteenth century, Thomas Aquinas ran into the same difficulty (4) in integrating the organic hylomorphism of Aristotle with the Christian tradition of the separability of man's spiritual soul. Aquinas could have taken the easy way and gone along with the prevalent neo-Platonic dualism, forgetting Aristotle. But he saw that the soundest course in the long run even for a theologian was to choose

[1] Mansi (Ed.) *Amplissima Collectio,* vol. 32, col. 843.
[2] *De Anima,* II, 2, 413b 26–27; III, 4, 429b 5. χωριστός can be separate, separated, or separable, but the first two meanings are ruled out by our discussion in the two preceding chapters. He goes on in III, 5, 430a 22 to say that the soul is ἀθάνατον (immortal) and ἀίδιον (everlasting). Needless to say, much of Aristotle's thought here is difficult to interpret, and we are undoubtedly inclined to read our own meanings into his words.

a philosophy which most accorded with experiential fact and rigorous logic, even though it did not come tailor-made to fit the needs of theology.

Aristotle, as a scientist-philosopher, was more concerned with universals, with essences. Thomas, as a philosopher-theologian, was more concerned with individuals, with existence. As a Christian he had even more reason than Aristotle to insist on the possibility of the soul's existence after death. According to hylomorphism the separated soul after death is not a complete human nature, a position not to the liking of some theologians. But this did not bother Aquinas so much as the apparent inconsistency in the dual role which the human soul plays in his doctrine, as form of the body yet spiritual and immortal. How could the soul be both a principle of being when it is the form of man, and a being after man's death? Is it a being and yet not a being? This is a metaphysical scandal.

That Aquinas felt a real challenge in presenting Aristotle to his contemporaries is evident from the number of times he treats this problem, and the long dialectical approaches which precede his own solution. In these, he gives about twenty reasons why it seems that the human soul cannot be both a form and a thing.[3] If it is only a form, a principle and not a being, then this individual's immortal destiny is a joke once the man dies. If it is capable of separate existence, then man before death seems to be two things.

In the present work we have emphasized the unity of man, even though in so doing we might seem to play down the nature of the soul as a spiritual reality capable of separate existence after death. This was a calculated risk, necessary if our task is to provide a concept of human nature representative of all the pertinent facts. Only thus could it be adequate to the needs of the biological and social sciences.

Perennial problem In our own age, the editor of a symposium on personality wrote that human nature always presents "a difficulty which has been central in psychology: man, while a biological organism, is not merely that, but something more."[4] History repeats itself, and the same facts keep demanding recognition in every century. We noted that J. B. Rhine of Duke University felt he had evidence for spirituality from his work on extrasensory perception and telepathy. Not basing our case on such disputable grounds, we preferred to examine other facts which have convinced a host of philosophers and psychologists that man is more than merely a biological organism.

[3] *Qp. Disp. de Anima,* q. 1; also *C. G.,* II, 56–71; S. T., 76, 1, and 5.
[4] J. L. McCary (Ed.) *Psychology of Personality: Six Modern Approaches* (New York: Logos Press, 1956), p. xiii.

Why does the editor quoted say that what his eminent symposiasts have hit upon is "a difficulty which has been central in psychology"? Partly for the same reason that it was a problem in the time of Aquinas: they approach it from a historical background of Cartesian dualism, much as the early medievals did from a background of Platonic dualism. But whereas the Christian Middle Ages were convinced of the reality of spirit, modern thought has been dominated by materialism. Only recently have leading psychologists such as Maslow, Cantril, Rogers, Allport, and others begun to make it scientifically respectable to talk of man's spiritual aspects. The above quotation indicates that others have discovered that man is "something more." We have already examined the nature of understanding and choice, and found them strictly immaterial in themselves, even though extrinsically dependent on matter. The conclusion can now be drawn that the ultimate formal principle of such operations must itself be spiritual, and only extrinsically dependent on matter.

MEANING OF IMMORTALITY

In the face of these varied arguments, and considering the extreme importance of the issue, it becomes important to define precisely what is involved.

Immortality means *unceasing duration of life*. An immortal being may have a beginning, but it will not end. (It thus differs from eternal, which means having neither beginning nor end.)

"Life after death" here certainly does not mean that the body will live when it is dead. "To live" is analogous, and we are speaking of the spiritual life of man, not biological life. Nor do we mean some temporary revival after apparent death, or continuance of some functions for a short time. We are not speaking metaphorically of immortality in memory or symbol, nor of identification with the eternal existence of God, but actual continued existence of the individual in one's own identity.

It is precisely here that Aquinas seems to have gone a step beyond Aristotle, in centering his metaphysics around the notion of *esse*, the "to be" or act of existence. Certain aspects of man's life have been seen to be spiritual. This spiritual life can continue in the same *esse* or existence. In this sense it is incorrect to say, "The soul leaves the body." The spiritual self continues to be what it always was, this human life. It is the matter that changes, in that it ceases to be a human body and becomes corpse. But the act of existence remains, and changes only in its relation with matter.

The details of this new relationship will hopefully be clarified in the rest of this chapter. While remaining admittedly mysterious in some ways, it should not imply any downgrading of matter. Man does not have two lives, but one. In and through his relations with the material universe and especially his fellow inhabitants of this planet, he works out his eternal destiny which is just a continuation of the present life. If he is to find God at all, he must find Him therein. Meanwhile, the student must judge for himself the adequacy of the solution to the metaphysical puzzle proposed: as form the soul is incomplete substance and co-principle with prime matter, but as spiritual it has the possibility of independent existence. It is both a being and a principle of being, but not at the same time. The change of relation to matter at the time of human death may well be unique and fit no pre-conceived categories, since the matter undergoes substantial change but the form does not. The question is whether there is any factual evidence against this position, since it does not seem to be absurd or contradictory.

Personal identity of the soul But before any resurrection of the body, if this does occur, how can the soul retain its individual identity after death? Separated from matter, will all souls coalesce into one confused mass of spiritual substance?

When we say that matter is the principle of individuation, this does not mean that prime matter confers some perfection. Being passive and of itself indeterminate, it cannot contribute individuality as a characteristic. Matter is the principle of individuation only in the sense that it makes possible the plurality of individuals within the same species.

One soul is not another soul, even though both are human, because each is united with different matter. This soul is not just any human soul, but is identifiable as the soul which united with matter to form John Q. Jones in a certain place at a certain time. This is true only of the soul of John Q. Jones, even though he has an "identical" twin. And it is historically and irrevocably true. Even after separation by death, for all eternity his soul retains this transcendental relation to the composite it formed with matter, that is, this man and no other.

This individual cannot be somebody else, regardless of changed material conditions. The senile psychotic may not be recognized by anyone who knew him at the age of twenty, much less at birth. But he is the same person. One may be in a fugue state and not know who he is; this hardly makes him somebody else, or nobody. Likewise, after death, the spiritual, though incomplete, life of this person is not subject to any change of existential identity.

FOR IMMORTALITY

We are now in a position to examine some of the traditional arguments for immortality. The first one reasons from the nature of the soul as analyzed, the second is more psychological. All three are deductive, since we have no direct experience of the afterlife.

Metaphysical or ontological argument

The proponents of this position reason that a being will continue in existence if they can eliminate all possibilities of its ceasing to exist. These seem reducible to corruption or annihilation. A thing can corrupt either of itself (per se) by breaking into parts, or incidentally upon corruption of that on which it is totally dependent for existence. If the soul is simple it can not break into parts; if it is spiritual it does not depend wholly on material being which is corruptible.

Soul is simple To be simple is to be undivided and indivisible, to lack parts. Since there are many different kinds of parts, there are many kinds of simplicity. *Spatial* parts are the result of extension. To have spatial parts is to be quantified. We can designate these parts in an extended being: this half, that third. *Constituent* parts are the result of composition in the order of essence or substance, e.g., by matter and form. Lack of the metaphysical "parts," essence and existence, would be *absolute* simplicity and proper only to God. Nor do we lack virtual or operative "parts," abilities—in this sense man is quite complex.

The human soul lacks spatial and constituent parts. The evidence for lack of spatial parts is the inextended nature of our acts of understanding and choice. These have no physical dimensions. Ultimately rooted in the whole man, their proper subject of inhesion must be also inextended, nonspatial. Again, the enduring personal identity of the spiritual self (Chapter 13) shows lack of composition. Extension and substantial change are our only infallible signs of composition, for they show potential multiplicity. Where these signs are absent, one may conclude that the human soul is simple in itself, extended only by reason of its union with matter.

Human soul is spiritual The above may not strike one as overwhelmingly conclusive. This is partly because our imagination gets in the way. We cannot picture these concepts, so the reasoning is hard to make very graphic. Another reason is that the attribute of simplicity itself is not very impressive. Any form, even that of beings below man, is simple per se, extended only by reason of its varying relation to matter. Spirituality is much more important, and peculiar to man's form.

What does spirituality add to simplicity? Independence of matter. A mathematical point, say the midpoint of this wooden table, is simple. It is inextended, has no spatial or constituent parts. But it is not spiritual, for it is wholly dependent on the table for its existence. Burn the table, and the midpoint vanishes. We do not destroy it by breaking it up into pieces, for it has no actual or potential parts. But we destroy it by destroying that upon whose existence it totally depends.

The same applies to the substantial form or "soul" of the plant or brute animal, though here is positive perfection beyond that of the mathematical point. These forms are simple, and cannot be broken into parts. But since they are wholly dependent upon the material composite for their existence, when the plant or animal dies the form simply ceases. Ceases what? To coexist, since the only existence it has is coexistence with matter in the being of the composite. But in the case of the human soul, its intellectual and volitional acts indicate a different relation to matter.

The first (1) of the philosophical arguments against immortality mentioned above reasoned from a parallel with the brute form. But men exhibit spiritual operations whereas brutes do not. The death of the body may be similar in the two cases, but man's spiritual operations do not involve the body intrinsically, as all brute activities do.

Spiritual means life or being without any material, physical qualities. Such was found to be the nature of concepts, early in Chapter 6. The precise relations between brain and thought were explored in Chapter 8, pp. 125–127. There the subordinate and instrumental role of organic activity in cognition was seen as congruent with the fact that matter does not enter into the internal nature of understanding and choice. If the human soul is spiritual in at least some of its activities, it is spiritual in its being. As such it is not wholly dependent on matter for its continued existence.

We say "in at least some" of its activities. Distinct but not separate from soul, matter enters directly and necessarily into vegetative and sensory operations. Neither an angel nor a separated soul can digest or feel, because neither has bodily organs, which are essential for such processes. The subject of organic activity is the composite of which soul and matter are coordinate causes. Though ultimately acts of the supposit or whole person, spiritual activities have the soul as their immediate subject.

This argument concludes that the human soul cannot corrupt of itself, for it is simple and inextended. It cannot break up into parts because it has none. Nor is it subject to incidental corruption, because it is spiritual. The human soul is thus immortal by nature.

Annihilation? The second objection (2) argued from the fact that the human soul is contingent being, hence does not have existence necessarily. A thing might be immortal by nature but not actually continue in existence. Regardless of its independence of matter or inability to decompose, it could cease to be if the First Cause did not conserve it in being. Annihilation removes existence absolutely. Such a being is open to the absolute possibility of annihilation, looking only to its contingent nature. But since only God can annihilate, one must look to His nature to see if it is also a possibility relative to His part.

To the question, "How can we know what God will do or will not do?" one can answer that God manifests His plan not only through revelation but also through the nature of what He makes. Without His telling us, we can see His design through an analysis of the soul, just as we can often figure out the manufacturer's idea just from the machine, even though we do not have any explanation from him. It is then an easy inference that He will not act like an inconsistent fool and contradict His own plan.

It is not necessary to appeal to faith to know this much about God. As First Cause discoverable by natural reason in philosophy, He is all-perfect and incapable of contradicting Himself. He cannot set up a nature and then go contrary to it. He is free to create or not, but He is free from doing the absurd. This is not because of any lack of power or self-determination in God, but because of His perfection and infinite wisdom. For God to annihilate what is immortal by nature would be inconsistent and unreasonable, a contradiction of His own design. Such imperfection is impossible to God.

One might object that an artist could paint an "immortal" picture and then destroy it, for it is his and he can do what he wants with it; so could God annihilate the human soul, since He has supreme dominion. The reply is that the picture is not truly immortal by nature, but only one we judge would deserve to be so because of its excellence. Also, the artist may be acting legally, since it is his own property, but one could question his wisdom if the picture were truly of such perennial worth. God's wisdom cannot be questioned. He cannot change His mind, nor could it be said that He did not know what He was doing when He freely made the soul immortal. For this reason some prefer to say that the human soul is "dependently necessary" rather than contingent.

Argument from natural capacities

A secondary argument for the immortality is drawn from an analysis of the unlimited capacities of intellect and will. It is sometimes called the argument from desire, but this suggests that the argument is reducible to "I desire to be immortal, therefore I am." This is hardly conclusive, for I might desire lots of things and not get them. Or one might not consciously desire immortality, preferring extinction at death because of a faulty conception of the afterlife, or because of a guilty conscience. Rather, it argues from the very nature of our two highest powers to the conclusion that we are made to live forever, whether we desire it or not.

It is a favorite paradox of the existentialists that man is open to infinity, yet mortal. Other animals do not seem to show *angst,* awareness of their finitude and eventual passing. Why does man ask the questions he does? The fact that he does is not self-explanatory, and when we investigate the conditions of its possibility we uncover potentialities never actualized to the full; we can always be better than we are. For this reason Karl Jaspers says that transcendence is the fulfilment of human existence.

The object of *the intellect* is being. This means that we can know whatever is or can be, all that is intelligible. This unlimited capacity for truth sets up in man an insatiable curiosity. We all want to know more and more, whether it be Mrs. Grundy's gossip or the conditions in outer space. Instead of being satisfied that he knows enough, the more a man knows the greater is his desire to learn. The most brilliant men are most painfully aware of all there is yet to know. A thousand lifetimes would not suffice to fill up one's intellect completely.

The will has a corresponding capacity for unlimited goodness. Its object being goodness as such, there is nothing which it cannot desire. However much it may possess, it can always want more. True, we may rightly expect a reasonable amount of happiness in this life, but even those who claim to be quite content are capable of more contentment. No matter how much we feel we are loved, we are all heart-hungry in the sense that we want fuller and more secure satisfaction of our desire to be loved and more adequate exploitation of our capacity to love. Our songs, our poetry, our world conquests all attest to the nature of the human will as made for unlimited good. Moreover, even the nicest finite things tire us after a while. True happiness demands an object which we can never exhaust, a never-ending fountain of new delights with which we can never become bored.

The unlimited capacities of intellect and will can never be fully satisfied in this life. Only when we can feed upon the inexhaustible intelligibility of Infinite Truth will our curiosity be sated. Only when we possess the infinite goodness and beauty of Goodness Itself will we live content. As the poet Browning says,

> Ah, but a man's reach should exceed his grasp,
> Or what's a Heaven for?

It is absurd to say that in a universe where other things reach their natural goals, for the most part and with admitted exceptions, only man should be necessarily and completely frustrated in achieving the end for which he was designed. Therefore man must continue to a state where his two highest basic capacities are satisfied by an adequate object: Infinite Knowledge and Love.

This argument is teleological, not theological. Purpose is as undeniable a reality as efficient cause. Even the most antiteleological person finds it impossible to talk for five minutes about the kidney or hormones without implying design or function. Nor is it a valid objection that not all seeds become trees, for the existence of forests is proof enough that by and large the purpose of seeds is fulfilled. There is no difficulty about the fact that nature achieves its goal in this case by making millions more seeds than ever become trees. They have no intrinsic value, and this is one way of arranging things to guarantee the desired result. But if the human soul is not immortal, it means that no man achieves his end, that the entire species is aimed at a nonexistent goal.

It is true that some people may not attain God, and thus they miss their end. This possibility is the inevitable consequence of free choice. But they do so by their own agency, not because their end was impossible of achievement or nonexistent. What is argued here is the absurdity of a world scheme in which *nobody* achieves his natural goal, and this by necessity.

Again, to say "necessarily and completely" frustrated admits that minor capacities of all men may not all be satisfied. At least our essential happiness is possible. Failure to grasp the essential nature of the future life indicated by this argument causes people to claim they do not desire heaven because they imagine it an eternity of playing the harp, instead of the enjoyment of God as Infinite Truth and Goodness. Any other objects or persons that might be desired are so minor a consideration as to be utterly negligible.

Argument from the moral order

The recent British philosopher A. E. Taylor and others add an argument for the logical necessity of a life after death from the experience we have of moral obligation.[5] To argue from moral obligation to immortality here, and then in ethics to argue from immortality to moral obligation would be a vicious circle. But quite apart from and prior to any ethical considerations, it is a fact that people generally *experience* moral obligation and a sense of responsibility. The question

[5] A. E. Taylor, *The Faith of a Moralist*, Series I (New York: St. Martin's 1951).

is whether this widespread phenomenological fact has any validity if the soul is not immortal.

Certainly investigation of the existing universe reveals order. The atomic table in chemistry made possible the prediction of the existence and properties of certain elements before they were discovered. Order underlies the classifications of zoology and botany. Astronomy finds order in the paths of the stars and allows very precise predictions. All physical laws attest the intelligible order of the observable world. Exceptions are recognizable as such only because there are laws to which they can be exceptions. Many apparent instances of disorder are found later to have meaning, as when the overenthusiastic followers of early evolutionary theory decided certain endocrine glands were vestigial because they could see no function for them. Cutting them out led to progress in our knowledge about hormones, but it was not the only time when nature embarrassed man because of his ignorance of her laws.

In such a universe, it is preposterous that disorder should reign only in the case of man. We see people trying to do what they think right, and receiving no reward in this life. Others literally get away with murder. Still others are punished unjustly for crimes they did not commit. What rationality is there in moral values? Why should anyone experience a sense of obligation and responsibility? There is certainly no adequate sanction in this life. Unless there is a life after death in which everything will be squared up and people will receive what they deserve, the whole notion of obligation makes no sense at all.

Everlasting sanction Some scholastic philosophers claim that this argument proves only that there will be some future life, but not that it will last forever. But is a sanction which is not everlasting really adaquate as an ultimate sanction? If the good knew that heaven would eventually cease, they would be tempted to feel that a virtuous life was not worth the effort. Moreover, the thought it was coming to an end would spoil their whole state of happiness. Happiness is the *stable* possession of the perfect good. Were we to achieve temporary satisfaction of our basic capacities either in this life or the next, but know that we were to lose out eventually, we would not be perfectly happy. In fact, the prospect of loss would sadden us all the more because the enjoyment was so intense. To enjoy perfect happiness, we must know that it is permanent. We can enjoy a party even though we know it will not last forever, because we implicitly accept that fact as part of the nature of things. But if we look to such temporary joys as sources of lasting happiness, we always find that sooner or later they turn to ashes in our mouths.

Likewise, if the bad knew that eventually they would be freed no matter what they did or how severe the punishment was, they could tell themselves they were willing to risk it. It would mean that in the end everybody would be the same, so the difference between moral and immoral would become zero eventually, and mere expediency would be at least as reasonable as obligation.

Against moral argument Some will argue that the sanction against bad conduct is that society will not approve. This makes no provision for the person whose attitude is, "To hell with society." Appeals to the good of posterity are likely to be met with an equally cynical, "What did posterity ever do for me?" Threats of punishment or physical force reduce morality to a question of adequate policing and to the matter of who has the biggest fists or atom bombs.

On the other hand, serious issue may be taken with the whole moral argument for immortality from the standpoint of humanitarian philosophy. There are many sincere people whose lives are morally superior to those of many believers, yet whose motivations are social utilitarianism or humanism rather than any belief in an afterlife. Genuine love for mankind and a need to be loved prompts many to live good lives. Their conduct may not differ from that of the believer, because the latter pursues his eternal goal precisely through love of neighbor in this life.

CONDITIONS OF AFTERLIFE

Knowledge The third difficulty (3) presents some real problems, for it argued that the immortal soul after the death of the body could not know, because of the lack of sense knowledge from which to abstract ideas. Now the manner of operation of the separated soul cannot be studied through observed experience. As philosophers we may not appeal to revelation, and theology offers only speculation on this point, for the most part anyway. Faith tells us that we shall enjoy the beatific vision, direct intuition of God Himself. This is not only beyond philosophical proof but a supernatural gift over and above (but not contrary to, as is clear from the second argument) our natural capacities. From unaided reason we can only conjecture that certain conditions will prevail.

Without some special supernatural aid we will be unable to know singular material objects or acquire further knowledge of the physical universe, for such operations demand sense experience and that is impossible without bodily organs. But there seems to be no intrinsic impossibility of our knowing spiritual realities, for they are intelligible and our intellect is immaterial. God, angels, our own and other human souls would thus be known without need to derive from sense. Again, we have habitual knowledge stored in the intellect which need not cease with the body.

The use of this and the acquisition of other knowledge does seem to call for something to supply the role now played by sense knowledge. But although we do not know just how, there seems no absurdity in this possibility because matter has only an extrinsic and subordinate part in human intellection. Even God could not supply for sense if matter entered intrinsically and essentially into the activity of the intellect. But we have seen that it does not. Therefore it seems legitimate to assume that He will somehow provide the necessary conditions for our intellect to function, perhaps through some new relation to matter of which man has never dreamed.

Resurrection of the body   The separated soul is not a complete man in any case. Even if its highest powers are satisfied, and happiness therefore essentially achieved, the soul still seems to have a certain incompleteness. It will be too much absorbed in enjoying God to be distracted by any desire for bodily pleasures, for He contains them all equivalently and to a supereminent degree. But it is still true that the soul is not an angel; its nature is to be united with matter to form a man.

This, plus the fact that it seems proper that the whole man should share in the reward or punishment, seems to constitute an argument from natural reason for the resurrection of the body. But although Aquinas seems to feel that the above reasons are quite compelling, we agree with Suarez that they are only suasive. Faith says that the future resurrection is a fact; philosophy seems only to demonstrate that it ought to be. In either case, it seems that the conditions of bodily life after the resurrection would be quite different from the present state. It would have all of the advantages and none of the disadvantages of a body: all the pleasure of eating without the need to depend on food, all of the beauty of full maturity with none of the defects of old age or failure to develop properly, and so of all other aspects of organic life.

Matter is indifferent   This conception finds no particular difficulty in the fact that the soul is united with different matter at various times, through the metabolic cycle. It is only necessary that it actualize *some* matter in order for it to form Jones's body. The soul is the subject of actual permanent identity, matter only the principle of potential multiplicity. For instance, matter which was once Jones may become fertilizer, then vegetable, then Smith (or may become Smith directly, if Smith is a cannibal and eats Jones). What makes this matter to be any of these is the fact that it is informed at the time by one substantial form rather than another.

Hence we see little problem in questions about the afterlife which vex those who apparently have not fully grasped hylomorphism. If this same matter once belonged to Smith and at another time to Jones, to whom will it belong at the resurrection? Our answer is that it makes no difference. As Shakespeare said about money, " 'twas mine, 'tis his, and has been slave to thousands." Smith's body will be *any* matter substantially united to his soul as potency to act, regardless of whether it had ever been previously his or not. One suspects some lurking Platonic dualism in those theologians who feel the dogma that each will be reunited with "his" body means that the same identical matter must be involved. If it means all matter in the resurrected body must be the same as in the previous life, the above facts of the metabolic cycle and cannibalism present difficult problems, which are no problem at all in hylomorphism. And if it means that all the matter previously used must now be united, then one who had eaten normally for a lifetime would be mountainous in size at the resurrection. If it means only that some matter must be the same, we are back at the question of why any matter is my body at all; according to this view, some of the resurrected body would be mine and some would not.

We have digressed only in the hope that this discussion may help toward a fuller understandang of the hylomorphic union. For the same reason, we might consider the frequent question of why the corpse should be given a Christian burial if it is only so much fertilizer in the shape of a man. The reason is twofold. First, it is out of reverence for the fact that this matter was once substantially united with the soul to form a human person, the object of our honor and remembrance—and, in the Christian scheme, the recipient of the sacraments, which are bodily signs of grace, conferred on the whole man. Secondly, it is a mark of belief in the eventual resurrection of the body, and hence of the future life of the soul. Cremation has been generally accepted in most cultures as a symbolic denial of immortality, a gesture which says that all is finished when the ashes are scattered to the wind. Where cremation is demanded by public health or other compelling reasons, it is clear that there is no symbolic denial of immortality.

Reincarnation With this fuller appreciation of the manner in which the individual human soul actuates matter to form this man's body, we find little in the theory sometimes proposed that souls could lose their personal identity and return to life on earth in a different body.

This is called metempsychosis, transmigration of souls, or reincarnation. The very notion of hylomorphism seems to rule out the possibility. For if Napoleon's soul were to return, any matter with which it would substantially unite would by that very fact be Napoleon's body. It might be necessary to appeal to theology for absolute proof that such a return cannot happen. But philosophically we can take the position that the burden of the proof lies with the affirmative, and examine any assertion very critically for evidence. None has been offered to date.

Even more preposterous is the theory that the soul could return as the form of a dog or other animal, for if the human soul actuated matter it could only be the formal cause of a human being, not any other kind. If a lion eats Napoleon, his body becomes lion. If Napoleon eats the lion, the lion becomes Napoleon. But Napoleon's soul retains its individual identity in either case.

REVIEW QUESTIONS

1. Read again the quotation from Strawson at the head of this chapter. (a) Can it be understood as a paraphrase of the personal immortality described in the chapter? (b) Do you think that was his meaning?
2. John Dewey, in *Human Nature and Conduct*, says, "The doctrine of a single, simple and indissoluble soul was the cause and effect of failure to recognize that concrete habits are the means of knowledge and thought." Is he saying that the soul is incompatible with habits, or that all knowledge is concrete? If the latter, does Gilbert Ryle's analysis of the dualism fallacy answer him?
3. Is incorruptibility the same as immortality?
4. Is immortality the same as eternity?
5. What are the chief reasons why some deny immortality?
6. Would you say that the majority of peoples on the earth believe in immortality?
7. Is it possible for a person to have no goal in life whatsoever?
8. What do you consider the hardest difficulty against immortality?
9. How do you answer it?
10. Is the human soul a being or a principle of being or both? Explain.
11. At death, does the soul undergo substantial change?
12. Show why the argument from natural capacities is not merely a matter of wishful thinking.
13. Does the argument from the moral order have any force with those who deny moral obligation?

14. What fact remains for these people to explain?
15. What facts indicate that the soul is what gives continued identity to the person?
16. If matter is the principle of individuation., what is the basis for the soul's identity as an individual after death?
17. Why is metempsychosis more compatible with a Platonic than with our notion of soul?
18. Since the soul can exist by itself, is it not a complete substance?
19. How does spirituality differ from simplicity?
20. Is the human soul in this life *entirely* independent of matter for any operations?
21. Is it intrinsically independent of matter for some operations? Which?
22. Is it extrinsically dependent on matter even for these?
23. Is it intrinsically dependent on matter for some?

FOR FURTHER READING

Kelly & Tallon: the selections from **Plato** on pp. 7–8, and from **Peters** on pp. 238–247. (Note also the passages from **Scheler** on pp. 125–126, and from **Strasser** on p. 270.)

Plato discusses immortality charmingly in three of his dialogues: the *Phaedo,* the *Apology of Socrates,* and *Alcibiades I.* While not agreeing with all of his reasoning, one cannot but be impressed with the thought of this ancient who was outside the stream of Judaeo-Christian thought. Also impressive is the stand of the British moralist **A. E. Taylor** in two books, *The Faith of a Moralist,* Series I, and *The Christian Hope of Immortality.*

Two who present a strong case against immortality are **Ashley Montagu,** *Immortality,* and **Corliss Lamont,** *The Illusion of Immortality.* The former dismisses personal immortality as wishful thinking and takes good advantage of the fact that the traditional arguments are sometimes poorly presented. The latter seems sometimes to confuse the issue.

R. A. Falconer gives a broad sweep in *The Idea of Immortality and Western Civilization,* as does **William E. Hocking** of Harvard in *The Meaning of Immortality in Human Experience.* As on will and soul, **Michael Maher,** S.J., in a lengthy chapter of his *Psychology* presents detailed arguments and rejects opposing views. Two other Jesuit writers are **Martin D'Arcy,** *Death and Life,* and the theologian **Robert Gleason,** *The World to Come.*

On metempsychosis, or reincarnation, an excellent collection from a wide variety of sources, including current thought, is that edited by **Joseph Head** and **S. L. Cranston,** *Reincarnation: An East-West Anthology.* Also of interest is the book by **Paul Siwek,** S. J., *The Enigma of the Hereafter: The Reincarnation of Souls.*

17   THE ORIGIN OF MAN

*It is impossible to conceive this immense and
wonderful universe including man with his capacity of
looking far backwards and far into futurity as the
result of blind chance or necessity.*   Darwin

Where did I come from? This is the final question in our
investigation of man. Although the origin of animals is
a matter of biology, the cause of the human soul presents
some rather knotty problems for the philosopher. We
shall consider first the cause of the human soul, then the
time of its origin, and lastly the evolution of man's body.

THE CAUSE OF THE HUMAN SOUL

Since being is a continuation of becoming, a thing's
existence tells us of its beginning. Now the substantial
forms of other animals, having no existence apart from
the composite, have no cause other than the cause of the
animal itself. We saw in Chapter 15 how the substantial
form is the result of the sum of efficient causes working
on an apt material cause and making it become this kind
of material being. Two parent dogs, disposing the matter
of the germ plasm in their reproductive organs, are the

proximate efficient cause of matter passing from potentially to actually puppy, and hence of the new dog form or soul.[1] Human parents prepare matter in a similar way to become a new human body; the question is whether this is adequate to cause the human substantial form.

Not educed from matter A thing can be made actually to be something else only if it potentially is the other thing to begin with. Hydrogen and oxygen become water, one worm can become two, food can become man, animal germ plasm can become a new animal, because in each case the terminal product is within the possibility of matter and all that is required is an adequate efficient cause.

The human soul is spiritual, and not within the potentialities of matter. No efficient cause, even God, can produce a spiritual effect from a material cause. Matter is in potency to become any other kind of matter, and hence any material form may be educed from it by a proper cause. But the spiritual human soul cannot arise by eduction from matter. The act of generation is a biological process, and therefore material.

Not generated by parents' souls One might argue that there is no need to postulate the origin of the human spiritual soul by a material process of generation. The parents' souls are also spiritual; could not they act as a spiritual cause producing a spiritual effect? Here there would be no violation of the principle of causality.

The difficulties arise when we attempt to explain precisely how this would happen. By composition? The soul is simple and could not be compounded from something received from each parent. There is no evidence that it arises from just one parent, to say nothing of the problems arising if we attempted to designate which one. By division? The parent's soul is simple and spiritual, so there is no possibility of dividing off a piece of it for the child's soul. By eduction? The new soul could not be educed from the potency of spiritual substance, for spirit does not contain a principle of substantial change: there is no possi-

[1] For this reason "be kind to the birds because God created their souls" is sentimental nonsense, as is much antivivisection propaganda. God is, of course, ultimately the First Cause of all being, but not in any special sense of plant or animal souls. The reason why we should avoid wanton cruelty to animals is not because of their dignity, but because of our own. Animals have no personal rights, and are for man to use. When a man abuses them, it is wrong because he is acting in a manner unworthy of his own rational nature, which is the norm of morality. Coleman (1956, p. 93) quotes an interesting pathological instance of the lack of logic which occurs here: an antivivisectionist advocates kindness to brute animals and proposes savage cruelty toward any fellowman who disagrees with his view.

bility in spirit for becoming other, analogous to prime matter in material being. The parents' souls would have nothing to work on, nothing out of which to make the soul. By production? One might consider whether it is necessary to talk of the parents' souls making the new soul "out of" any preexisting subject, i.e., whether they could simply produce it by their sheer reproductive activity.

Aside from the fact that the parental reproductive activity is entirely biological, this solution is rejected because no created cause gives being absolutely. Any efficient cause we know operates only by making something which already exists to be this way rather than that; never does it make something simply to be rather than not be. (Even in spiritual activity the idea, for example, is an actuation of the intellect and not creation from nothing.) The reason for this is that no creature has being of itself, and nothing gives what it has not. Contingent being is participated being, over which the recipient has no dominion. Act is limited only by the potency into which it is received; if "to be" were mine to give, it would be unlimited as act; and I could cause all finite existence including my own which is absurd.

Origin by creation Since only the First Cause has being of Itself and hence dominion over existence, only God can give being absolutely. He alone can make a thing simply be, rather than cause what already exists to be in another way. By a process of elimination, then, we arrive at the conclusion that the human soul can originate only through creation by God. Put positively, if the human soul is spiritual or strictly immaterial in its being, it must be essentially such in its becoming.

Unique creative cooperation

The precise nature of the cooperation between God and human parents is more complex and intimate than suggested by the old dualistic formula, "God creates the soul, the parents make the body." Both contribute to man's one act of existence, so it is incorrect to say that man's soul arises in *complete* independence of matter. Recent thinkers like Rahner and Teilhard de Chardin emphasize that God's causality is not the first link in a long chain of causality, but basic to and working within the framework of all causes, which are in a sense His instruments.[2] Precisely how to formulate the degree of immediacy with the parents of God's action in creating the human soul is beyond

[2] A favorite notion of Aquinas (cf. *De Pot.* 3, 7), long neglected in the centuries of vigorous opposition to occasionalism, which made creatures mere occasions for divine action, not true causes.

us, at least for the present. We cannot avoid the unique nature of the human soul as the terminus of the divine action, nor the existential unity of man as a spirit-flesh composite produced by the complex cooperation of many causes.

Creation Creation may be defined as *production in being by an efficient cause without any preexisting subject.* This definition is preferable to saying that to create is to "make out of nothing," because such an expression implies that God takes an already existing blob of "nothing" and makes something of it. The difficulty is really one of letting our imagination interfere with what must be a purely intellectual understanding. The potency for existence here is simply the objective possibility that something can be, and exists only in its efficient cause, not like the potency of a material thing to become something else.

Since efficient cause is always distinct from its effect, there is no question of the soul being God, or a part of God. Creation is the antithesis of pantheism. It is interesting that even the pagan Aristotle seems to have some awareness of this difference in the origin of the human soul,[3] although it is usually agreed that he had no clear idea of creation. Note that although we assume throughout this chapter the existence of a Creator as proved elsewhere in philosophy, we are not moving in a vicious circle, because the demonstration of God's existence through philosophy in no way presumes anything about the soul.

One might object that the body is potency to the soul, and therefore the soul must be educed from the potency of matter. This does not follow, for to be in potency to a form is not necessarily to have that form in potency. Matter is in potency to any form which can actuate it, and we have seen that the human soul does this. But only material forms can be educed from the potency of matter.

Again, this doctrine of creation might seem to detract from the fullness of parenthood, since the parents do not strictly generate the soul. But their offspring are truly theirs nonetheless, for it is not necessary that one produce all the component parts in order to be the true cause of a thing. Thus the artist is the real author of the picture, even though he does not make the canvas or oils. Relations like father and son are said of the *person*, not of the part: we do not say that his dad is the father of Junior's body, but of Junior. On the contrary, the notion proposed here rather enhances the human reproductive act, since it depicts the joint action of God and parent in producing the child. It

[3] *On the Generation of Animals,* II, chap. 3.

is the very opposite of puritanism, since it exalts sex to the sacred role of an invitation to the Creator for His most intimate cooperation. No other act in the natural order involves God so directly.

TIME OF SOUL'S ORIGIN

No preexistence In discussing the individuality of souls in the previous chapter, we saw that, unlike an angel whose nature it is to exist by itself as a complete substance, the human soul has as its proper role to unite with matter to form this man and no other. Hence any existence previous to the man is contrary to the very meaning of soul as substantial form. We saw that the separate existence of the soul after death does not contradict this, since it retains previously acquired knowledge, a transcendental relation to matter, and even a certain exigency to be united with matter. But *before* actual union with matter to form a body it can have no such relation. The notion that God has a supply of souls which are not anybody's in particular until He infuses them into human embryos is entirely unwarranted and lacks any evidence. They would have no personal human identity, and would be in an unnatural state because unable to acquire any knowledge in the way proper to man. In Chapter 6, we saw that the theory that we are born with ideas carried over from a previous life has nothing to support it, and much evidence against it.

Created when infused From this it appears quite certain that the soul is created at the time it is infused into matter, i.e., when it is substantially united with the embryo to form a complete living human being. The human parents produce germ cells (sperm and ovum) which unite to form a single cell (zygote). The soul is created and infused when this matter is appropriately disposed to receive it and form a man.

Exactly when this happens is more controversial, with scholastic philosophers of high standing on both sides. It is worth examining because among other things it illustrates some aspects of the relation between philosophy and science. The major premise of the argument is a philosophical principle, and hence perennially valid. The minor premise is one of fact, and on this modern biology can supply details not known to the medieval philosophers. Hence the conclusion could differ, even though there is no philosophical disagreement. The difference will not be about the essential nature of man; it can only be on an accidental point, viz., the precise time of the soul's origin.

At the moment of conception Granting that it is still an open question, this author wishes to take a position, as follows:

Since the soul is the formal principle of vital operations, the human soul is present when there is specifically human operation.

But there is evidence of specifically human operation from the first moment of conception.

Therefore the human soul is present from the first moment of conception.

The major premise is simply a restatement of the principle of causality. How do we know that there is a soul at all? As a necessary explanation to account for the facts. All the philosophers involved agree on this.

The minor is a question of evidence. Aristotle, although he held epigenesis rather than preformation centuries before the microscope was invented, did not have the technological devices necessary to uncover any evidence of specifically human organization and operation in the embryo during its first stages. He thought that he was unjustified in asserting true human life before the male embryo was 40 days old, and before 80 to 90 days in the female. Not a biologist himself, Aquinas followed him in this unwillingness to go beyond the evidence. They taught a succession of forms, the embryo having first a vegetative soul and later a sensitive one, before the human soul finally arrives. Aquinas postulates an exception by way of miracle to account for Christ's soul being present from the moment of conception, as he is apparently unwilling to let theological convenience dictate a systematic conclusion which would go contrary to scientific evidence as he knew it at the time.

Some modern scholastics seem reluctant to depart from this position, possibly because of an unconscious emotional repugnance against asserting that Thomas was wrong. But if Thomas were alive today, he would be the first to insist that factual evidence and not his say-so should determine the issue. The above argument seems to be not only within the framework of his general philosophical principles but actually more in accordance with his spirit.

What are the facts? The zygote is so tiny that a dozen could rest on the head of a pin, so we are not surprised that modern microscopes have revealed facts which were utterly inaccessible to the ancients. At the moment sperm and ovum unite and the two pronuclei fuse, an orderly process of development begins, with a definiteness compared by one professor of embryology to the action of a stop watch when you press the release. The new individual is characterized by its unique pattern in the DNA molecule, and its resulting peculiar constellation of genes and chromosomes, before the zygote divides for the first time.

This organization is not only intricate and vital; it is *specifically human.* The chromosomes contain determiners for specifically human eyes and ears, not just animals' eyes and ears in general. The offspring of all verterbrates may go through the same stages of embryological development, and in similar ways. But careful study on guinea pigs, rhesus monkeys, and other vertebrates has shown that each goes through those stages in ways which are characteristic and peculiar to its own species. The guinea pig goes through the stage when it superficially resembles a tadpole in a way that is proper to guinea pigs and different from the way the rhesus monkey goes through the tadpole stage. This has been observed even at the earliest levels of development and could hardly be different in the case of the human being. Embryologists make it quite clear from the way they write and speak that they consider the living body from the one-cell stage on to be a human individual, not some general plant or animal which will become human in forty or eighty days.

No father seriously doubts that his newborn son is a human being. If the child at birth has a human soul, mere passage down the birth canal does not change his essential nature and make human what was not before. Examination of the fetus back through earlier stages gives no clue as to when one can draw the line. The available evidence seems to force us back to the moment of conception.[4] If one were to wait until one had clear evidence of *rational* activity before concluding to the existence of a human soul, it would be a matter not of days but of years. As long as the embryo is clearly the product of human generation, it has a human nature, even if severe organic defect prevents it from ever exercising any rational activities, as in the case of some idiots. Recall our discussion in Chapter 12 on the indirect evidence we have about the sleeping man or the "hopelessly" insane. Before being awakened or cured, they retain their human rights.

In confirmation, it is interesting to note that our law courts concur in this, for they have held that a child *in utero* can inherit, and that only a human person can have rights.[5]

---

[4] C. Sherrington, *Man on His Nature,* 2d ed. [Garden City, N.Y.: Doubleday (Anchor), 1953], p. 74.

[5] For the believing Catholic there are also some interesting suasive theological arguments from the doctrine on the Immaculate Conception. The decree itself does not pretend to pronounce on this point. Theologians who are reluctant to abandon St. Thomas's position explain away this implication of the decree by terms like "second instant" and "passive conception," but the latter seems to stem from outmoded notions of the role of the wife in conception and of the true nature of the ovum. The liturgy (December 8 to September 8) clearly implies our position. There is also the fact that the Church changed her law so as to excommunicate all who deliberately procure an abortion, not only after forty to eighty days. But as a philosophical question it must be settled on its own merits, which means facts and reasoning.

Koren (1955, p. 268) says that for our doctrine the "main argument would seem to be that any other solution gets involved in all kinds of unnecessary complications." This criticism certainly does not apply to the above proof, which is based on positive evidence. One might retort that some opponents seem to base their adherence to the old doctrine on a desire to avoid complications, for example, in explaining human identical twins. Now we admit that this point is less neatly handled from our position. But we prefer to build our case on the ordinary situation and see if the exception can be fitted in without destroying it—this is the original meaning of "the exception proves (tests) the rule." There is no good reason to suppose that, in cases where the original fecundated ovum divides into two human beings, any insurmountable difficulty is encountered. Before division there can be only one soul; at the time of division a second soul is created for the second twin (it is irrelevant as well as impossible to say which one). This seems no greater a difficulty than to say that the intermediate vegetative soul is an instrument (Koren, p. 270), when in fact the embryo does not act as an instrument but as a nature.

ORIGIN OF MAN'S BODY

The origin of the individual human body is today a fairly well-understood biological process, and the general outlines of genetics and embryology are not a matter of controversy. Whether a body could be produced artificially will be discussed shortly. The origin of the whole human species, or of the first human being, could have been either by a process of evolution or by direct creation.

Evolution Around the beginning of this century, after Darwin's theories had received wide notice, it was a burning question whether man's body could have originally arisen by biological evolution from lower forms of life. Opposition came chiefly from formalistic Catholics who did not know the remote history of Catholic thought on the point, and from Protestants with a tendency toward a defensive literalness about Bible texts as their only stronghold against rising materialism. When the book of Genesis says that God made Adam out of the slime of the earth, many felt constrained to take this as meaning that He did so by a direct and separate act of creation.

Today there is a much more relaxed attitude toward evolution. Formerly thought to represent a clash between science and religion, it is now looked upon as an instance of science simply discovering more about how God does things.

This change has taken place for a variety of reasons. First, advanced scriptural studies have convinced scholars that the Bible is quite open to evolutionary interpretation, or at least contains nothing contrary to it. Secondly, a good look at Christian tradition shows that evolution is no novel idea dating from the time of Darwin, and that the changed attitude toward evolution is no instance of jumping on the bandwagon in a purely opportunist manner. Six centuries before Darwin, Aquinas had admitted the possibility,[6] and it accords with his Aristotelian doctrine of change by disposing matter. St. Augustine anticipated the modern discussions by nearly fifteen centuries in proposing the doctrine that evolution shows the glory of God even more clearly than separate acts of direct creation. Thirdly, as the dust of controversy has settled we see that much of the dispute involved false issues which have been eliminated by a careful philosophical analysis of what is really at stake. Scientific evolution as such, for example, is neither theistic nor atheistic; it has no concern with whether God as First Cause started the process or not, but only with the process. As implied by the quotation at the head of this chapter,[7] Darwin was a religious man; the atheism of his great popularizer Huxley did much to confuse the issue.

Finally, the theory of evolution itself has gained scientific respectability because the dogmatism adopted by some of its earlier proponents has been abandoned. It has good explanatory value, which is the criterion of a scientific theory. Gaps in our knowledge are admitted, and opinions vary as to the manner in which certain changes may have occurred. Nonetheless, evolution seems to afford the best explanation for the most facts, and is thus a useful, interesting, and legitimate hypothesis.[8]

Acceptable theory of evolution   For these reasons many philosophers and theologians now favor evolution as the preferred theory for the origin of man's body. There would seem to be nothing amiss if God had wished to make man's body out of the slime of the earth by putting into matter the potentialities of evolving through various stages until, under His Divine Providence, gene mutations in some anthropoid primate produced a zygote into which He could infuse a human soul.

Rahner aptly borrows the term "hominization" from Teilhard de Chardin in his description of the instrumental causality of creatures in the production of man. But contrary to his stand for mediate animation,

[6] *Qq. Disp. de Potentia Dei,* 3, 4 ad 7um.
[7] *Life and Letters* (New York: Appleton, 1898), vol. I, p. 282.
[8] See George P. Klubertanz, S.J., *The Philosophy of Human Nature* (New York: Appleton-Century-Crofts, 1953), appendixes G and N for an excellent delineation of the issues.

it seems a neater evolutionary scheme to hold for a human soul from the moment of conception also in the case of the first man. In our theory, there is no question of God making man out of an ape, but of His making a human zygote from previously evolved animal matter. The first man was human from the moment of his conception. This theory seems preferable to the anthropomorphism which pictures God on the banks of the Euphrates molding Adam's body by hand. Theologians agree that the Bible is not a scientific document, nor even a profane history as such; it teaches us that God made man, with no pretense of telling us precisely how. As indicated earlier, we are still groping for any full understanding of the cooperation between God and the reproductive process.

We have seen that every human soul must be created by God along with the natural causes by which matter was disposed to the point of being apt for its infusion. To try to explain the origin of intellect and will from animal life by postulating a new "emergent," derived from lower forms but not contained in them, still ignores the essential difference between material and immaterial and violates the logic of science itself. Even God could not put into matter the potency of evolving a spiritual soul.

On the other hand, the philosophical dialectic between change and stability has been going on since the opening round of Parmenides versus Heraclitus. Progress is a fact, and the real question is the degree of inner causality involved. Whether Bergson's *élan vital* or Teilhard's "radial impetus" or some other formula is used, we seek to comprehend better the inner dynamism by which nature progresses. Van Melsen would argue that any *special* causality by the Creator violates both His transcendence, since He is above acting as just one more cause, and His immanence, being so involved in all causality that no natural effect is special. Evolution seems to be still going on, including the important areas of cultural evolution and the exciting possibilities of artificial manipulation of human genetics. It seems that the notion of substantial change explained in Chapter 15 safeguards both the unity of man (evolution is not mere addition of angel to animal) and his difference from other animals (evolution is really *change*). The need is not for a closed system but for thinkers of vision, willing and able to change philosophical and theological formulations as science reveals more of reality to our purview.

God as First Cause and the creation of the human soul are known from philosophy. One further point seems demanded by theology. The whole economy of redemption in the Judaeo-Christian tradition implies some unity of all mankind as blood brothers of the Redeemer. This cannot be demonstrated either philosophically or scientifically, but we note that nothing here is contradictory. Gene mutations, either spontaneous or caused by cosmic rays and other natural radiations, could explain the different appearances of the various "races"—brown, white, black, yellow, red—just as we can change a strain of fruit flies by gamma rays. Actual trips (e.g., that of the Kon-Tiki) have demonstrated the possibility of worldwide migration of all peoples by primitive rafts from a common point of origin on the globe. The different so-called missing links are separated not only in space but in time; if truly human, they could easily be descendants of one pro-genitor. (If they were not human, there is no proof that the offspring of more than one actually became human.) Leading evolutionists such as Dobzhansky say that polygenism is not essential to evolutionary theory, while new explanations of original sin are being proposed by theologians. Whether other primates could evolve to the stage of uniting with rational forms, and whether Martians have rational souls, are open questions.

As for the six days mentioned in Genesis I, neither the Hebrew nor the Greek word means only a day of twenty-four hours, but can mean any period of time. The six "days" could have been six billion years of evolu-tionary process, and may not refer to chronological sequence at all. The point of the enumeration is that God is the author of every being. The Biblical account of the origin of the first woman has never been satisfactorily explained, but this is a problem for Scripture scholars. The language of the Old Testament is often metaphorical. Here it is at least expressing some dependence in origin of the first woman on the first man; precisely what that dependence was we do not know, but we need not be so literal-minded as to assume that God necessarily performed thoracic surgery in the Garden of Eden.

Could man synthesize living body? A final question allied to evolu-tion is the possibility that scientists in a laboratory could produce living protoplasm. One reason for considering it in this connection is because it helps clarify our thinking on the question, "Can life come from nonlife?"

When this issue is raised in discussions on evolution, it is assumed that nonliving matter is the total and adequate cause. Now life from nonlife in this sense is impossible. But neither does it happen in this way in evolution, for in addition to nonliving matter as a material cause we also have God as the efficient cause. Thus the effect is not above the total cause, for God is living and is quite adequate to produce living beings. He is the ultimate cause, and the problem is how He might use secondary causes as His instruments. These instrumental causes need not be alive, any more than the painter's brush needs to be artistic. The artist must be, or there will be no work of art; but the brush is never adequate cause.[9]

The same distinction must be made with regard to the artificial synthesis of living matter. By itself, nonliving matter is not an ade-quate cause. But the total cause here includes the scientist, who is not only alive but intelligent, and thus well above the minimum level of perfection demanded by the principle of causality. After all, we turn nonliving matter into living matter every day, when we digest the food we eat. There is no philosophical reason why science cannot

[9] See Klubertanz (1953), appendix L, "Efficient Causality in Material Things," for a good discussion of the nature of change by disposition, and appendix N for its application to the question of evolution.

understand the process well enough, in time, to duplicate it. We are certain that matter itself will never do so alone. But the scientist is more than mere matter.

If two parent dogs dispose matter so as to produce a new puppy dog, why cannot a scientist? It seems to be a question of how much biochemistry we can learn. Apparently we have synthesized a protein-like substance which produces amino acid; chemists have reconstructed the components back into an active virus; and it seems quite clear that we can synthesize artificial nucleotide chains in DNA. There would be little point in speculating about the possibility of what has already occurred.

Lest this again should seem like trimming our philosophical sails to the shift in scientific wind, we should recall that the ancient and medieval philosophers held a similar position. Before Reddi and Pasteur, *omne vivum ex vivo* was not the accepted formula, for it was supposed that maggots were spontaneously generated in decaying flesh, under the influence of the sun or other bodies. Our knowledge of the sun's action and cosmic rays has increased prodigiously since then, but the scientist in his laboratory may well accomplish things which the ancients attributed to heavenly bodies. The basic philosophical principles still hold. Recall our discussion of substantial change in explaining the nature of formal cause (Chapter 15).

Could this synthetic living matter be human? It is at this point that the problem becomes real for the philosopher. We have seen that not even God, much less the scientist, could dispose matter so as to produce from it the spiritual form of man. Plant and animal souls are within the potency of matter, and are caused by causing the composite plant or animal. For man, the most we could do would be to dispose matter so that it would be apt matter into which God could infuse a soul. The question is whether He would create one for this occasion. Philosophically, it seems that all we can say is that we do not know. This does not seem to be His plan; the normal way of human reproduction is by the generative act of the parents. The short-lived embryos produced in the laboratory by artificially fecundating a human ovum with a human sperm could conceivably have a human soul. If not, they could be animated by some infrahuman animal form.

CONCLUSION

Men have speculated for decades about the possibility of a man-made human being, a robot which would be a mechanical imitation of man. Between electronics and biochemistry we now have basis in fact for some of the fantasy one reads in science fiction. But so far we are more impressed by the essential superiority of living beings over nonliving, and that even the simplest plants have powers of self-repair, internal growth, and reproduction of their species which surpass the most fantastic electronic computers, not so much in degree as in kind.

This qualitative superiority becomes even more evident when we enter the realm of human experience. We may anthropomorphically attribute loyalty, excitement, perfectionism, and other reactions to a computer, but we have no evidence that it actually experiences such emotions or has any sense of values. Quite the contrary: we know that it reacts only in accordance with the way we built it. Man's spirit shows a contrasting independence of what others may try to make him. He is an individual, not a product. His creativity and appreciation of beauty far transcend the artificial poetry or music a computer might crank out.

Most important, he has a sense of his own dignity and responsibility, his historical roots and immortal destiny, which no machine can experience because it has neither these to know nor the means of knowing them. With this comes the fact that man is a social being. Because of the dignity of others and what he can share with them, he becomes committed to others: he cares about them, communicates with them, expects response from them. Man's nature makes him capable of unique relationships with other men, with the meaning of the universe, and with its Author.

REVIEW QUESTIONS

1. What reasons can you give against the existence of the human soul prior to its union with matter in the embryo?
2. Why cannot the human soul arise from the act of generation?
3. Why cannot the spiritual souls of the parents produce the child's soul?
4. To what extent would the scientific manipulation of human genetics (altering the DNA molecule, etc.) constitute intelligent cooperation with the Creator as an extension of the natural cooperation of parents?
5. Can responsibility for distant future generations through genetic upgrading be vested in public authorities? Can it be managed through the democratic process?
6. Do you feel the argument that the soul is present from the moment of conception is conclusive or merely suasive?
7. Would its rejection alter our understanding of the nature of man?
8. What practical consequences would its rejection have?

9. Supposing evolution, was the first man ever a subhuman animal if the human soul is infused at the zygote stage?
10. According to Teilhard, could the human soul be the product of evolution? in what sense?
11. Hegel's has been described as a system which tries to contain all truth, that of Aquinas as an attempt to order what truth we have. If so, how would each handle the question of the continuing evolution of man?
12. Distinguish between the two senses of the expression, "Can life come from nonlife?"
13. In terms of adequate causality, how does the theory of atheistic evolution differ from the theory that man could synthesize living protoplasm?

FOR FURTHER READING

Kelly & Tallon: the selection from Teilhard de Chardin on pp. 144–148.

Although theological, *Teilhard and Creation of the Soul,* by Robert North, S.J., is of real interest to the philosopher also. He explains some of the thinking of Karl Rahner, much of whose writing has not yet been translated into English. Rahner's influence is also felt in the writings of Joseph Donceel, whose article in *Thought,* 1965, on "Teilhard de Chardin and the Body-Soul Relation" was mentioned in the Readings for Chapter 15; see also his book *Philosophical Anthropology.*

George P. Klubertanz, S.J., and Donceel both say that the majority of scholastics today hold that the soul is present from conception. Opposed are the writings of E. C. Messenger, Henry J. Koren, Cardinal Mercier, Cannon Dordolot, and Robert LaCroix (the appendix to his *L'Origine de l'âme humaine*). The position of Aquinas is found in *Summa Theol.,* Ia, 90 and 118; *Summa Contra Gent.,* II, 83–89.

On evolution in its philosophical implications for man, the name of Pierre Teilhard de Chardin of course stands out. *The Future of Man* is perhaps less basic but easier reading than his *The Phenomenon of Man.* A leader in the scientific study of evolution is Dobzhansky, *Mankind Evolving.*

There has been a rash of speculations on reconciling the Bible with evolution. Many of them are concerned with the problem of original sin, which is not a philosophical question. The writings of **Cyril Vollert, S.J.,** e.g., **"Evolution and the Bible,"** in **B. Boelen,** *Symposium on Evolution,* strike this author as making good sense. Other writers on this topic include **Charles Hauret, Jean DeFraine, Raymond J. Nogar, John L. McKenzie, J. Franklin Ewing,** and **E. C. Messenger.**

John L. Morrison tells an interesting tale of reactionism in **"American Catholics and the Crusade against Evolution,"** *Rec. Amer. Catholic Historical Soc. Philadelphia,* 1953, 44:59–71. Though Catholics were by no means the worst reactionaries against evolution, this reactionary attitude has been misinterpreted as an official Church position, partly because of the unfortunate book by **Ernesto Cardinal Ruffini,** *The Theory of Evolution Judged by Reason and Faith.* In contrast are the ultraliberal opinions of some Dutch thinkers, reflected in **Andrew van Melsen,** *Evolution and Philosophy.*

APPENDIX
DO ANIMALS
HAVE INTELLECT?

*To expatiate upon the importance of thought would be
absurd. The traditional definition of man as "the
thinking animal" fixes thought as the essential difference
between man and the brutes—surely an
important matter.* Dewey

Whether brute animals think is really of no direct concern to the philosophy of man. One legitimate reaction to the question is that we simply do not care whether they do or not. As long as we are satisfied that analysis of our operations affords conclusive evidence that man thinks, our concept of man remains unchanged, regardless of what we decide may be the nature of other animals. If someone feels that intellect is necessary to explain animal activities, this does not invalidate the evidence for human intellect. At most, it would mean that such a person should be logically consistent and give animals the rights and responsibilities proper to an intelligent being.

The question can contribute indirectly to our study of man because it is sometimes said that man is not by nature a rational animal, but *acquires* rationality from his environmental experiences. This is an assertion which should be open to testing by empirical evidence. The facts which have been accumulated in the study of animals thus become pertinent. If man is just a high type of vertebrate who acquires rationality by social conditioning, others of the higher vertebrates should be able to acquire rationality if given similar environmental opportunities. And conversely, if other animals fail to develop rationality under identical social conditions, the difference would seem to be in the very nature of man and brute respectively.

Condition for rational development

Our account of the formation of ideas in Chapter 6 and our delineation of the subjective factors in perception in Chapter 5 both indicate the importance of environmental sensory experience in the development of even intellectual knowledge. Language is a sensory, social means of communicating thought, and its importance for rational development cannot be ignored. Evidence which confirms these assertions is available from the study of people who are born deaf, and from instances where children have been deprived of normal human environment.

It is always difficult to get accurate information on the latter cases, for if psychologists and social workers were around to record the data then there would not have been the complete lack of human social contact which is precisely the variable in question. But a few cases seem to be well enough authenticated to be considered. Two children, apparently abandoned in the jungle by their parents, were reported to have been raised by wolves in India. When found, they walked on all fours and were in a state of great mental retardation. One died shortly and the other lived only a few years after being brought into human society. Neither developed to any high degree of rationality. The French physician Itard studied and tried to help a wild boy found in the forest of Aveyron in similar circumstances. He likewise made some progress but never fully overcame the effects of early stultification. From these cases it seems that human social contact is an important condition for the development of rationality.

But a condition is not a cause. Having the wheels greased may be a necessary condition for having the car run, but it does not cause the car to move. Lack of proper environment may retard human development, just as failure to grease the wheels may mean that the car will not move. But in neither case will merely applying the condition produce the effect if the cause is not at work. Therefore, we cannot logically conclude from the low mentality of these children that environment is anything more than a condition for the normal actuation of man's rational nature.

Experiments with animals

We are not lacking in evidence for the other aspects of our problem. Many brute animals have been given educational opportunities vastly superior to those afforded the unfortunate children mentioned above. Yet even these children showed some evidence of true rational response in spite of severely retarded beginnings, whereas the animals never do, even when given ideal conditions right from the start. At least two experiments have involved human parents "adopting" a baby ape and raising it exactly the same as a human baby.[1] In both cases, careful scientific records were kept, and in both cases the early sensory and motor development of the ape was ahead of the child at the same age. This is to be expected, for the ape has a shorter life span and would be further developed when maturing at a proportionate rate. In both cases the experiment was abandoned when it became quite clear that the ape showed no signs of true intellect long after a human child had far surpassed it.

Robert M. Yerkes of Yale University studied primates for about half a century, and his colony of apes were given every advantage of civilization. Among other things, they showed signs of a crude barter, a sort of prostitution, and an ability to play slot machines. His reports of these superficial semblances to human behavior have often been appealed to in attempts to reduce man to mere animal. But Yerkes himself seems from his lifelong study to have drawn just the opposite conclusion: that as our knowledge and understanding of anthropoid life increases, so also does our thankfulness that we are man.[2]

Köhler's report of the chimpanzee who put the two sticks together to get the banana outside his cage is another instance of frequent distortion in secondary sources. Köhler's own report makes it clear that the ape put the sticks together accidentally after an hour or so of aimless play in which he apparently forgot all about the banana, and only later saw the new Gestalt in which the combined stick was long enough. Köhler himself does not claim perceptual insight to be an act of intellect.[3]

T. V. Moore made a comprehensive survey of the experimental data available and found that higher vertebrates manifest a grasp of concrete spatial configurations, to about the degree attained by a high-grade human idiot. This he attributes to the activity of the central

---

[1] W. N. Kellogg & Luella Kellogg, *The Ape and the Child* (New York: McGraw-Hill, 1933); Cathy H. (Mrs. Keith J.) Hayes, *Ape in Our House* (New York: Harper, 1951).

[2] Cf. Brennan (1945), p. 185.

[3] W. Köhler, *Gestalt Psychology* (New York: Liveright, 1947), p. 341. See F. L. Harmon, *Principles of Psychology*, rev. ed. (Milwaukee: Bruce, 1951), pp. 399–403 for a good discussion of Köhler's work.

sense. "But when we attempt to measure their power of abstract thought and their ability to see and form general principles in the logical order, we obtain zero scores, for such abilities are simply not present."[4]

Why don't animals talk?

There is no doubt about the fact that animals can communicate. Bees can transmit to other bees both the direction and the distance of a find. Most animals can make their wants known in some way. But the question is not whether they communicate, but whether they do so by the conventional symbols of conceptual language or by concrete natural signs. All the evidence points to the latter. To suggest that maybe they have a true conceptual language which we do not understand is an unwarranted assumption. To postulate that they have ideas and simply do not communicate is not only a gratuitous assertion but quite contrary to everything we know about the nature of knowledge as communicable. Moreover, to argue "Why should the animals manifest their thought to us?" admits that they do not. Since we can only go on the manifestations of evidence, this is tantamount to saying that for our purpose the issue is settled.

It is sometimes asserted (Garrett, 1955, p. 69) that the reason animals do not talk is that they do not have the equipment. But parrots and other animals do talk. Some species of apes possess vocal apparatus capable of modulating sounds. Parrots and any animals having lips, tongue, and larynx are far better equipped than many paralyzed or otherwise handicapped persons. Yet the latter somehow manage to communicate ideas, whereas the former never do. Yerkes says, "It may not be asserted that any of the anthropoid types speaks" (1929, p. 546; also p. 569). Garrett seems to contradict himself here, for on the same page he reports that Vicki, an ape raised as a child, was able to say three words, *mamma, papa,* and *cup*—quite impossible if she lacked the necessary equipment! The only conclusion is that the reason animals do not talk is that they have nothing to say, i.e., no concepts to express but only concrete sensory experiences.

Negative evidence

It is good to remind ourselves that we cannot expect to have the same kind of positive evidence as would be forthcoming if the conclusion were a positive one. What evidence do you have that there is not a

---

[4] T. V. Moore, "Human and Animal Intelligence," in H. S. Jennings and others, *Scientific Aspects of the Race Problem* (New York: Longmans, 1941), p. 152.

live alligator in the corner of the room as you read this? Only negative evidence; the burden of the proof is on him who asserts its presence. The closest you can come to positive evidence is to walk over to the corner and give the alligator a chance to snap at you if he is there. Similarly, we can only report on those experiments where conditions are created in which brute animals should manifest thought if they have any.

Note that this is a different matter from asserting that animals do stupid things, and that men do not. The question is whether animals *ever* show intellect; whereas man's has already been established, without implying that he always uses it. Neither does this involve a denial that animals do many extremely ingenious things. The explanation of how they do them will be discussed shortly. The question now is whether they manifest intellect when conditions warrant it.

Naturalists have set up many experiments to test whether animals understand why they are doing what they do. For instance, an elaborate series of seven steps is observed in the laying of an egg and storing it; at step four the experimenter removes the egg in full sight of the insect, who proceeds to go right on and complete the remaining steps even though the whole process is now pointless. Birds will continue to collect food for their young even when they have seen them killed. Again, the animal fails to modify his behavior when it would be logical to do so if he understood its purpose. It is proverbial that horses will follow their self-protective pattern even when it means burning to death in the stable.

Monkeys are great imitators. For centuries they have watched birds fly in the jungle. Yet they have never shown any evidence of abstracting out the principles of flight and applying them as did the Wright brothers. Nothing approaching the construction of machinery or mass production is ever observed in animals, nor the invention of any tool which shows more than concrete perception of spatial relations. Their language has no transposable signs, normative grammar, or abstract symbols. All these are signs of universal ideas.

Progress of some sort is almost infallibly a sign of intellect. Yet naturalists of ancient times observed exactly the same activities that we see animals doing today. It is incredible that the animals would have even rudimentary intellect and show no real accomplishment or transmission of anything they learn to their followers. Even the crudest primitives have some tradition. This is even more striking in the case of domesticated animals, where selective breeding and constant opportunities to learn from their association with man would be most conducive to progress. Yet even under these conditions we see no unequivocal evidence of genuine intellectual progress.

Akin to this is the animal's lack of any awareness of personal identity, and hence of self-reflectiveness or historicity. Man is the only animal that blushes; he alone seems to have a true sense of responsibility. Other animals show no appreciation of beauty, nor any attempts at art. Humor is completely lacking, even in the "laughing" hyena; it takes intellect to recognize incongruity and thus appreciate the ridiculous.

Ambiguous terms

We have already noted that such terms as intelligence, learning, trial and error, insight, and ability to adjust or solve problems are all ambiguous. Thus *insight* may mean a total perceptual awareness (Gestalt) in which concrete relations are seen, as in the case of the ape with the two sticks and the banana, or it may mean true intellectual understanding in terms of universal principles. *Trial and error* may mean chance connection in one of a series of random movements which is then associated with success, or it may mean an elaborate inductive reasoning process which involves the testing of hypotheses by a series of experiments. Even *concept* now often refers merely to concrete associations and generalized stimuli, perhaps associated with abstract symbol or satisfying experience. But a true intellectual concept is an understanding of what a thing *is*, not merely what it is *for*. These other uses of the term concept are analogous and involve generalized association of sense experience rather than abstraction. The fact that a monkey can learn to associate concrete reactions with the general shape of a triangle is not evidence that it understands the nature of triangularity, i.e., has a true concept. *Intelligence* may mean any ability to learn or adjust such as most animals manifest, or it may be the capacity for abstract thought such as we analyzed in Chapter 7. To say that an animal is more or less intelligent simply refers to the degree to which his internal senses are developed.

Internal sense powers ignored

It is the failure to appreciate the marvelous versatility of the internal senses which deludes most people into concluding that animals have intellect. They see animals do many wonderful things, which obviously surpass the power of mere reflex or sensation. Therefore they immediately conclude that intellect must be at work. The solution is not to deny that animals act in a very clever manner, but to study their central sense, imagination, memory, and estimative power. Imagination, for instance, is capable of forming an image of three-dimensional space wherein we can visualize generalized relations.[5] Associations and memories can pile up with incredible richness; sensory discrimination can be very acute. ("Kluger Hans," the counting horse, sensed when to stop counting out the answer from subtle cues, which even his master was unaware of giving him. Controlled experimentation showed he was helpless outside his master's presence.) These operations are possible at least to animals with well-developed brain and nervous systems, such as most higher vertebrates have. Such operations are quite adequate to explain the facts, without appealing to intellect. (See Chapter 5.)

True intelligence involved

Lastly, we readily concede that the activities of brute animals, including insects such as bees and ants, show definitely that there is intelligence in the strict sense of true understanding somewhere in the total picture. The leaf-roller beetle who cuts a perfect parabola may know no analytic geometry; the bee who constructs his honeycomb according to the best principles of structural design may not be a mechanical engineer. Like the navigation ability of homing pigeons and the built-in radar of bats, these manifest true intellect at work. The question here is, whose intellect is it?

Masterful understanding on just one point is contrary to the nature of intellect, which has being as its object. The intellect should be able to make some progress on other things. But these animals show no ability to generalize over into even allied areas. They do the same thing the same way for centuries, with no improvement and no application of their ability to other problems. This suggests that there is no real grasp of what is applied, but that they simply are following a concrete behavior pattern. There could hardly be such brilliance in one tiny area without its showing elsewhere. If they truly understand the solution to the problem, why do they always use the same solution when there are others? Why do they always solve it perfectly the first time, if it is really the result of their understanding? Man usually takes time to work things out, and is rarely as proficient in the beginning of his life as later on. All this indicates that it is not the animal's own intellect which is responsible for the wonders he performs.

The automatic pilot in a modern airplane certainly manifests in-

[5] Klubertanz (1953, p. 132) calls this an "abstract" image, but this seems a bit misleading. "General" image might be better. Similarly, the concrete associations obtained by the rhesus monkey can include the general image of "threeness" without this necessarily being a true concept of number as implied by Hicks (1956).

telligence at work, yet nobody argues that the device itself understands why it functions. The intellect of the designer is given full credit. A similar argument could lead to the conclusion that, if the animal does not have an intellect, the Designer of the animal does. But this would take us beyond the philosophy of human nature.

FOR FURTHER READING

Fabre, Jean Henri C. *Fabre's Book of Insects,* retold from **Alexander Teixeira de Mattos's** translation of Fabre's *Souvenirs entomologiques* by **Mrs. Rudolph Stowell.**

Fabre, Jean Henri C. *The Hunting Wasps.*

Gruender, Hubert, S.J. *Experimental Psychology.* Pp. 245–252, 286–300.

Katz, David. *Animals and Men.*

Köhler, Wolfgang. *The Mentality of Apes.*

Lorenz, K. Z. *King Solomon's Ring.*

Moore, Thomas Verner. "Human and Animal Intelligence," in H. S. Jennings and others, *Scientific Aspects of the Race Problem.* Pp. 95–158.

Romanes, George John. *Mental Evolution in Animals* (with a posthumous essay, "Instinct," by Charles Darwin).

Schiller, Claire H. (Ed.) *Instinctive Behavior: The Development of a Modern Concept.*

Teale, E. W. *The Insect World of J. Henri Fabre.*

Thorpe, W. H. *Learning and Instinct in Animals.*

Tinbergen, N. *The Study of Instinct.*

Von Frisch, K. *Bees: Their Vision, Chemical Senses, and Language.*

Wasmann, Eric, S.J. *Instinct and Intelligence in the Animal Kingdom.*

Wilm, E. C. *Theories of Instinct.*

Yerkes, Robert M., & Yerkes, Ada W. *The Great Apes.*

GENERAL BIBLIOGRAPHY

ADLER, MORTIMER J. *The Idea of Freedom*. Garden City, N.Y.: Doubleday, 1958, 1961. 2 vols.

ADLER, MORTIMER J. *What Man Has Made of Man*. New York: Longmans, 1937.

ADRIAN, EDGAR D. *The Physical Background of Perception*. Fair Lawn, N.J.: Oxford University Press, 1947.

ALLERS, RUDOLF. "Functions, Factors, and Faculties," *The Thomist*, 1944, 7:323–362.

ALLERS, RUDOLF. "Intellectual Cognition," in R. E. Brennan (Ed.) *Essays in Thomism*. New York: Sheed, 1942. Pp. 41–62.

ALLERS, RUDOLF. "The Intellectual Cognition of Particulars," *The Thomist*, 1941, 3:95–163.

ALLERS, RUDOLF. "Irresistible Impulses," *Amer. eccles. Rev.*, 1939, 100:209–218.

ALLERS, RUDOLF. "The Vis Cogitativa and Evaluation," *The New Scholasticism*, 1941, 15:195–221.

ALLPORT, GORDON W. *Becoming: Basic Considerations for a Psychology of Personality*. New Haven: Yale University Press, 1955.

ALLPORT, GORDON W. *Pattern and Growth in Personality*. New York: Holt, 1961.

ALLPORT, GORDON W. "Traits Revisited," *Amer. Psychologist*, 1966, 21:1–10.

AMES, A., JR. "Reconsideration of the Origin and Nature of Perception," in S. Ratner (Ed.) *Vision and Action*. New Brunswick, N.J.: Rutgers University Press, 1953. Pp. 251–274.

AMMERMAN, ROBERT R. (Ed.) *Classics of Analytic Philosophy*. New York: McGraw-Hill, 1965.

AQUINAS, ST. THOMAS. His works are probably most readily available in Anton C. Pegis (Ed.) *Basic Writings of St. Thomas Aquinas*. New York: Random House, 1945. His treatise on man is in vol. I, pp. 682–862; vol. II, pp. 225–411. Much of this is contained in Anton C. Pegis (Ed.) *Intro-*

duction to St. Thomas Aquinas. New York: Modern Library, 1948. Pp. 280–608.

AQUINAS, ST. THOMAS. *The Soul.* Trans. by John P. Rowan. St. Louis: Herder, 1949.

AQUINAS, ST. THOMAS. *The Summa Theologica.* Trans. by the fathers of the English Dominican Province. New York: Benziger, 1947. The most readily available Latin text is *Summa Theologiae.* Ottawa: Studium Generale, O.P., 1941–1944. References to *S. T.* can be located by question number in the Pegis or other editions. Questions 75–90 of part I (Ia) are especially pertinent.

AQUINAS, ST. THOMAS. *Treatise on Man.* Trans. by James F. Anderson. Englewood Cliffs, N.J.: Prentice-Hall, 1962. Questions 75–78 of part I of *S. T.,* in an excellent modern translation.

AQUINAS, ST. THOMAS. *Truth (De Veritate).* Trans. by R. W. Mulligan, S.J., J. V. McGlynn, S.J., & R. W. Schmidt, S.J. Chicago: Regnery, 1952–1954. 3 vols.

AQUINAS, ST. THOMAS. *On the Truth of the Catholic Faith (Summa Contra Gentiles,* abbreviated C. G.) Trans. by James F. Anderson. Garden City, N.Y.: Doubleday (Image), 1955. Book II, chaps. 46–90. Note that although the wording of the title of each *Summa* indicates theological content, we refer to them only as sources of philosophical argument.

ARISTOTLE. *On the Soul (De Anima)* may be found in *Basic Works of Aristotle* (ed. by Richard McKeon). New York: Random House, 1941; Modern Library, 1947.

ARISTOTLE. *De Anima* (in the version of William of Moerbeke and the commentary of St. Thomas Aquinas). Trans. by K. Foster & Silvester Humphries, with an introduction by Ivo Thomas, O.P. New Haven, Conn.: Yale University Press, 1951.

ARNOLD, MAGDA B. *Emotion and Personality.* New York: Columbia University Press, 1960. 2 vols.

ARNOLD, MAGDA B., & GASSON, JOHN A. *The Human Person: An Approach to an Integral Theory of Personality.* New York: Ronald, 1954.

AVELING, FRANCIS. *The Immortality of the Soul.* Vol. I. Westminster Lectures. St. Louis: Herder, 1906.

AVELING, FRANCIS. *Personality and Will.* New York: Appleton-Century-Crofts, 1931.

AYER, A. J. *Language, Truth, and Logic.* (2d ed.) New York: Dover, 1946.

AYER, A. J. (Ed.) *Logical Postivism.* New York: Free Press, 1959.

AYER, A. J. *The Problem of Knowledge.* London: Macmillan, 1958.

BAKAN, DAVID. *The Duality of Human Experience.* New York: Rand McNally, 1966.

BAKAN, DAVID. *On Method: Toward a Reconstruction of Psychological Investigation.* San Francisco: Jossey-Bass, 1967.

BAKAN, DAVID. "The Mystery-Mastery Complex in Contemporary Psychology," *Amer. Psychologist,* 1965, 20:186–191. (Also appears as chap. 4 in his book *On Method.*)

BARRETT, W. *Irrational Man.* New York: Doubleday, 1958.

BARUK, H. "Personality: Psychological and Metaphysical Problem," *Phil. Today*, 1957, 1:122–127.

BECK, WILLIAM S. *Modern Science and the Nature of Life.* New York: Harcourt, Brace, 1957.

BERENDA, CARLTON W. "Is Clinical Psychology a Science?" *Amer. Psychologist*, 1957, 12:725–729.

BERGSON, HENRI. *Matter and Memory.* Trans. by N. M. Paul & W. S. Palmer. New York: Macmillan, 1950a.

BERGSON, HENRI. *Time and Free Will.* New York: Macmillan, 1950b.

BERNARD, L. L. *Instinct: A Study in Social Psychology.* New York: Holt, 1924.

BERNSTEIN, MOREY. *The Search for Bridey Murphy.* New York: Doubleday, 1956.

BEROFSKY, BERNARD (Ed.) *Free Will and Determinism.* New York: Harper & Row, 1966.

VON BERTALANFFY, L. *Problems of Life: An Evaluation of Modern Biological Thought.* London: Watts, 1952.

BERTOCCI, PETER A. *Free Will, Responsibility, and Grace.* Nashville, Tenn.: Abingdon, 1957.

BIER, WILLIAM C., S.J. (Ed.) *Perception in Present-day Psychology: A Symposium.* New York: American Catholic Psychological Association (Fordham University), 1956.

BINET, ALFRED, & SIMON, TH. "Langage et pensé," *Année psychol.*, 1908, 14:284–339.

BLOCK, IRVING. "Three German Commentators on the Individual Senses and the Common Sense in Aristotle's Psychology," *Phronesis*, 1964, 9:58–63.

BOGANELLI, ELEUTHERIUS. "De Personalitate Psycho-physio-pathologica Delinquentis Enixe Expendenda in Judicio Ferendo de Culpabilitate Delicti," *Apollinaris*, 1937, 10:408–430.

BONNER, HUBERT. *On Being Mindful of Man.* Boston: Houghton Mifflin, 1965.

BORING, EDWARD G., "CP Speaks," *Contemporary Psychol.*, 1958, 3:361–362.

BORING, EDWARD G. *A History of Experimental Psychology.* (2d ed.) New York: Appleton-Century-Crofts, 1950.

BORING, EDWARD G. "Preface," in H. Misiak & V. Staudt, *Catholics in Psychology.* New York: McGraw-Hill, 1954. Pp. ix–xi.

BORING, EDWARD G. Review of James J. Gibson, *The Perception of the Visual World, Psychol. Bull.*, 1951, 48:360–363.

BORING, EDWARD G. *Sensation and Perception in the History of Experimental Psychology.* New York: Appleton-Century-Crofts, 1942.

BORING, EDWARD G. "When Is Human Behavior Predetermined?" *Scientific Monthly*, 1957, 84:189–196.

BORING, EDWARD G., LANGFELD, H. S., & WELD, H. P. *Foundations of Psychology.* New York: Wiley, 1948.

BOULOGNE, CHARLES-DAMIAN, O.P. *My Friends the Senses.* New York: Kenedy, 1953.

BOURKE, VERNON J. "Habitus as a Perfectant of Potency in the Philosophy of St. Thomas Aquinas." Unpublished doctoral dissertation, University of Toronto, 1938.

BOURKE, VERNON J. "The Role of Habitus in the Thomistic Metaphysics of Potency and Act," in R. Brennan (Ed.) *Essays in Thomism,* New York: Sheed, 1942. Pp. 103–109.

BOURKE, VERNON J. *Will in Western Thought.* New York: Sheed & Ward, 1964.

BOUTROUX, ÉMILE. *Historical Studies in Philosophy.* Trans. by Fred Rothwell. London: Macmillan, 1912.

BRAUNSHAUSEN, N. "Le Libre-arbitre à la lumière de la psychologie expérimentale et de la science moderne," *Rev. sci. pédag.,* 1947, 9:38–46 (*Psychol. Abstr.,* 1950, 24:1032).

BRENNAN, ROBERT E., O.P. *History of Psychology from the Standpoint of a Thomist.* New York: Macmillan, 1945.

BRENNAN, ROBERT E., O.P. *Thomistic Psychology.* New York: Macmillan, 1941.

BRIDGES, KATHERINE M. "A Genetic Theory of Emotions," *J. genet. Psychol.,* 1930, 27:514–527.

BRIDGMAN, PERCY W. "Remarks on the Present State of Operationalism," *Scientific Monthly,* 1954, 79:224–226.

BRIDGMAN, PERCY W. *The Way Things Are.* Cambridge, Mass.: Harvard University Press, 1959.

BRUNER, J. S., & GOODMAN, C. D. "Value and Need as Organizing Factors in Perception," *J. abnorm. soc. Psychol.,* 1947, 42:33–44.

BRUNER, J. S., GOODNOW, J. J., & AUSTIN, G. A. *A Study of Thinking.* New York: Wiley, 1956.

BRUNER, JEROME, and others. *Studies in Cognitive Growth.* New York: Wiley, 1966.

BUBER, M. *I and Thou.* New York: Scribner, 1958.

BUDDENBROCK, WOLFGANG VON. *The Senses.* Ann Arbor, Mich.: The University of Michigan Press, 1958.

BUGENTAL, J. F. T. (Ed.) *Challenges of Humanistic Psychology.* New York: McGraw-Hill, 1967.

CALDIN, E. F. *The Power and Limits of Science.* London: Chapman & Hall, 1949.

CAMERON, NORMAN. *Personality Development and Psychopathology.* Boston: Houghton Mifflin, 1963.

CAMMACK, J. S., S.J. *Moral Problems of Mental Defect.* London: Burns, 1938.

CAMUS, ALBERT. *The Myth of Sisyphus and Other Essays.* New York: Knopf, 1955.

CANNON, WALTER B. *Bodily Changes in Pain, Hunger, Fear and Rage.* (2d ed.) New York: Appleton-Century-Crofts, 1929.

CANNON, WALTER B. *The Wisdom of the Body.* (2d ed.) New York: Norton, 1939.

CANTRIL, HADLEY. "An Inquiry into the Characteristics of Man," *J. abnorm. soc. Psychol.,* 1950a, 45:490–503.

CANTRIL, HADLEY. *The "Why" of Man's Experience*. New York: Macmillan, 1950b.

CARNAP, R. "The Methodological Character of Theoretical Concepts," in *Minnesota Studies in the Philosophy of Science*. Vol. I. Minneapolis: The University of Minnesota Press, 1956. Pp. 38–76.

CARREL, ALEXIS. *Man the Unknown*. New York: Harper, 1939.

CARTWRIGHT, DORWIN. Review of Roy R. Grinker (Ed.) *Toward a Unified Theory of Human Behavior*, *Contemporary Psychol.*, 1957, 2:121–123.

CARUSO, IGOR A. *Existential Psychology: From Analysis to Synthesis*. New York: Herder and Herder, 1964.

CASSIRER, ERNST. *An Essay on Man*. New Haven, Conn.: Yale University Press, 1944.

CASTELL, ALBUREY. *The Self in Philosophy*. New York: Macmillan, 1965.

CASTIELLO, JAIMIE, S.J. *A Humane Psychology of Education*. New York: Sheed, 1936a.

CASTIELLO, JAIMIE, S.J. "The Psychology of Habit in St. Thomas," *The Modern Schoolman*, 1936b, 14:8–12.

CASTIELLO, JAIMIE, S.J. "The Psychology of Intellectual and Moral Habits," *Jesuit educ. Quart.*, 1941, 4:59–70.

CATTELL, RAYMOND B. "The Discovery of Ergic Structures in Man in Terms of Common Attitudes," *J. abnorm. soc. Psychol.*, 1950, 45: 598–618.

CHAPIN, MARY V., & WASHBURN, MARGARET FLOY. "Study of the Images Representing the Concept of Meaning," *Amer. J. Psychol.*, 1912, 23:109–114.

CHARLESWORTH, MAXWELL J. *Philosophy and Linguistic Analysis*. Pittsburgh: Duquesne University Press, 1959.

CHEIN, ISIDOR. *The Image of Man*. New York: Basic Books, Inc., Publishers, 1969.

CHEIN, ISIDOR, & IMMERGLUCK, L. Comment, *Amer. Psychologist*, 1967, 22: 77–79.

COADY, SR. MARY ANASTASIA. *The Phantasm According to the Teaching of St. Thomas*. Washington: The Catholic University of America Press, 1932.

COLE, LAWRENCE E. *Human Behavior: Psychology as a Bio-social Science*. New York: World, 1953.

COLEMAN, JAMES C. *Abnormal Psychology and Modern Life*. Chicago: Scott, Foresman, 1956.

COMBS, ARTHUR W., & SNYGG, DONALD. *Individual Behavior: A Perceptual Approach to Behavior*. (Rev. ed.) New York: Harper, 1959.

COMPTON, ARTHUR H. *The Freedom of Man*. New Haven, Conn.: Yale University Press, 1935.

COMPTON, ARTHUR H. "Science and Man's Freedom," *Atlantic Monthly*, 1957, 200(4):71–74.

COPLESTON, FREDERICK, S.J. *Contemporary Philosophy: Studies of Logical Positivism and Existentialism*. Westminster, Md.: Newman, 1956.

CROWELL, DAVID H., & DOLE, A. A. "Animism and College Students," *J. educ. Res.*, 1957, 50:391–395.

DALTON, ROBERT H. *Personality and Social Interaction.* Boston: Heath, 1961.

D'ARCY, MARTIN C., S.J. *Death and Life.* London: Longmans, 1942.

DARWIN, CHARLES. *Life and Letters.* New York: Appleton, 1898. 2 vols.

DAVIDSON, M. *The Free Will Controversy.* London: Watts, 1942.

DAVIDSON, M. *Free Will or Determinism.* London: Watts, 1937.

DAY, SEBASTIAN J., O.F.M. *Intuitive Cognition: A Key to the Significance of the Later Scholastics.* St. Bonaventure, N.Y.: Franciscan Institute, 1947.

DEFRAINE, JEAN, S.J. *The Bible and the Origin of Man.* New York: Desclee, 1962.

DEKONNINCK, CHARLES. *The Hollow Universe.* Fair Lawn, N.J.: Oxford University Press, 1960.

DEWEY, JOHN. *How We Think.* Boston: 1910.

DEWEY, JOHN. *Human Nature and Conduct.* New York: Holt, 1922.

DEWEY, JOHN. *The Quest for Certainty.* New York: Putnam, 1929.

DIEMERT, F. JEROME, S.J. "Thomistic Psychology and the Social Dimension of Man," *Proc. Jesuit phil. Ass.,* 1959.

DOBZHANSKY, THEODOSIUS. *The Biological Basis of Freedom.* New York: Columbia University Press, 1956.

DOBZHANSKY, THEODOSIUS. *Mankind Evolving.* New Haven, Conn.: Yale University Press, 1962.

DONCEEL, JOSEPH F., S.J. *Philosophical Anthropology.* New York: Sheed, 1967.

DONCEEL, JOSEPH F., S.J. "Theilhard de Chardin and the Body-Soul Relation," *Thought,* 1965, 40:371–389.

DONCEEL, JOSEPH F., S.J. "What Kind of Science Is Psychology?" *The New Scholasticism,* 1945, 19:117–135.

DRESSLER, ALWIN. "Can One Live without a Brain?" *Magazine Dig.,* 1934, 8:18–19. [Condensed from (Berlin) *Illustrierte Beobachter,* Sept. 9, 1933.]

DRIESCH, HANS. *Mind and Body.* London: Methuen, 1927.

DRIESCH, HANS. *The Science and Philosophy of the Organism.* London: Black, 1908. 2 vols.

DUNBAR, H. FLANDERS. *Emotions and Bodily Changes.* New York: Columbia University Press, 1954.

DUNBAR, H. FLANDERS. *Mind and Body: Psychosomatic Medicine.* (2d ed.) New York: Random House, 1955.

DUNLAP, KNIGHT. *Habits, Their Making and Unmaking.* New York: Liveright, 1932.

ECCLES, JOHN C. *The Neurophysiological Basis of Mind.* Fair Lawn, N.J.: Oxford University Press, 1953.

EDDINGTON, SIR ARTHUR. *The Nature of the Physical World.* Cambridge: Cambridge University Press, 1928.

ENGLISH, HORACE B. *Historical Roots of Learning Theory.* New York: Random House, 1954.

ENTRALGO, PEDRO LAIN. *Mind and Body: Psychosomatic Pathology.* New York: Kenedy, 1956.

ERICKSON, RAYMOND L. "Psychiatry and the Law: An Attempt at Synthesis," *Duke Law J.*, 1961, 30–73.

ESTABROOKS, G. H. "Your Brain," *Scientific American*, 1936, 155:20–22.

EWING, J. FRANKLIN, S.J. "Human Evolution—1956," *Anthrop. Quart.*, 1956, 29:91–139.

EYMIEU, ANTONIN, S.J. *Le Gouvernement de soi-même*. Vol. I, *Les Grandes lois*. Vol. II, *L'Obsession et le scrupule*. Vol. III, *L'Art de vouloir*. Vol. IV, *La Loi de la vie*. Paris: Perrin, 1925–1936. 4 vols.

FABRE, JEAN HENRI, C. *Fabre's Book of Insects*, retold from Alexander Teixeira de Mattos' translation of Fabre's *Souvenirs entomologiques* by Mrs. Rudolph Stowell. New York: Tudor, 1937.

FALCONER, R. A. *The Idea of Immortality and Western Civilization*. Cambridge, Mass.: Harvard University Press, 1930.

FARAON, MICHAEL J., O.P. *The Metaphysical and Psychological Principles of Love*. Dubuque, Iowa: Brown, 1952.

FARRER, AUSTIN M. *Finite and Infinite*. Chicago: Allenson, 1943.

FARRER, AUSTIN M. *The Freedom of the Will*. London: Black, 1958.

FEIGL, HERBERT. "Philosophical Embarrassments of Psychology" (invited address to the 1958 convention of the American Psychological Association), *Amer. Psychologist*, 1959, 14:115–128.

FEIGL, HERBERT, and others (Eds.) *Minnesota Studies in the Philosophy of Science*. Vol. I, "The Foundations of Science and the Concepts of Psychology and Psychoanalysis," 1956. Vol. II, "Concepts, Theories and the Mind-Body Problem," 1958. Minneapolis: University of Minnesota Press.

FELL, GEORGE, S.J. *The Immortality of the Human Soul*. St. Louis: Herder, 1908.

DE FINANCE, JOSEPH, S.J. "Being and Subjectivity," trans. by W. Norris Clarke, S.J., *Cross Currents*, 1956, 6:163–178.

FINGARETTE, HERBERT. *The Self in Transformation: Psychoanalysis, Philosophy and the Life of the Spirit*. New York: Basic Books, Inc., Publishers, 1963.

FLETCHER, RONALD. *Instinct in Man: In the Light of Recent Work in Comparative Psychology*. New York: International Universities Press, Inc., 1957.

FLYNN, THOMAS V., O.P. "The Cogitative Power," *The Thomist*, 1953 16:542–563.

FORGUS, RONALD H. *Perception: The Basic Process in Cognitive Development*. New York: McGraw-Hill, 1966.

FOTHERGILL, PHILIP G. "Towards an Interpretation of Evolution: The Teaching of 'Humani Generis,'" *The Tablet* (London), 1955, 205:543–544.

FREUD, SIGMUND. *Introductory Lectures on Psycho-Analysis*. 1916. Complete Works, vol. 15. London: Hogarth, 1963.

FREUD, SIGMUND. *Psychopathology of Everyday Life*. 1901. Complete Works, vol. 6. London: Hogarth, 1960.

FRIEDRICH, L. W., S.J. (Ed.) *The Nature of Physical Knowledge*. Bloomington, Ind.: Indiana University Press, 1962.

FRISCH, JOHN A. "Did the Peckhams Witness the Invention of a Tool by *Ammophila urnaria?*" *The Amer. Midland Naturalist,* September, 1940.

FROMM, ERICH. *The Art of Loving.* New York: Harper & Row, 1956.

FROMM, ERIC. *Man for Himself: An Inquiry into the Psychology of Ethics.* New York: Rinehart, 1947.

GAFFNEY, MARK A., S.J. *Psychology of the Interior Senses.* St. Louis: Herder, 1942.

GALLAGHER, KENNETH T. *The Philosophy of Knowledge.* New York: Sheed, 1965.

GANNON, TIMOTHY J. *Psychology: The Unity of Human Behavior.* Boston: Ginn, 1954.

GARRETT, HENRY E. *General Psychology.* New York: American Book, 1955.

GASSON, JOHN A., S.J., AND ARNOLD, MAGDA B. "The Internal Senses—Functions or Powers?" *The Thomist,* 1963, 26:1–34.

GEACH, PETER. *Mental Acts: Their Content and Their Objects.* New York: Humanities Press, 1957.

GENDLIN, EUGENE T. *Experiencing and the Creation of Meaning.* New York: Free Press, 1962.

GIBSON, JAMES J. *The Perception of the Visual World.* Boston: Houghton Mifflin, 1950.

GIBSON, JAMES J. *The Senses Considered as Perceptual Systems.* Boston: Houghton Mifflin, 1966.

GILBY, THOMAS, O.P. "Thought, Volition and the Organism," *The Thomist,* 1940, 2:1–13.

GILBY, THOMAS, O.P. "Vienne and Vienna," *Thought,* 1946, 21:63–82.

GILL, HENRY V., S.J. *Fact and Fiction in Modern Science.* New York: Fordham University Press, 1944.

GILSON, ETIENNE. *The Christian Philosophy of St. Thomas.* New York: Random House, 1956.

GILSON, ETIENNE. *Réalisme thomiste et critique de la connaissance.* Paris: Vrin, 1939.

GILSON, ETIENNE. *The Spirit of Medieval Philosophy.* New York: Scribner, 1936.

GILSON, ETIENNE. *The Unity of Philosophical Experience.* New York: Scribner, 1937.

GLEASON, ROBERT, S.J. *The World to Come.* New York: Sheed, 1958.

GOLDSTEIN, KURT. *Human Nature in the Light of Psychopathology.* Cambridge, Mass.: Harvard University Press, 1940.

GOLDSTEIN, KURT. *The Organism.* New York: American Book, 1939.

GRAHAM, C. H. "Behavior, Perception, and the Psychophysical Methods," *Psychol. Rev.,* 1950, 57:108–120.

GRAHAM, CLARENCE H. (Ed.) *Vision and Visual Perception.* New York: Wiley, 1965.

GRUENDER, HUBERT, S.J. *Experimental Psychology.* Milwaukee: Bruce, 1932.

GRUENDER, HUBERT, S.J. *Free Will, the Greatest of the Seven World Riddles.* St. Louis: Herder, 1916.

GRUENDER, HUBERT, S.J. *Problems of Psychology.* Milwaukee: Bruce, 1937.

GRUENDER, HUBERT, S.J. *Psychology without a Soul.* (2d ed.) St. Louis: Herder, 1917.

GUILFORD, J. P. "Creativity," *Amer. Psychologist,* 1950, 5:444–454.

GUITTON, JEAN. *Essay on Human Love.* Chicago: Franciscan Herald Press, 1966.

GURR, JOHN E., S.J. *The Principle of Sufficient Reason in Some Scholastic Systems, 1750–1900.* Milwaukee: Marquette University Press, 1959.

GURR, JOHN E., S.J. "Some Historical Origins of Rationalism in Catholic Philosophy Manuals," *Proc. Amer. Catholic Phil. Ass.,* 1956, 30:17–180.

GUSTAFSON, DONALD F. (Ed.) *Essays in Philosophical Psychology.* New York: Doubleday (Anchor), 1964.

HALL, CALVIN S., & LINDZEY, GARDNER. *Theories of Personality.* New York: Wiley, 1957.

HALSTEAD, W. C. *Brain and Intelligence.* Chicago: The University of Chicago Press, 1947.

HALSTEAD, W. C. & RUCKER, W. B. "Memory: A Molecular Maze," *Psychology Today,* (June) 1968, 2:38–41ff.

HAMLYN, D. W. *The Psychology of Perception: A Philosophical Examination of Gestalt Theory and Derivative Theories of Perception.* New York: Humanities Press, 1957.

HAMPSHIRE, STUART. *Freedom of the Individual.* New York: Harper & Row, 1965.

HARMON, FRANCIS L. *Principles of Psychology.* (Rev. ed.) Milwaukee: Bruce, 1951.

HARPER, ROBERT J. C., and others (Eds.) *The Cognitive Processes: Readings.* Englewood Cliffs, N.J.: Prentice-Hall, 1964.

HARRELL, W., & HARRISON, R. "The Rise and Fall of Behaviorism," *J. gen. Psychol.,* 1938, 18:401–402.

HARRIS, E. *The Foundations of Metaphysics in Science.* New York: Humanities Press, 1965.

HART, CHARLES A. *The Thomistic Concept of Mental Faculty.* Washington: The Catholic University of America Press, 1930.

HARTMANN, ERNEST. "The Psychophysiology of Free Will," in R. M. Loewenstein and others (Eds.) *Psychoanalysis—A General Psychology.* New York: International Universities Press, Inc., 1966. Pp. 521–536.

HAURET, CHARLES. *Beginnings: Genesis and Modern Science.* Trans. by E. P. Emmans, O.P. Dubuque, Iowa: The Priory Press, 1955.

HAYES, CATHY H. *Ape in Our House.* New York: Harper, 1951.

HEAD, J., & CRANSTON, S. L. (Eds.) *Reincarnation: An East-West Anthology.* New York: Julian Press, 1961.

HEBB, D. O. *A Textbook of Psychology.* Philadelphia: Saunders, 1958.

HERR, VINCENT V., S.J. "Gestalt Psychology: Empirical or Rational?" in Anton C. Pegis (Ed.) *Essays in Modern Scholasticism.* Westminster, Md.: Newman, 1944. Pp. 222–243.

HERRICK, C. JUDSON. *Fatalism or Freedom: A Biologist's Answer.* New York: Norton, 1926.

HESSE, MARY. *Models and Analogies in Science.* Notre Dame, Ind.: The University of Notre Dame Press, 1966.

HICKS, LESLIE H. "An Analysis of Number-concept Formation in the Rhesus Monkey," *J. comp. physiol. Psychol.*, 1956, 49:212–218.

HILGARD, ERNEST R. *Introduction to Psychology.* New York: Harcourt, Brace, 1953; 4th ed., 1967.

HILGARD, ERNEST R. *Theories of Learning.* (Rev. ed.) New York: Appleton-Century-Crofts, 1956.

HOBAN, JAMES H. *The Thomistic Concept of Person and Some of Its Social Implications.* Washington: The Catholic University of America Press, 1939.

HOBBS, NICHOLAS. "Science and Ethical Behavior," *Amer. Psychologist*, 1959, 5:217–225.

HOCKETT, C. F. "The Origin of Speech," *Scientific American* (Sept.) 1960, 203, n.3:88–96.

HOCKING, WILLIAM E. *The Meaning of Immortality in Human Experience.* New York: Harper, 1957.

HOCKING, WILLIAM E. *Types of Philosophy.* New York: Scribner, 1929.

HOENEN, PETER, S.J. *The Philosophical Nature of Physical Bodies.* West Baden Springs, Ind.: West Baden College, 1955.

HOENEN, PETER, S.J. *Reality and Judgment According to St. Thomas.* Trans. by H. F. Tiblier, S.J. Chicago: Regnery, 1952.

HOLT, ROBERT R., and others. "Ego Autonomy Reevaluated," *Int. J. Psychiat.*, 1967, 3:481–536.

HOOK, SIDNEY. (Ed.) *Determinism and Freedom in the Age of Modern Science.* New York: New York University Press, 1958.

HOOK, SIDNEY (Ed.) *Dimensions of Mind.* New York: Collier, 1961.

HOOK, SIDNEY (Ed.) *Psychoanalysis, Scientific Method and Philosophy.* New York: New York University Press, 1959.

HUDECZEK, METH. M., O.P. "De tempore animationis foetus humani secundum embryologiam hodiernam," *Angelicum*, 1952, 29:162–181.

HUNT, J. McVICKER. "Psychological Services in the Tactics of Psychological Science" (presidential address to American Psychological Association convention, Sept. 1, 1952), *Amer. Psychologist*, 1952, 7:608–622.

HYMAN, RAY. *The Nature of Psychological Inquiry.* Englewood Cliffs, N.J.: Prentice-Hall, 1964.

ITTLESON, W. H., & CANTRIL, H. *Perception: A Transactional Approach.* New York: Doubleday, 1954.

JAMES, WILLIAM. *The Principles of Psychology.* New York: Holt, 1896. 2 vols.

JASPERS, KARL. *Man in the Modern Age.* New York: Doubleday (Anchor), 1957.

JASPERS, KARL. *Way to Wisdom.* New Haven, Conn.: Yale University Press, 1951.

JOAD, C. E. M. *A Critique of Logical Positivism.* Chicago: University of Chicago Press, 1950.

JOAD, C. E. M. *Guide to Philosophy*. New York: Dover, 1936.

JOAD, C. E. M. *How Our Minds Work*. London: Westhouse, 1946.

JOHANN, ROBERT O. "A Matter of Character," *America*, 1967, 116:95.

JOHANN, ROBERT O. *The Meaning of Love*. Westminster, Md.: Newman, 1959.

JOHANN, ROBERT O. "Subjectivity," *Rev. Metaphysics*, 1958, 12:200–234.

JOHANN, ROBERT O. "Toward a Philosophy of Subjectivity," *Proc. Jesuit phil. Ass.*, 1958, pp. 35–75.

JUNG, CARL G. *Modern Man in Search of a Soul*. New York: Harcourt, Brace, 1933.

KAPP, ERNEST. *The Greek Foundations of Traditional Logic*. New York: Columbia University Press, 1942.

KATZ, DAVID. *Animals and Men*. New York: Longmans, 1937.

KATZ, DAVID. *Gestalt Psychology*. New York: Ronald, 1950.

KELLER, HELEN. *The Story of My Life*. New York: Grosset, 1904.

KELLOGG, W. N., & KELLOGG, LUELLA. *The Ape and the Child*. New York: McGraw-Hill, 1933.

KELLY, WILLIAM L., & TALLON, ANDREW (Eds.) *Readings in the Philosophy of Man*. New York: McGraw-Hill, 1967.

KENNEDY, F., HOFFMAN, H. R., & HAINES, WILLIAM H. "A Study of William Heirens," *Amer. J. Psychiat.*, 1947, 104:113–121.

KENNY, A. *Action, Emotion and Free Will*. New York: Humanities Press, 1965.

KIERKEGAARD, SØREN. *Either/Or, A Fragment of Life*. Princeton, N.J.: Princeton University Press, 1944. 2 vols.

KIERKEGAARD, SØREN. *Fear and Trembling, A Dialectical Lyric*. Princeton, N.J.: Princeton University Press, 1941.

KIERKEGAARD, SØREN. *The Sickness unto Death*. Princeton, N.J.: Princeton University Press, 1941.

KLAUSMEIER, H. J., & HARRIS, C. W. (Eds.) *Analyses of Concept Learning*. New York: Academic, 1966.

KLAUSNER, SAMUEL Z. (Ed.) *The Quest for Self Control: Classical Philosophies and Scientific Research*. New York: Free Press, 1965.

KLEIN, D. B. *Abnormal Psychology*. New York: Holt, 1951.

KLUBERTANZ, GEORGE P., S.J. *The Discursive Power*. St. Louis: The Modern Schoolman, 1952.

KLUBERTANZ, GEORGE P., S.J. *The Philosophy of Human Nature*. New York: Appleton-Century-Crofts, 1953.

KLUBERTANZ, GEORGE P., S.J. "St. Thomas and the Knowledge of the Singular," *The New Scholasticism*, 1952, 26:135–166.

KLUBERTANZ, GEORGE P., S.J. "The Unity of Human Operation," *The Modern Schoolman*, 1950, 27:75–103.

KÖHLER, WOLFGANG. *Gestalt Psychology*. New York: Liveright, 1947.

KÖHLER, WOLFGANG. *The Mentality of Apes*. New York: Harcourt, Brace, 1925.

KOLERS, PAUL A. "Bilingualism and Information Processing," *Scientific American* (March) 1968, 218, n.3:78–86.

KOREN, HENRY J., C.S.Sp. *An Introduction to the Philosophy of Animate Nature*. St. Louis: Herder, 1955.

KOREN, HENRY J. *Research in Philosophy*. Pittsburgh, Pa.: Duquesne University Press, 1967.

KRECH, DAVID, & CRUTCHFIELD, RICHARD S. *Elements of Psychology*. New York: Knopf, 1958.

KRUTCH, JOSEPH W. *The Measure of Man*. Indianapolis, Ind.: Bobbs-Merrill, 1953.

KUENZLI, ALFRED E. (Ed.) *The Phenomenological Problem*. New York: Harper, 1959.

KUHN, T. S. *The Structure of Scientific Revolutions*. Chicago: The University of Chicago Press, 1962.

KWANT, REMY C. *The Phenomenological Philosophy of Merleau-Ponty*. Pittsburgh, Pa.: Duquesne University Press, 1963.

KWANT, REMY C. *The Phenomenology of Language*. Pittsburgh, Pa.: Duquesne University Press, 1965.

LACROIX, ROBERT. *L'Origine de l'âme humaine*. Ottawa: Les Éditions de l'université, 1945.

LAMONT, CORLISS. *The Illusion of Immortality*. (3d ed.) New York: Philosophical Library, 1959.

LANDAUER, THOMAS K. "Two Hypotheses Concerning the Biochemical Basis of Memory," *Psychol. Rev.*, 1964, 71:167–179.

LASHLEY, KARL S. "Basic Neural Mechanisms in Behavior" (presidential address), *Psychol. Rev.*, 1930, 37:1–24.

LASHLEY, KARL S. *Brain Mechanisms and Intelligence*. Chicago: The University of Chicago Press, 1929.

LASHLEY, KARL S. "Cerebral Control versus Reflexology," *J. gen. Psychol.*, 1931, 5:3–20.

LAUER, J. QUENTIN. *Phenomenology: Its Genesis and Prospect*. New York: Harper (Torchbooks), 1965.

LEE, OTIS. *Existence and Inquiry*. Chicago: The University of Chicago Press, 1949.

LEPP, IGNACE. *The Psychology of Loving*. Baltimore, Md.: Helicon, 1963.

LEWIS, C. S. *The Abolition of Man*. New York: Macmillan, 1947.

LEWIS, C. S. *Four Loves*. New York: Harcourt, Brace, 1960.

LILLIE, RALPH S. *General Biology and the Philosophy of Organism*. Chicago: The University of Chicago Press, 1945.

LINDWORSKY, JOHANNES, S.J. *Experimental Psychology*. New York: Macmillan, 1931.

LINDWORSKY, JOHANNES, S.J. *The Psychology of Asceticism*. London: Edwards, 1936.

LINDWORSKY, JOHANNES, S.J. *The Training of the Will*. Milwaukee: Bruce, 1929.

LONERGAN, BERNARD, S.J. *Collection*. St. Louis: Herder, 1967.

LONERGAN, BERNARD, S.J. *Insight: A Study of Human Understanding*. New York: Philosophical Library, 1956.

LONERGAN, BERNARD, S.J. "St. Thomas' Thought on Gratia Operans," *Theol. Stud.*, 1941, 2:289–324; 1942, 3:69–88, 375–402, 533–578.

LORENZ, K. Z. *King Solomon's Ring.* New York: Crowell, 1952.

LOTTIN, DOM ODON. *La Théorie du libre arbitre depuis S. Anselme jusqu' à S. Thomas d'Aquin.* Louvain: Mont-Cesar, 1929 (extrait de la *Rev. Thomiste*, 1927–1929).

LUIJPEN, WILLIAM A. *Existential Phenomenology.* Pittsburgh, Pa.: Duquesne University Press, 1960.

LUIJPEN, WILLIAM A. *Phenomenology and Humanism.* Pittsburgh, Pa.: Duquesne University Press, 1967.

LUIJPEN, WILLIAM A. *Phenomenology and Metaphysics.* Pittsburgh, Pa.: Duquesne University Press, 1965.

McCALL, RAYMOND J. *Preface to Scientific Psychology.* Milwaukee: Bruce, 1959.

McCARTHY, RAPHAEL C., S.J. *The Measurement of Conation.* Chicago: Loyola University Press, 1926.

McCARY, J. L. (Ed.) *Psychology of Personality: Six Modern Approaches.* New York: Logos Press, 1956.

McCLELLAND, DAVID C. "Conscience and the Will Rediscovered," review of Karl Mierke's *Wille und Leistung* (Göttingen: Verlag für Psychologie, 1955), *Contemp. Psychol.*, 1957, 2:177–179.

McCORMICK, JOHN F., S.J. "The Burden of the Body," *The New Scholasticism*, 1938, 12:392–400.

McCORMICK, JOHN F., S.J. "The Burden of Intellect," *The Modern Schoolman*, 1935, 12:79–81.

McCOY, ALAN EDWARD, O.F.M. *Force and Fear in Relation to Delictual Imputability and Penal Responsibility.* Washington: The Catholic University of America Press, 1944.

McDOUGALL, WILLIAM. *Body and Mind: A History and Defense of Animism.* London: Methuen, 1915.

McGUIGAN, F. J. (Ed.) *Thinking: Studies of Covert Language Processes.* New York: Appleton-Century-Crofts, 1966.

McKIAN, J. D. "The Metaphysics of Introspection According to St. Thomas Aquinas," *The New Scholasticism*, 1941, 15:89–117.

McKINNEY, FRED. "Teaching Values and Psychology" (APA Div. 2, presidential address), *Amer. Psychologist*, 1960, 15:339–342.

McMULLIN, ERNAN (Ed.) *The Concept of Matter.* Notre Dame, Ind.: University of Notre Dame Press, 1963.

McMULLIN, ERNAN. "Realism in Modern Cosmology," *Proc. Amer. Catholic phil. Ass.*, 1955, 29:137–150.

McMULLIN, ERNAN. "Recent Philosophy of Science," *The New Scholasticism*, 1966, 40:478–518.

MacPARTLAND, JOHN. *The March toward Matter.* New York: Philosophical Library, 1952.

MADDEN, E. H. *Philosophical Problems in Psychology.* New York: Odyssey, 1962.

MAHER, MICHAEL, S.J. *Psychology: Empirical and Rational.* (9th ed.) London: Longmans, 1921.

MARC, ANDRÉ, S.J. *Psychologie réflexive.* Brussels: L'Édition universelle, 1949. 2 vols.

MARCEL, GABRIEL. *Homo viator.* Chicago: Regnery, 1951.

MARCEL, GABRIEL. *Man against Mass Society.* Chicago: Regnery, 1952.

MARCEL, GABRIEL. *The Mystery of Being.* Chicago: Regnery, 1951. 2 vols.

MARITAIN, JACQUES. *Art and Scholasticism.* New York: Scribner, 1930.

MARITAIN, JACQUES. *Distinguish to Unite: The Degrees of Knowledge.* New York: Scribner, 1959.

MARITAIN, JACQUES. *Freedom in the Modern World.* New York: Scribner, 1936.

MARITAIN, JACQUES. *The Range of Reason.* New York: Scribner, 1952.

MARITAIN, JACQUES. *True Humanism.* New York: Scribner, 1938.

MARTIN, OLIVER. "An Examination of Contemporary Naturalism and Materialism," in John Wild (Ed.) *The Return to Reason.* Chicago: Regnery, 1953. Pp. 68–91.

MARTIN, OLIVER. *The Order and Integration of Knowledge.* Ann Arbor: The University of Michigan Press, 1956.

MASLOW, ABRAHAM H. "Deficiency Motivation and Growth Motivation," *Nebraska Symposium on Motivation.* Lincoln, Nebr.: University of Nebraska Press, 1955. Pp. 1–30.

MASLOW, ABRAHAM H. *Motivation and Personality.* New York: Harper, 1954.

MASLOW, ABRAHAM H. *The Psychology of Science: A Reconnaissance.* New York: Harper & Row, 1966.

MAURER, ARMAND, C.S.B. "Introduction," in *St. Thomas Aquinas: The Division and Methods of the Sciences.* (2d rev. ed.) Toronto: Pontifical Institute, 1958.

MAY, ROLLO, and others (Eds.) *Existence: A New Dimension in Psychiatry and Psychology.* New York: Basic Books, Inc., Publishers, 1958.

MAYER, MAJOR WILLIAM E. "Why Did Many G.I. Captives Cave In?" *U.S. News and World Report,* Feb. 24, 1956, pp. 56–72.

MAYER, MARY HELEN. *The Philosophy of Teaching of St. Thomas Aquinas.* Milwaukee: Bruce, 1929.

MEISSNER, WILLIAM W., S.J. "The Epistemological Implications of Scientific Psychology," *The Modern Schoolman,* 1966, 43:111–132.

MEISSNER, WILLIAM W., S.J. "Neurological Aspects of the Sense Powers of Man," *The Thomist,* 1963,26: 35–66.

MELDEN, A. I. *Free Action.* New York: Humanities Press, 1961.

MELDEN, A. I. *Rights and Right Conduct.* New York: Humanities Press, 1959.

MERCIER, J. CARDINAL. *The Origins of Contemporary Psychology.* (2d ed.) London: R. & T. Washbourne, 1918.

MERLEAU-PONTY, M. *Phenomenology of Perception.* New York: Humanities Press, 1962.

MERLEAU-PONTY, M. *The Structure of Behavior.* Boston: Beacon Press, 1963.

MESSENGER, E. C. *Evolution and Theology*. New York: Macmillan, 1932.

MESSENGER, E. C. (Ed.) *Theology and Evolution*. London: Sands, 1949.

MICHOTTE, ALBERT. *The Perception of Causality*. New York: Basic Books, Inc., Publishers, 1963.

MILGRAM, S. "Issues in the Study of Obedience," *Amer. Psychologist*, 1964, 19:848–852.

MILLER, GEORGE A. "Some Preliminaries to Psycholinguistics," *Amer. Psychologist*, 1965, 20:15–20.

MISIAK, HENRYK. *The Philosophical Roots of Scientific Psychology*. New York: Fordham University Press, 1961.

MOBERLY, SIR WALTER. *Responsibility: The Concept in Psychology, in the Law, and in the Christian Faith*. Greenwich, Conn.: Seabury Press, 1956.

MONTAGU, ASHLEY. *Immortality*. New York: Grove Press, Inc., 1955.

MOORE, THOMAS VERNER. *Cognitive Psychology*. Philadelphia: Lippincott, 1939.

MOORE, THOMAS VERNER. "Consciousness and the Nervous System," *Catholic Univer. Stud. in Psychol. and Psychiat.*, 1938, Vol. IV, No. 3.

MOORE, THOMAS VERNER. *The Driving Forces of Human Nature and Their Adjustment*. New York: Grune & Stratton, 1948.

MOORE, THOMAS VERNER. "Human and Animal Intelligence," in H. S. Jennings and others, *Scientific Aspects of the Race Problem*. New York: Longmans, 1941. Pp. 95–158.

MOORE, THOMAS VERNER. "Image and Meaning in Memory and Perception," *Psychol. Monogr.*, 1919, 27(119):67–296.

MOORE, THOMAS VERNER. "The Process of Abstraction," *Univ. Calif. Publ. Psychol.*, 1910, I:73–197.

MOORE, THOMAS VERNER. "A Scholastic Theory of Perception," *The New Scholasticism*, 1933, VII:222–238.

MOORE, THOMAS VERNER. "The Temporal Relations of Meaning and Imagery," *Psychol. Rev.*, 1915, 22:177–225.

MORGAN, CLIFFORD T. *Introduction to Psychology*. New York: McGraw-Hill, 1956.

MORRISON, JOHN L. "American Catholics and the Crusade against Evolution," *Rec. Amer. Catholic Historical Soc. Philadelphia*, 1953, 44:59–71.

MOUNIER, EMMANUEL. *The Character of Man*. Trans. by Cynthia Rowland. New York: Harper, 1956.

MOUROUX, J. *The Meaning of Man*. Trans. by A. H. C. Downes. New York: Sheed, 1948.

MOWRER, O. H. "On the Dual Nature of Learning: A Reinterpretation of 'Conditioning' and 'Problem-solving'," *Harvard educ. Rev.*, 1947, 17:102–148.

MOWRER, O. H. "The Psychologist Looks at Language" (presidential address), *Amer. Psychologist*, 1954, 9:660–694.

MÜLLER-FREIENFELS, RICHARD. *The Evolution of Modern Psychology*. Trans. by W. B. Wolfe. New Haven, Conn.: Yale University Press, 1935.

MURPHY, GARDNER. *An Historical Introduction to Modern Psychology*. (Rev. ed.) New York: Harcourt, Brace, 1949.

Murphy, Gardner. *Human Potentialities*. New York: Basic Books, Inc., Publishers, 1958.

Nogar, Raymond J. *The Wisdom of Evolution*. New York: Doubleday, 1963.

North, Robert, S.J. *Teilhard and the Creation of the Soul*. Milwaukee: Bruce, 1966.

du Noüy, Lecomte. *Human Destiny*. New York: Longmans, 1947.

Nuttin, Joseph. *Psychoanalysis and Personality: A Dynamic Theory of Normal Personality*. New York: Sheed, 1953.

Nuttin, Joseph. *Psychology, Morality and Education*. Springfield, Ill.: Templegate, 1959.

O'Connor, William R. *The Eternal Quest*. New York: Longmans, 1947.

O'Connor, William R. "Molina and Bañez as Interpreters of St. Thomas Aquinas," *The New Scholasticism*, 1947, 21:243–259.

O'Connor, William R. *The Natural Desire for God*. Milwaukee: Marquette University Press, 1948.

Odier, Charles. "Les Deux sources, consciente et inconsciente, de la vie morale," *Cahiers de philosophie*, November, 1943–February, 1947, pp. 4–5 (Neuchatel: Editions de la Baconniere).

Oligiati, Francesco. *The Key to the Study of St. Thomas*. Trans. by J.S. Zybura. St. Louis: Herder, 1925.

O'Neill, Reginald F., S.J. *Theories of Knowledge*. Englewood Cliffs, N.J.: Prentice-Hall, 1960.

Orne, Martin T. "On the Social Psychology of The Psychological Experiment," *Amer. Psychologist*, 1962, 17:776–783.

Osgood, Charles E., and others. *The Measurement of Meaning*. Urbana, Ill.: University of Illinois Press, 1957.

Pap, Arthur. *An Introduction to the Philosophy of Science*. London: Eyre & Spottiswood, 1963.

Peghaire, Julien. "A Forgotten Sense, the Cogitative, According to St. Thomas Aquinas," *The Modern Schoolman*, 1943, 20:123–140, 210–229.

Pegis, Anton C. *The Problem of the Soul in the Thirteenth Century*. Toronto: Institute of Medieval Studies, 1934.

Pegis, Anton C. "St. Thomas and the Unity of Man," in J. A. McWilliams, S.J. (Ed.) *Progress in Philosophy*. Milwaukee: Bruce, 1955. Pp. 153–173.

Peirce, Chas. S. "How to Make Our Ideas Clear" (*Pop. Sci. Monthly*, 1878, 12), *Collected Papers of Charles Sanders Peirce*. Cambridge, Mass.: Harvard University Press, 1931–1938.

Penfield, Wilder. "The Permanent Record of the Stream of Consciousness," *Proc. 14th Int. Congr. Psychol.*, Montreal, 1954.

Piaget, Jean. *Logic and Psychology*. New York: Basic Books, Inc., Publishers, 1957.

Piaget, Jean. *The Moral Judgment of the Child*. New York: Free Press, 1948.

Piaget, Jean. *The Origins of Intelligence in Children*. New York: International Universities Press, 1952.

Piaget, Jean. *The Psychology of Intelligence*. New York: Harcourt, Brace, 1950.

PLANCK, MAX. *The New Science.* New York: Meridian Books, Inc., 1959.

PLATO. *Phaedo; the Apology of Socrates; Alcibiades I.* New York: Random House, 1941.

POLANYI, MICHAEL. *Personal Knowledge.* Chicago: University of Chicago Press, 1958.

POLANYI, MICHAEL. *The Study of Man.* Chicago: University of Chicago Press, 1959.

POPPER, KARL R. *Conjectures and Refutations: The Growth of Scientific Knowledge.* New York: Basic Books, Inc., Publishers, 1963.

POPPER, KARL R. *The Logic of Scientific Discovery.* New York: Basic Books, Inc., Publishers, 1959.

PRICE, H. H. "Some Objections to Behaviorism," in S. Hook (Ed.) *Dimensions of Mind.* New York: Collier, 1960. Pp. 79–84.

PROTHRO, TERRY E., & TESKA, P. T. *Psychology: A Biosocial Study of Behavior.* Boston: Ginn, 1950.

RAHNER, KARL, S.J. *Theological Investigations.* Baltimore, Md.: Helicon, 1964–1967. 5 vols.

REGIS, L. M., O.P. *Epistemology.* Trans. by I. C. Byrne. New York: Macmillan, 1959

REGIS, L. M., O.P. *St. Thomas and Epistemology.* Milwaukee: Marquette University Press, 1946.

REINHARDT, KURT F. *A Realistic Philosophy.* Milwaukee: Bruce, 1944.

RICHARDSON, WILLIAM J., S.J. *Heidegger: Through Phenomenology to Thought.* (Preface by Heidegger.) The Hague: Martinus Nijhoff, 1963.

RICKABY, JOSEPH, S.J. *Free Will and Four English Philosophers.* London: Burns, 1905.

RICOEUR, PAUL. *Fallible Man.* Chicago: Regnery, 1965.

RICOEUR, PAUL. *Freedom and Nature.* Evanston, Ill.: Northwestern University Press, 1966.

RICOEUR, PAUL. *History and Truth.* Evanston, Ill.: Northwestern University Press, 1965.

RIMAUD, JEAN. "Les Psychologues contre la morale," *Études,* 1949, 263: 3–22.

ROE, ANNE, & SIMPSON, GEORGE (Eds.) *Behavior and Evolution.* New Haven, Conn.: Yale University Press, 1958.

ROGERS, CARL. "Toward a Science of the Person," in T. W. Wann (Ed.) *Behaviorism and Phenomenology.* Chicago: University of Chicago Press, 1964.

ROHDE, ERWIN. *Psyche: The Cult of Souls and Belief in Immortality among the Greeks.* Trans. by W. B. Willis. New York: Harcourt, Brace, 1925.

ROMANES, GEORGE JOHN. *Mental Evolution in Animals* (with a posthumous essay "Instinct" by Charles Darwin). London: Kegan Paul, Trench, Tubner & Co., 1883.

ROMERO, FRANCISCO. *Theory of Man.* Trans. by Wm. F. Cooper. Berkeley, Calif.: University of California Press, 1964.

ROUSSELOT, PIERRE, S.J. *The Intellectualism of St. Thomas.* Trans. by James E. O'Mahony, O.M.Cap. London: Sheed, 1935.

ROYCE, JAMES E., S.J. "The Ghost of Free Will" (Div. 24, presidential address, American Psychological Association), *APA Div. 24 Newsletter*, 1964, 2:3–5.

ROYCE, JAMES E., S.J. "How Puritanism Persists," *Insight*, 1963, 1:3, 3–6.

ROYCE, JAMES E., S.J. "Life and Living Beings," *The Modern Schoolman*, 1960, 37:213–232.

ROYCE, JAMES E., S.J. *Man and His Nature*. New York: McGraw-Hill, 1961.

ROYCE, JAMES E., S.J. *Personality and Mental Health*. (Rev. ed.) Milwaukee: Bruce, 1964.

ROYCE, JAMES E., S.J. "St. Thomas and the Definition of Active Potency," *The New Scholasticism*, 1960, 34(4):431–437.

ROYCE, JOSEPH R. *The Encapsulated Man*. Princeton, N.J.: Van Nostrand, 1964.

ROYCE, JOSEPH R. (Ed.) *Psychology and the Symbol*. New York: Random House, 1965.

ROZWADOWSKI, A., S.J. "De distinctione potentiarum a substantia," *Gregorianum*, 1935, 16:272–281.

RUFFINI, ERNESTO, CARDINAL. *The Theory of Evolution Judged by Reason and Faith*. Trans. by Rev. Francis O'Hanlon. New York: J. F. Wagner, 1959.

RUGG, HAROLD. *Imagination*. New York: Harper & Row, 1963.

RYLE, GILBERT. *The Concept of Mind*. New York: Barnes & Noble, 1949.

RYLE, GILBERT. *The Revolution in Philosophy*. London: Macmillan, 1960.

SANFORD, F. H. *Psychology: A Scientific Study of Man*. Belmont, Calif.: Wadsworth, 1961.

SARTRE, JEAN-PAUL. *Being and Nothingness*. Paris: Gallimard, 1943.

SARTRE, JEAN-PAUL. *The Emotions: Outline of a Theory*. New York: Philosophical Library, 1948.

SARTRE, JEAN-PAUL. *Existential Psychoanalysis*. Trans. by Hazel E. Barnes. New York: Philosophical Library, 1954.

SARTRE, JEAN-PAUL. *Nausea*. New York: New Directions, 1949.

SAYRE, K. *Recognition: A Study in the Philosophy of Artificial Intelligence*. Notre Dame, Ind.: University of Notre Dame Press, 1965.

SCHEIN, EDGAR H. "The Id as Salesman," review of Vance Packard's *The Hidden Persuaders* (New York: McKay, 1957), *Contemp. Psychol.*, 1957, 2:308–309.

SCHILLER, CLAIRE H. (Ed.) *Instinctive Behavior: The Development of a Modern Concept*. New York: International Universities Press, 1957.

SCHNEIDERS, ALEXANDER A., "Psychology as a Normative Science," in Magda B. Arnold & John A. Gasson, S.J., and others, *The Human Person: An Approach to an Integral Theory of Personality*. New York: Ronald, 1954. Pp. 373–394.

SCHRODINGER, ERWIN. *What Is Life?* New York: Macmillan, 1945.

SCHUBERT-SOLDERN, R. *Mechanism and Vitalism*. Notre Dame, Ind.: University of Notre Dame Press, 1962.

SCRIVEN, MICHAEL. "The Compleat Robot: A Prolegomena to Androidology," in Sidney Hook (Ed.) *Dimensions of Mind*. New York: Collier, 1961. Pp. 113–133.

SCRIVEN, MICHAEL. "An Essential Unpredictability in Human Behavior," in B. Wolman & E. Nagel (Eds.) *Scientific Psychology.* New York: Basic Books, Inc., Publishers, 1965. Pp. 411–425.

SCRIVEN, MICHAEL. *Primary Philosophy.* New York: McGraw-Hill, 1966.

SERTILLANGES, A. D. *Foundations of Thomistic Philosophy.* Springfield, Ill.: Templegate, 1956.

SERTILLANGES, A. D. *The Intellectual Life.* Westminster, Md.: Newman, 1948.

SEVERIN, FRANK, T. "The Humanistic Psychology of Teilhard de Chardin," in J. F. T. Bugental (Ed.) *Challenges of Humanistic Psychology.* New York: McGraw-Hill, 1967. Pp. 151–158.

SEVERIN, FRANK T. (Ed.) *Humanistic Viewpoints in Psychology.* New York: McGraw-Hill, 1965.

SEVERIN, FRANK T. "Teilhard's Methodology for the Study of Cosmic Psychology," *Catholic psychol. Record,* 1967, 5:1–7.

SHERRINGTON, CHARLES S. *Man on His Nature.* (2d ed.) New York: Cambridge, 1940. Garden City, N.Y.: Doubleday (Anchor), 1953.

SIMON, YVES. *Traité du libre arbitre.* Liège: Sciences et Lettres, 1951.

SIMON, YVES, & PEGHAIRE, JULIEN. "The Philosophical Study of Sensation," *The Modern Schoolman,* 1945, 23:111–119.

SINNOTT, E. W. *Cell and Psyche: The Biology of Purpose.* Chapel Hill: University of North Carolina Press, 1950.

SIWEK, PAUL, S.J. *The Enigma of the Hereafter: The Reincarnation of Souls.* New York: Philosophical Library, 1952.

SIWEK, PAUL, S.J. *Experimental Psychology.* New York: J. F. Wagner, 1959.

SIWEK, PAUL, S.J. *Psychologia metaphysica.* (5th ed.) Rome: Gregorian University, 1956.

SIWEK, PAUL, S.J. *La Psychophysique humaine d'après Aristote.* Paris: Alcan, 1930.

SKINNER, B. F. *Cumulative Record.* New York: Appleton-Century-Crofts, 1961.

SKINNER, B. F. *Science and Human Behavior.* New York: Macmillan, 1953.

SKINNER, B. F. *Verbal Behavior.* New York: Appleton-Century-Crofts, 1957.

SKINNER, B. F. *Walden Two.* New York: Macmillan, 1948.

SLAVIN, ROBERT J. *The Philosophical Basis of Individual Differences.* Washington: The Catholic University of America Press, 1936.

SMITH, GERARD B., S.J. "A Date in the History of Epistemology," *The Thomist* (Maritain volume), 1943, 5:246–255.

SMITH, M. BREWSTER. Editorial. *J. abnormal soc. Psychol.,* 1961, 63:461–465.

SNIDER, LOUIS B., S.J. "A Research Method of Validating Self-determination," in Magda B. Arnold & John A. Gasson, S.J., and others, *The Human Person: An Approach to an Integral Theory of Personality.* New York: Ronald, 1954. Pp. 222–263.

SOLOMON, HARRY C., COBB, STANLEY, & PENFIELD, WILDER (Eds.) *The Brain and Human Behavior.* Baltimore: Williams & Wilkins, 1958.

SOROKIN, P. *Social and Cultural Dynamics.* New York: American Book, 1937–1941. 4 vols.

SPEARMAN, CHARLES. *The Abilities of Man.* New York: St. Martin's, 1927a.

SPEARMAN, CHARLES. *The Nature of "Intelligence" and the Principles of Cognition.* (2d ed.) New York: St. Martin's, 1927b.

SPEARMAN, CHARLES. *Psychology down the Ages.* New York: St. Martin's, 1937.

SPEARMAN, CHARLES, & JONES, L. W. *Human Ability.* New York: St. Martin's, 1950.

STAFFORD, JOHN W., C.S.V. "Freedom in Experimental Psychology," *Proc. Amer. Catholic phil. Ass.,* 1940, 16:148–153.

STOCK, MICHAEL, O.P. "Conscience and Superego," *The Thomist,* 1961, 24:544–579.

STONE, L. JOSEPH, & CHURCH, JOSEPH. *Childhood and Adolescence: A Psychology of the Growing Person.* New York: Random House, 1957.

STOTLAND, EZRA. "Mentalism Revisited," *J. gen. Psychol.,* 1966, 75:229–241.

STRASSER, STEPHAN. *Phenomenology and the Human Sciences.* Pittsburgh, Pa.: Duquesne University Press, 1963.

STRASSER, STEPHAN. *The Soul in Metaphysical and Empirical Psychology.* Pittsburgh, Pa.: Duquesne University Press, 1962.

STRATTON, G. M. "Vision without Inversion of the Retinal Image," *Psychol. Rev.,* 1897, 4:341–360, 463–481.

STRAUS, ERWIN W. *Phenomenological Psychology.* New York: Basic Books, Inc., Publishers, 1966.

STRAWSON, PETER F. *Individuals: An Essay in Descriptive Metaphysics.* New York: Doubleday, 1963.

SULLIVAN, ROBERT P., O.P. "Man's Thirst for Good," *Thomistic Stud.* No. 4. Westminster, Md.: Newman, 1952.

SULLIVAN, ROBERT P., O.P. *The Thomistic Concept of the Natural Necessitation of the Human Will.* River Forest, Ill.: Pontifical Faculty of Philosophy, 1952.

SYMONDS, PERCIVAL M. *Dynamics of Psychotherapy.* New York: Grune & Stratton, 1956.

SYMONDS, PERCIVAL M. *The Ego and the Self.* New York: Appleton-Century-Crofts, 1951.

TANQUEREY, A. *The Spiritual Life.* (2d ed.) Trans. by H. Branders. Tournai, Belgium: Desclee, 1930.

TAYLOR, A. E. *The Christian Hope of Immortality.* New York: Macmillan, 1947.

TAYLOR, A. E. *The Faith of a Moralist.* Series I. New York: St. Martin's, 1951.

TEALE, E. W. *The Insect World of J. Henri Fabre.* New York: Dodd, Mead, 1949.

TEILHARD DE CHARDIN, PIERRE, S.J. *The Future of Man.* New York: Harper & Row, 1964.

TEILHARD DE CHARDIN, PIERRE, S.J. *The Phenomenon of Man.* New York: Harper, 1959.

TERRUWE, A. A. A. *Psychopathic Personality and Neurosis*. Trans. by Conrad W. Baars, M.D. Ed. by Jordan Aumann, O.P. New York: Kenedy, 1958.

THURSTONE, LOUIS L. *Vectors of Mind*. Chicago: University of Chicago Press, 1935.

THURSTONE, LOUIS L., and others. *The Measurement of Values*. Chicago: University of Chicago Press, 1959.

TINBERGEN, N. *The Study of Instinct*. Fair Lawn, N.J.: Oxford University Press, 1951.

TITCHENER, EDWARD B. "Decription versus Statement of Meaning," *Amer. J. Psychol.*, 1912, 23:164–182.

TITCHENER, EDWARD B. *Experimental Psychology*. Part I, *Qualitative Experiments*. Part II, *Teacher's Manual*. New York: Macmillan, 1918.

TITCHENER, EDWARD B. *Lectures on the Experimental Psychology of the Thought Processes*. New York: Macmillan, 1927.

TITCHENER, EDWARD B. *Systematic Psychology: Prolegomena*. New York: Macmillan, 1929.

TITCHENER, EDWARD B. *A Text-book of Psychology*. New York: Macmillan, 1912.

TOMKINS, SILVAN S. *Affect, Imagery, Consciousness*. London: Tavistock, 1964.

DE TONQUÉDEC, JOSEPH. *La Critique de la connaissance*. Paris: Beauchesne, 1929.

TOURNIER, PAUL. *The Meaning of Persons*. New York: Harper, 1957.

TRAVIS, L. E. "Brain Potentials and the Temporal Course of Consciousness," *J. exp. Psychol.*, 1937, 21:302–309.

TYLER, LEONA B. "Toward a Workable Psychology of Individuality," *Amer. Psychologist*, 1959, 14:75–81.

VAN MELSEN, ANDREW. *Evolution and Philosophy*. Pittsburgh, Pa.: Duquesne University Press, 1965.

VERCORS (pseudonym for J. Bruller). *The Murder of the Missing Link*. New York: Pocket Books, 1958. (Also as *You Shall Know Them*. New York: Little, Brown, 1953.)

VOLLERT, CYRIL, S.J. "Evolution and the Bible," in B. Boelen (Ed.) *Symposium on Evolution*. Pittsburgh, Pa.: Duquesne University Press, 1959.

VOLLERT, CYRIL, S.J. "Evolution of the Human Body," *The Catholic Mind*, 1952, 1071:135–154.

VON FRISCH, K. *Bees: Their Vision, Chemical Senses, and Language*. Ithaca, N.Y.: Cornell University Press, 1950.

VYGOTSKY, L. S. *Thought and Language*. New York: Wiley, 1962.

WALKER, LESLIE J., S.J. *Theories of Knowledge*. (2d ed.) New York: Longmans, 1924.

WANN, T. W. *Behaviorism and Phenomenology* (Rice Symposium). Chicago: The University of Chicago Press, 1964.

WARNOCK, G. J. *English Philosophy since 1900*. Fair Lawn, N.J.: Oxford University Press, 1958.

WASMANN, ERIC, S.J. *Instinct and Intelligence in the Animal Kingdom.* St. Louis: Herder, 1903.

WECHSLER, DAVID. "Engrams, Memory Storage, and Mnemonic Coding," *Amer. Psychologist,* 1963, 18:149–153.

WEISS, PAUL. *Man's Freedom.* New Haven, Conn.: Yale University Press, 1950.

WEISS, PAUL. *Nature and Man.* New York: Holt, 1947.

WELLMUTH, JOHN J. *The Nature and Origins of Scientism.* Milwaukee: Marquette University Press, 1944.

WHITE, ROBERT W. *Lives in Progress.* New York: Dryden, 1952.

WHITEHEAD, ALFRED N. *Science and the Modern World.* New York: Macmillan, 1925.

WHORF, B. L. *Language, Thought, and Reality: Selected Writings of Benjamin Lee Whorf.* Ed. by John B. Carroll. Cambridge, Mass.: Massachusetts Institute of Technology Press, 1956.

WILD, JOHN. *Introduction to Realistic Philosophy.* New York: Harper, 1948.

WILD, JOHN (Ed.) *The Return to Reason: Essays in Realistic Philosophy.* Chicago: Regnery, 1953.

WILHELMSEN, FREDERICK S. *Man's Knowledge of Reality.* Englewood Cliffs, N.J.: Prentice-Hall, 1956.

WILLIAMS, ROGER J. *Biochemical Individuality.* New York: Wiley, 1956.

WILLIAMS, ROGER J. *You Are Extraordinary.* New York: Random House, 1967.

WILM, E. C. *Theories of Instinct.* New Haven, Conn.: Yale University Press, 1925.

WINDLE, SIR BERTRAM C. A. *Vitalism and Scholasticism.* St. Louis: Herder, 1920.

WINDLE, SIR BERTRAM C. A. *What Is Life? A Study of Vitalism and Neovitalism.* St. Louis: Herder, 1908.

WITTGENSTEIN, LUDWIG J. *Philosophical Investigations.* Oxford University Press: Blackwell, 1953.

WITTGENSTEIN, LUDWIG J. *Tractatus logico-philosophicus.* New York: Harcourt, Brace, 1933.

WOLMAN, B., & NAGEL, E. *Scientific Psychology.* New York: Basic Books, Inc., Publishers, 1965.

WOODWORTH, ROBERT S. "Non-sensory Components of Sense Perception," in *Psychological Issues.* New York: Columbia University Press, 1939. Pp. 80–88.

WOODWORTH, ROBERT S. "A Revision of Imageless Thought," *Psychol. Rev.,* 1915, 22:1–27.

WUELLNER, BERNARD, S.J. *A Christian Philosophy of Life.* Milwaukee: Bruce, 1957.

YERKES, ROBERT M. *Chimpanzees: A Laboratory Colony.* New Haven, Conn.: Yale University Press, 1943.

YERKES, ROBERT M., & YERKES, ADA W. *The Great Apes.* New Haven, Conn.: Yale University Press, 1929.

YOUNG, P. T. "Auditory Localization with Acoustical Transposition of the Ears," *J. exp. Psychol.,* 1928, 11:399–429.

YOUNG, P. T. "The Role of Hedonic Processes in Motivation," in *Nebraska Symposium on Motivation, 1955*. Lincoln, Nebr.: University of Nebraska Press, 1955. Pp. 193–238.

ZEDLER, BEATRICE G. "Averroës and Immortality," *The New Scholasticism*, 1954, 28:436–453.

INDEX

INDEX